W9-BXA-623

THE ROUTLEDGE COMPANION TO RACE AND ETHNICITY

"Not only does it contribute to our understanding of race and globalization, it makes a powerful statement about race and ethnicity and taken altogether it leaves no stone unturned."

Anthony Lemelle, *City University of New York, USA*

"This is a very wide-ranging, scholarly and accessible collection that will be of interest to a variety of academics, students, and other interested parties concerned with the intellectual and public policy implications of race and ethnicity globally."

Nasar Meer, *University of Northumbria, UK*

The Routledge Companion to Race and Ethnicity is a comprehensive guide to the increasingly relevant, broad, and ever-changing terrain of studies surrounding race and ethnicity. Comprising a series of essays and a critical dictionary of key names and terms written by respected scholars from a range of academic disciplines, this book provides a thought-provoking introduction to the field and covers:

- the history and relationship between "race" and ethnicity
- the impact of colonialism and postcolonialism
- emerging concepts of "whiteness"
- changing political and social implications of race
- race and ethnicity as components of identity
- the interrelatedness and intersectionality of race and ethnicity with gender and sexual orientation
- globalization, media, popular culture and their links with race and ethnicity.

Fully cross-referenced throughout, with suggestions for further reading and international examples, this book is indispensible reading for all those studying issues of race and ethnicity across the humanities and social and political sciences.

Stephen M. Caliendo is Professor of Political Science at North Central College, Naperville, Illinois.

Charlton D. McIlwain is Associate Professor of Media, Culture and Communication at New York University.

Also available from Routledge

The Routledge Companion to Film History
Edited by William Guynn
9780–415–77657–8

The Routledge Companion to Children's Literature
Edited by David Rudd
978–0–415–47271–5

The Routledge Companion to Critical Theory
Edited by Simon Malpas and Paul Wake
9780–415–33296–5

The Routledge Companion to English Language Studies
Edited by Janet Maybin and Joan Swann
9780–415–40338–2

The Routledge Companion to Gothic
Edited by Catherine Spooner and Emma McEvoy
9780–415–39843–5

The Routledge Companion to Postcolonial Studies
Edited by John McLeod
9780–415–32497–7

The Routledge Companion to Postmodernism (second edition)
Edited by Stuart Sim
9780–415–33359–7

The Routledge Companion to Russian Literature
Edited by Neil Cornwell
9780–415–23366–8

The Routledge Companion to Semiotics
Edited by Paul Cobley
9780–415–44073–8

THE ROUTLEDGE COMPANION TO RACE AND ETHNICITY

Edited by Stephen M. Caliendo
and Charlton D. McIlwain

Routledge
Taylor & Francis Group

LONDON AND NEW YORK

First published 2011
by Routledge
2 Park Square, Milton Park, Abingdon, Oxon OX14 4RN

Simultaneously published in the USA and Canada
by Routledge
270 Madison Ave, New York, NY 10016

Routledge is an imprint of the Taylor & Francis Group, an informa business

© 2011 Stephen M. Caliendo and Charlton D. McIlwain for selection and editorial matter;
individual contributors for their contributions

The right of Stephen M. Caliendo and Charlton D. McIlwain to be identified as editors
of this work has been asserted by them in accordance with sections 77 and 78 of the
Copyright, Designs and Patents Act 1988.

Typeset in Times New Roman by
Book Now Ltd, London
Printed and bound in Great Britain by
TJ International Ltd, Padstow, Cornwall

All rights reserved. No part of this book may be reprinted or reproduced or utilized in any
form or by any electronic, mechanical, or other means, now known or hereafter invented,
including photocopying and recording, or in any information storage or retrieval system,
without permission in writing from the publishers.

British Library Cataloguing in Publication Data
A catalogue record for this book is available from the British Library

Library of Congress Cataloging-in-Publication Data
The Routledge companion to race and ethnicity / edited by Stephen M. Caliendo
and Charlton D. McIlwain.
p. cm.
1. Race. 2. Ethnicity. I. Caliendo, Stephen M., 1971– II. McIlwain, Charlton D., 1971–
HT1521.R685 2011
305.8—dc22
2010022459

ISBN13: 978–0–415–77706–3 (hbk)
ISBN13: 978–0–415–77707–0 (pbk)
ISBN13: 978–0–203–83686–6 (ebk)

To my students – past, present and future – who inspire and challenge me on a daily basis. It is with genuine affection that I approach my work with you each day.

SMC

To Drs George Henderson and Dorscine Spigner-Littles, my first mentors in the study of race and ethnicity.

CDM

CONTENTS

List of contributors		ix
Acknowledgements		xxi
Introduction		xxii

Part I 1

1 Origins of the concept of race 3
  F. Carl Walton and Stephen Maynard Caliendo

2 Ethnicity 12
  Vivian Ibrahim

3 Whiteness 21
  Robert Jensen

4 Colonialism/postcolonialism 29
  William Muck

5 Race, politics and public policy 38
  Charlton D. McIlwain and Stephen Maynard Caliendo

6 Race-based social movements 47
  Charlton D. McIlwain

7 Motivation, immigration and the immigrant 55
  Eric M. Kramer

8 Race, gender, and sexuality 64
  Nina Asher

9 Race, media and popular culture 73
  Stephen Maynard Caliendo

10 Race, ethnicity, and globalization   82
    S. P. Udayakumar

Part II   **93**

Names and terms   95

    Index   238

CONTRIBUTORS

Nina Asher is Associate Professor and the J. Franklin Bayhi Endowed Professor of Education in the Department of Educational Theory, Policy, and Practice at Louisiana State University, USA. She is co-director of the Department's Curriculum Theory Project and Book Review Editor for the *International Journal of Qualitative Studies in Education*. She is also on the faculty of LSU's Women's and Gender Studies Program and Program in Comparative Literature. Her work in the areas of postcolonialism and feminism, multiculturalism, and Asian American studies in relation to education has appeared in such journals as *Educational Researcher*, *Teachers College Record*, *Discourse: Studies in the Cultural Politics of Education*, and *International Journal of Qualitative Studies in Education*, among others.

Stephen Maynard Caliendo is Professor of Political Science at North Central College, where he studies political psychology and political communication, particularly as it relates to US elections and race. He is the author of *Teachers matter: The trouble with leaving political education to the coaches* (Praeger, 2000) and *Inequality in America: Race, poverty and fulfilling democracy's promise* (Westview, forthcoming). He is also co-author of *Race appeal* (Temple, 2010) and co-director of the Project on Race in Political Communication (RaceProject.org). He is a frequent contributor to international, national, state and local print and broadcast media stories related to race and ethnicity in the context of US politics and elections.

Vivian Ibrahim completed her PhD at the School of Oriental and African Studies, University of London, where she was a Teaching Fellow in Middle Eastern History. She is currently a post-doctoral researcher examining European-Muslim identities in Ireland. Her areas of interest include the Middle East, sectarian divisions along ethnic and religious lines, Islam in Europe and minority–majority relations. Ibrahim has published in the *Arab Reform Bulletin* for Carnegie Endowment and is an Executive Board member of the Association for the Study of Ethnicity and Nationalism as well as the *International Journal for Arab Studies*. She is the author of *The Copts of Egypt: The challenges of modernisation and identity* (I.B. Tauris, 2010).

Robert Jensen, a journalism professor at the University of Texas at Austin, is the author of *All my bones shake: Seeking a progressive path to the prophetic voice* (Soft Skull Press, 2009); *Getting off: Pornography and the end of masculinity* (South End Press, 2007); *The heart of whiteness: Confronting race, racism and white privilege* (City Lights, 2005); *Citizens of the Empire: The struggle to claim our humanity* (City Lights, 2004); and *Writing dissent: Taking radical ideas from the margins to the mainstream* (Peter Lang, 2002). Jensen is also co-producer of the documentary film *Abe Osheroff: One foot in the grave, the other still dancing*, which chronicles the life and philosophy of the longtime radical activist.

Eric Kramer is Professor of Communication/Film and Video Studies, and Affiliate Professor of International and Area Studies at the University of Oklahoma. He has taught in Boston, Seattle, Virginia, Xalapa (Mexico), Taichung (Taiwan), Kyoto and Tokyo. He lived and worked for over a year in Sofia (Bulgaria) as a Fulbright scholar, in Taiwan as a visiting fellow at Feng Chia University, and was the first "Western" academic elected to faculty status in the prestigious school of journalism and mass communication at the National University Saint Kliment Ohridsky, Sofia. He is the author of *Modern/ Postmodern: Off the beaten path of anti-modernism* and other books related to race and culture, mass communication, and philosophy of communication.

Charlton D. McIlwain is Associate Professor of Media, Culture and Communication at New York University. His current research focuses on the use of racial appeals in political communication, including the semiotic construction of racial appeals in language and visual images; the effects of racial appeals on public opinion and voting behavior; framing and priming effects of race in various media; and media coverage of minority political candidates. He is the co-author of *Race appeal* (Temple, 2010), as well as *When death goes pop: Death, media and the remaking of community* (Peter Lang, 2004) and *Death in black and white: Death, ritual and family ecology* (Hampton, 2003). He is co-director of the Project on Race in Political Communication (RaceProject.org) and a frequent analyst for international, national, state and local print and broadcast media.

William Muck is Assistant Professor of Political Science at North Central College. His research interests are in the fields of international peace and security, foreign policy, and the practice of overt and covert military interventionism by the United States. His most current work explores the causal roots of religious conflict and the process of religious identity formation. He recently published a paper in *Politics and religion* (Autumn 2009) titled "The secular roots of religious rage: Shaping religious identity in the Middle East," which examines the role that US foreign policy plays in shaping conceptions of religious identity in the Middle East.

S. P. Udayakumar is Research Fellow at the Kirwan Institute for the Study of Race and Ethnicity, the Ohio State University. He has written widely on issues involving globalization, race and ethnicity, including *Presenting the past: Anxious history and ancient future in Hindutva India* (Praeger, 2005) and *Handcuffed to history: Narratives, pathologies and violence in South Asia* (Praeger, 2001). The author is indebted to Professor john a. powell, Director of the Kirwan Institute, for all his help and guidance.

F. Carl Walton is an Assistant Professor in the Department of History and Political Science and Director of the Honors Program at Lincoln University. He holds an MA and a PhD in Political Science from Purdue University and a BA in Political Science from Morris Brown College (1984). He was an American Political Science Association Congressional Fellow in the Office of Congressman Sanford D. Bishop (Dem., Georgia) from 1995 to 1996, and he participated in the New York University Faculty Resource Network Scholar-in-Residence Program during the summer of 2001. His major research focus is on legislative politics and Black political organizations; he is currently working on a manuscript that explores the work of the Congressional Black Caucus (CBC).

KEY TO NAMES AND TERMS CONTRIBUTORS

(AAL) Andrea A. Lunsford is the Louise Hewlett Nixon Professor of English and Director of the Program in Writing and Rhetoric at Stanford University. She received her PhD from the Ohio State University in 1997. Recent publications include the *Sage handbook of rhetorical studies, writing matters: Rhetoric in public and private lives* and the *St. Martin's handbook*, 7th ed.

(AEA) Amy E. Ansell is Dean of Liberal Arts and Professor of Sociology at Emerson College. She has written widely on racial politics, color-blind racism, whiteness, and reparations in the United States, Britain, and South Africa. Her current research is on the politics of race and land in contemporary Zimbabwe.

(AL) Alana Lentin is Senior Lecturer in Sociology at the University of Sussex. She is a political sociologist and social theorist focusing on the critical theorization of race, racism and anti-racism. She is the author of *Racism and anti-racism in Europe* (2004) and *Racism: A beginner's guide* (2008), and co-editor of *Race and state* (2006) (www.alanalentin.net).

(ALC) Arica L. Coleman is Assistant Professor of Black American Studies at the University of Delaware. Her areas of specialization include race and ethnicity issues in African American–Native American relations, mixed race identity, eugenics, and the intersection of race and gender.

(AO) Anthony Oberschall is Emeritus Professor of Sociology at the University of North Carolina, Chapel Hill. He earned a BA degree at Harvard and a PhD at Columbia. He has published extensively on conflict and conflict management, social movements, and social change. His latest book is *Conflict and peace building in divided societies: Responses to ethnic violence* (2007).

(BB) Barbara Bush is a Professor of Imperial History at Sheffield Hallam University, UK. She has published widely on culture and resistance in slave and post-slave societies. More recently, her research has focused on aspects of twentieth-century British imperialism.

(BM) Beza Merid is a PhD candidate in the Department of Media, Culture and Communication at New York University.

(CC) Chi-yue Chiu is Professor of Management at the Nanyang Technological University and Professor of Psychology at the University of Illinois. His research focuses on the psychology of culture and globalization.

(CCM) Carol C. Mukhopadhyay, Professor of Anthropology, San Jose State University, California, researches, consults, and publishes on issues of cultural diversity and education related to race and gender in the United States and India. She was a Key Advisor for the American Anthropological Association's public education project, RACE: Are We So Different?

(CMM) Carol M. Motley is Associate Professor of Marketing at the School of Business and Industry, Florida A&M University. Her research includes cross-cultural issues in popular culture and marketing messages.

(CVS) Cigdem V. Sirin is an Assistant Professor of Political Science at the University of Texas, El Paso. Her areas of interest include ethnic conflict, political psychology, military interventions, and foreign policy decision making.

(DB) Davina Bhandar is Associate Professor of Canadian Studies at Trent University, where she specializes in feminist theory, critical race studies, diaspora, contemporary social and cultural theory, and the politics of immigration, migration, and resettlement.

(DBhugra) Dinesh Bhugra is Professor of Mental Health and Cultural Diversity at the Institute of Psychiatry, King's College London and an Honorary Consultant at the Maudsley Hospital. Since 2008, he has been President of the Royal College of Psychiatrists. Recent publications include *Textbook of cultural psychiatry* and *Culture and mental health.*

(DBrown) Donathan Brown resides in the Department of Communication at Texas A&M University in College Station, Texas, where he studies race and public policy, particularly, African American and Latino politics.

(DCD) Davia Cox Downey is a doctoral student at Michigan State University. She studies issues of race and ethnicity as they relate to the development of policy at the state and local level.

(DCT) Darryl C. Thomas is the head of African and African American Studies at Penn State. He has published widely on the international politics of the Third World, African and Africana studies, globalization, democratization, and global Africa resistance to globalization and US hegemony and empire. His research and teaching revolve around Africana studies, African studies, world politics, comparative politics, Black politics, urban politics, and political theory. He is a graduate of the doctoral program in Political Science at the University of Michigan, emphasizing world politics, comparative politics, and political theory.

(DGE) David G. Embrick is an Assistant Professor of Sociology at Loyola University, Chicago. His areas of research include US race and ethnic relations and racial and gender diversity in the workplace.

(DH) Daniel HoSang holds a joint appointment in the Departments of Ethnic Studies and Political Science at the University of Oregon. His book on race and political ballot initiatives in post-Second World War California is forthcoming from the University of California Press. He teaches courses on racial politics, culture, and theory.

(DLM) Deborah L. Madsen is Professor of American Literature and Culture, Department of English, University of Geneva. She works in the field of Postcolonial American Studies, with a focus on issues of national rhetoric and cultural exclusion. Her approach is fundamentally historical, exemplified by her work on American Exceptionalism and the ideology of Manifest Destiny.

(GB) Galen Bodenhausen is the Lawyer Taylor Professor of Psychology at Northwestern University. His research addresses cognitive and affective aspects of intergroup relations, particularly the role of stereotypes in intergroup judgment and behavior. He is currently editor-in-chief of *Personality and Social Psychology Review*.

(GDS) Gregory D. Squires is Professor of Sociology and Public Policy and Public Administration at George Washington University. His research focuses on racial segregation, concentrated poverty, and the role of public policy in shaping the uneven development of metropolitan areas.

(GEH) George E. Higgins is an Associate Professor in the Department of Justice Administration at the University of Louisville. He received his PhD in criminology from Indiana University of Pennsylvania in 2001. His most recent publications appear in *Criminal Justice Studies, Deviant Behavior, Criminal Justice and Behavior, Youth and Society,* and *American Journal of Criminal Justice.*

(GG) Gabriel Greenberg is a graduate of Wesleyan University. He is an environmental and inter-faith educator in the Northeast. Currently, he is a student at YCT rabbinical school in New York. He is the co-author, with Peter Gottschalk, of *Islamophobia: Making Muslims the enemy* (Rowman & Littlefield, 2008).

(GJSD) George J. Sefa Dei is Professor (and immediate past Chair) of the Department of Sociology and Equity Studies, Ontario Institute for Studies in Education of the University of Toronto (OISE/UT). His teaching and research interests are in the areas of anti-racism, minority schooling, international development, Fanonian studies and anti-colonial thought.

(HB) Heidi Beirich, PhD, is the director of research and special projects for the Southern Poverty Law Center's Intelligence Project. A specialist on white nationalism and fascism, she co-edited *Neo-Confederacy: A critical introduction.*

(HC) Hilary Cunningham is Associate Professor of Anthropology at the University of Toronto. Her research has focused on borders and boundary-making. She is author of numerous publications on the politics of borders and border-crossings, including articles on biotechnology and genetic enclosures. Her current research focuses on what she terms "gated ecologies," especially those pertaining to transfrontier nature reserves and wilderness areas.

(JAK) John A. Kirk is Professor of US History in the History Department, Royal Holloway, University of London, UK. He has written extensively on African American history, race relations, and the civil rights movement.

(JC) Jillian Maynard Caliendo is a doctoral student at the Adler School of Professional Psychology with interests in mental health in college populations, public education on mental health issues, and access to mental healthcare. She has additional interests in social barriers to mental wellness, stigma and mental illness, and socially responsible psychological practice.

(JCH) John C. Hawley is Professor of English at Santa Clara University, author of *Amitav Ghosh: An introduction,* and editor of 14 books, including the *Encyclopedia of postcolonial studies* and *Postcolonial, queer.* He is associate editor of the *South Asian Review* and president of the United States Association for Commonwealth Literature and Language Studies.

(JD) John Duckitt is Professor of Social Psychology at the University of

Auckland, New Zealand. His primary research interests are the study of prejudice and intergroup relations, ideological social attitudes, and group identification.

(JEDC) Juan E. De Castro is Assistant Professor at Eugene Lang College, the New School for Liberal Arts, where he teaches Latino/Latina and Latin American Literatures.

(JEY) Joseph E. Yi was Assistant Professor of Political Science at Gonzaga University, Spokane, WA (2006–09), with expertise in political theory, civil society, urban politics, and race and ethnicity. He published *God and karate on the Southside* (2009), and is currently writing a new book on assimilation and bridging social capital among urban immigrant groups in Southern California. He received his doctorate in political science from the University of Chicago.

(JFD) John F. Dovidio is Professor of Psychology at Yale University. His research interests are in stereotyping, prejudice, and discrimination; social power and nonverbal communication; and altruism and helping. Much of his scholarship has focused on "aversive racism," a subtle form of contemporary racism, and ways to reduce it.

(JJEG) Jorge J. E. Gracia is State University of New York Distinguished Professor and holds the Samuel P. Capen Chair in the Department of Philosophy and the Department of Comparative Literature at the University at Buffalo. He works on issues of race, ethnicity, and nationality, with particular emphasis on Latinos/Hispanics.

(JMC) Jung Min Choi is a member of the Sociology Department at San Diego State University. He holds a doctorate from York University and is the co-author of several books, including *The politics of culture: Race, violence and democracy* (1995) and *Globalization with a human face* (2004).

(JN) Joane Nagel is University Distinguished Professor of Sociology at the University of Kansas. She is Director of the NSF Integrative Education and Research Traineeship (IGERT) program, C-CHANGE: Climate Change, Humans, and Nature in the Global Environment. She is the co-author, with Thomas Dietz and Jeffrey Broadbent, of *Sociological perspectives on global climate change* (National Science Foundation 2009).

(JWM) John W. Murphy is Professor of Sociology at the University of Miami, where he researches social theory/philosophy, cultural studies, and race and ethnic studies. He is the author or co-author of numerous books, including *The politics of culture* (1995) and *The politics and philosophy of political correctness* (1992).

(LCS) Louis Chude-Sokei is a scholar and writer who is currently an Associate Professor of Literature at the University of California, Santa Cruz. His book *The last darky: Bert Williams, black on black minstrelsy and the African diaspora* (Duke University Press, 2005) was a finalist for the 2006 Hurston/Wright Legacy Award.

(LE) Louwanda Evans is a PhD student at Texas A&M University in College Station, Texas. Her interests are racial and ethnic relations.

(LG) Lisa Gannett is Associate Professor of Philosophy at Saint Mary's University in Halifax, Canada. She specializes in the history and philosophy of biology and is particularly interested in the use of group categories (such as population, race and ethnicity) in genetics.

(MC) Michael Collyer is Lecturer in Human Geography at the University of Sussex in Brighton, UK. He has held visiting fellowships at universities in Morocco, Egypt, and Sri Lanka. His research focuses on the relationship between migrants and states, particularly in South Asia and the EuroMediterranean region.

(MGD) Meenakshi Gigi Durham is Associate Professor of Journalism and Mass Communication at the University of Iowa. Her research centers on feminist and critical approaches to media culture. She is the co-editor, with Douglas M. Kellner, of *Media and cultural studies: KeyWorks* (Blackwell, 2006) and the author of *The Lolita effect* (Overlook, 2008).

(MH) Mike Hawkins is Visiting Professor in the School of Social Science, Kingston University, UK. His research is in the history of Social Darwinism and in nineteenth-century French republican political theory.

(MHjerm) Mikael Hjerm is an Associate Professor at the department of Sociology, Umeå University. He is currently focusing on explaining the relationship between social cohesion, xenophobia, and nationalism. He is the national coordinator for the European Social Survey.

(MJC) Michael J. Coyle is Assistant Professor in the Department of Political Science at California State University, Chico. He studies language, public policy, and everyday life to expose the social construction of discarded persons (the deviant, the homeless, the imprisoned, and a variety of racial/ethnic/sexual orientation/etc. minorities) as "criminals" and "punishment-worthy."

(MK) Dr Maulana Karenga is Professor of Africana Studies at California State University, Long Beach, the creator of the pan-African cultural holiday Kwanzaa, and author of numerous scholarly articles and books, including:

Introduction to black studies; *Kwanzaa: A celebration of family, community and culture* and *Maat, the moral ideal in Ancient Egypt: A study in classical African ethics* (www.MaulanaKarenga.org).

(MKA) Molefi Kete Asante is Professor, Department of African American Studies, at Temple University, and the major proponent of Afrocentricity. He is the author of 70 books including four seminal works on Afrocentricity.

(ML) Mikhail Lyubansky, PhD, teaches Psychology of Race and Ethnicity (and other courses) in the Department of Psychology at the University of Illinois, Urbana-Champaign. He has co-authored a book on immigration and over a dozen academic articles and is a regular contributor to anthologies about popular culture (e.g., work on Harry Potter). His *Psychology Today* blog, Between the Lines, focuses on racial issues in politics and media.

(MP) Mark Potok is the director of the Southern Poverty Law Center's Intelligence Project. He edits the award-winning investigative quarterly, *Intelligence Report*, the country's only magazine devoted entirely to monitoring the radical right.

(NCG) Nigel C. Gibson is director of the Honors Program, Emerson College Boston and Research Associate University of KwaZulu Natal, Durban. He is the editor of the *Journal of Asian and African Studies*.

(NG) Nancy Gallagher is Chair of the Middle East Studies program and a Professor of History at the University of California, Santa Barbara. She is co-editor, with Sondra Hale, of the *Journal of Middle East Women's Studies* (JMEWS), published by Indiana University Press, and past-president of the Association for Middle East Women's Studies, the parent organization of JMEWS. Her last book was *Quakers in the Israeli–Palestinian conflict: The dilemmas of NGO humanitarian activism* (American University in Cairo Press, 2007). She is currently working on a study of women and microfinance in Afghanistan.

(PG) Peter Gottschalk is Professor and Chair of Religion at Wesleyan University. Along with works investigating religious identity in British and independent India, such as *Beyond Hindu and Muslim* (Oxford University Press, 2000), he is co-author, with Gabriel Greenberg, of *Islamophobia: Making Muslims the enemy* (Rowman & Littlefield, 2008).

(PH) Dr Paul Hanson teaches anthropology and sociology at Cuyahoga Community College in Cleveland, Ohio. His research focus is on ritual communication and conservation/development as a political technology in eastern Madagascar.

(RB) Dr Richard Broome is Associate Professor of History at La Trobe University, Melbourne, Australia. He is the author of *Aboriginal Australians* (1981), the only comprehensive overview of Aboriginal history, published in a fully rewritten fourth edition in 2010, and the prize-winning *Aboriginal Victorians* (2005).

(RD) Rutledge M. Dennis is Professor of Sociology and Anthropology at George Mason University. He is the author, co-author, editor, and co-editor of more than ten books and the recipient of the Joseph S. Himes Lifetime Achievement Award (given by the Association of Black Sociologists) and the Du Bois-Johnson-Frazier Award (given by the American Sociological Association).

(RH) Reza Hasmath is a Lecturer in Sociology at the University of Toronto. His research examines the education and labor market experiences of ethnic minorities in urban entities in China and North America.

(RKS) Dr Robinder Kaur Sehdev is an Assistant Professor in the Department of Gender Equality and Social Justice at Nipissing University, Canada. Her research examines the practices and politics of solidarity formation amongst anti-racist feminists and Aboriginal resurgence and resistance movements in what is now called Canada.

(RW) Rebecca Wittmann (PhD, University of Toronto) is Associate Professor of History at the University of Toronto. Her research focuses on the Holocaust and postwar Germany, trials of Nazi perpetrators and terrorists, and German legal history. She has received fellowships from the Alexander von Humboldt Foundation, the Social Sciences and Humanities Research Council of Canada, the United States Holocaust Memorial Museum, and the DAAD (German Academic Exchange Service). She has published articles in several journals, and her book, *Beyond justice: The Auschwitz trial* (Harvard University Press, 2005) won the Fraenkel Prize in Contemporary History.

(SC) Sapna Cheryan is an Assistant Professor of Psychology at the University of Washington. Her research interests include identity, stereotypes, and prejudice, and she has published articles on how Asian Americans respond to stereotypes of their racial group in *Psychological Science* and the *Journal of Personality & Social Psychology*.

(SEV) Sabina E. Vaught is Assistant Professor of Urban Education and American Studies at Tufts University. She studies educational equity and the political economy of urban schooling. Her current research is an ethnographic investigation of the school-to-prison pipeline through work with incarcerated youth.

(SG) Susham Gupta is a dually trained General Adult and Old Age Consultant Psychiatrist working in the East London NHS Foundation Trust. His areas of interest are dementia, management, and public health.

(SM) Sheng-mei Ma is Professor of English at Michigan State University in Michigan, USA, specializing in Asian Diaspora/Asian American studies and East–West comparative studies. He is the author of multiple books, including *Asian diaspora and East–West modernity* (2010) and *East–West montage: Reflections on Asian bodies in diaspora* (2007).

(SMC) Stephen Maynard Caliendo (see entry under Contributors).

(SMG) Shamira M. Gelbman is an Assistant Professor of Politics and Government at Illinois State University. Her research deals with the dynamics of social movement activity, party competition, and democratization in the United States and South Africa.

(SOP) Sherrow O. Pinder is Assistant Professor of Political Science and Multicultural and Gender Studies at California State University, Chico. She is the author of *From welfare to workfare: How capitalist states create a pool of unskilled cheap labor (A Marxist-Feminist social analysis)* (2007) and *The politics of race and ethnicity in the United States: Americanization, de-Americanization, and racialized ethnic groups* (2010).

(SS) Dr Steve Spencer is a senior lecturer in Sociology at Sheffield Hallam University. His research interests include the sociology of race and ethnicity, media, identity, and use of visual methods. Publications include: *Race and ethnicity: Culture, identity and representation* (2006) and a series of videos including: *Framing the fringe dwellers* (2004), *Under the skin of multiculturalism* (with Keith Radley 2006) and *Identities in transition: Interviews with 5 African-Canadian women* (2008).

(TDH) Thomas D. Hall is Professor Emeritus in Sociology and Anthropology at DePauw University in Greencastle, Indiana. His key interests are long-term social change, frontiers, and indigenous peoples. His most recent book is *Indigenous peoples and globalization: Resistance and revitalization* co-authored with James V. Fenelon (Paradigm Press 2009).

(TF) Teri Fair is an Assistant Professor at Suffolk University in the Department of Government. She studies medium-sized cities, the relationships between race and public policy, and various aspects of black politics.

(US) Utku Sezgin is a PhD candidate in Political Science at the Graduate Center, City University of New York (CUNY). He studies the assimilation and citizenship practices of second-generation immigrants in New York and Berlin. He is also a research fellow at the CUNY Dominican Studies Institute at City College of New York.

(VC) Valerie Chepp is a doctoral student in the Sociology Department at the University of Maryland. Her academic interests include intersectional theory, sociology of knowledge and ethnographic field methods. Her current work focuses on Black feminist thought, women's rap music, and representations of race, gender, and sexuality in American popular culture.

(VL) Vincent Lloyd is Assistant Professor of Religious Studies at Georgia State University. He studies philosophy of religion, religion and politics, and race.

(ZL) Zhi Liu is a PhD candidate in Management at the Nanyang Technological University. She studies the psychological benefits of multiculturalism.

ACKNOWLEDGEMENTS

As anyone who has been in our shoes knows, putting together a volume of this scope is no easy task. While our names are on the front of the book, there are scores of people who deserve credit for making this come together. First and foremost, of course, are the 78 contributors. They come from around the globe and from very diverse academic traditions and trainings, and they are in various stages of their professional development. While some are finishing doctoral degrees, others are established academics, and some of those are among the most well-respected scholars in their fields. For both groups, it is an arduous undertaking to offer a concise response to such involved topics. For those who are "stars" or otherwise established, such an effort is particularly admirable, as entries such as these do not often "count" toward promotion or tenure. This is, indeed, a service to the readership, and we are extremely grateful for all of their participation.

We had a series of administrative assistants who contributed to this effort, as well: Shannon Lausch helped to compile a list of potential contributors some two years before the volume was to go to print; Etienne Mashuli provided valuable counsel in the final stages; and Rebecca Mortland Valero and Julie Saflarski helped with early edits. We would still be in early stages, however, without the work of Sidra Hamidi, who, for two years, corresponded with scholars from around the globe with professionalism and efficiency, all while working on an undergraduate degree and holding down a part-time job. We can never thank her enough for helping this project blossom into what you are holding in your hands now. The editorial staff at Routledge, particularly Katherine Ong, Sophie Thomson, David Avital and Andy Humphries, were tremendously supportive and helpful throughout the process. We appreciate their interest in the project and their patience with us throughout. A number of reviewers were also helpful in their criticisms of and suggestions on multiple early drafts. We have included many of their suggestions, and the result is a stronger book. Any remaining weaknesses are ours.

Finally, we want to express our deep appreciation to our families for their patience and support as we worked to pull this project together. Our spouses and children were denied our attention at various points throughout this process; their love and encouragement is invaluable to us.

INTRODUCTION

Perhaps no two concepts are as central to modern human life and civilization as **race** and ethnicity. For many people across the globe, race and ethnicity, in addition to gender (and, increasingly, in many contexts, sexual orientation), help to define our individual and collective **identities**, our social worlds, our personal dreams, and our shared visions. Race and ethnicity function as code – shorthand, if you will – reminding us and telling others who "I" am, who "we" are, what we do, how we live and what we value, not to mention what we look like. Race and ethnicity – as well as the interrelationship with and intersectionality of gender, class and sexual orientation – uniquely (though not clearly) position us and provide a perspective from which to see and interpret the world and others in it. Race and ethnicity influence the range, scope and boundaries of that perspective. Beyond personal and collective identities, race and ethnicity provide key foundations for organizing our societies – our tribes, neighborhoods, villages, cities and nations.

Despite being central to individual and collective identity and formations of larger organized groupings such as nation-states, the terms "race" and "ethnicity" are fraught with misunderstanding. As detailed in the first two essays of this book, people often disagree and variably rely on the existence of racial categories and the salience of ethnic groupings across the globe. The original biological and genetic basis for the concept of race has been thoroughly debunked by scientists the world over. The scientific community, armed today with the tools to analyze the depth and breadth of the **human genome**, point out that, despite differences in body type, bone structure, cranial size, hair texture, skin pigmentation or any other human variation, human beings are more genetically similar than they are different. Irrespective of the fact that race is not a biologically valid construct, however, few would reject the notion that race is very real in terms of individuals' lived experiences. This is especially so given the fact that, since its inception, biological notions of race have largely functioned as an accepted truth about the nature of human difference.

Further, "race" and "ethnicity" are not often clearly delineated constructs. For example, many social justice activists and scholars were surprised to learn that "**Latino**" was listed as an ethnicity rather than a race on the 2010 United States census, despite the fact that most Americans consider Latinos to be a racial group parallel to African Americans. Since "race" is not "real" in the sense that it is not a valid biological classification, the construction of race and ethnicity is inherently blurry. In this book, the scholars who weigh in on the most salient elements of contemporary considerations of race and ethnicity do so with full awareness of this dilemma, centering their observations on the most relevant scholarship in the various fields and generally considering "race" to be a social construction rooted in physical differences, among the most prominent of which is skin color/tone, and ethnicity to be centered largely on geographical origin of one's ancestors and/or shared cultural elements.

But race and ethnicity, as an experience, are more salient for some than others. Whether related to colonialism (Chapter 4), contemporary public policy (Chapter 5) or the myriad aspects of immigration (Chapter 7), citizens are counted and labeled in a way that renders members of some racial and ethnic groups more dominant than others. As Robert Jensen explains in Chapter 3, whites are in privileged positions in most sociopolitical contexts – so much so that their race and/or ethnicity is often perceived to be non-existent. In this way, "race" is "seen" by those who possess the dominant racial characteristic wholly in terms of "**otherness**." As such, resistance to racial and ethnic preferences is often manifested in non-white groups engaging in social movements designed to dismantle systems of oppression (Chapter 6).

Compelling individuals to identify themselves – in highly race-conscious countries such as the United States, for instance – in racial terms reinforces this dynamic between race, **whiteness** and otherness in a way that magnifies a fundamental element of both racial and ethnic distinctions – the dimension of **power** and control that underlies them both. Categorizing people (and compelling people to define themselves accordingly) is a means of exercising power and control over them. We often think of ethnic grouping as being a more realistic and civilized way of defining groups of people, in part because ethnic groups have not generally been defined by dubious, self-serving, biological evidence. But what do we find if we, for instance, launch an Internet search for "How many ethnic groups exist across the globe?" In 2010, the highest (most reliable) source atop the list was the *World Factbook*, by the United States' Central Intelligence Agency. This speaks volumes on the reality that, like racial groups, ethnic groupings were created for the purpose of exploiting the natural resources provided in various geographical regions, as well as the human populations that inhabit them – in large part for their labor potential. The reality – as William Muck explores in Chapter 4 – is that many ethnic groups were named by colonizers. In a **postcolonial** world, many ethnic groups retain their colonized ethnic designations, while some shed them for more self-determined ethnic group titles. (Burma, now called "Myanmar," and the "Burmese" people, provide a recent example.)

The pride and **prejudices** that accompany individual and collective racial and ethnic identities, the annexation of racial and ethnic group designations with matters of state and nation, international struggles for self-determination, and power struggles for equal access to resources and equal opportunity for socioeconomic mobility all complicate the contemporary terrain of race and ethnicity in a way that continues to manifest itself in racial and ethnic tension and conflict throughout the world. According to the Uppsala Conflict Data Program (part of the Department of Peace and Conflict Research at Uppsala University in Sweden), there are currently 33 armed conflicts (conflicts resulting in more than 1,000 deaths, annually) taking place across the globe, from Afghanistan to the Sudan to Mexico (the US–Mexican "war on drugs") to Thailand. Many of these represent ethnic group conflicts in national or regional civil wars. In this context, wars in the former Yugoslavia during the early 1990s starkly highlighted both new and old (and sometimes overlapping) concepts related to ethnic conflict: **ethnic cleansing** (expulsion of certain ethnic group populations) and **genocide** (essentially, tribal or ethnic-group-based murder).

While ethnic conflict in national and regional civil wars accounts for some of this conflict, much of the widespread conflict across the globe related to race and ethnicity comes in the form of national tensions resulting from the contemporary reality of globalization (Chapter 10). In an environment where national borders are more fluid and porous, the exportation and importation of everything from new technologies to global media products to the values embodied in these material objects (originating primarily among "developed" Western nations to the "developing" or "underdeveloped" world) threaten traditional ethnic, racial and national identities. Proponents of Western-dominated globalizing patterns argue that they contribute to world progress, while critics point out that it does nothing more than reduce the world's rich diversity to a set of singular cultural values destined to leave the West more economically dominant and the rest of the globe more dependent on the West for resources.

But large-scale violent conflict is only one of the ways that racial and ethnic tensions play out in today's world. The more routine, mundane, less visible, everyday tensions and struggles around race and ethnicity come in the form of contesting state-controlled public policy, countering **stereotypical representations** that circulate in mass media and other forms of popular culture (Chapter 9) and trying to promote increased recognition of the ways that issues of gender and sexuality contribute to the character and power dimensions of racial and ethnic politics across the globe (Chapter 8). The degree to which race, especially, is an important dimension of the public policy concerns of citizens and state representatives depends to a great extent on the degree or level of race consciousness expressed within certain national boundaries. As we point out in Chapter 5, significant elements of policy debate in countries such as Britain and the United States either specifically relate to racial issues or make racial designations a significant factor in policy deliberations. In Chapter 7, Eric Kramer discusses (in a style that differs from the other authors of the primary chapters) a shared policy concern among most contemporary democracies that generally accept foreign-born persons' temporary or permanent residence.

With a greater number of channels for distribution, more accessible media technologies and increased global demand for popular music, television, film, art and the like, transnational popular culture flourishes in many places across the globe. On the one hand, the extent of media technologies coverage has the effect of solidifying certain race-related norms, such as perpetuating the notion that light and white is "right" when it comes to dominating standards of beauty. On the other hand, it allows groups to produce and circulate artistic creations that lend themselves to a more positive valuation of one's racial group (such as global hip-hop) or extend the reach of non-Western media products. The style of animation known as *anime*, which originated in Japan – whose popularity spread from East and Southeast Asia, and eventually throughout the Western world – is one prominent example.

It is crucial to remember, however, that race and ethnicity are just two related elements that have been used to divide and oppress individuals based on group identification. As Nina Asher illustrates in Chapter 8, gender and sexuality intersect with race and ethnicity in ways which are sometimes unpredictable, to provide additional factors by which persons can be labeled and controlled. Increased reliance on technology, in conjunction with economic and cultural globalization, adds weight to this tendency, as religious practices and interpretations, ideological beliefs and other cultural traditions come under increased scrutiny and face increased pressure as a result of the sharing of ideas and stories – not just by published authors, scholars and public figures, but by ordinary citizens through websites, "blogs" and social networking sites such as Facebook and Twitter. It is far too early, and things are moving far too quickly, to make solid evaluations about the effect of these emerging information-sharing tools on helping to bring about increased social justice relating to race, ethnicity, gender, sexuality and/or a host of other characteristics that have posed challenges for people in various contexts for centuries.

THE BOOK

Consistent with the aims of this series, the *Companion to Race and Ethnicity* is designed to be a one-stop shop for information about, and discussion of, the foundational and most relevant concepts and scholarship concerning the contemporary, broad and ever-changing terrain of race and ethnicity. The book is organized into two primary sections. The first section contains a series of longer essays, designed to introduce students to some of the most fundamental concepts and issues related to race and ethnicity, both historically and in our contemporary world. These essays – outlined in this introduction – focus on the following topics: the origins of the concept of race and ethnicity, the idea of "whiteness," the relationship of race and ethnicity to social movements and the establishment of public policy, and the ways that race and ethnicity affect broader socio-political realities, such as immigration, gender and sexuality, popular culture, globalization and postcolonialism. The contributors to this section provide an overview of the topics they consider and offer a firm foundation from which to explore these issues in greater depth. To be clear, this book is not designed to be an exhaustive, authoritative treatment of the topic; quite the contrary. Rather, it provides an excellent starting point for understanding the complexity of these issues. To that end, each author provides a set of "key readings" so that readers can "jump off" to pursue more advanced study.

Accordingly, the second section of the book provides A-to-Z coverage of the terms, concepts and figures with which any student of race and ethnicity should be familiar. From "Aboriginal" to "xenophobia," the essays in this section – some longer than others – will help students become conversant with the language and scholarship related to race and ethnicity studies. The essays in both sections share several characteristics. The authors of each of the essays span a wide array of disciplines, including sociology, political science, media and communication, racial and ethnic studies, psychology, international relations, geography, history and anthropology. Additionally, the contributors bring an international perspective to the study of the issues of race and ethnicity covered in this book. They represent institutions in (and are writing from) North and South America, Europe, Australia and Africa. The interdisciplinary and international background of these authors provides a wide range of perspectives from which to view and discuss issues that have been and continue to be relevant for individuals, groups and nations across the globe. Readers will note the overlap in many of the pieces. This is quite intentional, as we wish to highlight the degree to which many of these concepts and terms are interrelated. However, it is inarguable that there are many terms that are relevant to the study of race and ethnicity that do not appear in this section. Concepts such as "hybridity," "modernity" and "slavery," as well as important figures such as Collette Guillaumin and Ashley Montague, among many others, would fit naturally into this section. Of course, we only had the space to include a certain number of entries; our original list contained nearly twice as many as we were finally able to include. We trust, however, that this section will provide an excellent starting point for students of race and ethnicity wishing to explore key concepts that inform sophisticated discussion of this important topic.

As a final note, we want to point out that the contributors to this volume were all asked to do something that is very difficult for them: write in a thoughtful way without including formal citations. Volumes in the *Companions* series are designed to be written in a fluid, accessible style, so we asked the authors to write as though they were giving a lecture or other presentation, noting important landmark works in the text and providing a list of suggested reading at the end of their piece. We hope that you find this style digestible and useful.

PART I

1

ORIGINS OF THE CONCEPT OF RACE

F. CARL WALTON AND STEPHEN MAYNARD CALIENDO

The concept of **race** can be considered in both cultural and political terms. In that regard, race has been used to create a dividing line between those who were white and those who were non-white and to determine who would and would not have political rights (and, by extension, political **power**). In addition, cultural traditions created and adhered to by persons of European descent have come to be the "norm," while those from non-white races are deemed to be a less significant "**other**." In the end, race (and, by extension, racism) has been constructed as a great divider and the avenue by which people of certain ethnic groups have come to be framed as inferior to whites.

BIOLOGICAL JUSTIFICATION AND IMPLICATIONS

There is a long history of linking broad categories of difference to physical features. In the sixteenth century, for instance, racial classification was largely understood to differentiate humans from other species (i.e. "the human race"). While differences between and among humans is reflected in evidence from ancient times, it is not surprising that, as Europeans began to explore the globe and encounter persons who looked, spoke and acted differently from themselves, and from what they understood to be "normal," there was increased discussion of classification. Thus, an "ideology of race" took shape in the seventeenth, eighteenth and nineteenth centuries, such that the mixing of common understanding and scientific evidence opened the door for widespread abuses on the basis of race.

As exploration gave way to colonialism, the usefulness of racial classifications became enmeshed with power – the opportunity to control entire populations. In 1684, the French physician François Bernier identified four groups of humans: Far Easterners, Europeans, blacks and Lapps. As scientific methods advanced in the eighteenth century, a number of writers offered more nuanced classifications. Perhaps the most notable of these was German physician, physiologist and anthropologist, Johann Friedrich Blumenbach, who, in 1775, created a racial classification system that divided humans into five races: Caucasian (white), Mongolian (yellow), Malayan (brown), Negroid (black) and American (red).

By the nineteenth century, there were dedicated searches for a universal definition of race that would be applicable across time and geographic location.

Scientists went to work measuring bones and craniums in an attempt to justify racial distinctions on the basis of biology. Beyond physical differences related to these and other factors (it should be noted that skin color, for instance, continued to be a relevant variable), there were explicit attempts to link such differences to moral and intellectual judgments. It is this step that renders troublesome the otherwise benign study of humans on the basis of biological difference. In other words, it became widely accepted that, not only were some physical differences reflective of fundamental biological differences between groups, but that some groups were inherently superior to others. As early as the nineteenth century, however, there were arguments to the contrary. Charles Darwin, for instance, believed that there was only one race of humans, noting that attempts to classify had resulted in confusion and disagreement over how many "races" there really were. It is this logic that has led to contemporary scientists widely rejecting the notion of race.

Essentially, the meaningful construct has to do with measuring the degree of difference between groups compared to the degree of difference found within groups. In other words, while there are certainly biological characteristics – some of which appear to be quite obvious – that link persons of different races to one another and separate them from persons of other races, there is considerable evidence that the differences among people of the same "race" are greater than differences between them and those of other races.

We should be clear, however, that Darwin's objections did not signal the end of biological models of race. Ostensibly scientific models of identifying races continued throughout the nineteenth and early part of the twentieth centuries, through the writings of such notable figures as Louis Agassiz, Joseph Arthur Compte de Gobineau, and Carleton Coon. A number of writers engaged in the study of **population genetics** have interpreted scientific data to reveal that there are genetically based differences in IQ that would explain (and even justify) the widespread and seemingly durable socioeconomic gaps between whites and members of other racial groups in the United States and throughout the world. As recently as the 1990s, in fact, Richard Hernstein and Charles Murray offered *The bell curve*, in which they suggest, through the study of intelligence, that genes and environment have a connection to race difference. Critics of these interpretations note that the enmeshed social and environmental factors that contextualize human development and functioning cannot be appropriately isolated.

Further, there might be normatively benevolent reasons to consider biological differences among persons of common ancestry. There are current discussions within the field of epidemiology that center on the degree to which biological similarities amongst individuals with a common racial classification can, and should, be used to cue health-care practitioners with respect to diagnosis or treatment. For example, sickle cell anemia is a dangerous medical condition that is found in a disproportionately high number of persons of African descent, so it is useful for physicians treating persons with such heritage to be aware of those unique risks. However, sickle cell anemia is also found in whites (particularly those with ancestry tracing back to the Mediterranean), so it would be equally unwise to construct rigid classifications based on this type of information.

Arguably more important – and certainly more salient – than the medical issues involved with biologically based classifications of race is the way that such identification has been used to privilege members of some races and disadvantage members of others. In the next section, we briefly consider the degree to which racial classifications have become normalized, along with the ways that assumptions about members of racial groups have been used to control power in multiple contexts.

RACE MATTERS

As noted above, if the differences used to identify racial categorizations were limited to their usefulness in medical diagnoses and treatment, it would be unlikely that entire bodies of scholarship (such as those reflected in this book) would have surfaced. To borrow a phrase from **Cornel West**, "race matters" because it has mattered so much in the lives of millions of people throughout the world. Far from being a harmless classification system, the concept of race has come to embody a series of assumptions that subconsciously affect our thoughts and behaviors and which have been incorporated into our social and political institutions.

In the American context, A. Leon Higginbotham has identified four essential steps that contributed to the establishment of black inferiority and white superiority in what would become the United States. It was necessary, he argued:

1   to convince white colonists that, regardless of their social or economic status, they were superior to blacks;
2   to convince blacks that they were inferior to all others;
3   to enforce the inferiority of blacks and superiority of whites in the most open and public manner; and
4   to explain the inferiority of blacks and superiority of whites by reference to Christianity.

These ideals provided the basis for a long period of legalized racial oppression and **segregation** (the results of which can still be observed today). Such attempts were often both bolstered and perpetuated by reliance on religion, as Higgenbotham's fourth step reveals. From colonists' work in preaching Christianity in Africa and the Americas to the United States based **white suprem-acist** group, the Ku Klux Klan, Higgenbotham's first two steps were achieved, in part, by interpreting references to lightness and darkness (not to mention slavery) in the Bible as relating to skin tone. The public acknowledgement of such differences (Higgenbotham's third step) serves to legitimize the attitudes and create an aura of inevitability about race-based segregation and white supremacy.

Further, James Horton argues that the race-based separation during the colonial period, which provided the philosophical justification for slavery, was economically opportunistic, not simply rooted in beliefs about the superiority of whites. Africans could be embraced by the colonists as a source of free labor because of the inherent belief that they were inferior but, implicit in those racial distinctions, was the fact that they had different physical features from Europeans and, thus, were easily distinguishable if they tried to escape. In this way, the moral distinctions between races combine with the prospect of economic success such that the interaction of these ideas was more powerful than either on its own. Slavery in the American context is an example of the way that conceptualizing race based on biology can serve as a justification for, as well as a perpetuation of, deeply held assumptions and expectations that are deemed to be consistent with the categorization. In this way, we can understand racism as a related construct that emerged from such attempts to classify.

Classifications, however, must be constructed. It is important to be attentive to the process by which a group is "racialized," or assigned a label of race (by those in a dominant position). Members of groups with access to power have the privilege of determining labels. It is not uncommon, for instance, for whites to tacitly assume that they are race neutral and that only those who are members of racial (power) **minority** groups have a race. Put another way, merely mentioning "race" almost always immediately calls to mind members of racial minority groups, not whites. This unstated reference point of **whiteness** and the subsequent racialization that occurs has effects that reach far beyond an individual's resentments or even hatred for members of another racial group.

RACISM

The emergence of the concept of race and the realization that it could be used to distinguish groups from each other has led to the presence of racism, which is the imposition of political, social, and economic power, as justified by racial categorizations. Because race was used as a means to distinguish between, and ultimately separate, groups of people in a way that would preserve power for the dominant group, a discussion about the concept of race is inherently couched in the struggle for preservation of power on the one hand and the struggle to gain equality on the other. In *Black power*, Stokely Carmichael and Charles Hamilton define racism as the predication of decisions and policies on considerations of race for the purpose of subordinating a racial group and maintaining control over it.

One of the most vivid examples of racist action occurred in Europe in the middle of the twentieth century. German leader Adolf Hitler, driven by the precept of Aryan superiority, took the position that Aryans were a superior race – the chosen people. In 1933, Hitler's Nazi Party issued a degree that sought to legally classify citizens as Aryan or non-Aryan and, in the context of economic hardship, those of Jewish descent provided a convenient scapegoat for society's troubles. Jews were identified as the enemy – "the other" – and that distinction served as justification for them being denied access to land and power, beginning in the 1930s, and, ultimately, to their imprisonment and mass murder in the 1940s.

More recently, the system of **apartheid** in South Africa comprised a system of legal racial segregation enforced by the National Party Government between 1948 and 1994. Although whites were the overwhelming numerical minority in the colonized nation, they controlled virtually all meaningful access to power. Now that blacks have access to the levers of power in South Africa, all is not settled. Besides that hostility and resentment that follows decades of race-based oppression, the residual disadvantage that black South Africans face after generations of being denied access to education and wealth and the accompanying policies that the black-run government has implemented, continues to affect the day-to-day lives of citizens.

Ancestral classifications in Rwanda that were reaffirmed and institutionalized under colonial rule have had lasting effects on attempts to govern effectively. As discussed further in Chapters 4 and 9, the establishment of strict racial **identities,** combined with power attributions, led to a civil war and to a **genocide** in 1994, that left an estimated 800,000 people dead, most of them Tutsis, who were killed brutally by Hutu militiamen. Now, the Tutsi-dominated government is accused of **authoritarianism**, exclusion based on ethnic identity, and abuse under the direction of former rebel leader Paul Kagame. It is such long-term, far-reaching effects of racial classification and conceptualization that we turn to in the final section of this chapter, where we use the United States as a case study.

SYSTEMIC DISADVANTAGE OF AFRICAN AMERICANS IN THE UNITED STATES

The first slave ships arrived in Virginia in 1619. In the American slave era, one's birth in Africa or condition of being a descendent of Africans relegated an entire segment of the population to be maintained as property and seen as less human than persons of European descent. Even though the Founders of the United States escaped the oppression of Britain and declared Independence in 1776 as an act of separation from the British Crown, they formed a government that accepted, codified and perpetuated oppression of "others."

Slavery in the New Republic

As the transition was made from Confederation to constitutional government between 1781 and 1789, the new United States was plagued by the controversy over the institution of slavery. While the Southern states wanted to count slaves as population for the purposes of determining **representation**, the Northern non-slave states were in opposition. The concern was primarily over power sharing in the new government rather than morality; the slaves were but a by-product or pawn in the broader North-South struggle.

Ultimately the framers of the Constitution decided on the Three-Fifths Compromise, which provided that each slave would count for three-fifths of a person for purposes of calculating the populations of the slave holding states. The Compromise is but one of the legal avenues by which Africans were mitigated to a status of less than a full person. With this action, the Constitution of the United States legally established a two-tiered society based on racial difference.

The Civil War and Reconstruction

Although slavery is not explicitly mentioned in the United States Constitution, the United States Supreme Court ruled, in the 1857 *Dred Scott* v. *Sandford* case, that citizenship was not possible for slaves or former slaves, who were considered to be "property." In this case, the former slave, Scott, did not have the right to citizenship regardless of the fact that he had been freed and taken to a non-slave state. His status as a former slave (and thus, property) was to be a lifetime condition. The decision arguably set the stage for the US Civil War, through which slavery would be confronted and, ultimately, abolished. The Emancipation Proclamation was signed by President Abraham Lincoln in 1863, and the Civil War Amendments were subsequently passed: the Thirteenth Amendment (1865) abolished slavery, the Fourteenth Amendment (1868) brought citizenship rights for the former slaves and established their equal protection and the Fifteenth Amendment (1870) was designed to give black men the right to vote. Despite the legal advances, designed to move away from slavery and the denial of political and legal rights to former slaves, white citizens and governments in the American South did not readily accept the new status of their former property.

The period between 1865 and 1876 is characterized as the Reconstruction era. During this time, blacks were elected to the United States House of Representatives, the United States Senate and to many of the state legislatures. However, this came to a halt as Reconstruction ended. The election of 1876 was controversial in that Samuel Tilden, a Democrat, won the popular vote but Rutherford B. Hayes, a Republican, won the plurality but not majority of votes in the Electoral College, which is a mechanism of state power-sharing by which Americans elect their head executive. The US Constitution requires that a candidate receive a majority of the Electoral College vote, otherwise the House of Representatives decides the presidency. To avoid this option, Hayes agreed to a political deal that involved the withdrawal of federal troops from the Southern states. These troops had been posted there to ensure that blacks were able to participate in the political process through voting. In the aftermath, the

Southern states began to repeal many of the laws that had come into effect during Reconstruction, and the era of Jim Crow segregation emerged, whereby a series of laws that separated citizens along the lines of race were established, further institutionalizing the significance of the concept of race and, ultimately, the practice of racism.

In 1896, the U.S. Supreme Court established precedent for a legal system of segregation of public facilities and (in the case of schools) institutions, so long as they were "equal." This created a legal hierarchy between the races that lasted for 58 years. It was overturned in 1954, when the Court decided in *Brown* v. *Board of Education* that children of color are inherently disadvantaged by being forced to attend all-black schools. Although the narrow question in *Brown* related to public schools, its legacy was that of rendering the so-called "separate but equal doctrine" unconstitutional.

The Civil Rights Movement

That decision served as legal justification for groups opposed to racial inequality to petition government in various ways to rectify the system of racial inequality that had characterized the United States and, before that, the American colonies, for nearly 400 years. From Rosa Parks' stand in Montgomery, Alabama in 1955 (which launched a powerful bus boycott) to the emergence of **Dr Martin Luther King, Jr** as a spokesperson for the **Civil Rights Movement**, a decade of social unrest led to landmark legislation being passed in the 1960s.

Though the legal precedents that perpetuated racial superiority have been slowly deconstructed, the concept of **white privilege** has not disappeared. This is a particularly elusive concept because all whites experience a degree of white privilege regardless of whether they hold conscious racial hostilities or believe in white supremacy. In other words, they benefit from American racism whether they subscribe to it or not.

America's "post-racial" era

The election of Barack Obama as the first black President of the United States is an illustration of what can be accomplished by a non-white citizen of the United States. President Obama unapologetically sought to run a campaign that was without direct racial appeals and seeks to govern in the same way. This approach to politics can lead to resentment from the segment of the population that does not view the United States as being "post-racial." Obama's recognition of the racial reality of his electoral context provides an opportunity for us to examine the degree to which such an attempt to "transcend" race might negate the existence and significance of race.

However, Obama's election reawakened feelings of racism and racial superiority that were latent in the minds of many whites. Further, while Obama identifies himself as African American, he is bi-racial with respect to his parents' racial classifications (his mother was white and his father was black). This led to some discussion about whether Obama was "black enough" to represent the interests of the black community. This concern over black **authenticity** relates to more than voting preference. In the Obama era, African Americans are forced to consider how they view their accomplishments. Because some do not want to be seen as less qualified for a position or do not want their achievements to be second guessed, they may overcompensate to ensure that whites will not question their achievement.

All of this sets up a peculiar dynamic because, when one considers the history of race relations in the United States and throughout the world, whites have gained advantage because of their race, whether they have sought to do so (as some have) or, as is most often the case today, whether they are awarded privilege automatically. This is particularly difficult in the United States, where young citizens are taught that every person has an equal chance to succeed, which means that those who do not have only themselves to blame. Any recognition of systemic explanations is perceived as an "excuse" by those who subscribe to the myth of meritocracy, which turns racism on its head such that the very term itself has come to connote any consideration of race at all. That is, the concept of power has been removed from the notion of "racism," which has resulted in the steadfast insistence on colorblindness in a way that continues to disadvantage persons of color. In this way, the ultimate power of racial classifications seems nearly impenetrable, as a failure to properly consider context has resulted in conscious attitudes that resist any consideration of race at all.

CONCLUSION

The continued responses of white America to the accomplishments of racial minority groups in the United States is reflective of broader trends in the ways that classification based on race has come to "matter" in the lives of people around the globe. Specifically, despite the scientific discrediting of race as a biological construct, there are vestiges of what Higginbotham refers to as the "precept of inferiority" and the desire to maintain superiority. Although few nations operate in an actual colonial context, there are whites who may consider themselves superior to blacks regardless of their socioeconomic or political status.

More important, notions such as "superiority" and "inferiority" are, in many ways, unhelpful to understanding how the concept of race "works" in contemporary social contexts. Where there are resentments of non-whites, they are usually latent; where there are **prejudices**, they are often explained by personality traits. In other words, persons in Western democracies in particular spend time trying to identify who is "a racist" rather than contemplating the complexity of "racism" as a system of privilege and disadvantage that is pervasive in a given **culture**. The individualization of racism only serves to shift the burden from the shoulders of well-meaning, racially inclusive whites to persons of colors and overt bigots; the former group is disproportionately denied access to power, while the latter is patently uninterested in helping to rectify racial injustice.

As a result, the racial classification system that has been in place – though largely discredited – continues to be very "real" for people around the world. Scholars, then, such as those who have contributed to this book, are very interested in "race," even though it could be argued that it is not "real." Though its roots are not set in biology, the social and political importance of the concept renders it very "real" to millions of people around the world and, thus, is important to understand in all its complexity and historical context.

KEY READINGS

Alland, A. (2002). *Race in mind: Race, IQ and other racisms.* New York: Palgrave Macmillan.

Barker, L. J., Jones, M. H., & Tate, K. (1999). *African Americans and the American political system* (4th ed.). Saddle River, NJ: Prentice Hall.

Carmichael, S. & Hamilton, C. (1967). *Black power: The politics of black liberation.* New York: Vintage Books.

Dyson, M. E. (2007). *Debating race.* New York: Basic Books.

Fredrickson, G. M. (2002). *Racism: A short history.* Princeton, NJ: Princeton University Press.

Graves, J. L. (2003). *The emperor's new clothes: Biological theories of race at the millennium.* New Brunswick, NJ: Rutgers University Press.

Herrnstein, R. J. & Murray, C. (1994). *The bell curve: Intelligence and class structure in American life.* New York: Free Press.

Higginbotham, A. L. (1996). *Shades of freedom.* New York: Oxford University Press.

Ifill, G. (2009). *The breakthrough: Politics and race in the age of Obama.* New York: Doubleday.

Marable, M. (2006). *Race, reform and rebellion: The second Reconstruction and beyond in black America 1945–2006.* Jackson, MS: University of Mississippi Press.

Mukhopadhyay, C. C., Henze, R. & Moses, Y. T. (2007). *How real is race? A sourcebook on race, culture and biology.* Lanham, MD: Rowman and Littlefield Education.

Race: The power of an illusion. (2003). Film produced by California Newsreel in association with Independent Television Services.

Terrante, J. & Brown, P. Jr (1998). *The social construction of race and ethnicity in the United States.* New York: Longman.

Wagner, R. (2001). *The anthropological treatises of Johann Friedrich Blumenbach.* Chestnut Hill, MA: Adamant Media Corporation.

West, C. (1993). *Race matters.* Boston: Beacon Press.

2

ETHNICITY

VIVIAN IBRAHIM

The term "ethnicity" is commonly used in everyday parlance; however, the concept can be, and indeed has been, interpreted in a number of different manners depending on time and different socio-political contexts. Often used interchangeably with the term "**race**," I argue here that it is distinguishable by its social construction of certain identifying boundaries.

THE ORIGINS OF ETHNICITY

Given how much we use the term today, it may surprise many that the term "ethnicity" first appeared in the *Oxford English Dictionary* only in 1972. Despite this, however, the concept has long-founded roots: the term is derived from *ethnos*, the Greek word for "people" or "tribe." By the Middle Ages, the term "ethnic" had appeared in the English language. It referred to those who were pagan or heathen and was most likely derived from the Greek New Testament, which used it as a synonym for gentile. The usage of *ethnos*, or *ethnie* (plural) has been subject to much discussion and variation. Often associated with what Edward Said would term the "**other**," today, as in ancient Greece, the term is often reserved to differentiate "us" from "them." For the Greeks, the foreign barbarians were the *ethnea*, while they would commonly refer to themselves as *Genos Hellenon* or the "family of Hellenes." Today, in many parts of the world, and particularly the Western world, one is more inclined to refer to "nation" for themselves and "ethnic" for immigrant peoples, as in the frequently used term "ethnic minorities." This undoubtedly opens up the question of **power** dynamics that is involved in the usage of the term "ethnicity" – one that is often associated with differentiation and boundaries of, or indeed from, the "other," who in turn is often, although not exclusively, viewed as "exotic." This view of the exotic "other" may be based on a question of race, color of skin or simply being a recent immigrant. Thus, for example, one in the "Western world," which usually encompasses Europe, America and Australia, is far more likely to refer to African-inspired jewelry as "ethnic." Similarly, long-established North African communities of second and third generation in France are often denoted as "fringe" or ethnic communities that are characterized by their exotic *tagine* cooking and cous-cous and rai music. What is important to stress here is that this adoption or usage of the term "ethnic" in these situations has potential,

12

significant underlying issues in relation to power dynamics between majority communities and **minority/ies**.

If one is to assess the term from within the field of social sciences, however, a different usage of the concept emerges that is less concerned with the content of ethnicity than the mechanisms that convert "ethnic attributes" into "ethnic communities." At the forefront of this was the German sociologist Max Weber (1864–1920), who came to some significant conclusions during his research on agrarian life in East Germany during the 1890s. Examining the difference between German and Polish farmers and laborers, Weber concluded that historical and social causes could explain why there were discrepancies in the social and economic behavior of Poles and Germans on the land. This was an important breakthrough, as this negated the idea that a certain group had inherent characteristics. Instead, Weber argued that both Germans and Poles were a product of historical circumstances rather than a permanent cultural or biological attribute. Visiting the United States a few years later, Weber set out to examine why there was such a contrast in the status of African Americans and Natives. He argued that the differentiation could not be purely attributable to color, since neither was white (in contrast to large sectors of the population in the USA). Weber concluded that the only difference was related to the institution of slavery. Historical and social circumstance had created a group marker that differentiated the communities – the Native Americans, the African Americans and the white Americans – from one another.

Weber's argument rested on defining ethnic groups as "human groups (other than kinship groups) who cherish a belief in the common origins of such a kind that it provides a basis for the creation of 'community.'" Weber viewed all ethnic groups as socially constructed or *künstlich*, as they were based on a subjective belief of a shared community *Gemeinschaft*. Therefore, for Weber, beliefs were at the forefront of understanding the formation of ethnic groups. This was different from what historian and Marxist Harold Isaacs would later identify as *diacritics*, or distinguishing markers, such as language, religion and biological characteristics. While Weber argued that common ancestry was important, this was largely due to the fact that it assisted in the identification of a shared origin, which was often largely fictitious. For instance, he negated the fact that the Roman Empire fell when the "barbarian blood" of other communities was mixed with that of the Romans and, in fact, argued that this strengthened the empire through a widening of its boundaries. Indeed, he went on further to argue that supposed ethnic membership did not automatically result in the emergence of an ethnic community, and that historical circumstance was often responsible for the mobilization of certain political and social movements. For instance, he viewed **nationalism** as an extension of the ethnic community as members and leaders searched for a unique political structure by establishing an independent state. For Weber, it was clear that the central themes in understanding ethnicity were power, authority, legitimization and domination, which, even today, are useful in the analysis of racial and ethnic conflict.

THEORIES OF ETHNICITY

Weber's definition of communities as socially constructed has had an enormous effect on the body of literature that has emerged, largely in the Western world, since the 1960s concerning ethnicity and ethnic groups. Approaches to ethnicity are complicated and can be split between those who view *ethnies* as long-established and those who treat ethnicity as a political, social and cultural resource for their own interest. Beginning with the former, known as primordialists, the main supporters were sociologist Edward Shills and anthropologist Clifford Geertz, who argued that ethnicity could be defined as an overpowering bond that one was born with. This, for example, could include blood, race and language. Primordialists have, however, been greatly criticized since their explanation is largely viewed as being stagnant and failing to consider the flexibility of ethnic **identity**. To take an example to illustrate this, have Arabs always been a homogenous and defined "ethnic" group, the members of which have always inter-married with fellow Arabs and spoken Arabic? This view would undoubtedly fail to take into consideration those who converted to Islam from Judaism and Christianity following the expansion of the Islamic empires in the seventh to tenth centuries, and it would also fail to recognize those who consider themselves to be politically and linguistically "Arab," having once spoken Aramaic, Greek, Coptic, etc. Similarly, such definitions fail to take into account interactions between Arabs and Africans, traders from the Indian Ocean, and invading empires like the Mongols. Most social scientists today would agree that the primordial interpretation for ethnicity fails to stand strong.

In contrast, those known as the Instrumentalists view/ed ethnicity as a resource for various interests; for them, membership of an ethnic group is a question of rational choice. This involves elite strategies by which those who require power, wealth, and other sources of strength or benefit, etc., gain it by joining national or ethnic communities in order to achieve their own ends. Other instrumentalists, like **postcolonialist** Homi Bhabha, have argued that ethnicity is merely a "cut and paste job," where individuals pick and chose which parts of their identity they wish to highlight. Indeed, the author Amin Maalouf argues that

> [i]n every age there have been people who considered that an individual had one overriding affiliation so much more important in every circumstance to all others that it might legitimately be called his or her "identity." For some it was the nation, for others religion or class. But one has only to look at the various conflicts being fought out all over the world today to realize that no one allegiance has absolute supremacy. Where people feel their faith is threatened, it is their religious affiliation that seems to reflect their whole identity. But if their mother tongue or ethnic group is in danger, then they fight ferociously against their co-religionists.
>
> (Maalouf, 2000: 12)

Instrumentalists have, however, been criticized for dissociating individual cultural identity from institutional bases. Transactionalists, the most prominent of whom is social anthropologist Fredrik Barth, have argued that ethnicity is not unchangeable:

> ethnic distinctions do not depend on an absence of mobility, contact and information, but do entail social processes of exclusion and incorporation whereby discrete categories are maintained despite changing participation and membership in the course of individual life stories [...] The features which are taken into account are not the sum of the objective differences, but only those which the actors themselves regard as significant.
>
> (Barth, 1969: 10, 14)

This transactional nature of ethnicity comes in two basic kinds: internal definition and external definition. Barth suggests that internal definition of one's ethnicity is how an individual or "actor," as he denotes them, signals their own self-identification, for example "I am Croat." External definitions take place when a person defines others either consensually, in which case it is validated by the other, or conflictually, that is to say imposed. Creating further distinctions, Barth argues that there is a difference between groups and categories. A social group is self-defined, whereas a category, he argues, is delineated by others. Applying Barth's general approach, sociologist Anthony D. Smith has developed an understanding of ethnicity using the ethno-symbolist approach. Smith has argued that myths and symbols play an important role in unifying populations and ensuring that they continue. Emphasizing the cultural contents of myths, Smith argues that there has been a resurgence of ethnicity in the modern world as a reaction to bureaucratic rationalism.

ETHNICITY, THE NATION STATE AND MULTICULTURALISM

In his seminal work, *Imagined communities*, political scientist Benedict Anderson argues that a nation is an "imagined political community [that is] imagined as both inherently limited and sovereign." Nations and indeed nationalism developed with the rise of the modern bureaucratic state and, as a result, the national boundaries in many ways became synonymous with the state. In the Ottoman Empire, for example (1299–1922), religious minority communities, such as the Greek Orthodox, were dealt with as a *millat* in contrast to the Muslim majority. This effectively meant that they were autonomously recognized communities largely administered by their communal head (usually a patriarch) in affairs to do with the religious upkeep of the community. In a modern nation state, however, this autonomy would undermine the concept that all citizens should be equally integrated and homogenous within the nation state. This poses serious problems for those states that transitioned into nations but also housed "multi-ethnic" communities. On one hand, some nations were able to **assimilate** all individuals into a "civic nationalism," which effectively meant that all citizens would be equal if they adhered to the ideals of the new nation, which promoted perceived common cultural values and allowed people of different origins to assimilate within the nation. The most pronounced example of this was during the French Revolution with the concepts of *liberté, égalité, fraternité* or liberty, equality and brotherhood. Even these broad concepts were rejected by some factions during the revolution, however.

On the other hand, nations today face new preoccupations when it comes to the concept of ethnicity. The aforementioned Harold Isaacs has argued that the collapse of certain political systems in the modern world, which had, up until 1945, held clusters of people together, has had an important impact on ethnic groups and the types of societies that followed. For example, post-**imperial** states like France, following its departure from Algeria in 1962, were faced with a new challenge: Algerians migrating to France for socio-economic motivations. The essential question, therefore, is how this impacts French society, which prides itself on its apparent civic nationalism. How do Algerians interact with French ideals and, if they do not participate, do they become a "fringe" ethnic community? The influx of migrants from ex-colonies therefore poses an interesting question when it comes to the identity of an "established" nation state. On one hand, some states, like France, have felt a strong friction between these former colonial community migrants as their ideals, including their engagement in religious practices, sit at complete odds with French secularism. On the other hand, other nation states have prided themselves on becoming successful **multicultural** entities, with hybridized cultural communities. Here, it is worth noting the plurality of communities that act as polyethnic states. For example, India is the most multicultural nation state in Asia with its diverse languages, religions, and cultural practices. These boundaries, which are often used in day-to-day parlance to describe ethnic communities, can be seen in the state boundaries of the nation, which are largely drawn across linguistic lines. Indeed, the constitution of India recognizes 22 languages.

The most prominent multicultural societies in the Western world include Australia and Canada. In particular, Canada passed an "Act for the Preservation and Enhancement of Multiculturalism in Canada," in 1985 (later updated in 1991), which is more commonly known as the "Canadian Multiculturalism Act." Multiculturalism in Canada refers

to the presence and persistence of diverse racial and ethnic minorities who define themselves as different and who wish to remain so. Ideologically, multiculturalism consists of a relatively coherent set of ideas and ideals pertaining to the celebration of Canada's cultural diversity. Multiculturalism at the policy level is structured around the management of diversity through formal initiatives in the federal, provincial and municipal domains. Finally, multiculturalism is the process by which racial and ethnic minorities compete to obtain support from central authorities for the achievement of certain goals and aspirations.

(Dewing and Leman, 2006)

This act is hugely important, as Canada has one of the highest per capita immigration rates in the world. Its immigrants are largely, although not wholly, driven by economic motivations. On a local level, federal money is distributed to ethnic groups to help preserve **cultures**, and it is not uncommon for it to be used for the creation of ethnic-orientated community centers. Successive Canadian governments have argued that promoting a policy of multiculturalism strengthens national identity by breaking down social and cultural barriers, thereby promoting a single moral community. This policy can be described as either a celebration of difference or alternatively as the creation of a "melting pot," in many ways similar to America's national metaphor that emerged from the late nineteenth century. This idea is based on the notions that different immigrant communities brought their own practices and cultures, which later amalgamated to create a unique "American" identity.

THE FAILURE OF MULTICULTURALISM AND THE FEARS OF "BALKANIZATION"

Multiculturalism has, however, been rejected by a number of Western societies in recent years, the most prominent of which is the Netherlands, particularly since the late 1990s. The Netherlands has largely regarded itself, up to the post-Second World War era, as a monocultural society. The Netherlands has always had a strong classical national identity that romanticized a "Dutch Golden Age." This was to evolve as the Netherlands social composition changed from the 1960s, as large-scale labor migration to the Dutch nation was encouraged for lower-paid jobs. While the intellectual elites and political class expressed the language of multiculturalism and encouraged migration, there was a silent assumption that immigrant communities would return "home" once they were no longer needed. As numbers of migrants grew and many stayed to have children, who became second- and third-generation Dutch citizens, this idea of "returning home" began to diminish. Today, although the majority of the population is still ethnic Dutch, up to one-fifth is of non-Western origin. By the late 1990s, a series of intellectuals, both Dutch-born and assimilated immigrants, had attacked multiculturalism. For instance, a professor at Leiden University, Paul Cliteur, attacked **political correctness** and argued that Western cultures and values were, and indeed still are, superior to those of non-Western origin. As a result, Cliteur argues that political correctness allows immigrant communities to continue what he terms "barbaric practices," including homophobia and **discrimination** against women. This view has since been adopted by a number of prominent Dutch politicians who have argued that immigration and the presence of certain ethnic communities has led to a decay of Dutch ideals. These criticisms against immigrant minority and ethnic communities have mostly been aimed at Muslims, mainly from Morocco. Pim Fortuyn, who ran for the position of Prime Minister, argued vehemently against what he termed the

"Islamicization of the Netherlands." While it is clear that Muslims are not an ethnic minority, the assertion of these claims affects ethnic minorities in the Netherlands, the vast majority of whom are practicing Muslims. This suggests that this problem of ethnic group identification is far more complex than initially understood and that some religious identities are increasingly being attributed to race. Fortuyn was assassinated by an animal rights activist in 2002, who later argued that the politician was exploiting the weakness of minority communities in an election campaign. Since then, a number of prominent figures have emerged in the Netherlands, including Ayaan Hirsi Ali, who attacked minority practices of Islam as oppressive. Claiming that "all human beings are equal, but all cultures are not," she commissioned director Theo van Gogh to make a short film on women and Islam – the latter was subsequently murdered as a result of the inflammatory nature of the film.

Indeed, the Netherlands is not the only country to reveal signs of rejecting multiculturalism, often dubbed the retreat from liberalism. From the 1980s, prominent critics in the United States argued that multiculturalism undermined national unity. Instead, they argued that the celebration of difference through multiculturalism has led to the demonization of American culture, often closely associated with anti-globalizationists and the creation of a "cult of ethnicity." Indeed, some have gone further to argue that **ethnocentrists** who live in the West see only the negatives in Western/American society. It is, in turn, argued that this would lead to fragmentation of society and eventually "Balkanization." This term, though not completely accurate, is a reference to the disintegration of the Balkans, from the collapse of the Ottoman Empire to the present day, and has come to symbolize the worst case of social division and disintegration. The region has seen the creation of numerous new nation states that are divided along ethnic and religious lines and are largely the result of a series of wars throughout the 1990s. Most prominently, the Bosnian War (1992–95), saw mass **ethnic cleansing** of non-ethnic Serbs. The Srebrenica **genocide**, which took place in July 1995, when up to 8,000 Bosnian men and boys were killed and 25,000–30,000 refugees in the surrounding regions of Srebrenica were ethnically cleansed, is just one of a series of atrocities that have happened in recent history. While it is not the suggestion of the author that that the eradication of multiculturalism will lead to mass genocide, the case of Bosnia, like that of the Jews in the Second World War and, more recently, Rwanda, highlight the potential dangers of discriminatory behaviors and practices led by nation states and ethnic majorities against ethnic minorities.

BEYOND ETHNICITY

While sociologist and social anthropologist Ernest Gellner argued, in 1983, that the homogenizing tendencies of nationalism would leave little space for sub-nationalisms and ethnic identities, it seems that he has not been proven to be wholly correct. While it is impossible to conclude what the future holds for ethnic groups, advances in technology have led to stronger sub-state ethnic groups being forged, if not in "real" places, then at least in cyberspace. For example, the role played by Tamil Sri Lankans through the medium of the Internet, particularly in the vicious and violent fighting of May 2009, has led to greater awareness of the Tamil cause. The increasingly common use of the Internet as a medium by **diaspora** groups, amongst others, highlights that "non-traditional spaces" are being used to nurture and expand some ethnic and national identities.

KEY READINGS

Anderson, B. (1983). *Imagined communities: Reflections on the origin and spread of nationalism.* London: Verso.

Avruch, K. (2003). Culture and ethnic conflict in the new world disorder. In J. Stone & R. Dennis (Eds.), *Race and ethnicity: Comparative and theoretical approaches.* Oxford: Blackwell, pp. 72–82.

Barth, F. (1969). *Ethnic groups and boundaries: The social organization of culture difference.* Oslo: Universitetsforlaget.

Bhabha, H. (2002). *The location of culture.* London: Routledge.

Dewing, M. & Leman, M. (2006). *Canadian multiculturalism.* Available at www.parl.gc.ca/information/library/PRBpubs/936-e.htm.

Geertz, C. (1963). *Old societies and new states.* New York: Free Press.

Hecter, M. (1986). Rational choice theory and the study of race and ethnic relations. In J. Rex & D. Mason (Eds.), *Theories of race and ethnic relations.* New York: Cambridge University Press, pp. 264–279.

Hutchinson, J. & Smith, A. (Eds.) (1996). *Ethnicity.* New York: Oxford University Press.

Isaacs, H. (1975). *Idols of the tribe: Group identity and political change.* New York: Harper & Row.

Jenkins, R. (2003). Rethinking ethnicity: Identity, categorization and power. J. Stone & R. Dennis (Eds.), *Race and ethnicity: Comparative and theoretical approaches.* Oxford: Blackwell, pp. 59–71.

Maalouf, A. (2000). *On identity.* London: Harvill Press.

Margry, P. J. (2003). The murder of Pim Fortuyn and collective emotions. Hype, hysteria and holiness in the Netherlands? *Etnofoor: Anthropologisch tijdschrift*, 16, 106–131.

Melucci, A. (1989). *Nomads of the present.* Philadelphia, PA: Temple University Press.

Richmond, A. H. (2003). Post-industrialism, post-modernism, and ethnic conflict. In J. Stone & R. Dennis (Eds.), *Race and ethnicity: Comparative and theoretical approaches.* Oxford: Blackwell, pp. 93–94.

Runciman, W. G. (Ed.). (1978). *Weber: Selections in translation.* New York: Cambridge University Press.

Said, E. (1995). *Orientalism: Western conceptions of the Orient.* London: Penguin.

Schlesinger, A. M. (1998). *The disuniting of America: Reflections on a multicultural society.* New York: W. W. Norton & Company.

Smith, A. D. (1992). Nationalism and the historians. *International Journal of Contemporary Sociology*, 33, 63.

Stone, J. (2003). Max Weber on race, ethnicity and nationalism. In J. Stone & R. Dennis (Eds.), *Race and ethnicity: Comparative and theoretical approaches*. Oxford: Blackwell, pp. 28–42.

3

WHITENESS

ROBERT JENSEN

In recent years the study of, discussion about, and political organizing against racism have increasingly turned toward a consideration of **whiteness**. Recognizing that white people often do not think of themselves as part of a racial category, this approach can promote a clearer analysis of the racial system and a more honest self-assessment on the part of individual whites. Understanding **race** and racism requires an understanding of the pathology of whiteness that is at the core of our racial system.

Paradoxically, shifting whiteness closer to the center of the analysis offers a way to de-center whiteness by making visible the category of white, challenging the unspoken assumption of white-as-norm, and stripping away whiteness's always-present claim (whether explicit or implicit) of superiority. The goal is the recognition that the color of the race problem is white – racial conflict is a product of historical and ongoing claims of **white supremacy**. Though originally crafted and imposed by white elites, white supremacy eventually was accepted by most of the white community. The end of racism, therefore, requires the end of whiteness. To end whiteness, it first must be identified and analyzed.

This essay is focused on the idea of whiteness, not on the consequences of white supremacy on non-white people. The evidence of those consequences is clear and is dealt with throughout this volume. Studies from sociology and psychology demonstrate that white people, including those who reject racism and white supremacy, still often act in the world in a way that is based on white-supremacist assumptions. Extensive data outline the racialized disparities in wealth and well-being that have long existed in US society and endure decades after the significant legislative achievements of the **Civil Rights Movement**. The focus here will be on the concept at the core of those realities, looking primarily at the United States, where these ideas developed most distinctly and remain most visibly at the center of contemporary social life.

Like many concepts deployed in the study of complex social realities, "whiteness" can illuminate or obscure reality, depending on framing and focus. In this essay, the focus will be primarily on questions of **power** and wealth; I will use a political and economic framework. The modern notion of whiteness was created by elites who wanted to maintain and deepen political and economic power, and white supremacy today protects the status and wealth of a range of whites. Out of that political and economic system, white people have developed collective practices to shore up white control (the culture of white supremacy) and come to hold certain ideas and experience certain emotions about race (the psychology of white supremacy). Those cultural and psychological factors are important, but to most effectively analyze whiteness, white supremacy, and **white privilege**, we must remain grounded in the political and economic sphere. This is crucial in a period in which popular terms such as "**multiculturalism**" and "diversity" often signal a focus on the cultural and psychological that minimizes or ignores political and economic dimensions.

WHAT ARE WHITE PEOPLE?

White people often have white skin, which actually is not really white, of course, but a pale/pinkish/off-white shade that has come to be labeled as white. Associated with that skin pigmentation are a variety of other physical traits regarding, especially, the shape of noses and lips and the texture of hair. White people typically can trace their ancestors to Europe, especially the United Kingdom, northern Europe, and Scandinavia – what many think of as the places that are the source of the people who are most **authentically** white. But being white is not really about how people look or where our ancestors came from.

White people are most clearly defined as those people living in a white-supremacist society who are understood to be white by other individuals, especially those who make and/or execute political, economic, and social policies in the institutions of that society. People are white, in this sense, when they are perceived as being white by a police officer, by the person interviewing job candidates, or by the loan officer of a bank. A person is white if people with power believe the person to be white.

This means that people whose physical attributes may make it hard to categorize them in racial terms can be perceived as white in one situation and not in another; such decisions about racial classification result, not just from qualities in the individual who is being evaluated, but from the expectations of those doing the evaluating. A fair-skinned person with white and black ancestors might be classified differently by two different police officers, for example. Markers other than physical appearance also are relevant; light-skinned people who would be categorized as white based on physical appearance can shift into the **Latina/Latino** classification after someone hears them speak with an accent.

Although the terms "multi-racial" or "bi-racial" are used frequently today to describe people with parents from different racial groups, in the political and economic sense there are few people who straddle racial categories in ways that defy classification. A person may have relatives from many different racial categories and hence be multi-racial in cultural terms, in the sense of having connections to different traditions and practices. But in interactions with others, a multi-racial person is most often going to be treated based on the perceptions people have of the racial group that they assign to the person. In such cases, the actual family history of the multi-racial or bi-racial person is irrelevant to the perceptions of others. There are some mixed-race individuals whose characteristics are so ambiguous that others will be unable to categorize them, but that is rare.

Beyond such individual ambiguity, entire groups of people who were not initially classified as white in the United States – the Irish and Jews, along with immigrants from parts of southern and eastern Europe – "became" white by accepting the structure of a white-supremacist system. For example, Noel Ignatieff has described how Irish were the targets of intense bigotry and **discrimination** when they first came in large numbers to the United States but strove as a group to have themselves identified as white to secure a place in the United States' racial hierarchy. At the collective level, therefore, "white" also is not a description of biology but a term that simply means an identifiable group of people are perceived as white by those with power.

WHERE DID THE IDEA OF WHITENESS COME FROM?

Despite the common assumption that human beings have always categorized each other on the basis of race, the practice is relatively recent. The creation of modern whiteness, and accompanying rigid notion of racial categories, is connected to the "divide and conquer" strategies that elites throughout history have used to control the majority of a population and maintain an unequal distribution of wealth and power.

In the early years of the British colonies in North America, indentured servants, typically working under harsh conditions, made up the majority of the labor force. Eventually, slaves began arriving from Africa, often working alongside those indentured servants. Rigid racial categories had not yet been created, there were no clear laws around slavery, and personal relationships and alliances between the indentured servants and slaves were not uncommon. As the workers from England began to demand better conditions, the planter elite saw those alliances as a serious threat to their power. The "solution" was to increase the use of African slaves and separate them from poor white workers by giving the whites a higher status with more opportunities without disturbing the basic hierarchical distribution of wealth and power. This successfully undermined the alliances of blacks and whites, leading white workers to identify more with wealthy whites while blacks were increasingly associated with the degradation inherent in slavery.

This strategy of elites, written into law in the slave codes, destroyed **solidarity** between poor blacks and whites and proved to be a model not only for undermining connections between white and all non-white workers, but also for pitting different non-white groups against each other. The limited benefits that elites bestowed on white workers have been referred to as "the wage of whiteness," which is, in large part, psychological – white workers in this system get to think of themselves as superior to non-whites, and especially blacks, no matter how impoverished they may be or how wide the gap between their lives and the lives of wealthy white people.

A powerful summary of this comes from the film *Mississippi burning*, in which a Southern-born white FBI agent in the United States tries to explain the state's racial politics to a Northern white colleague. The Southerner tells the story of how his father, jealous of the success of a nearby black farmer, poisoned that neighbor's mule. The father told his son, "If you ain't better than a **nigger**, son, who are you better than?" Challenged by his Northern colleague not to make excuses for racism, the Southerner says he is simply describing his father, "an old man who was so full of hate that he didn't know that being poor was what was killing him."

Notions of white supremacy also were important in white people's campaign to eliminate **indigenous people** in what is now the United States and in other parts of the Americas. If native peoples were less than fully human, or at least inferior humans to Europeans, then the extermination of those people and the expropriation of their land could be presented as the inevitable triumph of a superior group and, therefore, morally justified. For example, President Theodore Roosevelt defended the expansion of whites across the continent as an inevitable process

> due solely to the power of the mighty civilized races which have not lost the fighting instinct, and which by their expansion are gradually bringing peace into the red wastes where the barbarian peoples of the world hold sway.
>
> (Theodore Roosevelt, *The strenuous life*. New York: The Century Co., 1901: 38)

From these roots emerged an increasingly well-developed notion of white supremacy that became codified in law and embedded in cultural practices, with disastrous consequences not only for people of indigenous and African descent, but also every other non-white group. Although there have been several points at which the United States has been in a position to renounce this white supremacy – such as the abolition of slavery after the Civil War and the end of **apartheid** in the twentieth-century Civil Rights Movement – whiteness and white supremacy have "survived US history," to borrow historian David Roediger's phrase. White people's belief in their special status has demonstrated an incredible tenacity; even when it is widely agreed to be morally bankrupt and intellectual indefensible, the idea of whiteness and the accompanying white-supremacist system remain deeply woven into the fabric of society.

WHY IS WHITENESS SO HARD TO SHAKE?

Roediger's analysis reminds us that white-defined and -dominated institutions, and white people individually, must confront the gap between stated ideals around racial justice in a post-civil rights society and the actual working of that society. This leads to troubling observations about the white community in general. While it is easy to condemn the bigotry of those white people who are overtly racist – those whose conception of whiteness has never moved beyond the nineteenth century – the more vexing questions concern "polite" white society that rejects the ugly expressions of white supremacy but has been unable and/or unwilling to take serious steps to remake society on egalitarian principles.

It is widely accepted that race is real in social terms – political, economic, and cultural systems treat race as if it were a coherent way of categorizing humans – and that race is a fiction in biological terms. Work on the **human genome** reveals some patterns that correlate with our ancestors' continent of origin, but there are not distinct races. As discussed in Chapter 1 of this volume, modern scientific evidence clearly shows that there is one human race, and the people who are part of it have various kinds of physical differences.

So, there is a scientific consensus that the idea of biological race is incoherent and a professed moral consensus that rejects the claim that people in one socially constructed racial group could be inherently superior to others. Why, then, does white supremacy continue to structure US society and so much of the world? Why do people in the socially constructed category of "white" – even those who would agree with the scientific and moral consensus – avoid the implications of the relevant data about the unjust distribution of wealth and power? Why do white people hold onto a sense of themselves as white when, at the same time, they condemn white supremacy? If the concept of whiteness has no meaning outside of white supremacy, why do white people who believe in justice have so much trouble letting go of whiteness?

Given the complex interplay of the political, economic, cultural, and psychological, no simple answers are likely, but patterns can be identified. In societies in which people believe there always will be hierarchies, it appears to be in one's self-interest (defined in material terms with a short-range view) to accept the hierarchies and try to climb to, or stay in, the highest position possible. The potential rewards for this are access (or the promise of access) to wealth, greater social status, and an inflated sense of self-esteem. Only a small percentage of white people are wealthy, of course, and many white people in contemporary US society do not work or live in positions of high status. So, while all three types of rewards are available only to a relatively small group of white people, even the poorest and most vulnerable whites can extract some social value from whiteness – the state of being white, of being on top in a racial hierarchy.

The complexity of this is captured in the term "white trash," a slur used to describe white people with few financial resources and/or low social status. For such people, one response to the cruel hierarchy from which the insult emerges would be to openly reject white supremacy and make common cause with the people of color who are at risk in similar ways – to reject the "white" and embrace the "trash" as a source of solidarity and strength. Yet no sustained cross-racial movement of the dispossessed has taken root in that segment of the white community in the United States, despite the potential for political success of such a grassroots strategy.

Whiteness has the capacity to dull the moral sensibilities of privileged white people, while at the same time providing some way for those without wealth or status to dull the effects of life near the bottom of the hierarchy. Again, the tenacity of the idea of whiteness is striking.

WHITE REACTIONS TO "WHITE PRIVILEGE" IN THE UNITED STATES

In a white-supremacist society, white people will have advantages that are not a product of any individual effort or ability but are built into the structure of society. We call this white privilege. That is hardly a radical claim, yet it continues to be controversial in many sectors of US society.

Overt white supremacists argue that white people are now victimized in the contemporary racial order, although there is no data to support such a claim of "reverse racism." Others invoke the idea that US society is a meritocracy and reject the possibility that things they have accomplished could be in any way the product of such privilege. And many of those who concede that racism is still a serious problem attempt to divert attention from white privilege by suggesting that racial justice can best be achieved by adopting a "color-blind" approach to social life and public policy. Such a claim is coherent only if there existed a truly level playing field on which we could safely ignore color without fear that we would unconsciously replicate white-supremacist patterns. But because of whites' historical advantages in the accumulation of wealth, along with contemporary manifestations of unconscious racism, such a level playing field does not exist. To claim to be **color blind**, then, is to endorse blindness when assessing the effects of color and, therefore, to lend tacit support to white supremacy.

Resistance to the idea of white privilege in the white community comes from across the political spectrum. Part of this is no doubt rooted in calculations of self-interest, but it seems to be in part the product of a lack of clarity in the use of the term, and the tendency for the term to be used in isolation from analyses of other hierarchies.

The claim that white privilege operates in contemporary society does not mean white privilege dictates the outcome of every interaction, but rather that it simply is one significant factor that may affect the outcome of those interactions. Take the commonly cited case of "driving while black/brown," the experience of being targeted by law enforcement if one is perceived to be driving in the "wrong" part of town or in the "wrong" kind of car. The claim is not that every black or brown person will be pulled over for no legitimate reason, or that every such interaction will result in the use of unnecessary force by an officer. Nor is the claim that white people are never treated unjustly by law enforcement officers. But there are patterns of treatment based on race; non-white people must deal with that potential threat on a daily basis in ways that white people are privileged to ignore.

As the editors of this volume noted in the introduction, we can, and should, recognize the effects of other hierarchies, such as those involving gender, sexuality, and class. In certain situations a black manager could wield power unfairly over a white worker, given the inequality built into corporate capitalism. An indigenous man could sexually harass a white woman, given the power dynamics in patriarchy. A straight Latino might refuse to rent an apartment to a white gay man or lesbian, given the nature of heterosexism. Recognizing that white privilege exists does not require one to ignore how other systems of privilege operate alongside white supremacy. To claim that white people have privilege is simply to acknowledge that, all other social factors being equal, non-white people face a range of hostile behaviors – from racist violence to being taken less seriously in a business meeting, from discrimination in hiring to subtle exclusion in social settings. While all people, including whites, experience unpleasant interactions with others, white people do not carry the burden of negative racial **stereotypes** into those interactions. That advantage is what we call white privilege.

"WHITE HISTORY MONTH" AND THE PROBLEM OF FALSE EQUIVALENCY

White people sometimes point out that there is no White History Month to balance Black History Month, or no White Student Center to provide similar services to a Latina/Latino Student Center. If race is discussed only in cultural or psychological terms, such claims may appear to have some merit. But when evaluated in the context of the distribution of power and wealth, using a political and economic framework, the frivolous nature of arguments that are based on false equivalency is clear. There is no White History Month because history in a white-supremacist society is routinely taught from the perspective of white people. There is no White Student Center because the services on a campus typically are designed to serve the needs of the dominant white student population.

Embracing white identity is not equivalent to non-white peoples' embrace of racialized identities. Pride in being black need not come with a notion that there is something biological or essential about black people from which the pride emerges; instead, black pride can grow from the collective resistance to white supremacy that black people have maintained throughout history. A Chicano identity is a political statement about one's refusal to accept white dominance. Asian-American and indigenous organizations can create a space where members gather without having to deal with white norms.

No such equivalent pride, identity, or space is necessary or possible for white people, whose racial identity is rooted in domination, not resistance to domination. Whiteness is not an identity rooted in actual cultural traditions but was instead constructed for political and economic domination. Individual white people can be proud of their personal achievements and feel rooted in cultural traditions from specific places in Europe. But whiteness itself is either politically oppressive or culturally empty. White people who want to live the values of equality that we claim to hold should recognize that such a life requires us to abandon our belief in, and reliance on, whiteness.

THE COLOR OF THE RACE PROBLEM IS WHITE

In his 1903 classic *The souls of black folk*, **W. E. B. Du Bois** suggested that the question white people so often want to ask black people is, "How does it feel to be a problem?" Because white people do not know how to formulate such a question, Du Bois said they most often avoid the issue and deny reality. A focus on whiteness can help us reverse the direction of the question.

Race problems have their roots in a system of white supremacy. White people invented white supremacy. Therefore, the color of the race problem is white. Rather than asking non-white people how it feels to be a problem, it is long past time for white people to ask ourselves: How does it feel to be a problem? What will we do about it?

KEY READINGS

Allen, T. W. (1994). *The invention of the white race*. London: Verso.

Baldwin, J. (1998). *Collected essays*. New York: Library of America.

Bonilla-Silva, E. (2006). *Racism without racists: Color-blind racism and the persistence of racial inequality in the United States*. 2nd ed. Lanham, MD: Rowman & Littlefield.

Dyer, R. (1997). *White*. London: Routledge.

Feagin, J. R. (2000). *Racist America: Roots, current realities, and future reparations*. New York: Routledge.

——. (2009). *The white racial frame: Centuries of racial framing and counter-framing*. New York: Routledge.

Garner, S. (2007). *Whiteness: An introduction*. London: Routledge.

Ignatiev, N. (1995). *How the Irish became white*. New York: Routledge.

Jensen, R. (2005). *The heart of whiteness: Confronting race, racism, and white privilege*. San Francisco: City Lights.

Lipsitz, G. (1998). *The possessive investment in whiteness: How white people profit from identity politics*. Philadelphia: Temple University Press.

Lui, M., Robles, B., Leondar-Wright, R. B., & Adamson, R. (2006). *The color of wealth: The story behind the U.S. racial wealth divide*. New York: New Press.

Roediger, D. R. (1991). *The wages of whiteness: Race and the making of the American working class*. London: Verso.

——. (1998). *Black on white: Black writers on what it means to be white*. New York: Schocken Books.

——. (2008). *How race survived US history: From settlement and slavery to the Obama phenomenon*. London: Verso.

Singley, B. (Ed.). (2002). *When race becomes real: Black and white writers confront their personal histories*. Chicago: Lawrence Hill Books.

Wise, T. (2005). *White like me*. Brooklyn, NY: Soft Skull Press.

——. (2009). *Between Barack and a hard place: Racism and white denial in the age of Obama*. San Francisco: City Lights.

——. (2010). *Colorblind: The rise of post-racial politics and the retreat from racial equality*. San Francisco: City Lights.

4

COLONIALISM/POSTCOLONIALISM

WILLIAM MUCK

European expansion and colonization has had a deep and lasting impact on the economic, political, and social development of every population it touched. When Europe's great powers descended on Africa, Asia, and the Western Hemisphere, they established powerful institutions and structures that would frame the nature of social interactions in those communities for generations to come. These colonial institutions constituted the primary context for shaping the **identities**, interests, and modes of political organization for those living in the region. This colonial structure largely disregarded local customs and traditions. The colony essentially became an economic appendage intended to feed the growing needs of the European market. Equally problematic was the relative indifference shown by colonial powers toward the territorial distribution of **indigenous** groups. This was particularly the case in Africa, where European leaders imposed boundaries that paid little or no attention to existing cultural or political organization. The decision had grave consequences, as the political communities that emerged following colonialism rested upon dense and highly charged ethnic and racial cleavages. Many assumed that, with time and economic modernization, this sense of racial and ethnic identification would temper and ultimately disappear. This has not proven to be the case, and these identities continue to be a source of conflict, as well as economic and political underdevelopment, around the world.

There is a growing consensus among scholars who study the impact of colonialism that the origins of our modern conceptions of **race** and ethnicity can be traced directly back to the structures first established by colonial regimes. For instance, Queen's University, Ontario, political scientist Bruce Berman and others have shown that, prior to European colonization of Africa, the concept of ethnicity simply did not exist. Pre-colonial Africa was defined by a complex maze of overlapping and frequently changing identities. It was only with the introduction of colonial rule that ethnically defined social units took form. Barbara Jeanne Fields, a professor of American history at Columbia University, has similarly shown that the ideology of race in America can be tied to a fixed historical moment (the American Revolution). According to Fields, colonial Americans of European descent constructed the concept of race to resolve the growing contradiction between the individual right to freedom and the practice of slavery. In other words, race and ethnicity are social constructions with clear colonial origins. To suggest that these identities are social constructions implies that they are evolving and contested concepts whose contemporary meaning reflects the social, political, and legal discourse over time. This perspective directly contradicts earlier scholarly work, commonly known as primordialism, which understands these identities as a fixed cultural, biological, or even genetic condition. The anthropologist Clifford Geertz is one of the most widely known primordialists who argues that ethnicity is an a priori aspect of the human condition.

This chapter explores the lingering institutional footprint of colonialism and the role it has played in creating the ethnically and racially stratified societies that persist today. However, in order to do this, one must first acknowledge that colonialism was not a monolithic force that assumed a standard form in each and every state. Instead, the structural conditions or characteristics of colonial regimes varied widely. The French, British, Portuguese, Germans, Spanish, and Belgians all employed distinctly unique colonial regimes. This institutional diversity helps explain the dissimilar outcomes we see across **postcolonial** states on a range of issues such as economic and political development, respect for human rights, as well as the frequency and severity of ethnic conflict. It is also important to note that arguing that colonialism played a significant role in shaping contemporary systems of racial and ethnic stratification is not to suggest that colonialism was the only explanatory factor. Many factors contribute to its definition and meaning. Yet, the historical record indicates that colonialism stands as a critical paradigmatic moment in shaping the contemporary context of race and ethnicity. Its influence has been pervasive, but it is far from the only causal factor at work.

CREATING ETHNICITY AND ETHNIC CONFLICT IN AFRICA

Historians, anthropologists, and political scientists who study the concept of ethnicity in Africa are increasingly in agreement that our modern conception of "African ethnicity" was constructed during the latter part of the nineteenth century. The ethnically defined social units that emerged in colonial Africa replaced a much more fluid and pluralistic indigenous system. The political communities in pre-colonial Africa were extraordinarily diverse and most closely represented a confederation of multiple cultural and linguistic groups. Scholars have warned against over-idealized accounts of pre-colonial Africa, noting that, prior to colonization, Africa was not immune from conflict, competition, or acute wealth disparity. While far from perfect, the system was nonetheless a reflection of indigenous society, and dramatically different from the externally imposed colonial system based on European practices and principles.

At the Berlin Conference of 1884–85, commonly known as the "Scramble for Africa," European powers carved up the continent, dividing and/or combining African groups in ways that completely disregarded pre-colonial patterns. For example, the modern state of Uganda was created when Britain arbitrarily pooled the Bantu, Langi, and Acholi people. Nigeria was formed by merging the

Hausa, Igbo, and Yoruba communities. European colonists used this artificial partitioning to their advantage by enacting policies that intentionally accentuated differences among the local groups. Looking back, scholars now identify this practice as the conceptual birth of modern African ethnicity. Arguably the most prominent example of colonial-induced ethnic categorization was in Rwanda where Germany, and then most notably Belgium, engineered Hutu and Tutsi enmity.

When Belgian colonists took control of Rwanda in the early twentieth century, they brought with them the European belief in a natural racial hierarchy. Certain races were superior and destined to lead, while others were to be ruled. Their perception of Rwanda was that the majority Hutu, who constituted roughly 85 percent of the population, were the racially inferior serf workforce. By contrast, the **minority** Tutsi were deemed naturally superior and therefore deserving of better jobs and political opportunities. The Belgians were so convinced of Tutsi racial superiority that they concluded the Tutsi could not possibly be Rwandan, but instead were likely descendents of a long-lost European race (the Hamitic thesis). The Belgians encouraged the Tutsi to embrace their superiority and rightful position of **power**. Not surprisingly, the Tutsi welcomed the new arrangement and corresponding ethnic identity.

In 1933, the Hutu/Tutsi identity became legally binding when the Belgian government distributed identity cards, formally classifying Rwandans as Hutu or Tutsi. In his account of Rwandan history, Stephen Kinzer concluded that no aspect of colonial policy was more devastating to Rwanda than creating the myth that one group was indigenous while the other was a foreign presence. Prior to colonialism, Hutu and Tutsi lived together as neighbors in relative peace. The politicization of these two identities by the Belgians, would profoundly contribute to the postcolonial Hutu/Tutsi ethnic conflict, ultimately culminating in the horrific **genocide** of 1994. Colonial-induced ethnic categorization was not limited to Rwanda. Scholars have similarly detailed how countless other "ethnic" groups emerged from colonial categorization policies of the early twentieth century. It would not be an exaggeration to say that virtually every postcolonial conflict in Africa has its roots in the ethnic identities cultivated during European colonialism.

COLONIAL STYLE AND ETHNIC CONFLICT

More recent scholarship has narrowed the focus by attempting to account for the variation observed in the frequency and intensity of ethnic conflict across Africa. While the findings are far from conclusive, there is some evidence to suggest that former British colonies have experienced a slightly better record on human rights and democratic development than other European colonial powers. Much of this work has centered on the different structures or "styles" of colonial administration. The French, Portuguese, Germans, and Belgians all employed a highly centralized administration, which had the rather elusive goal of cultural **assimilation**. By contrast, the British used the decentralized system of "divide and rule." These two styles of colonial administration had very different strategies for dealing with the indigenous population.

The centralized system, employed most prominently by the French, would begin with a complete dismantling of traditional political and social structures and supplanting them with the colonial bureaucracy. The French would reach out to one indigenous group (the selection often driven by conceptions of racially superiority) and grant it disproportionate status and privilege within the colony. More often than not, the local elite were the only group granted access to French education and cultural assimilation. By contrast, the British did not dismantle the indigenous social structure, but instead encouraged and exploited existing factional rivalries. The British hoped that, by promoting internal ethnic division, they would prevent the formation of an anti-colonial alliance.

Not surprisingly, the two systems had important impacts on the configuration of ethnic and racial identity in postcolonial states and, in turn, on conflict among those groups. The French system encouraged the creation of a single dominant ethnic group who enjoyed hegemonic privilege over the rest of the population. The British system encouraged multiple competing ethnic groups who were equally capable of political mobilization. In their analysis of these two colonial styles, Robert Blanton *et al.* found that each approach led to a distinct form of ethnic conflict in postcolonial Africa. Their findings indicate that, in former French colonies, the privileged ethnic group was frequently able to maintain its hegemonic advantage and suppress the political mobilization of other ethnic minorities. This suppression of minority ethnic groups has led to a lower frequency of ethnic conflict in former French colonies. This type of dominance was simply not possible in former British colonies where Britain had encouraged the political mobilization and competition of multiple ethnic groups. Blanton *et al.* found that this more contested structure led to a higher frequency of ethnic conflict in former British colonies. While the frequency of ethnic conflict in former French colonies was lower, when ethnic violence did erupt it was of a much greater intensity and took a much more violent form.

SLAVERY AND RACE MAKING IN AMERICA

Just like in Africa, the origins of race in the Americas can be traced back to colonialism. Throughout North and South America, colonial powers instituted regimes that pursued policies of racial categorization and domination. Moreover, just as in Africa, the European powers that divided up the New World brought a variety of distinct colonial institutions and practices. The differences led to dramatically different outcomes. One of the most prominent scholarly comparisons is between the policy of colonial slavery in Brazil and the United States. In both countries, a brutal slave regime was established during colonial rule. Each system perpetuated a myth about the inferiority of non-whites and, in the process, encoded a system of enduring racial disparity.

Nevertheless, the unique institutional and historic context of each colonial regime brought about dramatically different systems of racial stratification.

To understand the development of racial identity in the United States, one must appreciate the complicated relationship between slavery and freedom in the burgeoning American polity of the late eighteenth century. The Founding Fathers were boldly declaring for the entire world to hear that the American democracy represented a ground-breaking political arrangement. In America, "all men were created equal" and enjoyed the individual right to life and liberty that God had bestowed upon them. This revolutionary extension of political rights, however, starkly contradicted the practice of slavery. Forced to justify the practice of slavery in the self-professed land of individual freedom, colonial Americans gravitated towards the ideology and science of race. If, as the Founding Fathers were suggesting, liberty was the natural order of things, the only way to deny a group of individuals that entitlement was to invent a category which defined that group of people as somehow different and naturally inferior.

Ironically, it was only with the movement towards democracy in colonial America that the conception of race formally took hold. Slavery has existed for nearly all of recorded human history and, on its own, does not require racial categorization. It is only when a political community asserts that individual freedom is an inalienable right, but does not extend that right universally, that it becomes necessary to categorize certain people as undeserving of freedom. In fact, prior to the democratic upheaval of the late eighteenth century, skin color was not a powerful identifying characteristic in colonial America. Africans who were brought to the country during the sixteenth and seventeenth centuries did not identify themselves as "black," but with their previous indigenous African identity. Moreover, during this early colonial period, it was not only African slaves who were deprived of individual freedom. Large groups of poor white Europeans worked alongside African slaves as indentured servants in the absence of individual freedom.

Historians have determined that, at some point during the middle of the eighteenth century, African slave labor proved to be more profitable and began to supplant the practice of white indentured servants. It is at this point, when the economic argument for African slave labor confronts America's democratic revolution, that the difference between people becomes defined along racial lines. Americans of European descent apply a racially inferior identity to people of African descent in order to resolve the contradiction between American democracy and the practice of slavery.

The socially constructed identities of black and white in the United States were reinforced by scientific research at the time, which claimed to corroborate the biological differences between races. In the early nineteenth century, the scientist Samuel Morton launched the anthropological field of craniometry. Morton studied skull sizes of groups from all over the world and claimed to find a positive correlation between skull size and intellectual capacity. According to

Morton, the "Negro" had a smaller brain than Caucasians, with American Indians somewhere in between. His work gave birth to a much larger field, known as scientific racism, committed to systematically proving the biological roots of racial hierarchy. Comparative scholarly analysis of slavery in the Western Hemisphere has shown that the United States was the only country to develop an elaborate racial justification for slavery. Brazil experienced a comparable colonial slave regime, yet, because the Portuguese were not facing similar democratic pressures, never felt the need to defend slavery along racial lines.

RACIAL DEMOCRACY IN BRAZIL

The long and sordid history of race relations in the United States stands in stark contrast to race relations in Brazil. Brazil has managed to avoid the open racial tension and **segregationist** policies of the United States. For many years, Brazil and the region as a whole were characterized as a "racial democracy." This has caused many to wonder what brought about these extraordinarily different racial outcomes. Some have gone so far as to suggest that the absence of overt racial tensions in modern-day Brazil stems from the sense of racial tolerance brought to Brazil by the Portuguese colonialists. In the first half of the twentieth century, Brazilian sociologists Gilberto Freyre (1933) and Frank Tannenbaum (1947) provided the first serious comparative analysis of slavery and race relations in the Western Hemisphere. Examining the cases of Brazil and the United States, each concluded that Brazilian slavery under Portugal was much more humane. According to Tannenbaum, the more benign Portuguese colonial regime was exceptional for acknowledging the inherent humanity of its slaves. This sense of racial tolerance then carried over into postcolonial Brazil and helps to explain why the country has not experienced the same type of racial confrontation that has played out in the United States. Unfortunately, the historical record does not corroborate the thesis offered by Freyre and Tannenbaum. Research coming in the second half of the twentieth century demonstrated in great detail just how brutal and oppressive the Portuguese colonial regime actually was.

By the 1970s, another argument, focusing on demographic factors, emerged to account for differences between Brazil and the United States. This explanation looked at the level of miscegenation between the Portuguese colonists and the local indigenous population. Miscegenation refers to the degree to which different racial groups mix through marriage or sexual relations. In a ground-breaking work of historical comparative analysis, historian Carl Degler found that the Portuguese had engaged in dramatically higher levels of miscegenation than other colonial powers. According to this explanation, the Portuguese colonists had engaged in such widespread miscegenation that it was simply impossible to develop a rigid system of bi-racial categorization. In other words, as the line between black and white was blurred, it became increasingly difficult to ascribe inferior characteristics to one group, much less implement a segregationist system based on those characteristics. Degler believed the result of this colonial practice was that it provided for greater social mobility in Brazil; what he referred to as the "mulatto escape hatch." For Degler, Brazil's high mixed-race, or "mulatto," population was the crucial factor for understanding the difference between race relations in Brazil and the United States.

However, once again historical reality does not match the theoretical account. It is indeed true that Brazil experienced very high levels of miscegenation. Yet a wave of recent scholarship examining race in Brazil has found persistent inequality between races. Income of the "white" Brazilian population is dramatically higher than that of its "black and brown" counterparts. The reality is that Brazil continues to struggle with an informal racial hierarchy. Despite this very tangible material inequity, a myth of racial democracy and social mobility persists among the public at large. This suggests that Brazil has been able to reconfigure its colonial past into a more benign image. Many credit the writing of Gilberto Freyre and Frank Tannenbaum for changing the perception of non-whites as racially inferior. Freyre's work may not have accurately portrayed Portugal's colonial slave regime, but it did help to change the public understanding of race in Brazil. Most importantly, it appears to have lowered the salience of racial identity in the country. Brazil still needs to confront the lingering economic inequality left by colonialism, but it has taken important steps to reconstruct the public's perception of its racial identity.

DISCOVERING RACE IN THE AMERICAN INDIAN

It took over two centuries for European colonists to "discover" race in Native Americans. When Europeans first arrived in the New World they struggled to explain the ancestral roots of the indigenous group they would ultimately come to label "Indians." Speculation ranged from the group being the mythical "wild men" of medieval Europe to the long-lost tribes of ancient Israel. Yet, somewhat surprisingly, what dominated early accounts of European colonists were the connections they drew between themselves and the Indians. Scholars are in general agreement that early European colonists believed the Indians were not a distinct race, but very much like themselves. In fact, the historical record suggests that they admired the physical characteristics and biological prowess of the Indians. Skin color was not an important characteristic throughout the sixteenth and much of the seventeenth century. There was an obvious bias against what the colonialists saw as the uncivilized cultural practices of the Indians, but it was believed this could be overcome through a broad policy of cultural assimilation. The objective of the colonists was therefore to educate the Indians about the Christian faith, the English language, law and governance, as well as proper commercial agriculture.

The process that transformed Indians into a distinct and inferior race in the eyes of colonial Americans was slow and played out over the course of the eighteenth century. The change was driven by multiple factors, most notably frustration among colonial Americans over the Indian's reluctance to part with their uncivilized cultural practices. The Indians stubbornly clung to their tribal language, law, and government, all the while resisting conversion to Christianity. This, along with the growing incidence of war between the two groups, led many colonial Americans to conclude that the Indians could never be broken of their "savage" practices. What could explain their innate desire to cling to such uncivilized practices? The conclusion drawn by an increasing number of colonial Americans at the time was that this "savage" population must be an entirely different and inferior form of humanity. By the end of the eighteenth century, Indian identity becomes defined entirely in racial terms. The color of Indian skin assumes a central role and begins to quickly darken, ultimately settling on red. In many ways, this was a convenient conclusion for colonial Americans to draw in that it enabled them to justify the forced removal of Indians from their highly coveted farmland. Indians were deemed to simply be incapable of making proper use of the land.

The radical perceptual transformation of Native Americans from being the long-lost tribes of ancient Israel to redskin savage, demonstrates the socially constructed nature of race and ethnicity. It also reinforces the powerful role colonialism played in dictating whether and which racial identities were salient. The construction of this racial identity for Native Americans would set the stage for the political and economic exploitation they would endure over the next two centuries. An examination of the economic, social, and health conditions of Native Americans today confirms a vicious cycle of poverty and underdevelopment. There is little doubt that Native Americans continue to struggle with the negative racial stereotypes first articulated by the colonial power. All told, the institutional legacy of colonialism has been difficult to overcome and continues to play a prominent role in determining the success or failure of former colonial populations around the world. Europe's colonial adventures stand as a sobering example of the profound impact that the imposition of foreign institutions can have on the construction of ethnically and racially stratified societies.

KEY READINGS

Berman, B. (1998). Patronage and the African state: The politics of uncivil nationalism. *African Affairs*, 97(388), 305–341.

Bernhard, M., Reenock, C., & Nordstrom, T. (2004). The legacy of Western overseas colonialism on democratic survival. *International Studies Quarterly*, 48(1), 225–250.

Blanton, R., Mason, T., & Athow, B. (2001). Colonial style and post-colonial ethnic conflict in Africa. *Journal of Peace Research*, 38(4), 473–491.

Carey, H. (2002). The postcolonial state and the protection of human rights. *Comparative Studies of South Asia, Africa and the Middle East*, XXII(1), 59–75.

Cassidy, J. (2003). The legacy of colonialism. *The American Journal of Comparative Law*, 51(2), 409–455.

Cramer, R. (2006). The common sense of anti-Indian racism: Reactions to Mashantucket Pequot success in gaming and acknowledgment. *Law & Social Inquiry*, 31(2), 313–341.

Davis, B. (1975). *The problem of slavery in the age of revolution, 1770–1823*. Ithaca, NY: Oxford.

Degler, C. (1971). *Neither black nor white: Slavery and race relations in Brazil and the United States*. New York, NY: Macmillan.

Fields, B. J. (1990). Slavery, race and ideology in the United States of America. *New Left Review*, May/June, 95–118.

Freyre, G. (1933). *The masters and the slaves: A study in the development of Brazilian civilization*. New York, NY: Knopf.

Geertz, C. (1973). *The interpretation of cultures: Selected essays*. New York: Basic Books.

Hochchild, A. (1998). *King Leopold's ghost: A story of greed, terror, and heroism in Colonial Africa*. Boston, MA: Houghton Mifflin.

Kinzer, S. (2008). *A thousand hills: Rwanda's rebirth and the man who dreamed it*. Hoboken, NJ: John Wiley & Sons.

Marx, A. (1996). Race-making and the nation-state. *World Politics*, 48(2), 180–208.

Poe, S. C., Tate, C. N., & Keith, L. C. (1999). Repression of the human right to personal integrity revisited: A global cross-national study covering the years 1976–1933. *International Studies Quarterly*, 43(2), 291–131.

Posner, D. (2003). The colonial origins of ethnic cleavages: The case of linguistic divisions in Zambia. *Comparative Politics*, 35(2), 127–146.

Tannenbaum, F. (1947). *Slave and citizen: The Negro in the Americas*. New York: Knopf

Vaughan, A. (1995). *Roots of American racism: Essays on the colonial experience*. New York: Oxford.

White, S. (2002) Thinking race, thinking development. *Third World Quarterly*, 23(3), 407–419.

5

RACE, POLITICS AND PUBLIC POLICY

CHARLTON D. MCILWAIN AND STEPHEN MAYNARD CALIENDO

Public policy encompasses a variety of formal and informal actions (or inactions) taken on the part of government actors to uphold agreed-upon societal principles or to meet the interests of one or more segments of a population. Public policy can be inscribed in formal documents such as legislation, constitutions, national charters, public directives and the like, yet policy is also made when governmental bodies and actors simply do nothing with respect to any given issue or problem apparent within a society, allowing the status quo to be affirmed. With respect to issues relevant to **race** and ethnicity, policy is often centered on

1   the labeling of individuals according to racial or ethnic categorizations and
2   addressing embedded inequality by actively prohibiting prejudicial behavior, rectifying systemic oppression or reversing existing policy.

Public policy represents a long-term effort to direct the course of societal functioning, though the process of public policymaking is typically seen as fluid, particularly in democracies. That is, once policy exists, it continues through a process of potential challenges and changes. Its reach may be extended or restricted. Government actors may choose to actively enforce it or do nothing until citizens apply pressure for them to do so.

It is important to keep in mind that public policy and politics are often closely interrelated. That is, public policy results from a process of debate, contestation and struggle over – as Aristotle once put it – ways and means. Public policy is the outcome of individual and interest group wrangling over who gets to decide the direction a given community of citizens will take and who gets access to the limited resources available to enforce political will. In short, enacting public policy is – like politics – an exercise of **power**.

Focusing on race and public policy simply delimits the range of public policies to those that are specifically designed to influence the social relations amongst people based on race and/or ethnicity, as conceived within that society. Additionally, we must consider policies that are ostensibly race-neutral but that have consequences that disproportionately affect persons of different racial or ethnic groups. Affirmative action policies (called "positive **discrimination**" in the United Kingdom), for instance, are designed to remedy racial disparities and unequal opportunities that exist in a society as a result of historical oppression.

In their most basic form, they award additional "points" for being a member of a racial **minority** group (or for being a woman) in a mathematical equation designed to facilitate selection for employment or admission into institutions of higher education. Thus, affirmative action is rooted in a philosophy that is directly and explicitly related to race and ethnicity. Education policy, on the other hand, targets how teachers teach and how students learn and insures that educational institutions have the means to properly educate citizens. There is no explicit racial component to such policies. However, in many nations where a racial gap in educational attainment perpetually exists, education policy and affirmative action interact.

In this chapter, we provide an overview of the intersection of race, politics and public policy by providing examples of the myriad ways in which these issues affect the lives of citizens. Our discussion is predicated on the ways that policy is made in industrialized democratic nations (though some similarities exist between these processes and those in states with other types of governance). Before turning to specific examples of policy areas related to race and ethnicity, however, we review the steps in the public policymaking process as they have been observed in and applied to Western democracies so as to provide a framework for understanding these complex interactions.

THE POLICYMAKING PROCESS

Policymaking is at the heart of the political process, and politics is central to the policymaking process. Political scientist Harold Lasswell once offered a concise definition of "politics" as "who gets what, when and how." The distribution of the resources referenced in that statement is central to the decisions that policymakers make. Legislators (who make laws), executives (whose responsibility it is to apply and enforce laws) and judges (who interpret the meanings and weigh the appropriateness of application of laws) are all involved in the policymaking process. For instance, when a legislative body passes a law relating to limiting pollution, it is left to an administrative agency to figure out how to make sure that companies and individuals are complying with the new rules (and how to punish those who are not). If there is a question about whether the law is being enforced appropriately (or, in some contexts, if the passed law is consistent with broader constitutional principles), courts may be asked to weigh in on the matter. In each of these cases, policy is being made.

Though space here does not permit an adequate overview of the scholarship on the ways that public policy is made, there is a useful five-step arrangement that social scientists have used (and altered) to explain the process. The first step, agenda setting, refers to the ability of members of a society to determine what issues are relevant for public consideration. This can be done through representatives (elected or appointed), through organized interest groups, or directly by citizens. Once an issue is considered to be ripe for action, policy is formulated through established channels. This step involves discussion and/or debate about the reason for action and the various anticipated outcomes of one or more policy options. If a decision is agreed upon, the third stage of the process – adoption – is reached. In this stage the institution or institutions involved formally institute the formulated policy. In the next stage, the new policy must be implemented, which involves the application and enforcement of the provisions. Finally, all public policy is subject to continual and sometimes constant evaluation so that adjustments can be made, if necessary. In some cases, a policy might be completely reversed as a result of the evaluation stage. If reversal or even adjustment do occur, the policy "loop" must continue such that the issue would be placed on the public agenda again, followed by formulation (or re-formulation) of policy in response to the findings in the evaluation stage, adoption, implementation and more evaluation. In fact, the policy process is most often referred to as the "policy cycle" by those who study it.

RACIAL STRATIFICATION AND POWER

Racial policy – like all public policy – involves the exercise of power. Taxonomists such as Johann Friedrich Blumenbach first developed the concept of race as a means to distinguish human beings based on visually observable physical traits – skin color, cranial size, bone structure, and the like (see Chapter 1 of this volume). Had this ostensibly benign attempt to make such distinctions ended with these classifications, we might have known nothing of what we now refer to as racism and all of its attendant outcomes. However, those who embraced the meaningfulness of such distinctions transformed the observed reality of physical difference into a racial ideology that connected physical characteristics with innate personality and societal fitness. In other words, policymakers added power to the classifications, thus allowing "difference" to make a difference, to borrow a phrase from feminist legal theorist Deborah Rhode. By doing so, they set the stage for a new ethic that would govern the relationship between human beings worldwide. That is, the ideology developed into the presumption that those who were deemed to be superior (based on their physical features) had not only the right, but also the obligation, to exercise power over those at the bottom. This racial ethic was subsequently mobilized on a mass scale with what we know as the modern origins of European colonization and, eventually, slavery.

Of course, colonization and slavery (which constitute the most explicit exercise of racial, ethnic group and national power over others) do not exist in the twenty-first century as they once did. Today, we have remnants of colonization (see Chapter 3 in this volume) and slavery in various forms exists in many areas of the world – some based on ethnic classifications while others are based on gender – but the most widespread forms of power exertion take place in more democratic frameworks that have long incorporated racial and ethnic differences within the confines of national boundaries. Broadly speaking, citizens of the world generally espouse the fundamental principle of human equality.

However, individual, group or national quests for power are still quite evident today. Thus, within these more contemporary democratic and racially tolerant national structures, racial group power (and racial group challenges for greater access to that power) plays itself out through the public policy process.

If one maintains – as did racial and **postcolonial** theorists such as **W. E. B. Du Bois** and **Frantz Fanon** – that the critical (and global) racial dividing line is between whites and the darker people of the world, then we can frame race-related public policy as the terrain for struggling to either maintain **white supremacy** (white domination over the prevailing social order) or achieve meaningful racial equality in which social and political power – especially in the form of monetary and natural resources – is more equitably distributed across the **color line**.

In this context, then, it is important to study the relationship between race and public policy because it provides a key perspective from which to consider and better understand how racial dynamics play out in various states. It helps us to understand how policy shapes not only the conception and lived reality of race across the globe, but also the ways that the flow of financial resources – controlled by governmental policy – works to maintain or disrupt the racial social order. Specifically, we examine two broad policy areas – census policy and equal opportunity policy – to further explore the ways that policymakers have dealt with race and ethnicity in various cultural and political contexts.

RACE CONSCIOUSNESS AND CENSUS POLICY

Census policy affects decisions about who is to be counted and how to count the people living within a state's borders. Such determinations at once shape our conception of race and reflect the racial dynamics within particular communities. Because race is a social construction, it means different things to different people, based on their lived experiences. The concept and meaningfulness is more salient for some than others, which is to say the degree to which people in any given country consciously live the reality of race can differ significantly. In part, this is due to the degree of racial and ethnic diversity that exists within a country. The United Kingdom, for instance, has numerically substantial racial diversity, while the former Soviet Union, for example, had very little racial (but significant ethnic) diversity. Differences regarding the meaning and salience of race also depend on a society's specific racial history. That is, people in a country like the United States, which colonized **indigenous peoples**, imported African slaves whose descendants later became citizens, and has had significant waves of immigrants from all over the world, are likely to view race differently than , say, those in Australia, whose racial history does not include slave importation or the dramatic waves of immigration but does include treatment of "black" natives – "**Aboriginals**" – who were colonized by European settlers.

The form and scope of a nation's racial consciousness are both reflected in and shaped by how it counts the people who live within its national borders.

Most countries – with differing degrees of regularity – conduct a census of their population. The degree to which a census process requires its citizens to identify themselves based on race says much about each nation's general level of race consciousness. For instance, the United States – a country whose citizens engage in regular, explicit public discussions about race (even if those discussions often do not deal with the root of racial conflict) — conducts a decennial census, as well as periodic interim population surveys. Through the 2000 census, citizens were asked to identify themselves by race using the following categories: American Indian or Alaska Native, Asian, Black or African American, Native Hawaiian or Other Pacific Islander, and White. There were (and are) two categories for ethnicity: "**Hispanic** or **Latino**" and "Not Hispanic or Latino." However, the 2010 census includes some 15 categories, including (in addition to the five categories previously used): Chinese, Filipino, Japanese, Hawaiian, Samoan and Guamanian or Chamorro. The policy of using these categories is developed and enforced by a federal executive agency (the Office of Management and Budget), and the results are relevant to a variety of national decisions, such as apportionment of legislative seats and funding for social programs.

The fact that the government has a policy of racially categorizing its citizens using the aforementioned groupings, and the fact that, in the case of the United States, the executive branch of the government controls how official data about racial groups will be collected, is indicative of several characteristic realities about how race is viewed in that nation. First, it indicates that the United States (both the government and its citizens) is highly race conscious. Second, it demonstrates that the United States views race as a set of fairly narrow categorical distinctions based on color and national origin. Third, the policy reflects a desire to statistically measure various forms of racial distinction. That is, it expresses the need to be able to see all forms of ostensibly nonracial difference within a population (e.g. where people live, how much money they make, what occupation they work in or what form of transportation they use) through the prism of race. Possession of such data lends itself to policies that are designed to either maintain or ameliorate racial disparities. In short, the need to statistically measure racial difference for the sake of efficient government oversight of whether a nation is living up to espoused principles of racial equality restricts one's ability to view race in ways that are more nuanced than the simplistic and discrete racial categories.

By contrast, we might consider the ways that several other countries ask their citizens to identify themselves.

- On Australia's census, citizens are asked, "Are you of Aboriginal or Torres Strait Islander origin," with the option to indicate: No; Yes, Aboriginal; or Yes, Torres Strait Islander. Another question asks: "What is your ancestry?" (with the instruction that one may "provide more than one if necessary").

- Brazil's census instructs its citizens to "Choose your race," giving six options from which to choose: White, Black, Yellow, Brown, Native, Aboriginal, or Undeclared.
- The United Kingdom's census asks, "What is your ethnic group," with a set of multi-optional categories: White (with choice of British, Irish or any other White background); Mixed (White and Black Caribbean, White and Black African, White and Asian, Any other mixed background); Asian or Asian British (Indian, Pakistani, Bangladeshi, Any other Asian background); Black or Black British (Caribbean, African, Any other background); and Chinese or other ethnic group (Chinese, Any other).
- The first post-**apartheid** census in South Africa asked, "How would you describe yourself in terms of population group?" Five options are provided: Black African, Coloured, Indian or Asian, White or Other.

The wording of identification questions and the choices provided reflect differences between groups whose members see race primarily as a phenomenon centered on skin color and those that privilege ethnic group affiliation and ancestry above observable color distinctions. Some reflect a wider range of racial and ethnic diversity, while others narrow their population into a few categories. Still others, like the United Kingdom, reflect a mixture of these, along with what are apparently the dominant racial, ethnic and nationality group marriage patterns among its people.

In addition to providing insight into the ways that government and citizens view racial and ethnic classifications, examining census and racial identification practices can help us to understand the grounding for race-based social policies that seek to address a society's problems that relate to such classifications. In the next section, we consider a number of policies that are designed to remedy discrimination or disadvantage based on race and ethnicity.

NON-DISCRIMINATION AND EQUAL OPPORTUNITY

The terms "non-discrimination," "equal opportunity" and "affirmative action" (or "positive discrimination") refer to policies adopted to address (and redress) historical oppression. In various contexts, they apply to categories that include race, ethnicity, gender/sex, sexual orientation, physical ability and other areas where there is an understanding that individuals may be at some disadvantage in a given society. In this chapter, of course, we limit our discussion to policies that center on race and ethnicity, but it is important to remember that these are rooted in a broader philosophy that recognizes systemic disadvantage as a barrier to full participation in a community.

The idea of systemic disadvantage is important to understand because, without it, policies that explicitly mention race or ethnicity may be considered to be improper (or even illegal), as taking such classifications into consideration would have no purpose other than to advantage one group over another.

A useful analogy is a foot race: if all contestants are of equal physical ability and start at the same line, it would violate norms of "fairness" or "justice" to impede or aid any one of the contestants on his or her way to the finish line. Systemic oppression refers to discrimination against individuals because of group membership that has become codified in one form or another as a result of historic practices that serve to disadvantage members of the group. For example, in the United States, African slaves were not permitted to receive education, which meant that the offspring of those slaves, even when free, were at a competitive disadvantage to whites, many of whom had long and rich traditions of receiving free and widespread education. As the generations passed, this disadvantage has become manifested in a cycle of disadvantage relating to the ability to earn money, which relates to housing opportunities, which (because of the way American public schools are funded – based on property taxes) is related to the ability to achieve a strong public education, which is related to admittance to and success in college, which, in turn, relates to ability to earn income, thus perpetuating the cycle. Apart from individual-level **prejudice**, this **"institutionalized racism"** has been recognized as detrimental to members of racial minority groups in the United States and, thus, has been addressed with public policies designed to overcome it. Returning to our analogy, these policies are designed to remove barriers or hurdles that exist in the running lanes of some competitors and not others.

Some countries have established quotas to ensure that a certain proportion of groups considered to be at a disadvantage populate various institutions. In Finland, for instance, some university programs feature a quota for Swedish-speaking citizens. Israel has a stated policy of "preferential treatment" relating to education, employment and housing for Jews of Ethiopian descent. In the Southwestern China province of Yunnan, ethnic minorities are permitted to marry earlier than members of the majority and to have more children, and those children are admitted to schools even if their test scores are lower than those of majority children. In Norway, some government agencies give "positive special treatment" to some immigrants who possess the same credentials as native Norwegians. In other countries, such as the United States, explicit quotas are illegal, but "targets" are sometimes identified and complex systems of "points" can be awarded to members of historically disadvantaged groups upon application to institutions of higher education or for employment.

The situation in a country such as South Africa is more complicated. Though whites make up a small fraction of the population, until the very end of the twentieth century, the system of apartheid mandated that they controlled nearly all institutions, public and private, as an offshoot of colonization. Therefore, the power majority was squarely white, though the numerical majority was (and is) overwhelmingly black. Now that apartheid has been dismantled, South Africa has adopted a widespread "affirmative action" policy that seeks to provide support for blacks in government agencies (including the military) and private companies. In this way, the numerical minority seems to be at a disadvantage.

The policy is justified on the grounds that the overwhelmingly majority of companies and capital are still owned and held by whites, which is a direct result of the privileges they were accorded during the decades of apartheid.

SUMMARY

Ultimately, members of organized societies have to consider how their historical context has shaped the way that members of racial and ethnic groups are identified, and privileged or disadvantaged based on those classifications. Conflict arises when members of groups are only able to view resulting policies through their own psychological lenses. That is, if the runners in our race analogy believe that there have never been – or no longer are – hurdles in other runners' lanes, it seems fundamentally unjust for some runners to be able to start ahead of the starting line. From their perspective, they are being disadvantaged as a result of policies that are ostensibly designed to promote fairness.

The struggle, then, relates to the degree to which the hurdles are recognized by policymakers. If those in positions to make public policy (legislators, administrators or judges) perceive that the barriers are nonexistent, the resultant policies will not provide remedies to power minorities. If, however, there is consensus that historical oppression has not been adequately addressed, or that remnants remain that sufficiently harm members of certain groups, policy will reflect that position. A central element of resolving differences in perception is related to the power of members of racial and ethnic groups in a cyclical way. Only through policies designed to rectify discrimination can members of historically oppressed groups gain access to the policy reins in order help bring an end to unjust practices. Effective systems of classification and policies of nondiscrimination, then, tend to rely on "allies" from the power majority to empathize and ideologically support active efforts to bring about racial justice.

KEY READINGS

Anderson, T. (2005). *The pursuit of fairness: A history of affirmative action.* New York: Oxford University Press USA.

Applebaum, N. P., Macpherson, A. S., & Rosemblatt, K. A. (2003). *Race and nation in modern Latin America.* Chapel Hill, NC: University of North Carolina Press.

Bailey, S. (2009). *Legacies of race: Identities, attitudes, and politics in Brazil.* Palo Alto, CA: Stanford University Press.

Bell, M. (2002). *Anti-discrimination law and the European Union.* New York: Oxford University Press.

Bleich, E. 2003. *Race politics in Britain and France: Ideas and policymaking since the 1960s.* Cambridge: Cambridge University Press.

Fischer, C. S., Hout, M., Jankowski, M. S., Lucas, S. R., Swidler, A., & Voss, K. (1996). *Inequality by design: Cracking the bell curve myth.* Princeton, NJ: Princeton University Press.

Ingram, D. (2004). *Rights, democracy, and fulfillment in the era of identity politics: Principled compromises in a compromised world.* Lanham, MD: Rowman and Littlefield.

Lieberman, R. C. (2005). *Shaping race policy: The United States in comparative perspective.* Princeton, NJ: Princeton University Press.

MacDonald, M. (2006). *Why race matters in South Africa.* Cambridge, MA: Harvard University Press.

Massey, D. S. & Denton, N. A. (1993). *American apartheid: Segregation and the making of the underclass.* Cambridge, MA: Harvard University Press.

Mirsky, G. (1997). *On ruins of empire: Ethnicity and nationalism in the former Soviet Union.* Westport, CT: Praeger.

Nobels, M. (2000). *Shades of citizenship: Race and the census in modern politics.* Palo Alto, CA: Stanford University Press.

Rata, E. & Openshaw, R. (Eds.). (2006). *Public policy and ethnicity: The politics of ethnic boundary making.* New York: Palgrave.

Rodriguez, C. (2000). *Changing race: Latinos, the census and the history of ethnicity.* New York: New York University Press.

Solomos, J. (2010). *Race and racism in Britain.* New York: Palgrave.

Steinberg, S. (2007). *Race relations: A critique.* Palo Alto, CA: Stanford University Press.

Wilson, W. J. (2008). The political and economic forces shaping concentrated poverty. *Political Science Quarterly*, 123(4), 555–571.

Yanow, D. (2003). *Constructing "race" and "ethnicity" in America: Category-making in public policy and administration.* Armonk, NY: M.E. Sharpe.

Zhou, M. (2010). *Affirmative action in China and the U.S.: A dialogue on inequality and minority education.* New York: Palgrave.

6

RACE-BASED SOCIAL MOVEMENTS

CHARLTON D. MCILWAIN

Social movements are a hallmark of democratic political life throughout the world. Regardless of the circumstance – the location of the movement, the issues that prompt it, or the people involved in them – all social movements share a single, general goal: change. Social movements are a form of collective, political action; though, as we will later see, the forms and types of actions vary. We set apart **race**-based social movements as a way of singling out movements aimed at changing – in part or whole – the manner in which societies formally or informally institutionalize the social and political relations among the disparate racial groups that live within a society. Talking about race-based social movements considerably narrows the terrain of the kinds of social movements we might generally discuss. This is to say, studying race-based social movements limits the scope of our considerations to movements that have taken, and continue to take, place in societies where race has historically been a salient construct. Given this description of social movements in general, and race-based movements in particular, this essay focuses first on the way that race is framed as the principal basis of social movements, and second, the way that race is deployed as an organizing and mobilizing tool for such movements.

Surveying the scholarly terrain for work about social movements in general, and race-based social movements more particularly, quickly, and more often than not, leads us to two prominent examples: the **Civil Rights Movement** in the United States and the Anti-**Apartheid** Movement in South Africa. Why is this the case? Primarily, because these two countries have long histories of racial divisiveness, such that race seems perpetually salient in the lives of its citizens. But their prominence in the scholarly literature also has to do with the fact that they took place relatively recently and because of the fact that many considered them to be relatively successful. Though each of these movements differs from one another in significant ways, they have each provided models for social movements – race-based and otherwise – that have come after them. In the remainder of this essay I aim to simultaneously explore both social movements in general and race-based social movements in particular. That is, I focus on some of the primary theories and components of all social movements as a lens to better understand race-based movements more specifically. I frequently use the US Civil Rights Movement and the Anti-Apartheid Movement in South Africa as examples along the way.

FRAMING RACE IN SOCIAL MOVEMENTS

The idea of frames, the concept of framing and the work of framing analysis are now commonplace in a variety of academic disciplines and fields, from sociology to media studies to political science, and complement many more social movement theories promoted over the past 50 years, such as the political process theory, resource mobilization theory, new social movement theory and others. As Robert Benford and David Snow articulate, talking about "collective action frames" emphasizes the reality that social movements are socially constructed – that, at their foundation, they are signifying events; their participants, signifying agents. Social movement participants operate alongside other signifying agents – be it opposing social groups or mass media – for the purpose of, as Clifford Geertz would put it, making meaning. This is to point out that social movements, inasmuch as they are a form of collective action, are continually in the process of asking and answering the question, "what does this (the movement) mean" – for those participating in the movement, for those who stand to potentially benefit or suffer loss, or for the larger society in general?

Practically speaking, collective action frames address this question of meaning with respect to three (among many) issues: the problem that calls for action, the people engaged in the action and the goal of the action. In other words, framing work in social movements aims to address the meaning of the problem (its significance), to define what it means to be one of "us," for whom this problem has particular significance that leads to action and to determine acceptable meanings of success. Race-based social movements distinguish themselves among movements in general by how members of such movements frame these principal concerns.

Race is the central organizing frame of race-based social movements and, as such, it distinguishes itself from other forms of social movements. More specifically, such movements aim to change the primary manner in which societies have historically – through formal and informal means – racially framed the **power** relations among their people. If one defines racism as a systemic and structural problem that preserves white dominance and limits non-whites' access to power, then we might say that race-based social movements frame the underlying problem that the movement seeks to address and reform.

How such racism is expressed might be meaningfully different, however, from movement to movement. For instance, similar conditions existed in the pre-civil rights period in the United States to those during the South African apartheid regime – primarily racial **segregation** and white domination. The difference between them was that, in the United States segregation was (generally) a de facto condition (speaking primarily about the Jim Crow era that preceded the height of the movement) and when racial segregation was a matter of law these were generally specific state and local laws and ordinances rather than federal. The principle of equality was already, however, inscribed in US federal law in a variety of ways. The similar situation that existed in South

Africa was *de jure*; that is, a policy of forced, legally grounded racial segregation. Perhaps more importantly in terms of its difference from the United States, apartheid legally imposed **minority** (white) rule over the country's black majority. What does this mean when we return to the idea of collective action frames and determining the underlying meaning of race-based social movements? We might simply ask ourselves how someone – blacks – in each of these two conditions might frame the question about their condition in a way that is meaningful for them. The black individual in the United States might ask, "Why is it that my country says it believes in human equality and does so enough that it would write it into our laws, but I still can neither freely live where and in conditions I would like, and am continually denied access to basic human rights and privileges afforded the white citizens of my country?" The black South African might ask the question differently: "How is it that most people around me look like me, yet the few who do not can and do forcibly control my movement and restrict my freedoms." For the most part, the conditions are the same, but they mean different things to those who were involved in the movement. This has much to do with the second question race-based social movements must address – "Who are we?"

RACIAL ORGANIZATION IN SOCIAL MOVEMENTS

As I proceed to address central questions related to the framing work of race-based collective actions, I am also generally identifying parts of Herbert Blumer's early (and since adapted) stage model that helps to explain social movements' trajectory. It is in the first stage – emergence – that the initial framing work of movements begins to address the question about what the problem is and what it means to those facing it. Throughout the overlapping second and third stages – coalescence and bureaucratization – movement participants begin to grapple with defining the meaning of the collective involved in the collective action. This is the point where race-based social movements can become particularly intense and fraught with controversy. Framing the meaning of the collective in race-based movements means not only sharpening collective **identity**, but also simultaneously sharpening individual identity. The inevitable result is that in-group/out-group distinctions become more strictly defined in ways that affect the organization of the movement and the collective frame that participants project.

The racial logic is consistent here. The primary problem facing those engaged in race-based collective action is racial in its attempts to either reform or revolutionize – in David Aberle's terms – the status quo of racial power relations. Racism, the concept we use to define the racial power inequities such movements seek to change, presents a relationship of white dominance over non-whites, most notably those who occupy the polar opposite on the color spectrum – black. Thus, the racial frame imposed on race-based social movements leads movement participants to ask the question, "What does it mean to be black?"

This question played out in two (of many) similar ways in both the US civil rights struggle and the movement against apartheid.

First, having to frame the participants involved in these movements led to an increasing black consciousness, that is, a new and renewed search to find meaning, value, worth and fulfillment in one's blackness. Black consciousness expressed itself in the United States in a myriad of ways. Garveyism was one of the original black **nationalist** movements that made race – blackness specifically – its chief concern. Based on the philosophy of Marcus Garvey and channeled through the Universal Negro Improvement Association (which Garvey founded in 1914), the movement was often expressed as a "back-to-Africa" movement. More generally, however, Garvey's goal was to develop a national structure for the advancement of people of African descent in the United States and throughout the African **diaspora**. Other forms of black **solidarity** movements were reflected in later outlets for black nationalist sentiment and African-centered worldviews, including black Muslim religious practice and black self-help movements. Such movements came to be institutionalized in the academy with the inception of Black Studies programs in US universities and filtered through the production of black-oriented branches of academic disciplines such as sociology, psychology, political science and others.

In South Africa, black consciousness was translated into what began as an actual organizational movement. The movement was influenced by the same philosophical interests in black life, history and development that fueled the emergence of black consciousness in the United States, and the same scholars – such as **W. E. B. Du Bois**, **Frantz Fanon** and others who spoke of various forms of white colonization of the black mind – that provided the intellectual under-pinnings for their endeavors. Different than in the United States however, the Black Consciousness Movement in South Africa became a principal organizing apparatus for anti-apartheid struggle, after the African National Congress had been stripped of most of its practical power. Built around the idea of raising black consciousness as a principal element of the collective action, this part of the movement accomplished what civil rights causes in the United States always struggled to do – promote racial (black) solidarity.

As such solidarity begins to strengthen, a second problem emerges for move-ment participants to contend with: the necessity of and role for white allies. There were countless numbers of formal civil rights organizations in the United States – from groups like the Student Nonviolent Coordinating Committee (SNCC) to the Congress on Racial Equality (CORE) to the Urban league, not to mention the hundreds and thousands of churches and other black institutions collectively engaged in the struggle. Each of them, in their own way, had to address the racial, ideological and practical question about the role that whites (who represented the dominant power structure they worked against) would play in the movement. This was similarly addressed by the myriad black anti-apartheid organizations, parties and interests who dealt with considerable inter-national, non-black support – from the Boycott Movement in Britain to the

Defiance Campaign, and the involvement of the United Nations and UNESCO in the transnational struggle against apartheid. While few would contend that whites did not play a role in these movements' successes, their participants, nevertheless, had to consistently deal with and address the question about what it means to be black, what it means to be white and whether the answer to both questions should affect how various movement organizations and organizers worked together towards their shared goals and interests.

RACIAL SUCCESSES, FAILURES AND DECLINES

Framing the problem underlying race-based social movements is quite non-problematic, inasmuch as the problem of racial inequality is quite apparent at the time a movement emerges. The process of defining racial meaning and identity for participants – while problematic and messy – is nevertheless generally agreed on as a necessity. That is, movement participants understood and continue to understand at least one of the observations made by early mass society theorists such as William Kornhauser – that is, that groups acting together are more powerful than individuals acting alone, and as the size of the group expands, so too does the potential to exert greater collective power to enforce change. Thus, race-based movement organizers and participants generally saw that, amidst their countless differences, their success was dependent on closing ranks – not to say that their differences were not important, but to emphasize that the strength of their solidarity was necessary to fight the seemingly insurmountable problem of racial injustice.

It is the third aspect of framing work – defining and framing the goal of the movement – that presents many obstacles, disagreements and differing interpretations of movements as they proceed through the fourth stage of Blumer's social movement evolution: decline. Of course, goals are something that we expect organizers to work out in the beginning. A reality of social movements in general, however, is that one's goals often become defined through a prolonged process of negotiation where what "we want" is continually redefined by "what we can get." It is also true that the work of determining meaningful goals is part and parcel of defining the problem. If racism is the fundamental problem challenged by a movement then, naturally, the decline or disappearance of racism is the ultimate goal. The goal of such a movement may also be shaped by a continual process of determining whether the movement is out to change the hearts and minds of others in society – particularly whites in this case – or whether one is simply looking to gain the tangible legal, political and policy changes that will provide the opportunity to solve the problem.

The civil rights struggle in the United States was framed in many ways as a hearts-and-minds type of movement. We can see this in the rhetoric of some of its most visible leaders. In his famed speech at the March on Washington – what is known as his "I have a dream" speech – **Martin Luther King, Jr**, for example, appealed to the conscience of a nation that had already taken the first steps towards equality in that its founding principles guaranteed racial equality and equal opportunity. Using a banking metaphor, King described the US Constitution as a document containing a written promise to pay a stated sum to a specified person or the bearer at a specified date or on demand (better known as a promissory note – King referenced this in his "I have a dream" speech, which we are prohibited from quoting here due to the unusual practice of the King family requiring payment for even minor quotations of the speech). King claimed that America had defaulted on its debt when it came to ensuring equality for its non-white citizens and appealed for justice, based on the fact that these principles were part of the country's founding beliefs.

With this language and framing of the gap between the nation's ideals and its failed pursuit to reach them, King appealed to the nation's sense of principle, fairness, responsibility and justice. In other parts of the speech, he appealed to the nation's sense of morality and spiritual duty. His approach was that US citizens needed to get their hearts right before they could get their acts right. That is, a change in mind and heart would be reflected in brokers and policymakers doing the right thing to craft legislation that would further guarantee and enforce racial equality.

Though it is constantly debated, the US Civil Rights Movement ended with a blend of social movement end-stage actions – success, co-optation and mainstream establishment, chief among them. Landmark legislation was passed with the Civil Rights Acts of 1964 and 1968 and a host of related legislation and policies meant to address the problem of racial **discrimination**. Some say the movement ended with these successes, while others say that it has never ended, principally because racial inequality still persists. Many critics say that, while the movement produced legislative success, it failed to accomplish its greater goal of changing hearts and minds and, thus, racial progress has been incremental and incomplete.

If we look at the smaller Black Consciousness Movement within South Africa and its role amidst the broader anti-apartheid struggle, this blend of success and failure is again apparent as contemporary critics look back at history. While many regard it as being a success in terms of raising black consciousness and elevating the value of blackness, others – including Nelson Mandela – criticized, or at least shied away from, this aspect of its success. Such critics asserted that the movement's emphasis on blackness worked to sharpen racial tensions and upset working relationships with allied organizations in the transnational anti-apartheid movement. The presence of the movement, however, continues to be seen by many as one influential piece of the larger struggle that eventually ended apartheid, arguably beginning with F. W. de Klerk's decision to repeal petty apartheid laws, moving through to Nelson Mandela's release from prison in 1990, and the eventual culmination of apartheid with the institution of multiracial, democratic elections.

While we could debate whether the apartheid struggle was, like the US Civil Rights Movement, a campaign for hearts and minds, it is clear that the type and form of goals sought and gained by each movement differed significantly. In the United States, change took the form of the passage of new laws that would better enable and, indeed, compel the government to act affirmatively to end racial discrimination. But, as previously mentioned, this step was about policy reform – the principles of equality and equal opportunity were already there; they just needed to be more detailed, strengthened and enforced. Besides the legislation that was passed, the only other change to the actual structure of the government was a marginal increase in the number of non-whites elected to Congress, primarily through the policy and practice of racial gerrymandering. The point, however, is that the system remained practically the same. The end of apartheid was essentially a revolution, however. It not only included the repeal of previous law and the institution of new ones, it meant a fundamental shift in the nature and structure of racial power and instituted a fundamentally different political relationship between white and non-white South Africans. As in the United States, however, such relationships remain strained at both the political and social levels.

CONCLUDING NOTE

At the beginning of this essay, I pointed out that a central component instigating race-based social movements is a heightened, visible and shared reality that makes race, racial consciousness and racial inequality particularly salient in the minds and experiences of groups in a particular society. The United States' long history of racial distinction and inequality, and South Africa's more recent history of minority rule are two examples of the kinds of conditions that must exist to bring about the racial realities that induce race-based social movements. This racial landscape is quite different today than when these movements first began. In an era of globalization, marked by open immigration, constant migration, porous borders for the continual flow of goods, services, values and cultural products, it is not so much that race has ceased to be a salient construct – though in many ways it has. More accurately in relation to social movements, however, race has become simply one of many salient features of inequality that contemporary social movements emerge to resist. As a result, inequality is increasingly framed in terms of several related factors and constructs – incomes, gender, class, sexual orientation and preference, religion, national origin, developed versus developing and underdeveloped nation status, labor economy and others. To some degree, New Social Movement (NSM) theory incorporates some of these distinctive elements characteristic of more recent social movements emerging (generally) beyond the late 1960s and early 1970s. While NSM theory tends to stress many of the same **identity politics** of previous social movements, the prevailing view is that such movements are more organizationally diffuse and less tied to creating or changing public policy as a primary outcome.

In a way, many see this growing intersectionality, that both retains and sublimates racial identity as a principal basis for organizing, as progress; it is the realization that race is but one of many characteristics that work in concert with others to produce, sustain and promote continued inequality, or even what some call a global racial divide. Thus, while race may continue to be a salient factor or lens through which to see persistent division, our contemporary political maturity tells us that, to effectively fight racial injustice in our contemporary world, we must be attuned to the ways that each of these related factors work together, as well as to the fact that future movements must be maximally inclusive.

KEY READINGS

Bond, P. (2000). *The elite transition: From apartheid to neoliberalism in South Africa.* New York: Pluto.

Blumer, H. (1951). Collective behavior. In A. M. Lee (Ed.), *Principles of sociology,* New York: Barnes & Noble, 67–121.

Carson, Clayborne (1981). *In struggle: SNCC and the Black awakening of the 1960s.* Cambridge, MA: Harvard University Press.

Foss, D. A. & Larkin, R. W. (1986). *Beyond revolution: A new theory of social movements.* South Hadley, MA: Bergin & Garvey.

Franklin, J. H. (2000). *From slavery to freedom.* New York: Knopf.

Goluboff, R. L. (2007). *The lost promise of civil rights.* Cambridge, MA: Harvard University Press.

Klandermans, Bert. (1997). *The social psychology of protest.* Oxford: Blackwell.

Kornhauser, W. (1959). *The politics of mass society.* New York: Free Press.

Ludors, J. E. (2010). *The Civil Rights Movement and the logic of social change.* New York: Cambridge University Press.

Mandela, N. (1994). *Long walk to freedom: The autobiography of Nelson Mandela.* Boston: Little, Brown.

Rosales, F. (1996). *Chicano! The history of the Mexican American Civil Rights Movement.* Houston, TX: Arte Publico Press.

Shelby, T. (2005). *We who are dark: The philosophical foundations of Black solidarity.* New York: Belknap.

Snow, D. A. & Benford, R. D. (1988). "Ideology, frame resonance, and participant mobilization". *International Social Movement Research,* 1, 197–217.

Tilly, C. (2004). *Social movements, 1768–2004.* Boulder, CO: Paradigm.

Winant, H. (2004). *The new politics of race: Globalism, difference, justice.* Minneapolis, MN: University of Minnesota Press.

7

MOTIVATION, IMMIGRATION AND THE IMMIGRANT

ERIC M. KRAMER

Immigration – the willing or forced movement of individuals from the land of their birth and/or native citizenship to become a citizen of another nation – provides the basis for many racial and ethnic issues that exist within countries around the world. With immigration comes the inevitable and increased confrontation with **otherness** – racial, ethnic, cultural and otherwise.

Rather than proceeding with a political examination and explanation of the topic of immigration as it relates to **race** and ethnicity, I approach the topic by looking at the cultural backdrop of what immigrants face when immigrating from one's native home (by birth, citizenship or longevity) to another. As a communication scholar with a background in language, I focus in large part on how the origins and historical development of the term "immigrant" and those related to it help us to better understand the tensions that immigrants and members of "host" societies confront when the issue of their "foreigness" and otherness – especially as it relates to one's racial, color and ethnic **identity** – takes center stage. One might view my aims in this piece in light of **W. E. B. Du Bois's** classic concept of **double consciousness** or **Frantz Fanon's** assertion that the black man's destiny is white. At bottom, both of these ideas are the essence of the immigrant reality – questions about adaptation, acculturation, acceptance, rejection and racial/ethnic/cultural **assimilation**. The essential issues surrounding immigration, though highly political, are at base questions about racial and ethnic identity and survival, dominance, acquiescence, fusion and change and the related motivations, consequences and implications involved. So I proceed first with an examination of etymology, embracing Fanon's claim that "mastery of language affords remarkable **power**," for both the immigrant and, in our case here, the student and scholar.

IMMIGRANT

The English word "immigrate" is a verb. "Immigrant" can be both a noun and an adjective. These words share the root "migrate." In English, they derive from the Latin immigrᵃre, immigrᵃt-, which means "to go into." We also have in-[2] + migrᵃre, meaning "to depart." The Indo-European root of "migrate," which has acceptations and adumbrations in many languages, not only English, is mei-, which superficially means, "To change, go, move; with derivatives referring to the exchange of goods and services within a society as regulated by custom or law" (*The American heritage dictionary of Indo-European roots*). English derivatives include *mad, molt, mutate, mistake* and *migrate.*

From the Latin *me^{a}re*, which means "to go," or "pass," we have the root of the English word "immigrant," meaning "to permeate." Like a liquid or gas, immigrants are mobile. They penetrate, interpenetrate, pass a boundary and enter into a larger preexisting body. They are not **indigenous** and, as such, they are foreign, often seen and defined as abnormal by the indigenous element. They communicate strangely and may follow alien mores. The emphasis on abnormal difference also appears in *mew*, the root of "molt," "mutate," "commute," "permute," "transmute," from Latin *m^{ü}t^{a}re*, "to change," and the suffixed zero-grade form **mi-t^{a}-* from Latin *s^{e}mita*, meaning "sidetrack, side path" (< "thing going off to the side"; *s^{e}-*, apart; see s(w)e-).

The unfamiliar behavior of the immigrant is often perceived as "wrong." Meanwhile, the immigrant may very well recognize the same mistakes she has made and be quite aware that she does not know all aspects of the host cultural ways but she attributes her mistakes to her lack of knowledge about the local environment. The immigrant does not see herself as evil or malicious or stupid; just ignorant. The immigrant will tend to attribute her mistakes to innocent ignorance, not to personal malice or disrespect for local folkways or to her own moral failing. The difference the immigrant embodies may well be attributed by the host as an inherent failing of the immigrant. For the immigrant, it is not an inherent failing but a matter of innocent misunderstanding that can be ameliorated with time and experience. Thus, attribution is in the eye of the beholder.

ADJUSTMENT, ADAPTATION, ADOPTION, CONFORMITY, INTEGRATION, ASSIMILATION, ACCULTURATION

The immigrant experience is in no way uniform, even inasmuch as all immigrants confront some degree of pressure related to the inevitable changes that take place when old and new, home and host, familiar and foreign collide. Identity and issues of change, conformity pressure, assimilation, etc. are highly charged and deeply affective matters for those immigrants who deeply embrace race, ethnicity and **cultural** constructs as essentially meaningful. Because race and ethnicity are often tied to one's sense of self, self-worth, and the collective self-worth of racial and ethic others within one's community, these attendant issues of immigration are simultaneously political, social, psychological and, in many cases, a matter of one's sense of physical wellbeing. To explore these issues, I proceed here too with linguistic roots.

There is confusion in the use of concepts among some writers that needs to be addressed. For instance, a few writers simply duplicate nearly everything that Park – an American journalist and sociologist who studied civilizational and cultural transformations, especially related to Africans and African Americans – said in 1950, except that they confound the concepts he employed with great rigor. Some writers replace Park's "adopt" with "adapt." But in both cases (adopt and adapt) the conformity pressure put on immigrants by the host culture, is just that. Conformity pressure is not the same thing as adaptation. Nor is adoption the same as adaptation. Park is more accurate in his description of reality than those who borrow from him when he says that immigrants adopt some local host ways and some locals adopt innovations brought to them by immigrants. Adaptation involves the emergence of a new form of living, not coerced conformity to the "mainstream" *status*. Conformity pressure, which has nothing to do with "adaptation," is real. Conformity is the opposite of adaptation. Adaptation is the emergence of a new form of life. However, it affects different immigrants differently and, in nearly all cases, at least some of their native culture, and racial/ethnic identity is retained.

As we follow the evolution of the idea of immigrant identity and assimilation theory from Park to Milton Gordon and beyond, the trajectories of the concepts adapt, adopt, adjust, assimilate and integrate, sometimes become entangled and confused. Like Park, Gordon was an American sociologist who recognized that the US immigrant landscape showed evidence of how immigrants' racial/ethnic/ cultural identities are simultaneously maintained, transformed and transformative. Most noted for outlining seven stages of immigrant assimilation, Gordon realized that the change that constitutes assimilation is on both sides of the equation, that the host culture is changed by the presence of immigrants just as they are changed by the host **culture**, a process I have referred to elsewhere as "co-evolution," which also involves the co-constitution of identities.

Park and Gordon were also very careful to distinguish between assimilation and integration, for integration presumes that cultural differences between the host and the migrant will endure so that there is something to integrate. While assimilation leads to the disappearance of the immigrant culture and the ethnic identity of a person in a process of socio-cultural homogenization, integration involves the continued vitality of immigrant identity as such. Some writers who borrow in whole or in part the Park/Gordon notion of cultural adaptation/ assimilation fail to be clear about the difference between assimilation and integration. They are mutually exclusive processes. Assimilation means the end of integration, for integration requires difference. Gordon updated Park's work, noting that assimilation is a multidimensional process and that the changes wrought by immigration affect everyone involved, including the host society.

In 1997, the Canadian social-psychologist John Berry set out to clarify the concept of acculturation, a process that takes two fundamentally different paths; assimilation and integration. As noted, these are mutually exclusive processes, for assimilation spells the end of integration, the end of the immigrant identity, way of behaving, thinking and feeling. While a few writers still adhere to the idea that a "functionally fit" immigrant is one who willfully "unlearns" or "deculturizes" herself via "psychic disintegration" in order to conform to the host society's "mainstream" versions of appropriate behavior patterns, cognitive patterns and affect patterns, Berry and Kramer note that attempts to impose assimilation often lead to resistance and social conflict. Immigrants themselves prefer to integrate and this is also most likely to be the "natural" path given the nature of hermeneutic horizons and cultural fusion. One cannot learn anything new except by making sense of it from one's perspective, which is always already operant. That perspective is one's hermeneutic horizon and interaction involves the fusion of two or more horizons.

CO-INTEGRATION

At the social level, integration is really co-integration. Communication is not a one-way process. While what intercultural communication scholars William Gudykunst and Young Yun Kim call "conformity pressure," which they claim is exerted one-way onto **minority** immigrants by the numerical majority of the host population, is real, such pressures cannot completely overwhelm the immigrant's mind. If it did the mind would be like an erased computer memory, having no operating system left with which to translate and interpret (make sense of) their new world, even if and even though that interpretation must be accented. Like the co-constitution of identity and the co-evolutionary process whereby a society both changes and is changed by immigrants who move in, joining the living process of society as a system, a semantic field, integration is also a communicative process. Integration is co-integration. In short "both sides" influence each other. Conformity pressure exists on "both sides" or in both directions. And the intensity of the pressure cannot be reduced to simple quantification. A single missionary entering a village can have tremendous influence.

ACCULTURATION STRATEGIES

Berry has identified four mutually exclusive acculturation strategies. These four strategies are: assimilation, integration, separation and marginalization. Berry accepts Park's definition of assimilation, whereby the immigrant eventually disappears. Integration, according to Berry is the process by which the immigrant, or immigrant group, becomes an active member of the host society, yet simultaneously maintains a distinct ethnic identity. Separation occurs when ethnic minorities refuse (or are rejected by the host society) to become active participants in that larger society. The host society may see their culture as fundamentally incompatible and therefore the immigrant as not "assimilable." In such a case, the host society may attempt to bar their entry while welcoming more compatible immigrants. An example of this was the passage of the Chinese Exclusionary Act of 1882 in the United States. After helping to build the transcontinental railroad, Chinese were excluded from further immigration by an act of the United States Congress. At the same time, the United States government welcomed more and more immigrants from Europe, who were seen as more culturally compatible.

Finally, marginalization, as defined by Berry, is what many contemporary writers such as Edward Said incorrectly call **diaspora**. Many peoples have found themselves displaced and unable to "go home." Diaspora, a term taken from the Jewish *Torah* (Christian *Old Testament*), means to be dispersed, scattered across the earth; homeless or wandering far from home. The first use of the word is in *Deuteronomy* 28:25, referring to the "wandering Jews": "thou shalt be a *dispersion* in all kingdoms of the earth." Marginalization is different. In some ways it is worse, because the ancient Jews never lost their sense of who they were. Marginalization, as defined by Berry, occurs in migrants when they neither identify with their original cultural home, nor with that of the host society.

This is common among immigrants in the modern world where change is great and swift, so that after an extended stay of many years in an adopted home country, when they return to their original home, they find that it is "gone." It has changed so much that they no longer feel like they belong. The diasporic condition means that a person feels as though she no longer belongs as a full citizen and cultural participant in either her new adopted country or in her old homeland. It is, in essence, a sense of alienation. However, it is may be impossible to avoid for any traveler or member of a modern society. As the novelist Thomas Wolfe observed, you can never go home, that is if you ever leave, and if you never leave then you may not fully appreciate home. It is a paradox. You have to leave in order to miss something or someone but then, upon return, that very experience changes who you are. Many very traditional conservative societies change very little. Other modern societies change rapidly. But, in either case, if a person leaves home, especially for an extended time, they are changed and so when they return the meaning of home for them also changes. One cannot return to one's childhood.

BRIEF ETYMOLOGY OF THE WORD "MOTIVE"

The word "motive" has as its root *mot* derived from the Indo-European root *mu* (meu³-). The word "motive" comes from the Middle English *motif*, motive, from Old French *motif*, from Late Latin *mōtᵢvus*, of motion, from Latin *mōtus*, past participle of *movᵉre*, which means "to move." The Indo-European root meu³- also means "to push away." Other contemporary words that share this root include motion, move, might and make. Notice that within the word "emotional" we find the word "motion."

Motive leads to motion; action. While inanimate objects move, humans act. While cause explains the movement of inanimate objects, motivation explains human action and it is essential to adjudicating moral culpability. Motive expresses an emotional (e-mot-ional) want more than a cognitive calculation. Motive is emotional. The words "morph" and "mob" articulate the phenomenon of emotional movement and motion toward change, such as loco-mot-ion. Myth shares the root *mu* with words such as "mouth" and "music," which emotionally inspire courses of action from dance to heroism. In modern mental-rational terms, it comes to mean making a motion within a deliberative directional forum, such as in a legislative body or formal meeting with an emphasis on logical disputation. Motion involves pathos, ethos and logos, with the latter suggesting a rational course of action to change reality via policy and resource allocation. Deliberative bodies are places where rhetoric employing logical and pathetic appeals is used to effect change, to motivate action. In his *ΤΕΧΝΗΣ ΡΗΤΟΡΙΚΗΣ* (his analysis of the "Art of Rhetoric") Aristotle argues that to move people to action one must do more than simply state the facts or a dispassionate argument. Logic alone does not inspire passion in most people. One must also appeal to their emotions to get them to move.

CONSCIOUS VERSUS UNCONSCIOUS MOTIVES

In the modern social science literature, an unconscious motive is defined as one of which the social agent is unaware. Here, the literature tends to introduce the concept of drive. Drives are often defined as intrinsic urges. Instinctual drives, such as the urges we call hunger and sexual arousal, motivate us to take action and seek food and sex. Maslow argued that attribution, or the reasons we give for our own behavior or assign to explain other people's behavior, is complex. The relationship between a conscious drive or desire and the actual unconscious aim that underlies it may not be obvious. Stated motives that people give to explain their behaviors often do not agree with the reasons inferred by observers of their behavior.

Behavior motivated by an unconscious drive is revealed by a divergence between the individual's explanation for their actions and what third-person observers see as the "real" reason for the action. For instance, a person who misses a dental appointment may explain her behavior as simply "forgetting" an unpleasant appointment. Or a person may fail to apply for a job because they fear rejection not because, as they explain, they are not interested. Research has demonstrated that some students cut classes more than others because they harbor aggression toward authority figures who evaluate their performance, not because they are sick or for other stated reasons.

INTRINSIC VERSUS EXTRINSIC MOTIVATION

An intrinsic motivation comes from the potential reward one experiences that is inherent to a task or activity. There is no motive, incentive or reward except from doing the activity itself. Thus, one may knit, not in order to produce a blanket for sale, but just for the sheer joy of knitting. Intrinsic motives tend to be process-oriented rather than goal-oriented. Thus, a person may enjoy playing piano, cooking or painting even though their "products" are not so good. They continue to pursue these activities for their own sake. The means are the ends. Many people travel across cultural and national boundaries just for the fun of seeing new sights and tasting new cuisine. They are motivated to travel for its own sake. But others migrate across borders in order to achieve a goal that is separate from the movement and even the destination itself.

THE MOTIVE TO MOVE ACROSS BORDERS AND AWAY FROM ONE'S "COMFORT ZONE"

Just as important as the act and psychological experience of crossing borders is the experience of leaving one's home, either willingly or under duress. When people flee their homes due to famine, war, disease, flooding or other external factors, they are being compelled by an extrinsic motive, which means a motivator that is external to their own actions. If a person chooses to migrate in the hope of making more money in a foreign land, they too are being compelled by an extrinsic motive external to their own bodies. In the first case, the person is being compelled by the extrinsic yet basic or primary need for safety and the need to eat. In the second case, the migrant is being compelled by an extrinsic yet secondary motivator – money.

A secondary motivator tends to be a cultural, as opposed to a physical, desire or need. Hunger is a basic physiological motivator or urge to get up and seek food. The desire for money, which does not directly but can only secondarily satisfy certain physical needs (one does not directly eat money), also satisfies "higher order" needs like self-esteem, which is not necessary for life to continue. Secondary motives tend to involve the quality of life rather than basic needs for an organism to endure. Psychologists often use the term "drive" as synonymous with "motive."

According to the originator of attribution theory, Fritz Heider, a person's motivation is also affected by how he or she evaluates a situation and whether or not he or she has what Albert Bandura calls "self-efficacy." In other words, a person's choice to act on an urge and try to achieve some stimulus or outcome will be affected by whether or not she believes she has some control over the situation and can consciously make a difference or if achievement is just a matter of random chance or luck. If a person thinks that the future is beyond their control, they are likely not to try very hard to change things.

Most migrants and refugees believe that by moving they can actively achieve a goal, such as making a better living or saving themselves from a military conflict. Migrants, and even refugees, thus exhibit optimism and self-efficacy – a sense that the future can be better and that they have some control over the future. They are thus resourceful, ambitious and energized.

As noted above, drive theory postulates that, once the target of a drive such as food as it relates to hunger is acquired, then the urge will subside and the individual will achieve a state of rest or homeostasis. However, this simple feedback notion of motivation fails to explain why people will explore their environment even if they are satiated or why secondary motivators that are not innate but culturally learned, such as the acquisition of money, are pursued, often without limit. It may be that humans are not satisfied with homeostasis and/or that the repetitive combination of an action followed by a reward becomes a habit. Then action may become compulsive, which is to say irrational, in that a person continues pursuit behavior, such as working to acquire money, long after all basic needs have been satiated.

A reward system, such as a monetary bonus, may be institutionalized in order to create a measurable increase in a desired behavior and to periodically reinforce motivation. This is basic behavior modification achieved by the use of rewards, as when we train a dog with treats. However, there is evidence that such extrinsic incentives often lose their motivational power on people over time. Also, it has been found that there are intangible motivators, such as recognition of a job well done, which generate longer sustained positive satisfaction than tangible motivators such as money.

Frederick Herzberg has identified what he calls "hygiene factors." The metaphor "hygiene" is used in relation to motivation because the presence of good physical hygiene will not make one healthier than he or she already is, but its absence may cause a deterioration in health. Likewise, the presence of hygiene factors, such as perceived appreciation for job performance, perceived job security, benefits, and the like, do not motivate a person more. However, their absence can demotivate a person. This has much to do with the violation of expectations.

If immigrants have their expectations violated, if they make the arduous effort to migrate in search of a better life for themselves and their families, only to find intense resistance from the host cultural environment, such as negative racial or ethnic **prejudice**, or if hopes of a brighter economic status do not pan out, they may well be demotivated and return to their home country. In fact, this has been seen occurring with the economic downturn in the United States during 2008 and 2009. Immigrant laborers from South and Central America have been returning to their homelands because their expected rewards for their risks and effort have not materialized. Their motives have not changed but the material conditions in the host environment have.

As I mentioned in the introduction, both Du Bois and Fanon intimate that colonization, forced migration especially, and immigration all subject individual and group racial and ethnic identity to the hegemonic impulse of the Western, the "modern" the "progressive" to dominate, erase and remake the foreigner into the image of those exercising their superiority. No doubt this accurately and genuinely reflects immigrant reality from their time up to the present. But it is not the full story. Putting one's racial/ethnic/cultural identity in play in the act of immigration is an act of confrontation, challenge and resistance not only to existing racial social order across the globe, but to the very constructs of race, ethnicity and identity themselves.

KEY READINGS

Berry, J. (1997). Immigration, acculturation, and adaptation. *Applied Psychology: An International Review*, 46(1), 5–34.

Gebser, J. (1949 Ger./1986 Eng.). *The ever-present origin.* (N. Barstad & A. Mickunas, Trans.). Athens, OH: Ohio University Press.

Glazer, N. & Moynihan, D. (1963). *Beyond the melting pot: The Negroes, Puerto Ricans, Jews, Italians, and Irish of New York City.* Cambridge, MA: MIT Press.

Gordon, M. (1964). *Assimilation in American life.* New York: Oxford University Press.

Habermas, J. (1998 Ger./2000 Eng.). *On the pragmatics of communication.* (M. Cooke, Trans.). Cambridge, MA: MIT Press.

Kramer, E. M. (2000). Cultural fusion and the defense of difference. In M. K. Asante & J. E. Min (Eds.), *Socio-cultural conflict between African and Korean Americans.* New York: University Press of America, pp. 183–230.

Kramer, E. M. (Ed.). (2003). *The emerging monoculture: Assimilation and the "model minority".* Westport, CT: Praeger.

Park, R. (1950). *Race and culture.* Glencoe, IL: The Free Press.

Sowell, T. (1995). *Race and culture.* New York: Basic Books.

Toennies, F. (1887 Ger./2001 Eng.). *Gemeinschaft und Gesellschaft*, Leipzig: Fues's Verlag. *Community and Society* (M. Hollis, Trans.). Cambridge: Cambridge University Press.

8

RACE, GENDER, AND SEXUALITY

NINA ASHER

As dimensions of the human experience, **race**, gender, and sexuality have been discussed in terms of physical characteristics and biology, as well as social and political implications. Differently put, all three can be analyzed in terms of the classic "nature–nurture" controversy. With regard to physical characteristics, race has been discussed largely in terms of skin color, hair, and facial features, and gender and sexuality in terms of female and male sexual features and relations. With regard to social and political implications, all three have been discussed in terms of associated behaviors and expectations, social relations, and hierarchies across various groups, in historical and present-day micro and macro contexts. While, in the past, race relations in the US context were discussed largely in terms of black-and-white, today this discussion has evolved to engage Native Americans, **Latinas/Latinos** and Asian Americans as well as multiraciality. While, in the past, gender relations were discussed primarily in terms of male–female, today, increasingly, the discussion also includes transgender and intersexed individuals and communities. Similarly, today, the discussion of sexuality has evolved beyond a primary focus on heterosexuality to engage homosexuality, bisexuality, and genderqueer identifications. Indeed, discussions of race, gender, and sexuality have evolved beyond the premise of predetermined, "essential" **identities** to consider also the choices and preferences individuals exercise in determining their own raced, gendered, and cultural identities. Witness, for instance, the presence of **rap** and hip-hop artists, not only in diverse racial and ethnic communities within the United States, but also in different countries across the world. Or, a young man/woman may choose the broader term "queer" as an identifier rather than the more defined, narrower "gay"/"lesbian," or "bisexual."

Before I proceed with a discussion of the complex interrelationship between these concepts, I want to be clear about my use of some key terms. In this essay, I use "LGBT" (lesbian, gay, bisexual, and transgender) and "queer" interchangeably, given that the term "queer" is used in critical discourses to represent a wide range of gender identities and sexualities that are typically construed as exceeding the norm, including lesbian, gay, bisexual, and transgender. Additionally, I prefer the term "people(s) of color," rather than such phrases as "racial and ethnic minorities." The word "**minority**" connotes a diminution. By contrast, "people of color" serves to assert the presence of diverse racial groups.

Finally, I also note that, given that I am a US-based scholar, my scholarship largely – but not exclusively – engages discourses of race, gender, and sexuality coming out of the US academy.

COMMON ISSUES TO CONSIDER ACROSS RACE, GENDER, AND SEXUALITY

Today, it is recognized that relations and hierarchies of race, gender, and sexuality intersect. For instance, in the US context, white, heterosexual males – who have, historically, been considered as representative of the "norm" – have, typically, been privileged over such "minorities" as peoples of color, women, and LGBT peoples. If we consider each dimension separately, we see how the forces of racism, sexism/gender-bias, and heterosexism have been operating. We see, for instance, that white (or Caucasian or European American) people have been privileged over peoples of color, whether US-born or immigrants. In fact, historically, white people have oppressed peoples of color – by such acts as seizing the land of Native Americans and creating "reservations" for them and exploiting African Americans through slavery, lynching, and **segregation**. Similarly, men have been privileged over women. Witness, for instance, the movement for women's suffrage in the United States, as recently as a century ago. And, even today, we encounter such issues as the persistence of inequities in income and the challenges women encounter in running for leadership positions (be it as leaders of major corporations or such offices as that of the U.S. President or a justice in the U.S. Supreme court). And, of course, heterosexuals have been privileged over LGBT peoples. High rates of hate crimes against LGBTs, and inequities in terms of civil rights (such as not being allowed to marry or not having access to domestic partner benefits in the workplace) are instances that come to mind. For instance, findings from the *National School Climate Survey* (2007) reveal that 86.2 percent of LGBT middle and high school students reported being verbally harassed, 44.1 percent reported being physically harassed and 22.1 reported being physically assaulted at school in the past year because of their sexual orientation. More than half (60.8 percent) of students reported feeling unsafe because of their sexual orientation and more than a third (38.4 percent) felt unsafe because of their gender expression. Historically, then, peoples of color, women, and LGBTs have been construed as "**other**" and relegated to the "margins." That is, unlike white, heterosexual men – who, traditionally, have represented the "norm," been at the "center," and held positions of **power** – these groups have not been in positions of power. They have been **discriminated** against, silenced, and rendered invisible in the larger social context. The **Civil Rights Movement** of the 1960s, followed by the women's movement, and, more recently, the movement for equal rights for LGBTs bear testimony to the prevalence of these issues and the efforts to redress them on the larger scale.

Despite these developments, even today, one common consideration across the dimensions of race, gender, and sexuality is that of addressing essentialized identities and **stereotypes**. For instance, such notions as "all women are nurturing and all men are tough" or "all Asians are good at mathematics and science" serve to box in people from those groups into specific, limited characterizations in a monolithic manner that allows for no deviation. Furthermore, such simplistic **representations** not only strip individuals and communities of the complexities and contradictions that are part of the human experience, but also they set up spurious binaries. For instance, women *and* men may be both "tough" and "nurturing" at the same time. And, an individual who has transitioned – either from male to female or from female to male – or, an individual who identifies as "genderqueer" may be able to speak to experiences in terms of both genders. In other words, behaviors and characteristics that have been traditionally identified as specific to a particular gender are, in fact, not biologically determined; rather "masculinity" and "femininity" are social constructs.

Furthermore, issues such as inequities in income, discrimination in the workplace, and facing grueling hurdles in running for and getting elected to public office remain common to all groups – peoples of color, women, and LGBTs. And, of course, in this regard too, we need to bear in mind that the three dimensions intersect. One may be a bisexual woman of color. One may also be from a working class or low socioeconomic status background. One may also be an immigrant, legal or not. One may also have a disability. All of these factors play into the options and opportunities to which individuals and communities have access. Despite historical and present-day constraints, there is a greater awareness of such issues and intersections in a hyperdigitized, globalized, **multicultural**, twenty-first century context in which diverse voices and perspectives are increasingly audible in public forums (such as the media, the workplace, and politics) at local, regional, national, and transnational levels.

In this context of widespread capitalism and increasing global interdependence, we also need to consider issues of race, gender, and sexuality beyond national borders. In today's rapidly changing world, we encounter a range of identifications – from the traditional to the modern and postmodern, from the colonial to the **postcolonial** and global. For instance, many who are located in metropolitan contexts, in the "East" and the "West," the global South and the global North encounter such diverse representations in their transnational interactions and exchanges, be they as quotidian as reading a newspaper, or calling – or responding to a call at – the customer service center of a credit card company or computer manufacturer, or as broad in scope as corporate mergers. Our assumptions about race, **culture**, gender, and sexuality are constantly challenged as we are compelled to engage in such worldly encounters.

CONCEPTUALIZING RACE, GENDER, AND SEXUALITY IN ACADEMIC DISCOURSES

Various academic discourses and areas of study engage the intersections of race, gender, and sexuality to consider the ways in which they are interrelated, the complex, nuanced representations evident in relation to each, and the contradictions that emerge in the process of negotiating raced and gendered identities. Such distinct and yet interrelated fields of study as ethnic studies, the study of race and racism, **cultural studies**, multiculturalism, postcolonial theory, women's and gender studies, feminist theory, LGBT studies, queer theory, and more recently, transgender studies engage issues that these different groups – peoples of color, women, and LGBTs – confront. These fields conceptualize and theorize the experiences and perspectives of marginalized groups, serving not only to represent their voices but also to transform academic discourse. In so doing, they rewrite the traditional, Western "canon," according to which "classic" works – authored by white, European males – are central, authoritative sources of disciplinary knowledge. For instance, cultural and postcolonial theorists (such as Edward Said, **Stuart Hall**, Gayatri Spivak, Chandra Mohanty, Dipesh Chakrabarty, and Homi Bhabha, among others) have written about issues of identity, culture, and nation to critique Eurocentrism in literature, history, women's studies, and so on. In 1978, Said's groundbreaking book, *Orientalism*, offered one of the early critiques of how Western discourses construed and represented the "East" as "other," as inferior to the "West." And, postcolonial and transnational feminist theorist, Chandra Mohanty wrote about how "third world women" were represented "under western eyes" in feminist discourses. Specifically in relation to the US context, writing about the intersections of race, class, and gender, a quarter of a century ago, feminist scholar, **bell hooks** critiqued feminist discourses for ignoring the writings of women of color. Around that time period, black, lesbian poet, Audre Lorde, who famously cautioned, "the master's tools will never dismantle the master's house," (Lorde, 1984: 110) also wrote about how academic discourses are rooted in patriarchal, racist, heterosexist structures and how we need to draw on difference as a "crucial strength" (Lorde, 1984: 112) to develop a culture of interdependence.

Such analyses are further complicated when we consider how individuals and communities of color, queers, women – again, US-born or immigrant – have themselves internalized hierarchies of race, gender, and sexuality. As critical and postcolonial theorists (**Frantz Fanon**, Paulo Freire, Audre Lorde, bell hooks and Trinh Minh-ha, among others) have noted, the oppressed/colonized internalize the oppressor/colonizer. That is the oppressed/colonized adopt – often for the sake of their own survival – the mannerisms and ways of thinking of the oppressors/colonizers, further validating the authority of the oppressor/colonizer and their own subjugation. For instance, in his classic work, *Black skin, white masks*, French-educated psychiatrist and theorist from Martinique, Frantz Fanon, wrote, nearly 60 years ago, of the colonized black man (in this case from Martinique), who, returning from the colonizing country (in this case France), has forgotten his own language and only speaks the language of the colonizer. And, more recently, feminist writers of color, such as Audre Lorde, bell hooks, and Trinh Minh-ha, have written about how, in order to succeed, women writers, including women of color, have to internalize the language of the "master." Thus, we see how race and gender intersect to influence the very language and discourse we use even to analyze and critique them.

ACCOMPLISHMENTS AND ONGOING STRUGGLES

Thus, in recent decades – mainly, post-the Civil Rights era in the United States – issues of identity, culture and representation pertaining to race, gender, and sexuality have become a part of academic discourse, with many universities housing departments and centers that focus on the aforementioned fields and offer degree programs or at least courses in these areas. Of course, even today, many programs in such areas as ethnic studies, women's studies, and LGBT studies continue to struggle for funding, faculty lines, and administrative support from their institutions. Even if we have succeeded in adding a few windows to the "master's house," we have not yet come close to accomplishing the task of "dismantling" it and creating a new house in which *all* are present equitably. In other words, even as the study of race, gender, and sexuality now has its place in academic discourse, it remains a contested area, one that does not quite fit within the structures that have been established to determine what knowledge and whose knowledge was worthy of study and, therefore, to be located at the "center."

Again, the process of transformation is neither uniform nor without its contradictions. As we see, above, even as feminism and women's studies first emerged as discourses representing women's experiences, perspectives, analyses, and critiques, they came in for critique for leaving out the voices of women of color, Third World women, and lesbian women. For instance, women of color – whether based in the "West" or the "Third World" – have critiqued "mainstream" feminist discourses as misrepresenting their particular struggles, perspectives, cultures, and identities, given that such discourses are located within and limited by a Eurocentric frame. Thus, even as feminism emerged as a liberating discourse, intended to confront the marginalization and othering (treating as "other,") of women, it perpetuated the marginalization of women of color and reinscribed hierarchies of race and culture.

Similarly, theorists who argue for critical approaches to multiculturalism have critiqued approaches rooted in cultural pluralism and cultural relativism. They argue that although multiculturalism may have "arrived" – as a discourse, in practice, in media representations – such approaches are still widely prevalent. Shallow and seemingly benign, cultural pluralism and cultural relativism focus on external, obvious aspects of diverse cultures – such as foods and fests, celebrations and customs – rather than examining in depth the relations of power that lead to and perpetuate hierarchies of race, culture, gender, and nation. Thus, such approaches ultimately acknowledge and even "celebrate" diversity only at the surface level, leaving intact extant power structures that operate to privilege white, heterosexual men. Rather than viewing diversity as an issue that is somehow to be "resolved," critical multiculturalists assert that we need to engage diversity and difference to enrich ourselves, and strengthen the fabric of our communities and the larger society. Such a critical approach to multiculturalism is useful in continuing the work of deconstructing "us–them" binaries and fostering alliances across differences. For instance, when white youth see that multiculturalism does not exclude them to focus only on communities of color, that it pertains to them, too, they can examine their own cultures in relation to others' and also participate as allies in the process of social change. Similarly, when diverse peoples of color consider how they can come together with others – of color or white – to attain shared goals, they can form coalitions and work to foster social justice in the larger context.

RELATIONS ACROSS COMMUNITIES

The internalization of the oppressor/colonizer is also evident in hierarchical relations that exist across different groups on the margins. For instance, different peoples of color may hold stereotypes about and have **prejudices** against each other. Oftentimes, such attitudes play into the "divide and rule" policy adopted by the oppressor, who benefits by pitting one marginalized group against another. Furthermore, seemingly benign or "positive" stereotypes can also factor in. For instance, according to the "**model minority**" stereotype, Asian Americans are construed as good workers, who uniformly excel in math and science and hold high-paying jobs. Not only does this stereotype pit Asian Americans against such communities of color as African Americans and Latinas/Latinos, who have often been represented as a drain on society's resources, but also it ignores the particular challenges and struggles they encounter. Ultimately, the model minority stereotype is a representation that the dominant group – whites, in this case – keeps in circulation to validate further their own power to determine the status of communities of color and keep them in their place as subalterns.

Similarly, some in communities of color may view homosexuality as a prevalent issue in white communities – "it is a white issue" – but not their own. Thereby, they succeed in further marginalizing those within their own racial and ethnic groups who are queer-identified. Furthermore, queers of color – again, whether US-born or immigrant – are a small percentage of the larger queer community and often find themselves on the margins in that context, too. For instance, queer Asian American theorists have discussed the challenges and contradictions queer Asian Americans encounter at the intersections of race, ethnicity, and sexuality within their own communities and within the larger social context, where they may be silenced and rendered invisible. Thus, we see that individuals and communities may be located at multiple margins in the larger social context. At the same time, it is important also to note that diverse individuals and communities *do* accept differences, engage the intersections (of race, class, gender, sexuality, nation, and so on), and establish collaborative efforts to address shared concerns. For instance, the Audre Lorde Project – a New York City-based organization for queer people of color – focuses on activism, education, and community-building across different groups, and social and economic justice. And, indeed, a number of scholars have made the case for dialoguing and building coalitions across diverse racial, ethnic, and gender communities in order to work towards social transformation.

INTERSTICES AND HYBRIDITIES

The complex intersections of race, gender, and sexuality – and the related contradictions – are evident in present-day hybrid and interstitial (existing in the interstices, the in-between spaces) identities and representations. For instance, the contradiction of racial segregation and racial miscegenation (mixing of different races) existing at the same time in the US context has been well documented. In the US context, the gendered nature of race relations has been most discussed in terms of black and white relations and the presence of mixed-race individuals in these communities. A related issue that has also been much discussed is "passing" – where some mixed race individuals have passed, typically (but, of course, not always), as white.

As noted earlier, current discourses also focus on interracial relations across various groups (Asian Americans, Latinas/Latinos, Native Americans, immigrant populations) and on issues of identity and culture as they pertain to multiracial individuals. Also, in a global context, there is increasing awareness of the wide range of representations of culture, gender, and sexuality in different contexts. For instance, the popular film *Bend it like Beckham* represents some of the contradictions and challenges that a young British girl from a South Asian immigrant family encounters as she pursues her interest – much against traditional mores pertaining to gender and culture – in playing soccer.

Similarly, today there is increasing awareness that there are various iterations of queer identities in different cultures (Native American, African, Asian), where such terms as "lesbian," "gay," and "bisexual," which are typically used in "Western" discourses, are limiting and do not serve as apt descriptors. For instance, "two-spirit" people are members of Native American/First Nations communities who fulfill one of many mixed gender roles **indigenous** to their communities. Such roles traditionally include wearing the clothing and performing the work of both male and female genders. In other words, "two-spirit" people are seen as embodying both the masculine and feminine in one body. This term, which breaks out of the male–female binary, was coined by contemporary Native American LGBT people to describe themselves and reclaim their diverse gender identities. The African documentary *Woubi Chéri* presents other examples of culturally specific queer identities. *Woubi Chéri* focuses on constructions of gender and sexuality as they pertain to homosexuals and bisexuals in the African country of Côte d'Ivoire (formerly Ivory Coast), where, for instance, a "woubi" is a male who chooses to play the role of "wife" in a relationship with another man and a "yossi" is a bisexual man, perhaps married, who accepts the role of a woubi's husband.

Finally, just as the issue of "passing" has been much discussed in terms of race, the issue of "closeting" has been much discussed in terms of queer sexualities. LGBTs who feel pressured (for instance, due to concerns about job security and acceptance by their families and communities) to hide their sexual preference, are "closeted," or "in the closet," or not "out."

RACE, GENDER, SEXUALITY AND SOCIAL CHANGE

Over the decades, a number of activist and community organizing efforts – large scale and local – have emerged to address issues of race, gender, and sexuality. From the Black Power movement and the feminist movement, which started in the 1960s, to the emergence in the 1980s of the Gay Pride movement and the Radical Lesbians movement, various efforts have been made to address the concerns of marginalized communities. Such organizations as the National Association for the Advancement of Colored People (NAACP), National Organization for Women, and Human Rights Campaign, among others, serve to represent these groups on a national level. And numerous local organizations now exist across the country to give voice to, lobby for the rights, and address the concerns of various communities on the margins. Such popular films as *My beautiful launderette*, *Boys don't cry*, *Ma vie en rose*, *Billy Elliot*, *Real women have curves*, and *Transamerica*, among others, speak to issues of race, culture, gender, and sexuality. The numerous resources available for educators include such films as *It's elementary: Talking about gay issues in school* and *Strange fruit*, as well as the publications issued by Rethinking Schools and films and videos available from such sources as California Newsreel and PBS (Public Broadcasting Service).

KEY READINGS

Allison, D. (1995). *Two or three things I know for sure.* New York: Penguin Books.

Anzaldúa, G. (1987). *Borderlands/La frontera: The new mestiza.* San Francisco, CA: Spinsters/Aunt Lute.

Asher, N. (2007). Made in the (multicultural) U.S.A.: Unpacking tensions of race, culture, gender, and sexuality in education. *Educational Researcher*, 36(2), 65–73.

Butler, J. (1990). *Gender trouble: Feminism and the subversion of identity.* New York: Routledge.

Fanon, F. (1967). *Black skin, white masks.* New York: Grove Press.

hooks, b. (1984). *Feminist theory: From margin to center*. Boston, MA: South End.

——. (1990). *Yearning: Race, gender, and cultural politics*. Boston, MA: South End.

Kumashiro, K. K. (Ed.). (2001). *Troubling intersections of race and sexuality: Queer students of color and anti-oppressive education*. Lanham, MD: Rowman & Littlefield.

Lorde, A. (1984). *Sister outsider*. Freedom, CA: The Crossing Press.

McCarthy, C. & Crichlow, W. (Eds.). (1993). *Race, identity, and representation in education*. New York: Routledge.

Mohanty, C. T., Russo, A., & Torres, L. (Eds.) (1991). *Third World women and the politics of feminism*. Bloomington, IN: Indiana University Press.

National School Climate Survey (2007), available via the website of the Gay, Lesbian and Straight Education Network (GLSEN) (www.glsen.org/cgi-bin/iowa/all/library/record/2340.html?state=research&type=research).

Pinar, W. F. (2001). *The gender of racial politics and violence in America: Lynching, prison rape, and the crisis of masculinity*. New York: Peter Lang.

Pratt, M. B. (1984). Identity: Skin, blood, heart. In E. Bulkin, M. B. Pratt, & B. Smith, *Yours in struggle: Three feminist perspectives on anti-Semitism and racism*. Brooklyn, NY: Long Haul.

Said, E. (1978). *Orientalism*. New York: Penguin.

Sears, J. T. & Williams, W. L. (Eds.). (1997). *Overcoming heterosexism and homophobia: Strategies that work*. New York: Columbia University Press.

Sedgwick, E. K. (1990). *Epistemology of the closet*. Berkeley, CA: University of California Press.

Trinh, T. M. (1989). *Woman, native, other: Writing postcoloniality and feminism*. Bloomington, IN: Indiana University Press.

Villenas, S. (1996). The colonizer/colonized Chicana ethnographer: Identity, marginalization, and co-optation in the field. *Harvard Educational Review*, 66(4), 711–731.

Weedon, C. (1999). *Feminism, theory, and the politics of difference*. Malden, MA: Blackwell.

9

RACE, MEDIA AND POPULAR CULTURE

STEPHEN MAYNARD CALIENDO

As technology advances, citizens increasingly rely on mass media for information about their political world. While the type and availability of media vary with levels of economic development and democratization, most of the world's citizens interact with mediated communication in some form, and much of that communication deals explicitly or implicitly with **race** and ethnicity. In post-industrial societies, print sources gave way to radio, radio to television, and television to the Internet, such that images and messages related to race continue to be pervasive. Whether it is found in news or entertainment sources, it is important to consider the mediated information that we encounter about race and ethnicity as distinct from (though related to) that which we experience ourselves.

Communication consists of an interdependent relationship between the message (which is related to the source of the message) and one who receives a message. In the next section, I detail some of the major theories that account for the potential effects that messages can have on individual or collective attitudes and behaviors. After that, I discuss some of the different ways that media content about or involving race and ethnicity is formed and appears in different contexts, with emphasis on the ways that racism can be reinforced and perpetuated or challenged. Finally, I provide a case study about the ways that radio messages helped to reinforce cultural **stereotypes** and, consequently, instigate mass killings throughout the countryside during the 1994 Rwandan **genocide**.

EFFECTS OF MEDIA MESSAGES

The content of mediated communication might be considered by most to be irrelevant if we cannot see clear connections to the ways that such messages affect individuals' thoughts and behaviors. Accordingly, it is helpful to understand the potentiality of media effects, spending time on the content of the messages. Of course, space does not permit a full discussion of these concepts, many of which are supported by extensive research by psychologists, political scientists and communication scholars. More detailed information can be found, starting with some of the readings listed at the end of this chapter.

Understanding cognitive processing

The key to understanding media effects is the realization that the human brain works in mysterious ways. Apart from the intricacies of the biological functions, there are two primary concepts to consider: conscious-level thinking and subconscious processing. Conscious-level thinking is fairly easy to understand because it is the more obvious of the two. We know what we think and, while we cannot always know what others think (unless and until they express those thoughts), nearly everyone can comprehend ideas about how others think, even if those attitudes are different than their own. What is much more difficult to understand is the effect that subconscious processing has on our thoughts and behaviors.

Information processing can be best understood as a function of how our brains receive and store information for our subsequent use. One dominant theory about how this happens involves the existence of schemata, which are organizing structures in our brains. A convenient (if simplistic) analogy is to think about a computer hard drive. While it is possible to simply store all files in one space (the c: drive, or the "My Documents" folder, for instance), most of us create a rather elaborate system of "folders" so that a structure exists. When we download or create a new file, we are careful to store it in a place that will make it easier for us to retrieve. When we retrieve a file from our computer, it is in exactly the same form as when we placed it there. Our brains work similarly, but not quite so cleanly. When we retrieve an item from memory, the schema within which it was stored is "activated," which means that other information stored there is also available to us as we think about the item. Therefore, the place where a piece of information is stored in our brains has a significant effect on how we think about it later.

This relates closely to the concept of stereotypes, which are sets of assumptions and generalizations that members of a society harbor, often subconsciously, about groups and members of those groups. If we are socialized to accept a stereotype about **Latinos** – for instance, that they are untrustworthy or prone to criminality – any encounter that we have with a Latino or Latina individual has the potential to activate schemata related to trustworthiness or crime. We might clutch our purse closer to us or check to make sure our wallet is still in our pocket without even consciously thinking about it. Indeed, racially progressive persons are horrified when they realize that they are prone to such expectations and assumptions, although doing so is not a sign of overt **prejudice**. As is explained more fully below, such tacit forms of racism are much more common and hard to combat than visible, explicit race-based messages.

Agenda setting, framing, and priming

Such subconscious processing about race and ethnicity can affect us in a variety of ways. Political communication scholars have identified three primary concepts related to media effects – agenda setting, framing, and priming – all of which have clear and identifiable relations to race-related attitudes.

Agenda setting refers to the ability of mass media to determine the topics about which citizens think. Often, public officials struggle with each other and with media professionals over control of the public agenda. For example, in the 2008 presidential campaign in the United States, Barack Obama became the first candidate who identified as African American to win the nomination of one of the two major parties. Because of the unique structure of American presidential elections (i.e. the Electoral College system) and the history of white Americans not voting for candidates of color, Obama tried to keep explicit discussions of race out of his campaign. There were two problems with his desire, however. First, since he was black in a context where whites have been and are the **power** majority, his "**otherness**" was obvious to everyone. Even if he did not talk about his race, his very presence served as a reminder. Obama's task, then, was to avoid activating racial schemata while trying to keep other types of schemata (leadership, common "American" values, etc.) active. The second problem was that his opponents understood that making race "matter" in this context would work to their advantage. Democratic candidates during the nomination contests and his Republican and conservative opponents during the general election all used various types of messages that activated Americans' racial schemata. As a result, the Obama campaign team had to deal with race directly, which meant that part of the agenda was about race.

Framing is the way that we think about information in different contexts. The term itself is a metaphor that refers to the fact that a picture can look quite different if it is placed in different frames. Even though the image itself might be identical, a frame can highlight certain elements, colors or shapes in a way that a different frame would not. Our world is, in a sense, organized by frames; everything we experience happens within a particular context, even if we do not recognize it as such. If someone were to enter a room with a stuffed monkey doll, waving it around and making monkey sounds, the act on its own is not infused with any racial meaning. If, for instance, that act were to take place in a daycare center with children of various races and ethnicities, few would ascribe any racial meaning to the act. However, were the same person to arrive at a gathering of a civil rights group acting in the same way, it would be hard to ignore the racial connotation. The act (the picture) did not change; what changed was the context (the frame).

Frames may be employed intentionally, but they need not be. Public officials have become quite savvy in manipulating frames to their own benefit (or to the detriment of their opponents). In 2008, South African president Thabo Mbeki employed a racial frame when discussing HIV/AIDS in a parliamentary debate. While the disproportionate number of HIV cases on the African continent – and South Africa in particular – cannot be ignored, the challenges surrounding the disease are complex and multifaceted. Mbeki chose to discuss the issue in the context of racism by Westerners who, he argued, harbor resentments and harmful stereotypes about blacks. His opponents claimed that he was intentionally trying to deflect the issue, but Mbeki believed that the perception of (black) South Africans and HIV by whites was a significant aspect of the crisis. Had he not framed the discussion in the context of race, the resultant news stories would probably not have mentioned race at all but, rather, would have focused on other elements of the pandemic discussed at the meeting.

Even without intentional invocation, though, all information that we encounter is framed. Sometimes the context is related to physical space, such as watching a television show about race in a room with persons of various races, as opposed to watching it in a room only of those of our own race. At other times, the context is related to time, as in experiencing a speech about race in 2010 as opposed to 1940. Further, time and space intersect to create unique contexts, such that watching the speech on race with a mixed-race audience in Mexico in 2010 would differ from the same experience in the same year in Russia, and so forth. Put simply, context – the frame – has a great deal to do with how we experience race and ethnicity.

Priming has to do most directly with the activation of schemata so that subsequent evaluations are informed by information stored within those structures. Even without a particular frame, information that is encountered prior to other information can "prime" schemata and, consequently, affect how we perceive the information. If we return to the example of President Mbeki's speech about HIV/AIDS, we can consider how race might have been primed even if he had not wrapped his speech in race that day. If there had been explicit discussion about race and racism in South Africa during the days leading up to the parliamentary discussion, it is possible that onlookers would have "read" Mbeki's comments through a racial lens because race-related schemata would have been previously activated, making them accessible as Mbeki spoke. Similarly, relating to our example about Barack Obama's presidential run, his skin color could serve to prime racial schemata even as he sought to avoid any explicit discussion about race. Such priming might have happened in that context anyway, but his opponents were able to actively engage in discussion that would make sure that race was primed. Whether those opponents did so intentionally is irrelevant to this discussion; the effects are meaningful irrespective of whether there was a deliberate attempt to capitalize on Obama's status as racial "other."

Explicit and implicit discussion of race

To this point, most of the examples we have considered dealt with race being spoken about explicitly. Indeed, mediated discussion of race today often centers on the degree to which race should or should not be taken into consideration during the political process involved in deciding public policy matters. What sort of considerations (e.g. **reparations**) should be made with respect to **indigenous peoples** who were displaced as a result of colonization? How does the history of black slavery and **segregation** in the United States contribute to the disproportionate suffering of African Americans? How does immigration from Africa, the Middle East, and South America and East and South Asian to Europe and North America relate to the allocation of resources in those areas? However, as civil rights progress, people are increasingly reluctant to allow race or ethnicity to dictate their conscious attitudes about political and social policy. This is what Tali Mendelberg has referred to as the "norm of racial equality." In other words, we know that race and ethnicity should not affect the evaluations we make of people or situations, so when we realize that they might, we resist those attitudes to bring our thoughts into congruence with the core value of racial equality.

As a result of this norm, it is perhaps more important in modern times to understand implicit media messages about race. These are images and language that contain information likely to activate our racial schemata but not bring race into our consciousness, which would, in turn, violate the norm of racial equality. Again, these messages might be employed with the designed purpose of tapping into latent racist predispositions, but they need not be (or be proven to be) intentional for the effect to occur.

We might consider the example of a television advertisement by the international chicken restaurant KFC that ran in Australia in 2010. The ad featured a white Australian man surrounded by (black) West Indians dancing, playing music and, apparently, making him feel uncomfortable during a cricket match. Asking us (by way of the camera), "Need a tip when you're stuck in an awkward situation?," he raises a container of KFC chicken as black hands grab for pieces, apparently settling down. The white man says, "Too easy," as the image of KFC products, referred to as "crowd pleasers," appears on the screen. The ad was posted on an international Internet server (YouTube) and drew the wrath of Americans who pointed out the stereotype about blacks eating fried chicken. KFC issued a statement defending the ad, but eventually removed it with a statement of apology for any offense that may have been taken. The controversy nicely captures many of the concepts discussed in this chapter.

The ad – or, more accurately in this case, the controversy surrounding the ad after it was re-posted on the Internet – affected the agenda of public discourse in a number of communities for several weeks. Many who were not thinking about racial stereotypes prior to this incident were forced to consider the issue once the story broke. The context of the story is important, too, as KFC argued in defending the spot. They point out that the "fried chicken" stereotype is a uniquely American construction, so that running such an ad in Australia was not designed to, nor did it, prime racist stereotypes. In other words, the Australian frame may have resulted in the spot not being considered to be racist, while an American frame would certainly lead to such a reading. This incident, as well as another incident involving an Indian student in Australia at about the same time, helped to prime racial attitudes in Australia and focus attention on problems of racial inequality in that nation in ways that were not particularly salient prior to these news stories. In short, when an implicitly racial message is highlighted as racial, it becomes explicit, and our conscious minds take over the processing duties from the subconscious.

CONTENT OF MEDIA MESSAGES

Mass media content can be broadly grouped into two categories: news and entertainment. Much of the explicit discussion of race and ethnicity is found in the news, either in the form of so-called "hard news," which is reporting based on facts and occurrences in particular contexts, or in the form of opinions and editorials, which are clear attempts to persuade the reader or viewer of a particular point of view.

News and editorial content

Many scholars believe that "hard news" is potentially more persuasive than editorial content because individuals approach the latter with cognitive filters relating to political ideology or policy preference in place and, therefore, are more likely to have their attitudes reaffirmed (if they agree with the writer or speaker) or be prepared to defend their own position (if they disagree with the message). In other words, if we know that someone is trying to persuade us, we are prepared to defend our positions; if we do not expect to have our attitudes challenged, we are more susceptible to having our attitudes changed. For example, if a newspaper story on the front page has a title "Whites outperform blacks in standardized tests" and contains statistics about recent results consistent with that headline, readers would be hard pressed to resist the information, even if it did not match their preconceived notion about whether black members of society were at a systemic disadvantage. On the other hand, if an editorial (either by the newspaper's editorial board or by a guest columnist) contains information about how white members of the community have advantages that lead to such results, a reader who believes that any racial discrepancy is the result of some members of society simply not working as hard as others will be likely to resist the message as "argument" and dismiss the content as "just opinion."

In this way, existing predispositions (conscious and subconscious) about race and ethnicity serve to shape the way we experience the news and the way news is written. For example, in the aftermath of Hurricane Katrina in Louisiana in 2005, and again in the days after the earthquake in Haiti in 2010, the phrase "searching for food" was used to describe the plight of white Americans while the term "looting" was applied to black Americans engaging in the same behavior.

Entertainment

It is important to remember that communication is an interactive process; no message has meaning without an audience, and the interaction of the message with the person determines what it "means." This phenomenon is at work perhaps most prominently with respect to entertainment. Whether we consider music, television, film, video games, or Internet content, messages have meaning dependent on the context and the way that audience members process them. In the United States, for instance, hip-hop (or "**rap**") music has come under scrutiny for perpetuating harmful stereotypes (specifically related to misogyny and physical violence) about African Americans. Its supporters argue that, rather than serving to reinforce and prime racist stereotypes and copycat behavior, hip-hop music is a reflection of the realities of life in much of black America. Both sides, of course, are correct. The music made is reflective of the lived experiences of some aspects of black Americans' lives, but because it is the only window to black life for many whites who live in suburban and rural areas of the country, its messages encourage extrapolation to the entire black population.

Similarly, so-called "reality" television programs have highlighted racial inequality and stereotyping in a number of cultural contexts. Great Britain's version of the international program *Big Brother*, for instance, has featured a number of racial conflicts amongst its participants. Controversy revolves around the degree to which such conflicts highlight deeply held racial resentment in society at large or are isolated to the persons involved. Because of our aversion to accepting the power of the subconscious on our attitudes and behaviors, it is convenient and comfortable for individuals to believe that our conscious attitudes are our "real" thoughts and that racism is a problem for those who harbor overtly bigoted attitudes. Combined with the tendency to dismiss entertainment programming as "just fun," these messages constitute what Dan Shea has referred to as a "Trojan Horse" effect, carrying powerful political messages in the guise of harmless escapism.

RADIO RACISM IN RWANDA

As is the case in most **cultures**, the line between news and entertainment was blurry in rural Rwanda at the end of the twentieth century. Some members of the Hutu majority referred to their ethnic Tutsi neighbors as "cockroaches," often playfully and in ways that were disarming and seemingly benign. The dehumanization of Tutsis on a regular basis over a sustained period of time, combined with historical resentment of Tutsis (who were the preferred "race" of colonial powers for decades) by Hutus, set a context within which otherwise peaceful Rwandans committed brutal acts of violence and murder against their compatriots over a 100-day period in 1994.

Radio-Télévision Libres des Mille Collines (RTLMC) began broadcasting in 1993, just before the historic signing of the Arusha Accords peace agreement between the Rwandan government's armed forces (FAR) and the Tutsi rebel force, the Rwandan Patriotic Front (RPF). Journalist Linda Melvern reports that broadcasts were characterized by crude jokes and vulgar language, often by intoxicated radio personalities. For nearly a full year before the killings began, listeners were treated to a steady dose of propaganda that demonized the Tutsis, celebrated the government, and (perhaps ironically) warned of unspeakable atrocities that the Tutsi rebels planned to commit on ordinary Hutu citizens.

Social psychologist Stanley Milgram's research helps to explain how ordinarily kind and gentle persons can commit the most heinous acts of brutality in certain situations. As he set out to determine how German citizens might have been permissive (at best) and complicit (at worst) during the Holocaust, Milgram demonstrated, through a series of laboratory experiments in which participants believed that they were administering electric shocks to persons to instigate learning of word pairs, that regular folks can be persuaded by a researcher to continue to inflict pain, even though they wish to stop. If the participants had been asked ahead of time if they would engage in this type of behavior, all of them would probably have adamantly denied that they were capable of such abuse. Yet, in the context of the experiment, many followed the orders of the experimenter.

In the Rwandan situation, the "laboratory" context is illustrated by decades of folklore about the ethnic differences (which were deliberately exacerbated and exploited by colonial Europeans) and a year-long campaign of fear and instigated resentment by the RTLMC. As a result, some ordinary Rwandans picked up machetes and hacked their neighbors to death in daily assaults throughout the rural countryside, as well as in the capital city of Kigali. When Jean Hatzfeld interviewed perpetrators after the killings had stopped, they overwhelmingly articulated psychological detachment from the activities, avoiding the term "genocide" but affirming ethnic differences that, by that time, had come to be accepted as **authentic**.

Did the radio broadcast cause ethnic killings? Such a question is overly simplistic and ignores the agency of individuals involved in the slaughter. However, the communication certainly contributed to preexisting negative predispositions about Tutsis and helped to establish a context within which mass killings could be perpetrated by citizens who ordinarily would never entertain the thought of such brutality. That is, the interaction between the content of the message and the lived experiences of the audience members had an effect that, in this case, led to one of the most widespread and horrific incidents of terror – primarily based on ethnic difference – in recorded history.

CONCLUSION

It would be inaccurate to say that racism continues because of messages that are contained in media and popular culture. However, it cannot be denied that the racism that exists is both reinforced and perpetuated by such messages, whether they are expressed explicitly or implicitly. The content of racialized messages interacts with audience members' lived experiences within cultural contexts, which means that no one message will "work" the same way all of the time. If we want to understand the effects of mediated communication involving race, we must be attentive to historical realities and the psychological processes that dictate how the information is understood.

KEY READINGS

Childs, E. C. (2009). *Fade to black and white: Interracial images in popular culture.* New York: Rowman and Littlefield.

Dallaire, R. (2003). *Shake hands with the devil: The failure of humanity in Rwanda.* New York: Carol and Graf.

Dolby, N. E. (2001). *Constructing race: Youth, identity and popular culture in South Africa.* Albany, NY: State University of New York Press.

Entman, R. M. & Rojecki, A. (2000). *The Black image in the White mind: Media and race in America.* Chicago: University of Chicago Press.

Gourevich, P. (1999). *We wish to inform you that tomorrow we will be killed with our families: Stories from Rwanda.* New York: Picador.

Hatzfeld, J. (2003). *Machete season: The killers in Rwanda speak.* New York: Picador.

Iyengar, S. (1994). *Is anyone responsible? How television frames political issues.* Chicago: University of Chicago Press.

Iyengar, S. & Kinder, D. R. (1989). *News that matters: Television and American opinion.* Chicago: University of Chicago Press.

Jamieson, K. H. & Waldman, P. (2004). *The press effect: Politicians, journalists, and the stories that shape the political world.* New York: Oxford University Press USA.

Lakoff, G. (2009). *The political mind: A cognitive scientist's guide to your brain and its politics.* New York: Penguin.

Luntz, F. I. (2006). *Words that work: It's not what you say, it's what people hear.* New York: Hyperion.

Melvern, L. (2000). *A people betrayed: The role of the West in Rwanda's genocide.* London: Zed.

Mendelberg, T. (2001). *The race card: Campaign strategy, implicit messages and the norm of equality.* Princeton, NJ: Princeton University Press.

Milgram, S. (1974). *Obedience to authority: An experimental view.* New York: Harper and Row.

Shea, D. (1998). *Mass politics: The politics of popular culture.* New York: St. Martin's.

Strausbaugh, J. (2007). *Black like you: Blackface, whiteface, insult & imitation in American popular culture.* New York: Tarcher.

Westen, D. (2007). *The political brain: The role of emotion in deciding the fate of the nation.* New York: PublicAffairs.

10

RACE, ETHNICITY, AND GLOBALIZATION

S. P. UDAYAKUMAR

> . . . I pointed out the tremendous advantages accruing to the white world
> from exploitation of undeveloped coloured lands and from exports of
> manufactured goods to coloured markets. The prodigious wealth thereby
> amassed has been a prime cause of white prosperity, has buttressed the
> maintenance of white world-hegemony, and has made possible much of
> the prodigious increase of white population. We little realize what the loss
> of these advantages would mean.
>
> (Lothrop Stoddard, 1920: 240–241)

The one word that is commonly used these days to sum up the rapid changes
occurring in human society is "globalization." This word has become the
catchphrase of the late twentieth century and often means different things to
different people. Globalization sounds rather innocuous and even seeks to
invoke some positive images in one's mind: that it is an altruistic geographical
notion that attempts to integrate the "globe"; that it rotates on its own moral
axis and revolves around the notion of universal peace and justice; and that this
"chance-discovery" of humanity has had no past and is completely devoid of the
political. Most of the discussions on globalization indeed reflect this naïve
understanding.

On the contrary, a closer look at globalization's actual workings would reveal
that it also **segregates** a large portion of the world's population and prevents it
from sharing the benefits provided by scientific advances and technological
progress. As Francisco Sagasti rightly warns, we can delineate "the emergence
of a fractured global order – an order that is global but not integrated" (quoted
in Edoho, 1997, p. 199). This order pulls all of us into contact with each other
but simultaneously maintains deep fissures between different groups of countries and people within countries. A good example to consider would be the
impact of globalization on the racial and ethnic minorities.

Such a critical scrutiny necessitates first locating globalization in a historical
and political context. According to Angus Maddison's 1995 book *Monitoring
the World Economy 1820–1992*, economic growth was paltry until the industrial
revolution. The world gross domestic product (GDP) went from $565 per
person in 1500 to $651 per person in 1820 (measured in 1990 US dollars). After
the industrial revolution, however, the world GDP per capita swelled from $651
to $5,145, and the total world GDP grew from $695 billion in 1820 to almost

$28 trillion in 1992. Charles Kindleberger's historical review of globalization identifies three periods along the lines of Maddison's periodization, namely traditional society before the industrial revolution, early globalism from 1500 to 1850, and modern globalism after 1850. The "distant trade" that took place between ancient empires, "Columbus's discovery of the New World," European colonization, and World War II are all considered by Kindleberger to be major milestones in the globalization highway.

In the 1950s and 1960s, world trade brought about "shallow integration," the early stages of accelerated economic growth for established market economies. By the 1970s, international trade also enhanced growth in the developing countries that had open and competitive market systems. The General Agreement on Tariffs and Trade (GATT) and the rules of the World Trade Organization (WTO) came to facilitate increased world trade in concurrence with several regional trade associations and bilateral trade agreements. Globalization, as we know it today, emerged in the early 1980s with the advancements in telecommunications and transportation technology and foreign direct investment (FDI) by transnational corporations (TNCs).

A sanitized and sacrosanct history of globalization is being written in the North, connecting it to the Enlightenment philosophy, the American revolution, the French revolution and now the "remarkable progress [that] has been made in all major dimensions of human development since the late 1960s" (Rondinelli and Behrman, 2000: 7) This glossy history of globalization conveniently hides the bitter squabbles between the "developed" countries and "developing" countries over trade and financial issues, the developing countries' demand for a "New International Economic Order," and the developed countries' complete disregard for socioeconomic justice. Even before addressing these legitimate claims meaningfully, globalization has been thrust down their throats.

FRAMING THE ISSUE

The existing global structure is stratified into three areas: a global universalistic dominant stratum of industrial states and TNCs; a dependent stratum of small industries, small agricultural units and liberal technocratic intellectuals linked to the former by unstable ties; and a third stratum of social sectors that are exploited and **discriminated** against and who are excluded from the benefits of the global economy. Most of the women, **indigenous people**, **minorities**, and exploited classes in the informal sectors belong to the excluded stratum.

Endowed with the capital, technology and know-how, the corporate masters of the North and their trading allies in the South have declared unilateral victory in the development war. According to them, the Holy Trinity of "Money, Market and Machine" alone can redeem human beings. In fact, globalization promotes a future-blind attitude toward the Earth and its resources. It consolidates the wrong and lopsided development of the world and destroys indigenous expertise, local industries, and sustainable development initiatives. Worst of all, it ties the welfare of the entire globe to the operation of a single economic scheme that is dominated by a few corporate groups and individuals. Aside from globalization's devastating impact on our living environment and on the chasm between the rich and the poor, among its worst crimes is its complete negation of the underprivileged and the unwilling. Racial and ethnic minorities, landless peasants, urban poor, minorities, women, children, the disabled, refugees, and migrant workers are some of the specific groups of people who get the rawest deal in the ongoing globalization.

It is important to see ongoing globalization as part of a historical process of socioeconomic-political domination and abuse. The perpetuation of the hierarchies of **race**, ethnicity, class, gender, and generation has to be situated in that larger context. Problematizing the danger of permanently re-inscribing a subordinated and life-threatening status for people of color all over the globe becomes very urgent.

The "people of color" are not an economically homogenous group either. The upper class and middle class sections of the South countries have fared rather well in the new economy and are closely tied to their Northern counterparts. Moreover, in countries such as Bangladesh and Ecuador, for instance, the plight of the minority communities is not much different from that of the poor sections of the majority community. Similarly, not all whites are rich and comfortable. There is a substantial group of poor whites in North America and Europe. The middle-income whites in North America have also lost jobs, income, and social stability due to globalization.

Thus, the "**color line**" and the "class line" are intertwined and operate discursively in the socioeconomic-political space. While the "color line" may be more prominent in the United States, the "class line" may be indomitable in other parts of the world. Other societies, such as India, may have added complexities like the "caste line." However unscientific they may be, race, color, and caste have been used to deprive many people of economic resources, political **power**, and fundamental human dignity. These harsh realities of the human society are still hanging heavy on our national and global affairs. Hence, it is premature to dismiss racism, casteism, sexism, and other forms of oppression as outdated or unimportant in assessing the plight of many oppressed communities around the world.

Several different approaches to racial/ethnic discrimination and oppression emerge. The moralists, for instance, would highlight the lack of ethics in the scheme. They question the basic operating principle of globalization by comparing the current situation with that which existed some one and a half centuries ago. The opium trade between the Chinese and the colonial British was draining the coffers of China and destroying its social structures and institutions in the process. The Western business community, however, focused on China's "internal problems" and not on the unhindered and unrestricted international trade. A Chinese official, Lin Tze-Hsu, wrote to Queen Victoria of Britain in

1839 and asked: "In coveting wealth to the extreme, they [persons who do harm to the people of China] have no regard for injuring others. Let us ask, where is your conscience?" The moralists claim that the same kind of indifference and discriminatory attitude is still perpetuated today. For instance, Asian precepts and practices are often derided as "ossified and prone to 'cronyism'," and the Asian governance systems are sought to be replaced by the US-style stock market-centered systems.

The **multiculturalists** try to evade the serious allegations of the moralists by claiming that they are fair and socially responsible. Their seemingly noble philosophy of "multiculturalism" allows them

> to buy inexpensively the perception that they are fair and socially responsible. And because multiculturalism takes the heat off transnational corporations by implying that a liberatory politics need not attack their power, it is harming the very communities it seeks to help. [The means to counter all this is] transracial political movement for community empowerment.
>
> (Anthony Taibi, quoted in Chandhoke, 2000)

Then there are the "egalitarians," the defenders of formal equality, who insist on treating everyone equally "without making any distinctions." They fail to realize the fact that the constituency they intend to treat equally is profoundly unequal. Inequality takes many forms: being powerless, poor, ineffective and non-authoritative, and numerically inferior. These people are underprivileged and unequal by virtue of the fact that they possess fewer resources, or no resources, for reasons that are outside their control, such as historical deprivation. Hence, they are profoundly vulnerable to majority decisions. And, if we treat all of them equally, we will end up reproducing inequality. In that process we may also make the situation worse for those who are already suffering.

There are human rights advocates who insist on using the human rights instruments to understand and act upon the plight of the oppressed. The Sub-Commission on Prevention of Discrimination and Protection of Minorities under the UN Commission on Human Rights passed Resolution 1999/30 (Trade Liberalization and Its Impact on Human Rights) on August 26, 1999, which, among other things, requests the UN High Commissioner for Human Rights

> to intensify efforts at dialogue with the World Trade Organization and its member states on the human rights dimensions of trade and investment liberalization, and to take steps to ensure that human rights principles and obligations are fully integrated in future negotiations in the World Trade Organization.

Racism, as much as racial discrimination, haunts society both as institutionalized government policy or as a result of racial superiority and exclusivity doctrines and as manifestations taking place in segments of society that are perpetrated by vested interests for socioeconomic-political purposes. It is quite pertinent to study how financial markets and the overall processes of globalization and liberalization contribute to racism and racial discrimination and segregation and also stand to gain from it.

My argument here is not that race, as such, causes economic exploitation. Neither do I intend to universalize the race problematic made by and for Americans or to fall into the trap of "globalization" of American problems and thereby verify the Americanocentric understanding of "globalization" as the Americanization of the entire universe, as sociologists Pierre Bourdieu and Loic Wacquant fear. All I posit here is that racism continues to be a social reality in many parts of the world, that it is an integral part of the ongoing globalization scheme, and that the oppressed ought to deal with this issue according to the logic of their own society.

After all, globalization undermines local communities and affects traditional ways of living and working. It skews income and wealth distribution, damages the environment, causes insecurity for workers, and entrenches the lopsided development that plagues the contemporary world. At the same time, international financial power is concentrated in a few hands in the North, and it is employed in secrecy and self-interest with a senseless fixation on monetary calculations rather than human considerations. These different realities make one wonder if race and ethnicity are factors in the political disenfranchisement, social exclusion, and economic abuse of minority communities. In this way, it is important to conduct an impact assessment of globalization on the development of the most vulnerable groups of people in the world.

ANGLO-SAXON GLOBALISM AND MARKET RACISM

The present style of financial globalization – a style of capitalism prevalent in the predominantly English-speaking nations such as the United States, the United Kingdom, Australia, Canada, and New Zealand with strong laissez-faire and individualist traditions, small welfare states, and rampant financial sectors – is often called "American." Although British writers refer to it as "Anglo-American," the French prefer the nomenclature of "Anglo-Saxon." Indeed, there is said to be an agreement among nations that a European should run the International Monetary Fund (IMF) while an American manages the World Bank.

The globalization scheme perceived and promoted by these industrialized and predominantly Christian countries with a bad track record of colonialism, slavery, racism, and systematic elimination of the indigenous population has intrinsic Western principles and values, such as property, ownership, intellectual property rights regimes, and so forth. Financial markets and the overall processes of globalization and liberalization are built on racism and racial segregation and they contribute further to racial and economic discrimination. Jeffrey Sachs compares the 30 highest-income countries in the world with the 42 Highly Indebted Poor Countries (HIPCs) and points out some specific problems. Rich-country research is on rich-country ailments such as cardiovascular diseases and cancer and not on the poor countries' problems like malaria, tuberculosis, and AIDS. Two-thirds of the world's 33 million individuals with HIV infection are sub-Saharan Africans, and about 95 percent of worldwide HIV cases are in the developing world.

Consider, for instance, the level of global responsibility for containing AIDS epidemic in sub-Saharan Africa. The total sum needed annually for AIDS prevention in Africa is approximately $2.4 billion, but the continent currently receives only $165 million a year from the world community. The imbalance of global science (that is directed by the rich countries for the rich-country markets), the disparity in technological capacity, global production of knowledge in crucial areas such as life sciences or energy, and the climatic damages the rich counties impose on the poor are some of the major issues that mark the rich–poor divide.

Globalization of racism plays out in many more discrete ways: "global environmental racism"; consolidation of racial and ethnic hatred through the Internet; giving rise to ethnic conflicts and **ethnic cleansing**; facilitating freedom of movement for select groups of people; exclusivistic measures such as the Proposition 187 of California (a 1994 ballot initiative that sought to create a citizenship screening system in order to prohibit illegal immigrants from accessing social services); unleashing racial harassment and violence on minorities, refugees, and migrant workers; police harassment, and so forth.

In defining biotechnology research agenda, for example, cosmetic drugs and slow-ripening tomatoes come higher on the list than a vaccine against malaria or drought-resistant crops for marginal land. Even as communications, transportation, and technology are driving global economic expansion, headway on poverty is not keeping pace. Breakthroughs in technology – such as the Internet – can open a fast track to knowledge-based growth in rich and poor counties alike but, at present, benefit the relatively well-off and educated. Statistics indicate that 88 percent of users live in industrialized countries, which collectively represent just 17 percent of the world's population.

DOMINATION, EXCLUSION, AND DISCRIMINATION

Ongoing globalization, which is marked by dispersion of production and finance capital, has pro-Western and pro-urban biases and has actually led to massive concentration of economic control, surveillance, management, and servicing of the global economy in major metropolises such as New York and London. Understanding the social restructuring of these "global cities" is an important prerequisite in seeing how social dislocations that include new class alignments, new social polarizations, and new norms of consumption take place. Rosemary Coombe posits:

A small class of workers, largely a white, male group of high-skill service providers who structure, communicate, and process the flows upon which transnational capital relies, impose visible transformations in many cities, in the nature of commerce, consumption, and the occupation of space, often in processes of gentrification.

(1995: 797–798)

As this cohesive core group of professionals grows, "an ethnically and culturally diverse 'periphery'," that includes female clerical workers, unskilled and low-skilled workers, and those involved in the informal economy, also expands concomitantly. The global city thus becomes a "dual city" with increased social and economic polarization.

The most important racial dynamic of globalism, however, is the systemic exclusion and increasing marginalization of people of color in the United States and around the world. Such social dislocation takes place in quite a few areas of globalization. Besides these "segmentized impacts," the segmentization itself is an important part of globalization. It is only eager to exploit the ethnic and cultural dynamics in order to fragment communities and perpetuate the exclusionary precepts and practices.

Although globalization seeks to override the national and cultural boundaries, it does promote local difference. As Maria Mies and Vandana Shiva point out, local **cultures** are deemed to have "value" only when they are fragmented and these fragments transformed into saleable goods as "ethnic food," "ethnic music," and "ethnic" objects for the world market. This commodification is crucial in organizing and managing the minoritized racial and ethnic groups within individual states. When these minorities try to exert control over their cultural resources, they are delegitimized by the invocation of "wider" national or universal interests. This simultaneous erasure and reification of racial and ethnic difference is a key component in the discourse of globalization.

This elusive interplay of globalism and racism also manifests itself in many other inscrutable ways. On the one hand, as William Greider points out, "the process of globalization is visibly dismantling enduring **stereotypes** of race and culture, ancient assumptions of supremacy" (Greider, 1997: 20). Mastering modern technology, and dispelling the notion that high-caliber work can be done only by well-educated white people in a few chosen countries, people of color who exist in surroundings of scarcity are making complex things of world quality for the global market. Thus, one of the major racial constructs of the modern world is being steadily shattered by globalization. On the other hand, emulating the Western science and technology and producing copycat products also creates the impression that the non-Western cultures have little else to offer other than trying to excel in Western technologies.

Focusing on the lop-sided global power and opportunity structure that is a system of domination, discrimination, and oppression, one can see how people of color are the ones who are left out. Even when whites are a numerical minority in some national societies, they control much of the national resources. For instance, in Zimbabwe, a predominantly black country, some 4,500 white farmers control most of the arable land. Similarly, in South Africa, Afrikaners, who make up hardly 7 percent of the national population, dominate the economy. Nonetheless, they complain about the affirmative action and other policies of the government and, according to a study by the Human Sciences Research Council, only a meager 11 percent of whites were satisfied with black rule in November 1999.

Thus, the globalized world plays a sort of socioeconomic-political "hide-and-seek" with racial and ethnic minorities. Their **identities** are reified for profit, but their voices are erased for any political claims. Some of the globalized world's precepts and practices appear to be rectifying a number of the defects of the established order only to turn the same into additional disadvantages. While the white center has emerged as the solid guiding spirit for the globalized world, the periphery stands dispersed, disorganized, and disturbed. While racism pervades globalization overtly and covertly, any acknowledgement or problematization is carefully avoided. After all, if "global" is the norm, "local" becomes an exception. The global market reigns supreme, and national sovereignty, safety nets, and benefits become not only outmoded but also subversive. Racial and ethnic minorities *are* there, and again they *are not* there. This is how minority identities are both reified for profit and delegitimized for any political claims.

GROWING ECONOMIC DISPARITY AND THE DENIAL OF OPPORTUNITIES

The relationship between race and ethnicity and globalization is not a tenuous one, since globalization is not neutral of class or nationality. However, supra-class and supra-nation advocacy could be quite misleading, as it conceals the dominant class and national interests. Globalization policies have diverse and often contradictory consequences for different classes, communities, regions, and sectors.

The racial and ethnic minorities around the world are worst affected by this growing economic disparity and the denial of opportunities. Consider the case of African Americans in the United States, a country that witnessed its longest economic expansion in the 1990s. A recent study reveals that a record 48 percent of American households own stocks, and stocks comprise 35 percent of all household financial assets. However, in this "stock-holder society," many African Americans are drowning in debt and have not saved a single cent for investments of any kind.

Globalization and the economic good times have not reached, and are less likely to reach, millions of people worldwide. Consider the situation of the Dalits (oppressed) in India, the largest minority group in the whole world. Within the country's oppressive caste system, Dalits are often forced to carry out tasks and undertake occupations that are considered by other caste groups to be ritually polluting. They are exploited in the agricultural sector, where they are paid a few kilograms of rice or Rs.15 to Rs.35 (US$0.38 to $0.88) a day.

Most of the 40 million people in India who work as "bonded laborers" are Dalits. Millions of them still work as manual scavengers cleaning public latrines and disposing of dead animals. Some 1.5 million Tharis in the Tharparkar region of Sindh province in Pakistan are in utter destitution because of prolonged and severe drought. Across the border in India, there are reports of tribal laborers and women dying.

LOSS OF SOVEREIGNTY

With loss of control over their land and other resources, many of the racial and ethnic minorities lose their sovereignty and tend to be even more vulnerable socially, economically, and politically. For instance, Eskimos, Indians, and Aleuts (the native people) were the majority in Alaska into the 1940s but now make up only 15 percent of the state's population. When they demand priority rights to fish and game as "subsistence gatherers" and to carry out their traditional way of life (which could restrict others' access to rivers, etc.), it irritates those who fish as a hobby or who make profits in commercial fishing.

Globalization imposes its own values and worldviews on the world's peoples and even tries to oversee the "not-so-efficient" peoples around the world. The foundational principles of contemporary globalism are quite detrimental to indigenous peoples, Africans and other racial groups. Indigenous peoples, for instance, contend in The Indigenous People's Seattle Declaration: "We believe that the whole philosophy underpinning the WTO [World Trade Organization] agreements and the principles and policies it promotes contradict our core values, spirituality and worldviews, as well as our concepts and practices of development, trade and environmental protection."

Africans, too, diagnose the problem of globalization along these lines in their recent call for "The International Tribunal on Africa":

> [I]t is no longer the colonial occupiers who are in charge – but colonial domination is still ever present [in Africa]. It is now the "experts" from the World Bank and the IMF who have taken charge of the economies of the African countries and who rule its states. In all the ministries of the African governments, one can find "experts" who exercise genuine power. This is done in the name of "good governance" and, therefore, implicitly, in the name of the so-called inability of black people to govern for themselves.

With loss of control over their land and other resources, many of the racial and ethnic minorities around the world lose their sovereignty and tend to be very vulnerable socially, economically, and politically.

CONCLUSIONS

There are visible links between globalization and the increasing abuse of workers and their rights without basic labor standards (such as allowing workers to form unions and negotiate with their employer, and the international trading system, etc.). Similarly, minorities are not proportionately represented in high-skilled jobs around the world. It is common knowledge that racial and ethnic hierarchy and poverty are interrelated. The racial and other minorities around the world deserve closer attention, as they are even more vulnerable because of their precarious social position, lack of political base, scant bargaining power, and other such in-built inadequacies. Indigenous peoples' rights, women's rights, children's rights, other general human rights principles and obligations, civil rights struggles, and safeguarding those accomplishments have all become serious concerns of informed citizens.

The global economy, as such, is not evil, but the fact that it is unbalanced is. Hence, we do not have to oppose globalization but only its harmful aspects. So, the contention here is not to abandon globalization and hark back to narrow **nationalistic** protectionism but to deal seriously with the anti-people precepts and practices of globalization. Of course, there are pockets of "First World" in the "Third World" and vice versa. This necessitates a closer and critical look at the existing opportunity structures and the need to see if globalization is poised to address the situation meaningfully or aggravate it drastically. Scholars expect that more than 60 percent of world income will originate in Asia by 2025 and that up to 400 million people will be added to the region. If racial parity concern is not raised, the lopsided development will be worsened and we may have a US-kind of situation, not just in Asia but all over the world.

One way to remedy the negative impacts of globalization is to enhance democracy, establish a strong welfare system, free and compulsory education, effective labor rights, environmental laws, and progressive taxation on not only on income, but also on wealth. There should be minimal guarantees regarding independent labor unions, companies' environmental practices, safety stan-dards, child labor, and democratic decision-making. Business elites can have a say and must have the right to a voice, but they cannot have a monopoly, and they have to share that right with others. The emerging "third perspective" with the intervention of Harvard University's Nobel Prize winning economist Amartya Sen, who insists that globalization and liberalization policies be accompanied by social spending, especially on education and health as the basis for an economy's success in the modern world, has to be taken seriously.

It is safe to conclude then that the globalized market, which includes the financial market, has not provided and does not even contemplate providing a level playing field for many disadvantaged sections of the human population; that it undermines the existing social insurance available for them at the national level without making any such arrangement to fall back on at the global level, and that it merely perpetuates the discriminatory beliefs and prac-tices that have marred the full blossoming of human potential and permitted the lopsided development that plagues us all.

KEY READINGS

Buchanan, P. J. (1998). *The great betrayal: How American sovereignty and social justice are being sacrificed to the gods of the global economy.* Boston: Little, Brown and Company.

Chandhoke, N. (2000). The illusions of formal equality. *The Hindu,* 2 May 2000.

Coombe, R. (1995). The cultural life of things: Anthropological approaches to law and society in conditions of globalization. *American University Journal of International Law and Policy,* 10(2), 791–836.

Edoho, F. M. (1997). Globalization and the new world order: Toward an inclusive framework in the twenty-first century. In F. M. Edoho (Ed.), *Globalization and the new world order: Promises, problems, and prospects for Africa in the twenty-first century.* Westport, CT: Praeger, pp. 197–204.

Frank, D. (1999). *Buy American: The untold story of economic nationalism.* Boston, MA: Beacon Press.

Gordimer, N. (2000). Africa's plague, and everyone's. *The New York Times,* 11 April 2000.

Greider, W. (1997). One world, ready or not: The manic logic of global capitalism. San Francisco: Jossey-Bass.

Jayaraman, R. (1999). Border and borderless culture: A study of the process of recreation and maintenance of ethnic boundary in a global society. In R. B. Browne & M. W. Fishwick (Eds.), *The global village: Dead or alive?.* Madison, WI: University of Wisconsin Press, pp. 146–163.

Kindleberger, C. P. (2000). The historical roots of globalization. *Global Focus,* 12(1), 17–26.

Knippers, J. (1999). *Inequity in the global village: Recycled rhetoric and disposable people.* West Hartford, CT: Kumarian Press.

Rondinelli, D. A. & Behrman, J. N. (2000). The promises and pains of globalization. *Global Focus,* 12(1), 3–16.

Sachs, J. (1999). Helping the world's poorest. *The Economist,* August, 14, 1999.

Sen, A. (1999). *Development as freedom: Human capability and global need.* New York: Alfred A. Knopf.

Stoddard, L. (1920). *The rising tide of colour against white world-supremacy.* New York: Charles Scribner's Sons.

Tripathi, S. (1999). Globalization and tribal problematique. In V. K. Pant & B. S. Bisht (Eds.), *Backward communities: Identity, development and transformation.* New Delhi: Gyan Publishing House.

Wilson, K. (1993). Globalization and "Muslim belt": Reshaping of British racism. *India Alert Bulletin,* 6(3).

PART II

NAMES AND TERMS

ABORIGINAL The word "aboriginal," from the Latin *ab origine* (meaning from the beginning), emerged in seventeenth-century English to mean "the original inhabitants of a land." It was used in the colonial context and has a long history, mostly in Australia and, more recently, Canada, to mean **indigenous people**, as opposed to the colonists.

In Australian colonization it did not initially take hold. The English discoverer of the east Australian coast, James Cook, who took possession for Britain in 1770, called the original owners, "natives" and occasionally "Indians" (terms also used in Canadian settlement). Early observers after settlement in 1788, such as Lt. Watkin Tench, used "natives," rarely "Indians." Early Australian colonists mostly used "natives," although "the blacks" also came into use on the frontier, as the language of **race** intruded. Both these terms remained in common usage until the twentieth century.

On May 4, 1816, a New South Wales government proclamation used "natives," "black natives" and "Aborigines," which was probably the first Australian use of this last term. The word "aborigines" did not become common until the 1840s in Australia and existed along with "natives" and "blacks," which had a long life. Indeed, "native" was used until the middle of the twentieth century, even in Australian legislation. The word "aboriginal," with "aborigine" as the alternate singular of "aborigines," did not overtake "native" in common usage until the late nineteenth century.

Its generalized adoption was curious in a sense, for most colonists were aware of the different cultural-linguistic groups among Australian indigenous people, which they eventually totaled at about 500. However, the lumping together of all groups under the one name was a convenience. It was also an essentializing mechanism that diminished indigenous peoples' significance.

For much of its usage in Australia, "aboriginal" was a term of disrespect, although more robust and cruder terms of racial abuse were in use among many whites. For most of its life in print in Australia, "aboriginal" languished without a capital "A." This was another indication of the contempt towards Aboriginal people and their **culture** as a "doomed race." This was how it was used in Canada in earlier times. The word graced the title of special legislation in Australia to control indigenous people and labeled the special places, missions and reserves, intended to confine them. When children of mixed Aboriginal and European descent were earmarked to be removed from their families, the reason for removal marked down in the register in the Aboriginal Protection Board's office was often: "aboriginal."

Indigenous people in Canada and Australia, since the invasion of their lands, continued to refer to themselves by their traditional local names of which there were thousands, if clan and band names are included. As groups were moved onto reserves and missions in new colonial conglomerations, they forged additional names associated with their new abodes. In

Australia, for instance, groups sometimes called themselves Framlingham people or the Hermansburg mob after their mission place.

In Australia at least, regional names gradually emerged as well, as people moved about in non-traditional ways, seeking work in the new colonial world. East coast people called themselves Murris in the north and Kooris in the south-east, while the Yolgnu inhabited northern Australia, Nyoongar the west and Nungah the south. But regional groups still termed themselves "Aboriginal people" or "Aborigines"/"Aboriginals," when referring to the continent-wide totality of indigenous people. Indeed, it is a reflection of their traditional local orientation that they continued to use the colonizers' general word and did not invent one for themselves. This was still the case once Aboriginal political movements emerged from the 1920s in Australia to fight for civil rights. Activist organizations included the word "Aboriginal" in their titles, to show their aspiration of a continent-wide reach.

Even when a national Aboriginal movement emerged in 1960s Australia, based on aspirations for Indigenous rights to land, the colonial word "Aboriginal" stuck. There were some proposals to adopt a regional word nationally, but regional loyalties again denied this. At least the word assumed a consistent capital letter in the 1960s, due to a growing respect from other Australians, and its use by Aboriginal organizations. Its derivative, "Aboriginality," began to be used as **identity politics** emerged.

In Canada, for much of its colonial history, words like "natives," "Indians," and "Eskimos" were used to describe indigenous peoples but, as in Australia, they have fallen out of fashion since the 1960s, as they applied to certain groups, particular legislative situations, or were perceived as offensive. "First Nations" emerged in the 1970s to replace "Indian" but has no legislative status and is not inclusive of all groups. "Aboriginal" has become widely used more recently to describe all first peoples of Canada. In 1996, an annual National Aboriginal Day was proclaimed.

In Australia, in recent times, more respect has been accorded Aboriginal people, due to a growing reconciliation between settler and Indigenous Australians, reflected in a growing intermarriage rate, as least in urban and settled Australia. The word "Aboriginal" has lost its edge of **otherness** and, indeed, now has a certain cachet. Foreign tourists seek an indigenous experience when travelling to Australia, and Aboriginal culture, which is assuming a renaissance, is admired by a growing number of Australians. Helped also by the washing out of Aboriginal skin tones and other physical identifiers through miscegenation, some non-indigenous Australians have attempted to pass as Aboriginal. Legal cases have been fought in the state of Tasmania in the 1990s by Aboriginal (Palawah) activists who resent this appropriation of their Aboriginality.

The word "Aboriginal" still has strong currency after 200 years in Australia and now Canada, where it is embraced by all first peoples. However, in Australia the existence of the Torres Strait Islanders off the north-east coast, and their increased movement to the mainland and intermarriage with Aboriginal people, has complicated matters. To be inclusive, in Australia, many bodies are beginning to use the word "indigenous" as "Aboriginal" refers to only the dominant mainland indigenous peoples. In Canada, the same problem with "Aboriginal" does not apply, and it is used widely as a collective term for First Nations (usually those formerly called "Indians"), Inuit and Metis (those of mixed European-Indian descent). But, "Indigenous" is gaining some acceptance in Canada due to international influences.

However, "indigenous" is simply another European name, and first peoples in Australia and Canada are again captive to another seventeenth-century Latin-derived English word for "original inhabitant." It is doubtful, but not impossible, that after two centuries of colonization, the original owners of these settler nations will invent an indigenous word for themselves; that is, for all descendants of first peoples in their land. Until that happens, the legacy of colonialism will not be fully shrugged off. [RB]

Key readings

Broome, R. (2010). *Aboriginal Australians: A history since 1788* (4th ed.). Sydney: Allen and Unwin, Sydney.

Chesterman, J. (2005). *Civil rights: How indigenous Australians won formal equality*. Brisbane: University of Queensland Press.

National Aboriginal Health Organization. (2003). Terminology guide. Retrieved from www.naho.ca/english/pdf/terminology_ guidelines.pdf.

Reynolds, H. (1990). *The other side of the frontier* (revised ed.). Melbourne: Penguin.

AFROCENTRICITY Afrocentricity is a contemporary philosophical movement deriving its name from the centrality of African people and phenomena in the interpretation of all data related to African people. The Afrocentric school of thought was founded in the late twentieth century with the launching of several books, numerous articles, and conferences under the leadership of Molefi Kete Asante. Afrocentricity may be thought of as placing African ideals and values at the center of any analysis of African phenomena inasmuch as Afrocentrists believe that there is nothing more correct for the study of Africans transcontinentally and transgenerationally than the historical experiences that have constituted the texture of African lives. Seeking to rid themselves of Eurocentric strangleholds on African knowledge, the Afrocentrists have pursued the path of conceptualizing Africa in its own terms and Africans, whether continental or **diasporan**, in their own terms.

Afrocentricity sought to address several crises in **culture**, **identity**, language, and analysis, by re-positioning the African person and African reality from the margins of European thought, attitude, and doctrines, to a centered, therefore positively *located*, place within the realm of science and culture. Afrocentricity finds its grounding in the intellectual and activist precursors who first suggested culture as a critical corrective to a displaced agency among Africans.

Inasmuch as Africans in the diaspora and on the continent of Africa had been deliberately de-culturalized and made to accept the conqueror's codes of conduct and modes of behavior, the Afrocentrists discovered that the interpretative and theoretical grounds had also been moved. Thus, synthesizing the best thought of African American and African thinkers, Afrocentricity projects an innovation in both criticism and interpretation. It is therefore, in some senses, a paradigm as articulated by Ama Mazama, a framework as seen in the writings of C. Tsehloane Keto, and a dynamic humanist quality of thought in the mind of Maulana Karenga. However, it is not a worldview and should not be confused with Africanity which is essentially the way African people, any African people, live according to customs, traditions, and mores of their society. One can be born in Africa, follow African styles, modes of living, and practice African religion and not be Afrocentric; to be Afrocentric one has to have a self-conscious awareness of agency possibilities and necessities. Thus, those individuals who live in Africa and recognize the de-centering of their minds because of European colonization may self-consciously choose to be demonstratively in tune with their own agency. If so, this becomes a revolutionary act of will that cannot be achieved merely by wearing African clothes or having an African name.

The arena of position

Afrocentricty contends that there could be no social or economic struggle that would make sense if African people remained trapped in the philosophical, linguistic, and intellectual positions of white hegemonic **nationalism** as it relates to Africa and African people. At base, therefore, the intellectual work of the Afrocentric school of thought is a political one in the sense that all social knowledge has a political purpose. No one constructs or writes about re-positioning and re-centering merely for the sake of self-indulgence; none could afford to do so because the African dispossession in material and cultural terms appears so great and the displacing myths so pervasive that simply to watch the procession of African *peripheralization* is to acquiesce in African de-centering.

The Afrocentrist contends that passion can never be a substitute for argument as argument should not be a substitution for passion. Afrocentric intellectuals may disagree on the finer points of interpretation and some facts, but the overall project of relocation and reorientation of African action and data has been the rational constant in all Afrocentric work. Interest in African people and opinions about African history are not sufficient for one's work to be called "Afrocentric." Indeed, Afrocentricity is not merely the discussion of African and African American issues, history, politics, or consciousness; any one may discuss these issues and yet not be an Afrocentrist. Furthermore, it is not a perspective based on skin color or biology and should not be confused with melanist or other essentialist theories. Africological terms such as *position, line, centeredness, agency*, and *location*, help to establish the objectives of Afrocentricity. What is more relevant for the Afrocentrist is the question, "what is the *location* of the person asking such questions or the location of the person needing to answer them?" Location theory is itself an aspect of the Afrocentric paradigm.

Distinguishing characteristics

As a cultural configuration, the Afrocentric idea is distinguished by five characteristics:

1 an intense interest in psychological location as determined by symbols, motifs, rituals, and signs;
2 a commitment to finding the subject-place of Africans in any social, political, economic, architectural, literary, or religious phenomenon with implications for questions of sex, gender, and class;
3 a defense of African cultural elements as historically valid in the context of art, music, education, science, and literature;
4 a celebration of "centeredness" and agency and a commitment to lexical refinement that eliminates pejoratives about Africans or other people; and
5 a powerful imperative from historical sources to revise the collective text of African people.

Thus, it is consciousness, not biology that decides how one is to apprehend intellectual data, because the key to the Afrocentric idea is orientation to data, not data themselves. Where do you stand when you seek to *locate* a text, phenomenon, or person? [MKA]

Key readings

Asante, M. K. (2008). *An Afrocentric manifesto.* London: Polity Press.
——. (1998). *The Afrocentric idea.* Philadelphia: Temple University Press.
Mazama, A. (Ed.). (2003). *The Afrocentric paradigm.* Trenton, NJ: Africa World Press.

GLORIA EVANGELINA ANZALDÚA Mexican American writer, editor, poet, and artist Gloria Anzaldúa (1942–2004) is known for her articulation of what it means to live on the borderlands – of language, of nationality, of sexuality, of **culture**. Born and raised in the border country of south Texas, Anzaldúa graduated from Pan American University and, three years later, earned a MA in English from the University of Texas. She later moved to Santa Cruz, California where she lectured, wrote, and pursued a strong activist agenda.

Throughout her work, Anzaldúa insists that the self is multiple. She is at once speaking as a lesbian, feminist, poet and artist, working-class socialist, and Mexican American, describing herself as "a wind-swayed bridge, a crossroads inhabited by whirlwinds." Much of Anzaldúa's work explores and enacts such multiple **identities**, particularly *This bridge called my back* (edited with Cherie Moraga in 1981); *Borderlands/La Frontera* (1987); and the collection *Making face, making soul/ Haciendo Caras* (1990).

At some generative moments, Anzaldúa argues, it is possible to find all others in one's self and one's self in all others. Learning to live such transformations calls for a "new **mestiza**" who has "a tolerance for contradictions, a tolerance for ambiguity," who "learns to be an Indian in Mexican culture, to be Mexican from an Anglo point of view. She learns to juggle cultures ... Not only does she sustain contradictions, she turns the ambivalence into something else" (Anzaldúa, 1987: 79).

Living in such transformations calls for a special writing style. Thus, Anzaldúa engages a mixture of genres, shifting from poetry to reportorial prose to autobiographical stream of consciousness to mythic chants to sketches and graphs – and back again, weaving visual images and words of her own and from others into a tapestry of language. In addition, she mixes languages – English, Spanish,

Nahuatl – as well as dialects and registers. In "How to tame a wild tongue," Anzaldúa denounces "linguistic terrorism," saying

> I am my language ... Until I can accept as legitimate Chicano Texas Spanish, Tex-Mex and all the other languages I speak, I cannot accept the legitimacy of myself. Until I am free to write bilingually and to switch codes without having to translate, ... my tongue will be illegitimate.
>
> (Anzaldúa, 1987: 59)

Anzaldúa's commitment to multiplicity and inclusivity led her to embrace collaboration – with artists in her children's books, with co-editors, and with various collectives. Anzaldúa presents herself as in constant dialogue among her many selves, her multiple audiences, and the texts that emerge in the process, with the intertexts and internal conversations that hummed along as she wrote.

At a time when many writers are experimenting with new forms of discourse, Anzaldúa stands as an early advocate of alternative styles and of mixed forms. Moreover, her attempt to embrace the contradictions of her own life, to claim a voice and identity that is recognized and respected while also embodying multiple cultures, languages and selves, addresses one of the core issues of our time.

The Nettie Lee Benson Collection, at the University of Texas, holds the Anzaldúa archive. [AAL]

Key readings

Anzaldúa, G. (1987). *Borderlands/La Frontera*. San Francisco: Aunt Lute Books.
——. (1990). *Making face, making soul: Creative and critical perspectives by women of color*. San Francisco: Aunt Lute Books.
Anzaldúa, G. & Moraga, C. (1981). *This bridge called my back: Writings by*

radical women of color. Watertown, MA: Persephone Press.

Barnard, I. (1997). Gloria Anazldúa's queer mestisaje. *MELUS: The Journal of the Society for the Study of Multi-Ethnic Literature of the United States*, 22(1), 35–53.

Keating, A. (2000). *Interviews/entrevistas*. New York: Routledge.

Keating, A. (2005). *EntreMundos/AmongWorlds: New perspectives on Gloria Anzaldúa*. New York: Palgrave MacMillan.

Lugones, M. (1992). On *Borderlands/La Frontera*: An interpretive essay. *Hypatia*, 7, 31–37.

Lunsford, A. (2004). Toward a Mestiza rhetoric: Gloria Anzaldúa on composition and postcoloniality. In A. A. Lunsford & Lahoucine Ouzgane (Eds.), *Crossing borderlands: Composition and post-colonial studies*. Pittsburgh: U Pittsburgh Press, pp. 33–66.

Yarbro-Bejarano, Y. (1994). Gloria Anzaldúa's *Borderlands/La Frontera*: Cultural studies, "difference," and the non-unitary subject. *Cultural Critique*, 28, 5–28.

ANTI-RACISM MOVEMENT Anti-racism is both an activist and intellectual movement, committed to challenging racism in its national and international, as well as its political, social and economic contexts. Because its scope is necessarily broad, there is no singular anti-racism movement. Though not ideologically or politically unified, anti-racism movements share common principles: that while **race** is not a biological fact it is nonetheless made a reality in the realm of human action and meaning; that racism is not restricted to individualized action, but pervades sociopolitical structures such as the education system and the law (in the institutional sense).

The roots of anti-racism movements can be traced to slavery abolitionist movements, which identified slavery as a violation of the humanity of slaves, as well as slaveowners and traders. These movements pressured states to divest their slave trading and owning interests in the service of the restoration of morality. In the United States, contemporary anti-racist movements are the beneficiary of the **Civil Rights Movement** where African-American activists and allies worked to challenge the ways that the civil liberties of African-Americans were systematically violated. Anti-racism continues this examination of the nation-state by focusing on racism as a violation of the rights of those so affected. The state is both potential violator and potential protector of the rights of victims of racism. The terrorist attacks of 9/11 have sparked reactionary **nationalist** rhetoric and action, which frames Muslim Americans as potential threats to American national security. Anti-racist activists and scholars have endeavored to expose the ways that the discourse of national security enables and obscures state-sanctioned racism against Muslim and turbaned citizens.

In Canada, anti-racism emerges in response to both the American Civil Rights Movement and the national discourses and policies of **multiculturalism**. Canadian anti-racists argue that national inclusion is potentially coercive. Many have examined official multiculturalism as ensuring a racist status quo. Official multiculturalism, they argue, identifies the existence of diversity but offers no framework for meaningfully identifying and challenging racism in Canada. Furthermore, multiculturalism, as the shorthand for inclusivity and harmony, dominates public discourse and pushes serious talk about systemic racism out of the public sphere.

Anti-racism movements in Europe similarly balance popular national discourses against the need for structural analyses of race and racism. The struggles of colonies to win independence from European imperialist nations and the subsequent migration of people from these colonies to these imperial centers challenges European anti-racists to consider the ways that their national communities are racially coded. Waves of migration following the retraction of empires have given rise to new kinds of citizens: former colonial subjects who, because of colonization, have migrated to colonial centers. As national **identity** is radically reconsidered, nations demand that their "new" citizens demonstrate their belonging in ways that the "old" citizens never had to. These demands have become far more strident, reactionary and divisive and are expressed through civic panic speculating how prepared immigrants are to become "full and proper" citizens according to the traditions and customs of that nation. Anti-racists in France, for example, have expressed concern about the nation's proposed laws banning religious dress (laws that, if passed, would prevent people wearing such dress from accessing public services), arguing that such laws discriminate against religiously observant people of color. Amongst the strongest critics of such proposed laws are anti-racist feminists who argue that the prohibition from public services of women of color who wear religious dress will focus the public's racial anxieties on the bodies of women of color. If passed, such laws will surely result in increased risk of alienation and violence.

Despite their geographic, political and strategic differences, anti-racists share common principles when thinking of race and racism, the first of which is that race is not a biological truth. This revelation is important to anti-racists who wish to challenge the ground upon which racism is structured. Race, they argue, is an arbitrary system of classification that is rooted in **power** imbalances and is historically shored up by scientific practices that were dubious at best. Race biology attempts to locate race within the body, rather than within the socio-economic and historical forces that give such bodily differences racial meaning. While, historically, phenotype (physical appearance) was the focus of scientific examination, scientific advancements culminating in genetic research (most notably, the **Human Genome Project**) attempted to locate the "truth" of race within the body, in the human genetic code. Such research has been unsuccessful in this regard. Anti-racists therefore struggle with the paradoxical nature of race: while it is not a biological truth, it is a social reality. This means that not only is racism a pervasive social construction, race is also a powerful way of organizing community, both as a technique of oppression and as a strategy of resistance and community among people of color. Such an observation enables anti-racists to focus a critical lens on the ways in which race comes to have social meaning.

Writing on his relocation from his native Martinique to France, **Frantz Fanon** observes that racial meaning was ascribed to his body there, while in Martinique it was not. He argues that the categorization of his body according to the racial schema was no innocent observation on the part of white French citizens, but a power-laden technique designed to impose an aura of intrinsic primitiveness and insurmountable difference. Anti-racists have since named the process whereby racial meaning is attached to people as *racialization*. When anti-racists use this term it is often with the understanding that race is invoked to secure the status quo by constricting the human potential of those so categorized. Racialization is not an even process; anti-racists interested in the interaction of **whiteness** and the process of racialization have argued that, according to the logic of racial categorization, whiteness is considered to be the de facto state of being. In other words, whiteness is the standard by which racialized **others** are judged.

Whiteness studies further explore this dynamic.

More than a matter of individualized acts of violence and oppression, racism is structural. Put another way, racism is embedded within social structures. Structural racism does not depend on individual actions, but on institutional practices and standards that disadvantage people of color. Moreover, structural racism is interactive, meaning that it is more than the idiosyncratic behaviors and practices of a single institution. The state's response to crime by implementing "tough on crime" policies is one example of structural racism. "Tough on crime" policies involve intensive policing practices in urban and impoverished neighborhoods that are predominantly populated by people of color. On the surface, such actions respond to the state's expressed goal of ensuring social order by appearing to dispassionately focus regulatory attention on geographic areas where more crime occurs. Such practices present urban and poor people of color as inherently criminal, thereby obscuring discriminatory rental practices which limit housing options, insufficient employment opportunities and financial supports for women of color and their children, and discriminatory policing practices that especially target young men of color. The European Network Against Racism employs a structural analysis of racism, arguing, for example, that the social anxiety resulting from economic instability felt across the European Union can be harnessed by neo-conservative factions to exclude and scapegoat minorities.

The anti-racist movement's concern with exposing racism in the nation forces them to reckon with the ways that this focus can be contradictory to their social justice goals. This is especially true in nations whose borders coercively extend to absorb **indigenous peoples** without regard for their sovereignty. The United States, Canada, Australia and New Zealand, for example, are the result of the reorganization of nations and societies in order to secure imperial interests. They are, in other words, settler states. Indigenous critiques to anti-racism challenge the movement to explicitly recognize indigenous sovereignty while confronting the coercion of settler nationalism. This means that the critique of racism in the nation must be grounded in an analysis of the ways that the nation is dependent upon the alienation of indigenous peoples from their lands. Beginning with this fundamental recognition, the anti-racist movement's work for social justice in settler states can begin to challenge the way that racism not only organizes community, but also cooperates with nationalism itself in the displacement indigenous nations. [RKS]

Key readings

Bannerji, H. (2000). *The dark side of the nation: Essays on multiculturalism, nationalism and gender.* Toronto: Canadian Scholar's Press.

Dei, G. J. S. (1996). *Anti-racism education: Theory and practice.* Halifax: Fernwood.

European Network Against Racism. (2010). *Every person matters – Ending poverty for all: ENAR messages for the 2010 European Year for Combating Racism and Social Exclusion.* Available at http://cms. horus.be/files/99935/MediaArchive/pdf/ ENAR%20messages%20EYAP%20final. pdf.

Fanon, F. (1967). *Black skin, white masks.* (C.L. Markmann, Trans.). New York: Grove Press.

Frankenberg, R. (1993). *White women, race matters: The social construction of whiteness.* Minneapolis, MN: University of Minnesota Press.

Gilroy, P. (2000). *Against race: Imagining political culture beyond the color line.* Cambridge, MA: Belknap Press of Harvard University Press.

Razack, S. (Ed.). (2002). *Race, space, and the law.* Toronto: Between the Lines Press.

Smith, A. (2008). *Native Americans and the Christian right: The gendered politics of unlikely alliances.* Durham, NC: Duke University Press.

APARTHEID Apartheid was a totalitarian racial ideology and policy program implemented by the National Party (NP) government in South Africa from 1948 until 1990. Prior to that time, South Africa had maintained a robust policy of racial **segregation**, including the exclusion of Africans from land ownership in most of the country and an employment "color bar" that restricted skilled positions to white workers. While apartheid drew upon many of these pre-1948 segregation policies, it reflected a novel way of thinking about **race** and went well beyond merely intensifying past practices to construct an unparalleled racialized polity, economy, and society.

Ideology

Apartheid grew out of several decades of intellectual discourse by Afrikaner theologians and academics who sought to develop an ideological framework for coming to terms with the Afrikaner population's conquest by the British in the Anglo-Boer War (1899–1902) and devising a practical strategy for advancing its political and socioeconomic interests. The term itself, which means "apartness" in Afrikaans, was first used in a racial policy context in 1929 to describe a Dutch Reformed Church mission policy designed to uplift the African population through segregated ministry. It was introduced into political parlance during the early 1940s and, by the end of that decade, "apartheid" was incorporated into the NP's official statements and campaign propaganda to encapsulate the party's plan to replace traditional segregation with an all-encompassing system of fundamental separation.

In contrast to earlier ideological formulations, which had justified segregation in terms of different racial groups' levels of civilization, apartheid was based on an understanding of racial and national divisions as divinely ordained and inviolable. In other words, it was believed that God had separated people into races and nations with different developmental needs and objectives, and that to override His distinctions would constitute the ultimate transgression. The policy upshot was the realization that merely segregating blacks' and whites' residences and use of public amenities, or even relegating them to different classes of citizenship within South Africa, would inevitably undermine the integrity of each one – and of the white race and Afrikaner ethnos in particular – and ultimately cause their extinction. Instead, politics and society should be organized so as to allow all racial groups to operate entirely within their own sphere of existence, thus ensuring their survival and maximizing their developmental potential.

Policy program

As a policy program, apartheid encompassed a wide array of laws aimed at both fulfilling the ideological vision articulated by the Afrikaner **nationalist** thinkers and enticing the support of white voters by promoting their economic self-interest. Its centerpiece was "separate development," a long-term plan to establish a system of nominally independent "homelands" (or "Bantustans") in the paltry rural areas that had been designated as "Natives' reserves" since the 1910s to serve as Africans' only rightful bastions of citizenship. South Africa proper would then be a whites-only country where Africans could enter and reside only as highly regulated temporary guest-workers.

Several apartheid laws, such as the Bantu Authorities Act of 1951, the Prohibition of Interdicts Act of 1956, the Promotion of Bantu Self-Government Act of 1959, and the Black Homelands

Citizenship Act of 1970 set the stage for separate development by creating an administrative apparatus for the homeland system, empowering the government to forcibly relocate residents from South Africa proper to their assigned homelands, and revoking Africans' South African citizenship. The first "homeland," Transkei, was declared autonomous in 1963 and independent in 1976 and, despite the South African government's failure to persuade any other country to recognize them, a total of ten "homelands" were created and granted nominal independent status by the late 1970s.

While the "homeland" system was designed to enforce a rigorous correspondence between race and national citizenship, it also served to facilitate the government's efforts to exert full control over the mobility and allocation of African labor. A number of laws were enacted to bolster this aim, including the Native Laws Amendment Act of 1952, which established government labor allocation bureaus; the Native Labour (Settlement of Disputes) Act of 1953, which excluded Africans from the official definition of "employee," prohibited African workers from participating in strikes, and denied official recognition to African trade unions; and the Industrial Conciliation Act of 1956 and its 1959 amendment, which prohibited interracial unionization and extended the Minister of Labour's power to impose and enforce racial hiring restrictions.

Still other laws were concerned with promoting "petty apartheid," or the prevention of miscegenation and interracial contact in public spaces. The very first apartheid law to be passed, the Prohibition of Mixed Marriages Act of 1949 and the Immorality Act of 1950, made it illegal to marry or have non-marital sexual relations across racial lines. These Acts were bolstered by the Population Registration Act of 1950, which provided for all South African residents to be officially classified into one of four racial groups at the discretion of government officials, who would make the determinations based on crude generalizations about physical appearance, socioeconomic status, and lifestyle. The Reservation of Separate Amenities Act of 1953, meanwhile, provided for the segregation of virtually all public services, vehicles, and premises. It further stipulated that separate amenities would not have to be provided on an equal basis and that an amenity could be simply reserved for members of one racial group to the total exclusion of all others.

Finally, several laws were passed to minimize opposition to the new racial order. The most prominent was the Suppression of Communism Act of 1950, which allowed the government to ban individuals, organizations, and writings that were deemed subversive. Under the auspices of this law and others, the NP government moved quickly to consolidate its **power**, rigorously enforce its racial policy program, and effectively silence all non-parliamentary opposition to its regime.

Protest, reform, and dismantlement
The South African government largely succeeded in demobilizing antiapartheid activism in the wake of the Sharpeville Massacre of 1960. Following its brutal suppression of antiapartheid protests in Sharpeville and other townships, the government banned the major antiapartheid movement organizations and imprisoned their leaders, ushering in a period of relative domestic stability that lasted into the early 1970s. Nevertheless, a resurgence of antiapartheid protest by workers, political activists, and students during the mid-1970s prompted the government to contemplate reforming apartheid as a means of coopting some of its opposition, even as it continued to uphold apartheid's core policies and repress overt antiapartheid activism.

In 1977, two commissions were appointed to propose recommendations regarding industrial relations and urban employment conditions. Provisions were subsequently made for the legalized registration of African labor unions and the cultivation of a new class of African urban-dwellers who would be accorded preferential employment treatment relative to others, who would have to migrate to the cities for job opportunities. Nevertheless, antiapartheid protest and international pressure intensified during the 1980s, leading President P. W. Botha to push through a new wave of reforms, including the 1984 establishment of a "Tricameral Parliament" in which two intermediary racial groups ("Coloureds" and Asians) would be represented, but on a very limited and segregated basis. Botha's effort to "divide and conquer" the non-white population in this way backfired, however, as the Coloured and Asian communities by and large rejected the new arrangement and the continued exclusion of Africans only exacerbated the antiapartheid movement's surging momentum.

A vicious cycle of protest and repression persisted for the remainder of the apartheid regime's existence until finally, on February 2, 1990, President F. W. de Klerk announced that the NP government would concede to negotiations with representatives of all of South Africa's racial groups in order to produce a new constitution that would enable "every inhabitant [of South Africa to] enjoy equal rights, treatment, and opportunity in every sphere of endeavour." Shortly thereafter, antiapartheid organizations were unbanned, African National Congress (ANC) leader Nelson Mandela was released from his life prison sentence, and Parliament began voting to repeal the apartheid laws that had been enacted during the previous four decades. Four years later, after two rounds of tense negotiations that nearly broke down at points, South Africa held its first ever nationwide multiracial election, which resulted in a resounding victory for the ANC and signaled apartheid's final demise as a governing formula.

Legacy

Apartheid's significance and influence extend well beyond the historical space and time in which it was originally conceived and implemented. In 1973, the United Nations defined "the crime of apartheid" in broad terms as "inhuman acts committed for the purpose of establishing and maintaining domination by one racial group of persons over any other racial group of persons and systematically oppressing them." Since then, the term has been applied – albeit controversially – to several other contexts and situations, including Israel's occupied territories and race relations in the United States. In South Africa itself, meanwhile, apartheid's repercussions are still very palpable despite the passage of two decades since the announcement of its termination. Racial socioeconomic inequality remains extremely high and the structural effects of decades-old disparities in education and employment continue to undermine the country's economic growth possibilities. [SMG]

Key readings

Clark, N. L. & Worger, W. H. (2004). *South Africa: The rise and fall of apartheid.* London: Pearson Education Ltd.

Hamilton, C. V., Huntley, L., Alexander, N., Guimarães, A. S. A., & James, W. (Eds.). (2001). *Beyond racism: Race and inequality in Brazil, South Africa, and the United States.* Boulder and London: Lynne Rienner.

Louw, P. E. (2004). *The rise, fall, and legacy of apartheid.* Westport, CT: Praeger.

MacDonald, M. (2006). *Why race matters in South Africa.* Cambridge, MA: Harvard University Press.

O'Meara, D. (1996). *Forty lost years: The apartheid state and the politics of the National Party, 1948–1994.* Athens, OH: Ohio University Press.

Seekings, J. & Nattrass, N. (2005). *Class, race, and inequality in South Africa.* New Haven: Yale University Press.

ASSIMILATION From the Greek *assimilatio* ("to render similar"), "assimilation" refers to the complex processes by which immigrants and their descendants integrate themselves into the host country. In the United States, theories of assimilation were initially shaped by the huge wave of immigrants (roughly 24 million) between 1882 and 1924, mostly comprising groups outside of the dominant Anglo-Protestant stock, such as Irish Catholics, Polish Jews, and Chinese Confucians. Anglo Protestant nativists doubted the compatibility of other ethnic and religious groups with American society and pushed for restrictive laws, such as the Immigration Act of 1924, which sharply curtailed immigration from Eastern and Southern Europe and banned it completely from East and South Asia.

Social scientists, however, claimed that non-Anglo, non-Protestant "ethnic" groups gradually become similar in values, behaviors, and characteristics to the native-stock population. University of Chicago sociologist Robert Park (1921) described "a process of interpenetration and fusion in which persons and groups acquire the memories, sentiments, and attitudes of other persons or groups, and by sharing their experience and history, are incorporated with them in a common cultural life." Robert Dahl (1961) claimed that, as large segments of the ethnic group become part of the middle and upper strata of American society, they share similar political values and interests. In summary, assimilating ethnic groups attain higher socioeconomic status (such as defined by education, occupation, and income), lower spatial-residential concentration and more dispersion into various neighborhoods, more proficiency in the English language, and greater intermarriage.

The sociologist Milton Gordon (1964) theorized three possible outcomes of assimilation: Anglo conformity (**minority** immigrants conform to the "superior" norms, values, and institutions of the majority Anglo group); the melting pot (different racial/ethnic groups interact and collectively create a new **culture** that incorporates elements from all groups); and cultural pluralism (different racial/ethnic groups keep their unique cultural norms, traditions, and behaviors, while still sharing some common national values, goals, and institutions). Gordon claimed that Anglo conformity represented the dominant mode of assimilation in America.

After the 1960s, however, intellectuals mostly abandoned the traditional assimilation paradigm on empirical and normative grounds. The post-1965 wave of immigrants came mostly from non-European regions, such as Latin America, Asia and the Caribbean. Theories of "downward" and "segmented" assimilation (Portes and Zhou 1993) highlighted factors that blocked traditional paths to middle-class assimilation, such as white racism, the decline of high-paying manufacturing jobs, and dysfunctional public schools. Economically and racially disadvantaged minorities, such as low-income, dark-skinned **Hispanics**, were considered vulnerable to joining an urban "underclass."

In addition, the idea of assimilation to one core American culture was deemed racist and intolerant of differences. The alternative concepts of cultural pluralism and **multiculturalism** support the right of each ethnic and national group to preserve its separate culture and to participate equally in mainstream institutions, such as through bilingual education and affirmative action policies. Harvard professor

Diana Eck defines the new pluralism as inviting newcomers to "come as you are, with all your differences, pledged onto the common civic demands of citizenship." Variants of multiculturalism have been officially promoted in traditional melting-pot societies such as Australia, Canada and Britain, and in the public schools and universities in the United States.

Theories of segmented assimilation and multiculturalism prevailed in educated circles during the 1990s; but the opening years of the twenty-first century have seen renewed empirical and normative interest in traditional assimilation. New scholarship shows that worries about downward mobility for post-1965 groups were exaggerated. An extensive study of five immigrant groups (Dominican, South American, West Indian, Chinese, and Russian Jew) in metropolitan New York finds continuing patterns of upward mobility and acculturation: "the second generation [children of immigrants] is mostly speaking English, working in jobs that resemble those held by natives their age, and creatively combining their ethnic cultures and norms with American ones" (Kasinitz et al. 2008).

Rather than separating themselves from the larger society, the new second generation are actively shaping and "remaking the American mainstream," in the words of Richard Alba and Victor Nee. Racially diverse politicians, such as President Barack Obama and L.A. Mayor Antonio Villaraigosa, call for shared ties and common ground among diverse ethnic and racial groups, in order to promote health care or education reform. They reflect the melting pot idea of a dynamic, composite American culture that is continually remade by successive immigrant groups and generations.

Most Western intellectuals debate the respective merits of the multicultural and the melting pot models for incorporating new immigrant groups. A few scholars, and some politicians, however, argue for the old model of assimilating immigrants to the core culture of the historic majority. After the 9/11 terrorist attacks in the United States, Harvard political scientist Samuel Huntington argued for reaffirming the country's Anglo-Protestant heritage, which includes the English language, Christian religion, and the Protestant work ethic. He strongly opposed bilingual and multicultural policies that would deter immigrants from learning English and from assimilating to the core WASP (White Anglo-Saxon Protestant) culture. In the European Union, increasing numbers of intellectuals and politicians, such as the first Moslem French Justice Minister Rachida Dati and the late Dutch politician Pim Fortuyn, insist that Moslem immigrants conform to the secular, democratic traditions of their host countries.

Advanced, industrial countries in East Asia are also experiencing a recent, rapid influx of foreign-born residents, including manual workers from developing nations and highly educated, Western professionals. For example, in the historically homogeneous, insular nation of South Korea, "In just the past seven years, the number of foreign residents has doubled, to 1.2 million, even as the country's population of 48.7 million is expected to drop sharply in coming decades because of its low birth rate" (*New York Times*, November 1, 2009). Korean government officials are setting up Korean language institutes and other measures to ease the assimilation of foreigners to Korean society. [JEY]

Key readings

Alba, R. D. & Nee, V. (2003). *Remaking the American mainstream. Assimilation and contemporary immigration.* Cambridge, MA: Harvard University Press

Dahl, R. (1961). *Who governs: Democracy and power in an American city.* New Haven, CT: Yale University Press.

Gordon, M. M. (1964). *Assimilation in American life: The role of race, religion, and national origins.* New York: Oxford University Press.

Huntington, S. P. (2004). *Who are we? The challenges to America's identity.* New York: Simon & Schuster.

Kasinitz, P., Mollenkopf, J. H., Waters, M. C., & Holdaway, J. (2008). *Inheriting the city: The children of immigrants come of age.* Cambridge, MA: Harvard University Press.

Park, R. E. & Burgess, E. W. (1921). *Introduction to the science of sociology.* Chicago: The University of Chicago Press.

Portes, A. & Zhou, M. (1993). The new second generation: Segmented assimilation and its variants. *Annals of the American Academy of Political and Social Science,* 530, 74–96.

Warner, W. L. & Srole, L. (1945). *The social systems of American ethnic groups.* New Haven, CT: Yale University Press.

AUTHENTICITY Authenticity is one of the more controversial terms in the contemporary lexicon related to issues of **race** and ethnicity. Authenticity, the notion of a true and original racial or ethnic **culture**, society, and **identity**, is seen to be bound in complex ways to the equally fraught term "essentialism." Indeed, authenticity is the expression of a racial or ethnic "essence," an unchanging and unchangeable foundation of being. Perhaps most frequently used in relation to the fixing of **indigenous peoples** in a static "primitive" past, the term applies to all racialized identity categories. In a philosophical context, authenticity points more positively to efforts at self-creation rather than social construction, through resistance to the identity categories represented by essentialism. Thus, existentialist "inauthenticity" refers to conformity to social roles (including racial and ethnic **stereotypes**) while "authenticity" in this context refers to an individual ethical commitment to a mode of being that is freely adopted, a commitment that demands the right of recognition as an autonomous individual that Charles Taylor describes as fundamental to effective **multicultural** societies.

Authenticity in indigenous contexts can function positively as a claim to historical precedence, in support of claims to land and its uses. Also, membership of a defined racial group can carry with it protections, rights, and material benefits. Native American "authenticity" is measured by the US government in terms of tribal membership. This can mean membership of a tribal community that has obtained federal recognition; it can also mean individual membership by virtue of genetic inheritance or blood quantum. The requirement of a specified percentage of Native American Indian blood descent is a form of identification formulated and imposed by the federal government as part of the 1887 General Allotment Act. Under the Act, those Native people who qualified to receive a federal land grant, together with other payments and benefits, could prove that they possessed one-half or more Indian blood. However, those who could not prove themselves "authentic" in this way were dispossessed of their previous treaty entitlements. The connection between blood quantum and entitlement to rights and protections accorded to "authentic" American Indian tribes is sometimes cited to explain why some Native communities themselves enforce this colonialist system. Alternatively, identity as an "authentic" tribal person or group could be denied in the interests of opening tribal lands to white settlement. Thus, the definition of "authentic" tribal identity, the criteria for judging the racial status of a person, is historically contingent within an ongoing US colonialism. The debate concerning Native American authenticity is, in the words of Jace Weaver, "a process rendered more dysfunctional by the fact that for many years, for its own colonialist reasons, the United States government intruded itself into the questions of definitions, an intrusion that still has a significant impact on Indian **identity politics**."

Blood quantum has been used in other racial contexts to define identity: as evidenced by the complex vocabulary developed in the context of slavery for measuring degrees of "African-ness" or "blackness," such as mulatto, quadroon, octoroon, etc. Authenticity provides the basic assumption of racial purity upon which these categorizations are built. These categories control the conditions under which it is possible to "be" of a particular race or ethnicity. Referring not to any lived reality, the concept of authenticity operates within a colonialist strategy for regulating perceptions of racial difference and access to particular racial identities. [DLM]

Key readings

Cheung, V. J. (2004). *Inauthentic: The anxiety over culture and identity.* New Brunswick, NJ: Rutgers University Press.

Lopez, I. (1997). *White by law: The legal construction of race.* New York: New York University Press.

Sequoya, J. (1993). How(!) is an Indian? A contest of stories. In Arnold Krupat (Ed.), *New Voices in Native American Literary Criticism.* Washington, DC: Smithsonian Institution Press, pp. 453–473.

Taylor, C. (1994). *Multiculturalism and "The Politics of Recognition"* (expanded paperback edition). Princeton, NJ: Princeton University Press.

Vizenor, G. (1994). *Manifest manners: Postindian warriors of survivance.* Hanover, NH: Wesleyan University Press.

Weaver, J. (2001). *Other words: American Indian literature, law, and culture.* Norman, OK: University of Oklahoma Press.

AUTHORITARIANISM The term "authoritarianism" can describe forms of government and the state, group and social organization, ideologies and belief systems, styles of leadership and command, and individual social attitudes and values. Authoritarianism, as a set of social attitudes and beliefs held by individuals, has been extensively studied in psychology, where it has been seen as a relatively stable individual difference dimension encompassing, at one extreme (high authoritarianism), socially conservative beliefs favouring traditional and religious values and morality, respect and obedience for established authority, and coercive control of individual behavior versus, at the other extreme (low authoritarianism), socially liberal beliefs favouring individual freedom and self-expression, social change, diversity, and innovation.

The first systematic research on authoritarianism as a relatively stable individual difference dimension was published in 1950 in the classic volume, *The authoritarian personality*, by Adorno, Frenkel-Brunswick, Levinson, and Sanford. As the title indicates, they viewed this social attitude dimension as a direct expression of a particular kind of personality structure. Their theory proposed that this authoritarian personality arose out of inner conflicts originating from harsh, punitive childhood socialization. This created underlying feelings of resentment and anger towards parental authority, which were repressed and replaced by deference to and idealization of all authority. The repressed anger was displaced as hostility towards deviant persons and outgroups. Adorno and his colleagues also developed a psychometric scale (the F scale) to measure this authoritarian personality.

This theory initially attracted enormous attention and the F scale was widely used in research. The research, however, did not support their theory of the origins of authoritarianism and, with time, serious psychometric deficiencies of the F scale became apparent. Alternative theories and measures of authoritarianism were developed but these largely shared the flaws of the original theory and of the F scale. Eventually, in 1981, a new measure was developed by Altemeyer, the Right Wing Authoritarianism (RWA) scale, which did prove to be psychometrically robust, and which rapidly became the measure of choice for research on authoritarian attitudes in individuals.

Research by Altemeyer and others confirmed that the social attitudinal dimension measured by the RWA scale was highly stable in individuals over periods of as long as 20 years, and was powerfully associated with right-wing political orientation, religious fundamentalism, social traditionalism, resistance to change, preferences for structure, and being generally **prejudiced** and **ethnocentric**. The research has also suggested that that right-wing authoritarian attitudes are largely formed through social learning and personal experiences and crystallized during late adolescence, which suggested that that they might be better conceptualized as a dimension of social values rather than as personality.

A new development in authoritarianism research came in the 1990s when Sidanius and Pratto proposed and measured the concept of Social Dominance Orientation (SDO). The items of their SDO scale express a general attitudinal preference for intergroup relations to be hierarchical rather than equal, with more **powerful** groups having the right to dominate weaker ones. Research has shown that the SDO scale, like RWA, powerfully predicts generalized prejudice, intolerance, right-wing political orientation, anti-democratic sentiments, and militarism, but is uncorrelated (or only weakly correlated) with RWA. It has therefore been widely concluded that there seem to be not just one, but two, distinct dimensions of authoritarian social attitudes in individuals. [JD]

Key readings

Altemeyer, B. (1981). *Right-wing authoritarianism*. Winnipeg, Canada: University of Manitoba Press.

——. (1996). *The authoritarian specter*. Cambridge, MA: Harvard University Press.

——. (1998). The other "authoritarian personality". In M. Zanna (Ed.), *Advances in experimental social psychology* (Vol. 30). San Diego: Academic Press, pp. 47–92.

Duckitt, J. (in press). Authoritarianism and dogmatism. In M. Leary & R. Hoyle (Eds.), *Handbook of individual differences in social behavior*. New York: Guilford Publishers.

Sidanius, J. & Pratto, F. (1999). *Social dominance: An intergroup theory of social hierarchy and oppression*. Cambridge, UK: Cambridge University Press.

BELL HOOKS Born Gloria Jean Watkins in Hopkinsville, Kentucky in 1952, bell hooks is a distinguished author, feminist, **critical race** and education **theorist**, cultural critic, and social activist. She is the author of more than 30 critically acclaimed and influential books and numerous academic and popular magazine articles on gender, **race**, popular **culture** and teaching. hooks is a celebrated public figure, a subject of documentary films, a teacher in both elite and working class colleges and universities, and is widely considered to be one of the leading public intellectuals of her generation.

hooks came of age in a small, segregated town in rural Kentucky. Her family was poor working class. Her father worked as a janitor and her mother as a maid for white families. She portrays her early life as deeply impacted by the experience of being an African American in a society characterized by a color caste system and racial

apartheid. hooks describes her encounter with racism as one that both brought hardship and provided a context in which to develop personal strength and skills of resistance.

In her autobiographical works, hooks discusses her education as one of the definitive experiences of her life. Her development as a thinker and a writer is deeply related to her educational experiences. Initially a product of segregated schools, hooks finds that in this environment she benefited greatly from the young black women teachers who were deeply dedicated to building the self-esteem and confidence of African American children. While the 1960s brought school integration and a consequent move to a "white school," hooks' experience was one of loss. She describes her new teachers as less interested in building critical minds than in passing on large bodies of frequently irrelevant and seemingly colorless information. She also describes the "white schools" as locations that were interested in obedience rather than any kind of thinking that questioned white male authority.

The insights of hooks' early education were only deepened by the scholarships that led to a higher education. She obtained a BA from Stanford University in 1973, an MA from the University of Wisconsin in 1976, and a PhD from the University of California, Santa Cruz in 1983 – all in English. In university life, hooks reports encountering a racism she did not expect, and one that combined with a gender bias to produce an alienating experience. For instance, hooks demonstrates how black women were frequently ignored by citing the example of literature classes that did not explore African American women authors. Her experience of earning advanced degrees as a black woman in a post civil rights environment of a white "sisterhood" empowerment movement awakened her to the complexities of **power** and hegemony and came to

have an enormous impact on the development of her thought and teaching.

The disillusionments hooks experienced in her education became fodder for some of her most important contributions to critical race studies, feminism and pedagogical theory. Hers was an early voice in the critique of the racism that flourished in the feminist movement – academic or otherwise. Her insight into the persistent and twin logics of racism and sexism led her to decry the impact of domination of those two hegemonic forces that travel together. Her first book, *Ain't I a woman: Black women and feminism* (1981), which she began to write at 19, immediately made her an important name in feminist debate and is widely still recognized as one of the most important and influential books of the period. In this book, she began the pursuit of what would become a lifelong central theme: the intersection of culture, race, gender, and class. With this text, hooks explores the impact of sexism on black women during slavery, the devaluation of black womanhood, black male sexism, and racism within the recent feminist movement

In her 1989 work, *Talking back: Thinking feminist, thinking black*, she coined the term "**white supremacist** capitalist patriarchy" to point to the interlocking systems of domination that define everyday life. She also uses this term to point out that the problem of race is one of institutional structure, not individual beliefs.

In her writings, hooks has not only challenged antiracist, feminist and anti-**imperialist** movements to work together instead of in competition with each other, but she has also pushed them to think and operate out of a concern for the lives of women of color. For example, in *Breaking bread: Insurgent black intellectual life* (1991), co-authored with **Cornel West**, she argues that intellectuals should be deeply concerned with fusing in their work a moral depth and a political engagement that is necessary both to rescue the colonized and suppressed **others** (especially black women) and to produce a public intellectual community capable of critical thought.

In her work, hooks is also deeply interested in pedagogy. She writes about how racism and sexism is learned and about the value of learning itself. In her frequent studies of contemporary culture, hooks analyzes movies, television, and events of everyday life to point to the ways in which mass media supply deeply racist and sexist depictions. In *Black looks: Race and representation* (1992), hooks demonstrates that black **representation** is characterized by African Americans' inability to exert any substantial influence on how they are portrayed.

hooks also calls for a pedagogy that questions the imperialist, capitalistic, and patriarchical ideology of the status quo. In this work she is enormously influenced by Paolo Freire, who argues for literacy as liberation. In her first work on education, *Teaching to transgress: Education as the practice of freedom* (1994), hooks calls for a pedagogy that will teach students, not just bodies of knowledge, but how to recognize their **multicultural** histories and how to transgress against the oppressions of racism, sexism, and classism. In *Teaching community: A pedagogy of hope* (2003), she calls for the "decolonisation of ways of knowing" to be replaced by a widespread and rigorous training of critical thinking. For hooks, it is the use of critical skills in reading, thinking, and everyday life that is the essential element in ending the nexus of the various forms of **discrimination** and domination; developing such capacities is a necessary step to accomplishing the just society. [MJC]

Key readings

hooks, b. (1981). *Ain't I a woman: Black women and feminism.* Boston, MA: South End Press.

——. (1989). *Talking back: Thinking feminist, thinking black.* Boston, MA: South End Press.

——. (1990). *Yearning: Race, gender, and cultural politics.* Boston, MA: South End Press.

——. (1994). *Teaching to transgress: Education as the practice of freedom.* New York: Routledge.

——. (1995). *Killing rage: Ending racism* (first ed.). New York: H. Holt and Co.

——. (2006). *Outlaw culture.* London: Routledge.

hooks, b. & West, C. (1991). *Breaking bread: Insurgent black intellectual life.* Boston, MA: South End Press.

CIVIL RIGHTS MOVEMENT The Civil Rights Movement can be characterized as the social, political, and legal struggle towards racial equality. The beginning of the movement is often marked by the events of 1955, which include the arrest of Rosa Parks for refusing to give up her seat to a white man, the Montgomery Bus Boycott that followed, and the rise of **Dr Martin Luther King, Jr** as the national figure of the movement. Notwithstanding, the roots of the movement can be traced to the foundation of this country. From the American slave's appropriation of Thomas Jefferson's declaration that "all men are created equal" to Barack Obama's historic election, the Civil Rights Movement has been a continual thread, weaving its way through the fabric of American society.

The American Revolution was more than a revolt against British tyranny. The revolution led by the Founders was largely influenced by the freedom struggles already occurring within the 13 colonies of those excluded from Jefferson's definition of equality, namely slaves. While the enslaved population had long challenged the legality of their enslavement, the revolutionary rhetoric of liberty and equality provided the best line of defense against the tyranny of slave ownership, which denied Africans and their American-born descendants liberty and citizenship. As the nation's first Attorney General, Edmond Randolph asserted that not only were slaves to be excluded from American society, but also that the language of liberty and citizenship did not apply to them. In 1856, Dred Scott, a slave, challenged this sentiment by attempting to sue his master for his freedom. Scott contended that his prolonged residence in a free state made him a free man and, therefore, a citizen of the United States. The Supreme Court disagreed, declaring that no person of African descent, whether slave or free, was included or intended to be included under the term "citizen" as defined by the Constitution.

The free Black population, largely located in the North, fared little better than their slave counterparts as they too faced the harsh reality of racial inequality. One of the ways in which free Blacks chose to push back was to hold local, state, and national conventions to address issues specific "to the **race**." From 1830 to 1861, 11 national conventions were held in states including, New York, Pennsylvania, and Ohio. Delegates passed resolutions and wrote manifestos demanding the abolition of slavery, equal protection under the law, and universal suffrage. The notion that Blacks fared better in the North was indeed a matter of perspective. Northern Blacks were well aware that many of their white allies adhered to racist **stereotypes** held by their southern counterparts. Even the staunchest abolitionist baulked at the idea of social equality. Blacks chided the Anti-Slavery Society for refusing to include social equality as a part of its agenda. Hence, North or South, slave or free civil rights formed the cornerstone of Black activism which begin with the American Revolution and continued throughout the antebellum period.

The Civil Rights Movement gained a sense of urgency in the immediate post-Civil War era known as "Reconstruction." The radical legislation passed by a Republican-dominated Congress in the first decade following the war inspired a new sense of hope in Blacks nationwide. In 1866, Congress adopted the Thirteenth Amendment to the Constitution, which abolished chattel slavery and overrode President Andrew Johnson's veto to pass the Civil Rights Act of 1866. This Act granted citizenship to every person (except Indians) born in the United States regardless of race. In 1868, Congress passed the Fourteenth Amendment guaranteeing equal protection under the law. In 1870, the Fifteenth Amendment granted suffrage to Black men. The Civil Rights Act of 1875 guaranteed equal treatment in public accommodations, regardless of race, color, or previous condition of servitude.

While the civil rights project was nowhere near its completion, the drastic measures taken by Congress gave reason for those in the **anti-racism** campaign to be optimistic. As the decade wore on, however, the North tired of its Reconstruction effort. Wishing to reestablish financial ties with the South, the Civil Rights Movement was abandoned in what is known as the compromise of 1877. The compromise settled the dispute regarding the outcome of the 1876 presidential election between Democrat Samuel J. Tilden and Republican Rutherford B. Hayes. When the final agreement was reached in March 1877, two days prior to inauguration, Hayes was named President and the Republicans agreed to withdraw Federal troops from the South. Consequently, Reconstruction was dealt a fatal blow, and civil rights gains became unenforceable as the doctrine of states rights trumped individual rights.

Another doctrine, "separate but equal," gained ground in the years following Reconstruction as **segregation**, also known as Jim Crow, situated Blacks as second-class citizens. While poll taxes and literary tests were enacted to prevent Black men from exercising the franchise, thus nullifying the Fifteen Amendment, segregated public accommodations, which were later sanctioned by the Supreme Court, completed the roll-back of civil rights gained during Reconstruction. As a case in point, in 1873 the Supreme Court ruled in favor of Catherine Brown, a Black woman, who sued the railroad station for violently ejecting her from the "ladies car" (the first car) in 1868 as she traveled from Alexandria, Virginia to Washington, DC. This was the first racial public transportation case decided by the Court; nevertheless, the decision would prove the exception and not the rule.

In 1896, in the landmark decision *Plessey* v. *Ferguson*, the Supreme Court sanctioned segregation legalizing the "separate but equal" doctrine. The plaintiff, Homer Plessey, could pass for white but was known to have a Black great-grandmother. Although Plessey paid for a first-class ticket to travel from New Orleans to Covington, Louisiana, he was told to sit in the colored section. When he refused to leave the "white only" car, Plessey was violently dragged from the train by police. He sued on the basis that segregation violated his Fourteenth Amendment rights and that the railroad company violated his civil rights as outlined in the Act of 1875. The Court disagreed, stating that the Civil Rights Act of 1875 only guaranteed separate but equal accommodations, but did not outlaw segregation. Consequently, the Plessey decision not only legitimized Jim Crow in the Southern states, but numerous states nationwide adopted segregation laws, which enforced the Jim Crow way of life. Schools, restaurants, public transportation, hospitals, and cemeteries were all subject to Jim Crow. Not even Hattie McDaniels, the first Black woman to win an Oscar for her supporting role as Mammy in the movie adaptation of *Gone with the wind*, was allowed to be buried in the famous Hollywood Memorial Park in 1952 because of its "whites only" policy.

The twentieth century witnessed a steady effort in the continued fight towards civil rights. In 1909, The National Organization for the Advancement of Colored People (NAACP), a multiracial organization which served as the vanguard for civil rights was formed to resist the systematic **discrimination** of minorities. While the NAACP worked to organize civil rights activities on a national level, community organizations garnered support to fight against racism on a local level. In the 1930s, Adam Clayton Powell, pastor of the famous Abyssinian Baptist Church of Harlem, New York, organized the Greater New York Coordinating Committee which initiated boycotts, picketed for jobs, and broke the political stronghold in Harlem. Activists in Arizona, Wyoming, Texas, Oklahoma, Kansas, and New Mexico were instrumental in dismantling Jim Crow in the west.

From 1947 to 1950, Black students at the University of New Mexico in Albuquerque staged boycotts to demonstrate against discrimination practiced by local businesses. The 1952 Albuquerque Civil Rights Ordinance and 1955 Civil Rights Bill were results of their efforts. In 1951, the NAACP Legal Aid Division won a lawsuit against the Tolleson School District in Phoenix, Arizona, due to its practice of segregating Mexican-American students. When Phoenix Union High School refused to comply with the order, the NAACP bought a suit and won in 1953. The ruling not only led to the collapse of segregation throughout the state, which opened the door to Black student enrollment in white Arizona schools, it also served as a precedent for the landmark decision in the 1954 Supreme Court case of *Brown* v. *the Board of Education*, which declared the doctrine of "separate but equal" unconstitutional.

The nonviolent philosophy of Dr Martin Luther King, Jr, carried the Civil Rights Movements throughout the decades of the 1950s and 1960s as the struggle for racial equality intensified in the South. Civil disobedience in the form of boycotts, sit-ins, marches, and peaceful protest were used to chip away at the stronghold of racial injustice resulting in the Civil Rights Act of 1964, which outlawed segregation in schools, public places, and employment. The Voting Rights Act of 1965 outlawed discriminatory voting practices used to disenfranchise Blacks. However, passing legislation was one thing, enforcing it was another. Hence, the Civil Rights Movement, for the remainder of the twentieth century, focused on the protection and enforcement of civil rights gains, which were under constant attack by neo-conservatives.

The historic election of Barack Obama in the eyes of some signifies the achievement of racial equality in America. Others believe it only mirrors the possibility of racial equality and that the work of dismantling structural inequality must continue. For certain, the Civil Rights Movement is central to American **identity** and will continue to influence the nation for years to come. [ALC]

Key readings

Clar, D., Garrow, D. J., Gill, G., Harding, V., & Carson, C. (Eds.). (1991). *Eyes on the prize civil rights reader: Documents, speeches, and firsthand accounts of the black freedom struggle*. New York: Penguin (Non classic).

Crawford, V. L., Rouse, J. A., & Woods, B. (Eds.). (1990). *Women in the civil rights movement: Trailblazers & torchbearers, 1941–1965*. Bloomington, IN: University of Indiana Press.

Ezra, M. (2009). *Civil rights movement: People and perspectives* (perspectives in American social history). Santa Barbara, CA: ABC-CLIO.

Taylor, Q. (1999). *In search of a racial frontier: African Americans in the West 1528–1990*. New York: W. W. Norton & Co.

Williams, J. & Bond, J. (1988). *Eyes on the prize: America's civil rights years.* New York: Penguin.

COLOR BLINDNESS Within the field of racial politics, "color blindness" typically refers to the concept of "racial non-recognition" – the assertion that racial identities, categories or distinctions should not be formally acknowledged or acted upon, especially with regard to legal doctrine and government policy. Some supporters of this concept assert that a commitment to color blindness represents the full realization of the ideals of the US **Civil Rights Movement**, sometimes invoking **Dr Martin Luther King, Jr's** call from the 1963 March on Washington that his children would hopefully one day "not be judged by the color of their skin but by the content of their character." Critics of this position argue that Dr King believed that, to fully eradicate racial distinctions, government policy had to proactively address the lived realities of racism.

Thus, contemporary disputes over whether public policy can or should aspire to be "color blind" index a much broader debate over whether the racial hierarchies that dominated the nation's past continue in the present, and what role the government should play to remedy or address these inheritances and their contemporary consequences. As such, recent controversies over the meaning and rationale for color blindness have been expressed through disagreements over **race**-conscious affirmative action programs in public employment and education, debates over the boundaries of voting districts, and disputes over the collection of race and ethnicity data by the government.

Historical origins of color blindness

An early articulation of color blindness as

a legal and moral claim can be found in the well-known dissent by Justice John Harlan to the Supreme Court's 1896 *Plessy* v. *Ferguson* decision. In *Plessy*, by a 7–1 majority, the Court validated the "separate but equal" doctrine of formal racial **segregation**. In his passionate dissent, often celebrated as a bold, **anti-racist** claim, Justice Harlan declared: "Our Constitution is color-blind, and neither knows nor tolerates classes among citizens." Legal scholars note, however, that Harlan preceded this statement with an important qualification:

> The white race deems itself to be the dominant race in this country. And so it is in prestige, in achievements, in education, in wealth and in **power**. So, I doubt not, it will continue to be for all time if it remains true to its great heritage and holds fast to the principles of constitutional liberty.

For Harlan, a color-blind Constitution would not necessarily disrupt or eliminate the trenchant racial hierarchies within the broader society. Harlan's dissent thus raises some of the vexing questions and contradictions which continue to animate debates about color blindness today. If racial inequities persist in the economic, cultural, and social spheres, as Harlan suggests, then what role should the government play in rectifying or mitigating those inequities?

In the wake of the Supreme Court's unanimous decision in the 1954 *Brown* v. *Board of Education* case, formally overturning the "separate but equal" doctrine and subsequently committing to end formal segregation in public schools with "all deliberate speed," rhetorical allusions to an idealized principle of color blindness grew more frequent in public discourse. In his landmark June 1963 Civil Rights Address, President John F. Kennedy declared his intention to ask Congress to

"make a commitment...to the proposition that race has no place in American life or law." Kennedy also coupled this claim with the assertion that "the old code of equity under which we live commands for every wrong a remedy" and noted the continued ways in which "wrongs are inflected on Negro citizens." This invocation of color-blind rhetoric, in which the government is called upon to help realize a society without formal racial distinctions by adopting ameliorative race-conscious policies, dominated much of the public discourse during the 1960s and 1970s. Within this framework, legacies and practices of racial subordination had to be addressed through affirmative action and other equal opportunity programs so that a substantive "color blindness" could be achieved.

This particular articulation of color blindness came under increasing attack in the late 1970s, most notably in the Supreme Court's 1978 *Regents of the University of California* v. *Bakke* decision. In a 5–4 decision, the Court declared that a medical school's affirmative action program violated the Equal Protection Clause of the Fourteenth Amendment because it set aside a particular number of admission slots for applicants from racial **minority** groups. The *Bakke* case set a legal precedent which held that, in order for a government agency or program to formally take race into account, it had to demonstrate that the remedy and criteria employed could be justified by a compelling governmental interest, meeting the standards of "strict scrutiny." Supporters of the *Bakke* decision declared that limiting affirmative action programs in this way advanced rather than retarded progress towards a "color-blind" ideal because the state could not formally recognize race unless it demonstrated a compelling governmental interest. In his dissent, Justice Harry Blackmun declared that the recognition of race was a fundamental prerequisite to realizing a society free of racism: "In *order* *to move beyond race*, we must first *take race into account.*" Thus, invocations of a commitment to color blindness were used by figures on both sides of the debate.

Recent debates

In the 1990s, disputes over the meaning, definition and application of color blindness within public policy and the law re-emerged in a series of contentious debates over the status of extant affirmative action programs. In 1996, Republican California Governor Pete Wilson and Sacramento business-consultant Ward Connerly spearheaded a successful statewide ballot measure that effectively banned most public affirmative action programs in higher education and employment. Named the "California Civil Rights Initiative," the measure's proponents regularly invoked iconic figures such as Dr King and President Kennedy, declaring their measure would help "*all* California children" to "succeed on a fair, color-blind, race-blind, gender-blind basis."

Connerly, an African American with libertarian political leanings, insisted that it was race-conscious programs, rather than legacies of societal racism, that prevented the realization of a "race-blind" government and nation. With support from several conservative foundations, Connerly continued to press this articulation of color blindness into service through successful anti-affirmative action ballot measures in Washington state in 1998, Michigan in 2004 and Nebraska in 2008. In 2003, however, a Connerly-sponsored measure in California, dubbed the "Racial Privacy Initiative," which sought to ban the collection of most race and ethnicity data by state and local governments, lost by a large margin. In that contest, civil rights groups opposed to the measure began their ballot argument by affirming, "We all want a color-blind society," before cautioning voters that the initiative's ban on collecting racial and ethnic data could be harmful to

important medical research and treatment. Their invocation of the ideal championed by Connerly demonstrated that color-blind political rhetoric had appeal across the political spectrum.

In 2007, the U.S. Supreme Court further declared its support for an extremely limited framework for government agencies to formally consider race in their *Parents Involved in Community Schools v. Seattle School District No. 1* decision, which prohibited the use of race in assigning students to public schools for the purposes of desegregation or achieving racial balance. Writing for the Court's majority, Justice John Roberts asserted, "The way to stop **discrimination** on the basis of race is to stop discriminating on the basis of race." Roberts' contention that all forms of racial recognition by the state were equally insidious and unjustified expressed one of the primary logics of contemporary color-blind discourse. From this perspective, the government must remain strictly "neutral" and avoid all recognition and acknowledgement of racial difference, identity or categories. Most opinion polls suggest that, framed in this way, the proposition of formal government neutrality with regard to racial recognition has widespread public support.

Criticisms of color blind discourse

Contemporary critics of this color-blind discourse offer a number of arguments. First, legal scholars have noted that the very concept of "racial non-recognition" is implicitly flawed, as it requires us to know what race is (and how to recognize it) in order to ignore it, thus marking and reifying race as a stable and coherent category of human difference, rooted in biology or nature rather than society and history. Thus, the requirement to ignore race is actually a mandate to recognize race as a fixed characteristic and condition. In addition, critics charge that, while formal government recognition of racial distinctions may be prohibited under a color-blind framework, racial hierarchies and inequities can continue to flourish in many other realms of public life. They point, for example, to continued racial disparities in employment and housing markets, disproportionate levels of poverty and incarceration, and biased **representations** in popular **culture**, among other areas. By choosing to tolerate such conditions, detractors maintain, the state is hardly acting in a "racially neutral" fashion. From this perspective, professions of formal government color blindness implicitly sanction such group-based racial inequities and hierarchies as inevitable, or beyond the pale of state action.

Finally, opponents of contemporary color-blind discourse raise questions concerning whether color blindness (the inability to visually distinguish between particular colors), a condition which is typically classified as a visual impairment, serves as the best metaphor for an idealized state of racial justice. Given the extent to which racial subordination is articulated through diverse forms, symbols and relationships, rather than just formal and intentional bigotry or discrimination, they ask whether a genuine commitment to addressing racial disparities and inequities is not better served by a heightened, rather than restricted, perception of racial dynamics and power. [DH]

Key readings

Bonilla-Silva, E. (2003). *Racism without racists: Color-blind racism and the persistence of racial inequality in the United States*. Lanham, MD: Rowman & Littlefield.

Brown, M., Conroy, M., Currie, E., Duster, T., Oppenheimer, D., Shultz, M., & Wellman, D. (2003). *Whitewashing race: The myth of a color-blind society*. Berkeley, CA: University of California Press.

Connerly, W. (2002). *Creating equal: My fight against race preferences*. New York: Encounter Books.

Crenshaw, K. W. (1997). Color blindness, history, and the law. In W. Lubiano (Ed.), *The house that race built*. New York: Pantheon Books.

Gotanda, N. (1991). A critique of "Our constitution is color-blind". *Stanford Law Review*, 44, 1–68.

Steele, S. (1991). *The content of our character: A new vision of race in America*. New York: Harper Perennial.

COLOR LINE The idea of the "color line" became widely used after **W. E. B. Du Bois** declared that the color line is the biggest "problem of the twentieth century." Most notably, the term identifies the sometimes hidden hierarchy of "**races**," the critical dividing line between "races" of people – that is, primarily between whites and people of color. Since Du Bois called it out, the color line has been used to signify domestic and international racial relations, often as a way of noting the everyday impacts of Western racism.

Even before the beginning of the slave trade, the color line had served as a symbol of considerable gain for "white" peoples and a great loss for "red" peoples (indigenous Americans). The early theft of indigenous lands was based on the European and European American notion of an inherent division of "races," with indigenous Americans deemed by whites to be inferior peoples. During this time, many North American and European laws were instituted to ensure the great import of the color line. The systemic nature of Western racial oppression was now solidly in place, based in part on the "obvious" (to whites) new color line. Indeed, the color line served as a key marker of condition and status – of freedom or oppression, of superiority or inferiority.

During the earliest times in North American history, many groups experienced implicit hardship based in large part on their racially defined differences. The lower position on the color hierarchy belonged primarily to African and indigenous Americans and this ensured that they would remain segregated from whites, that their labor would be exploited, and that they would remain highly oppressed. Throughout the centuries of slavery, Civil War, and Reconstruction, the US color line became a well-institutionalized form of racism. African Americans, indigenous Americans, and some other people of color (by the 1850s, Mexican and Chinese Americans) remained disenfranchised in most major spheres of institutional life. During the Civil War, many formerly enslaved (and free) African Americans in the North sought to contribute to the Union cause by volunteering to fight. However, initially they were prevented, by President Abraham Lincoln and other white officials, from enlisting to fight for their freedom because of the longstanding color line and its deeming of blacks as inferior.

The color line cemented the denial of socioeconomic opportunity and political participation for African Americans and other people of color. Jim Crow notions of "separate but equal" became law and encapsulated further the belief that skin color was a significant indicator of intelligence, status, and privilege, or lack thereof. Due to the new US laws, "free" people of color were legally barred from gaining significant resources, wealth, education, and, thus, prosperity. The demonization of black Americans and other people of color guaranteed that they would remain residentially, educationally, and economically segregated on the other side of the color line. Because of this, many African Americans found themselves blocked from gaining access to most important institutions, which would have granted them upward mobility.

The systemic and institutionalized reality of the color line continues to shape national and international understandings of "race." Evident in the emigration of people of color around the world, many find themselves placed by whites with **power** and privilege within the confines of the old socially constructed color line. Many Asian, African, and South American immigrants to the United States find themselves subject to the harsh realities of the color line – not only through color-based discriminatory practices, but also through more subtle "English Only" efforts and policies. The systemic nature of the color line remains and is evidenced in blocked opportunities in employment, in the criminalization of people of color, and in the continuing residential and educational **segregation**. [LE]

Key readings

Bonilla-Silva, E. (2004). "From bi-racial to tri-racial". *Ethnic and Racial Studies*, 27, 931–950.

Du Bois, W. E. B. (2003 [1903]). *The souls of black folk*. New York: Routledge.

Feagin, J. R. (2009). *Racist America: Roots, current realities, and future reparations*. New York: Routledge.

Karenga, M. (2003). "Du Bois and the question of the color line: Race and class in the age of globalization". *Socialism and Democracy*, 17, 141–160.

Quillin, F. (1969). *The Color line in Ohio: A history of race prejudice in a typical Northern state*. New York: Negro University Press.

CORNEL WEST Cornel West is an African American cultural critic, academic, and orator. Acclaimed for his ability to weave together philosophical ideas, popular culture, and social justice advocacy, West has reached a broad audience through his articles, books, media appearances, and, especially, through his frequent public lectures.

His scholarly work has contributed to renewed interest in pragmatism, to black theology, and to explorations of the relationship between **race** and **culture**.

Born in Tulsa, Oklahoma on June 2, 1953, West spent much of his childhood in Sacramento, California. As a young man, he coordinated a citywide student strike to protest the lack of African American history in the Sacramento school curriculum. As an undergraduate at Harvard, West continued his involvement in progressive social activism, including as co-president of the Black Student Association. The injustice West worked against was not distant or abstract: at Harvard West found himself, along with his two black roommates, accused of raping a white woman. He was held in jail overnight before the woman recanted.

West's doctoral training, at Princeton, was in philosophy. He was especially influenced by Richard Rorty, an analytically trained philosopher who was beginning to argue that the discipline of philosophy problematically closes itself off to the significance of history, literature, and culture. With Rorty, West came to consider himself an epistemic antifoundationalist: he rejected the claim that we have direct access to how the world really is. Instead, West asserted that access to the world is always mediated by historical and cultural context. West saw two options for anti-foundationalists: postmodernism or pragmatism. While sympathetic to the critique of **power** and embrace of hybridity associated with postmodernism, West was suspicious of postmodernism's accompanying nihilism and his primary allegiance was to pragmatism. In the writings of C. S. Peirce, William James, and John Dewey, West found intellectual resources that addressed the significance of critical inquiry, historical and cultural rootedness, and the American experience – including the African American experience. In *The American evasion of philosophy*, West

presented pragmatism as an expansive tradition of thought, and public intellectual performance, stretching from Ralph Waldo Emerson to **W. E. B. Du Bois** to Reinhold Niebuhr and finally, implicitly, to West himself.

The grandson of a Baptist minister, West professes a serious, not superficial, personal religiosity. It is his Christianity, he writes, that prevented him from becoming a Marxist, or a Black Panther, or a postmodernist, despite being very sympathetic to these views. In contrast to Rorty, who saw philosophy's secular foundationalism as replacing the discredited foundationalism of Christian theology, West takes Christianity to be intellectually defensible when its focus is on Jesus as a model of love and on the existential resources of the Christian tradition, resources which can be tapped in the face of suffering and death (he is particularly fond of Kierkegaard). West has brought together his philosophical and religious commitments in "prophetic pragmatism," a term West coined to refer to a genre of cultural criticism that is antifoundationalist but also energetically calls upon the resources of a tradition to call out the ways that tradition is not living up to its ideals. West has pointed to homophobia in African American churches as a target for such criticism, but he has also pointed to targets and resources in the Jewish and Islamic traditions, particularly in the context of the conflict in Israel and Palestine.

Just as West unabashedly identifies himself and his work as Christian, he also embraces an African American **identity**. It was with *Race matters*, a series of reflections on black culture and politics, that West first entered the public spotlight. West brings his prophetic pragmatism to these reflections: he is critical of claims to racial **authenticity** on the part of blacks, claims which can hurt the most vulnerable within the black community; he is critical of leaders of the black community who are self-aggrandizing and who cater to the desires of whites; he notes the detrimental effects of weak civil society institutions amongst blacks; and he commends a "love ethic" as a means of improving blacks' sense of self-worth while also encouraging political resistance. Most of all, West gives voice to frustrations widely felt by African Americans in a thoughtful and nuanced way. His method, in *Race matters*, is to use the tools of analysis – for example distinguishing types of black intellectuals and types of responses to racism – and to note the shortcomings of both sides of an issue as it is conventionally framed. But West writes that the intellectual should be like a jazz performer, and he tries to put this into practice, using his analytic categories only as a starting point to explore the complexities that they both name and elide.

Just as he is committed to Christianity and to African American identity, West is also committed to democracy; specifically, to what he calls radical democracy. He has not permanently aligned himself with particular positions or parties (though he supported the presidential campaigns of Bill Bradley, Ralph Nader, and Barack Obama); instead, West has aligned himself with a democratic ethos. This ethos is maintained by the cultural critique of prophetic pragmatism, and it is an ethos that encourages such critique. This ethos is endangered by the rise of American **imperialism**, West argues, but the American tradition also contains resources that could revitalize democracy. These resources include the writings of Herman Melville, Walt Whitman, and James Baldwin; they also are found in contemporary youth culture, including in hip hop music (West himself has recorded spoken word albums). Especially important to the radical democratic ethos West envisions is dialogue, fueled by a love of truth and a questioning of others and of oneself.

West's influence has been felt on those students who studied directly with him (including the public intellectual Michael Eric Dyson), those many academics who have studied West's writings on race, religion, philosophy, and culture, and by the thousands of individuals who have heard West speak in person in the more than one hundred public lectures West gives each year. West has faced criticism from some academics for a lack of intellectual rigor. West's defenders have responded that West has shown his intellectual capacity in scholarly works but also takes the intellectual vocation to include speaking in many registers, and speaking to a broad audience. Other critics worry that the love ethic and focus on dialogue West commends may not be sufficient to solve intractable problems like those faced in the Middle East – or, perhaps, amongst African Americans. In response to this, West's defenders may note West's perennial emphasis on the tragic nature of our world, which necessitates faith. [VL]

Key readings

Cowan, R. (2003). *Cornel West: The politics of redemption*. Cambridge: Polity.

West, C. (1982). *Prophecy, deliverance! An Afro-American revolutionary christianity*. Louisville, KY: Westminster John Knox Press.

——. (1989). *The American evasion of philosophy: A genealogy of pragmatism*. Madison, WI: The University of Wisconsin Press.

——. (1993). *Race matters*. Boston: Beacon Press.

——. (2004). *Democracy matters: Winning the fight against imperialism*. New York: Penguin.

Yancy, G. (Ed.). (2001). *Cornel West: A critical reader*. Malden, MA: Blackwell.

CRITICAL RACE THEORY

Critical race theory (CRT) is a scholarly, political movement that originated in legal studies when a group of US scholars of color worked collectively to address shared concerns: first, critical and conservative scholarly legal traditions that did not explain the role of **race** and racism in the law and society; and, second, civil rights law and action that had been severely blunted or dismantled. In particular, this group of scholars challenged critical legal studies (CLS). CRT scholars were influenced by the Frankfurt School and so focused almost exclusively on class-based analyses of inequality and **power**. Significantly, CLS failed to address race as a mechanism of power. Instead, CRT scholars suggested that legal language, and the law itself, were false constructs and should be deconstructed and ultimately abandoned. CLS offered no alternative to the existing legal structures and practices.

CRT scholars argued pointedly that the CLS proposal to discard the law without providing alternatives utterly ignored the structurally tenuous position of disempowered people, who often found in the law their only hope of **representation** or remedy, even if it was terribly uneven and biased. And, as evidenced by those historical advances made by people of color in the United States – voting rights, school desegregation, etc. – the law provided one of the few viable channels of challenge to institutional and societal inequity. CRT scholars rightly suggested that CLS was a fundamentally privileged body of thought. The failure of CLS to incorporate race and racism as mechanisms of power in the law marked the central intellectual, ideological, and political differences between CLS and the CRT movement.

CRT scholars also responded to what they perceived as both shortcomings in civil rights legal strategy and the dismantling of those victories that were won. Specifically, CRT scholars explained that civil rights legal strategy was limited by its liberal approach. Legal strategy that sought incremental change within existing institutional arrangements, they argued, was neither viable nor sustainable. Instead, CRT scholars proposed that the transformation of racist, oppressive structures would only occur through radical change. Importantly, CRT scholars, beginning with Derrick Bell, argued that racism was not merely an individual pathology – a psychological disease of sorts – but rather an organizing mechanism of society. Many CRT scholars defined racism as the participation in a system of racial inequality marked by the institutional protection of white dominance. Scholars variously described this system as systematically controlled unequal access to material and informational resources, protections, and representation, reinforced by cultural and ideological practices that maintain explanations for **white supremacy**.

Early CRT scholars were largely materialists and, as such, challenged the very organization of systems and institutions. Various scholars took differing conceptual and analytical approaches to this issue. For example, Cheryl Harris argued that **whiteness** was not merely a badge of racial privilege that garners benefits for some individuals, but a structural form of property that has been legally constructed and protected throughout US history. Neil Gotanda debunked the myth of Constitutional **color blindness** and revealed the pernicious structural impact of color blindness. Mari Matsuda, Charles Lawrence III, Richard Delgado, and others conceptualized hate speech as systemic oppression rather than individual expression. Kimberlé Crenshaw detailed the intersectionalities of oppressions. There are many other equally significant scholars and salient concepts.

Through rigorous dialogue and rich scholarship, the early CRT scholars formed a body of work that shaped this powerful movement. This body of work engaged race and racism as explanatory and analytical tools. And, from this process of analysis, the movement emerged with core tenets, including:

1 racism is endemic to the United States and as such is a permanent, though shifting, organizing force of American social and political life;
2 scholarly and legal claims to positivism, neutrality, and ahistoricism are false and should be challenged;
3 race and racism are historically constructed and as such adequate understandings of present conditions of racial inequity necessarily include historical analyses;
4 the experiences, voices, and stories of people of color are legitimate and important knowledge and must be mobilized to counter dominant narratives and ideologies;
5 CRT is multidisciplinary and interdisciplinary;
6 the end of racism and other forms of oppression is tied to radical societal transformation, so CRT rejects liberal projects grounded in incremental change.

While CRT is shaped by these shared basic tenets, it is also a movement that is not bound by scholarly discipline or content. So, out of this set of shared purposes, CRT expanded into an extraordinarily rich body of scholarship that included LatCrit (**Latino** Critical Theory), Critical Race Feminism, OutCrit or QueerCrit (Queer Critical Race Theory), AsianCrit (Asian American Critical Theory), and so on. CRT embarked on a second generation, in which scholars challenged a perceived black–white binary in earlier work, analyzed globalization, and debated anti-essentialism, for example. Areas of law explored expanded to include corporate tax law, among others. This second generation of CRT expanded the content, disciplinary approach, and conceptual bases, and also solidified CRT as a very specific

scholarly and political project. While scholars from various disciplines and fields have long studied race, and while individual scholars have used race as an analytical tool (such as **W. E. B. Du Bois** and Carter G. Woodson, among others), CRT is a collective body of work and a movement that conceptualizes race at the center of its explanatory framework. Further, the overarching theoretical focus is systemic and structural.

Scholars outside legal studies have made significant forays into CRT. Education scholars, in particular, have adopted CRT and expanded its analytical and methodological capacities in addressing racial and other inequities in schooling. In addition to incorporating conceptual frames from CRT, Education scholars have emphasized the importance of counterstorytelling – the methodological highlighting of narratives and experiences of people of color – as requisite to challenging and transforming institutionalized schooling practices and organization (from policy to pedagogy) to create viable equity.

CRT is a complex, sophisticated body of scholarship that continues to provide a framework for scholars and activists to challenge structural oppression. The future of CRT is connected in part to the movement's ability to respond to current prevailing mainstream notions in the United States that we are now a "post-race" society. [SEV]

Key readings

Crenshaw, K., Gotanda, N., Peller, G., & Thomas, K. (Eds.). (1995). *Critical race theory: The key writings that formed the movement*. New York: The New Press.

Delgado, R. & Stefancic, J. (2001). *Critical Race Theory: An introduction*. New York: New York University Press.

Dixson, A. & Rousseau, C. (2006). *Critical race theory in education: All God's children got a song*. New York: Routledge.

Ladson-Billings, G. & Tate, W. (1995). Toward a critical race theory of education. *Teachers College Record*, 97, (1) 47–68.

Matsuda, M., Lawrence, C., Delgado, R., & Crenshaw, K. (Eds.). (1993). *Words that wound: Critical race theory, assaultive speech, and the first amendment*. San Francisco: Westview Press.

Taylor, E., Gillborn, D., & Ladson-Billings, G. (Eds.) (2009). *Foundations of Critical race theory in education*. New York: Routledge.

Valdes, F., Culpe, J. C., & Harris, A. (Eds.) (2002). *Crossroads, directions, and a new Critical Race Theory*. Philadelphia: Temple University Press.

CULTURAL STUDIES Cultural Studies is an interdisciplinary intellectual and social movement that brings the study of **culture** – particularly the uses of popular culture in everyday life – to the forefront of theoretical analysis. It draws on literary, sociological, political, anthropological, and communication theory to interrogate the production, content, and reception of cultural texts and to engage culture as a dynamic and multifaceted social process. The genesis of Cultural Studies was in Great Britain, but its roots reach back to the Frankfurt School and Marx, while its scope now extends worldwide. Cultural Studies is, at its core, a radical and subversive intervention in the academy, because of its basic goal of troubling the term "culture" and linking it to social **power** and the construction and dissemination of knowledge.

British roots of Cultural Studies

Cultural Studies was established as an academic discipline in 1964, when the Centre for Contemporary Cultural Studies (CCCS) was founded at the University of Birmingham in England. The term was coined by the center's first director,

Richard Hoggart, author of a key text in the field, *The uses of literacy* (1957), which challenged the low culture/high culture divide of orthodox scholarship by legitimizing popular culture as an object of serious scholarly critique and analysis.

The work of Hoggart and his contemporary, Raymond Williams, were the cornerstones of the emerging field of Cultural Studies. Both Hoggart and Williams understood cultural texts to be the keys to understanding society as a whole. In Williams' 1958 essay "Culture is ordinary," he defined culture as "a whole way of life," a dynamic and complex production that shed light on the priorities, power structures, economics and politics of a society. This key concept shaped the field of Cultural Studies, giving rise to the seminal works in the area as well as to later challenges and critiques.

The writings of another British scholar of the period, the historian E. P. Thompson, also impacted the development of Cultural Studies. Thompson's book *The making of the English working class* (1963) similarly celebrated working-class culture, interpreting it as a resistant response to urban industrialization and the homogenizing and hegemonic effects of capital-driven mass media.

Hoggart and Williams both engaged Marxism in their analyses of culture, in many ways echoing the concerns of Frankfurt School scholars such as Theodor Adorno and Max Horkheimer in their ideological critiques of mass culture as well as the approach of the French literary critic Lucien Goldman, who interrogated the relationship between textual forms and history. Marxist theory was a pivot for early British Cultural Studies; in particular, the Gramscian concepts of hegemony and ideology offered a framework for the analysis of cultural texts. But British Cultural Studies transformed Marxist thought in a variety of ways, especially by destabilizing the classic base/

superstructure model in which the economic circuits of production drive the development of artistic and cultural forms. Rather, British Cultural Studies understood the superstructure – culture – to be constitutive of society apart from any economic underpinning. Thus, British Cultural Studies broke with traditional Marxism to embrace a critical, revisioned Marxism. British Cultural Studies was also impacted by structuralism, particularly semiotics.

Hoggart's founding of the CCCS was instrumental in the development of the field. The CCCS served as an incubator for a number of scholars who became leading figures in Cultural Studies, publishing working papers, pamphlets, and books that are to this day considered canonical theoretical texts. Well-known CCCS scholars include **Paul Gilroy**, **Stuart Hall**, Dick Hebdige, Richard Johnson, Angela McRobbie, David Morley, Paul Willis, and Janice Winship. Not only did these theoreticians focus their work on the mass media, but they also incorporated a multimethodological approach to media analysis that became a hallmark of Cultural Studies, integrating ethnographic field observations, in-depth interviews, semiotics, critical textual analysis, and production studies into investigations of culture in society.

Controversies and challenges

Cultural Studies scholarship at the CCCS was marked by significant theoretical shifts that expanded and reshaped the field. In the late 1970s, Angela McRobbie published blistering feminist critiques of some of the male CCCS scholars' works, taking them to task for neglecting the role of gender in their analyses and for relegating girls' adolescence and cultural engagements to the sidelines. Her work brought gender politics to the forefront of Cultural Studies. On the heels of this development, in the early 1980s, the Race and Politics

Group, under the leadership of Paul Gilroy and influenced by the writings of Stuart Hall, turned its attention to the ideology of race in the construction of nation, a research agenda that led to the publication of *The empire strikes back* in 1982. The CCCS group redefined race as an open political construction – a shifting signifier whose meaning is contested and rearticulated vis-à-vis power and resistance; their work also paved the way for **postcolonial** theory in Cultural Studies. As Stuart Hall would later reflect in "Cultural Studies and Its Theoretical Legacies," these two interventions represented "real ruptures" in Cultural Studies that "reorganized the field in quite concrete ways."

Arguably because of these theoretical developments, the mighty triumvirate of class, gender and race has become a key trope in Cultural Studies, with the recognition of these concepts as mutually imbricated, dynamic social formations linked to power and resistance.

Another major theoretical development stemmed from interpretations of Stuart Hall's groundbreaking "Encoding/ Decoding" essay (1980). In this essay, Hall proposed a model of mass communication that parsed out the conditions of production of media messages, the meanings encoded into media texts, and the varying possibilities for audience interpretation, which he outlined as dominant, negotiated and oppositional readings of the texts. The implications of this model are that texts are polysemic (i.e. that they have multiple meanings), so that varied interpretations of a single text are possible. For the British communication scholar John Fiske (1986), the polysemy of media texts render them open to resistant readings by audiences. Such resistant reading has the potential to undermine the text's ability to perpetuate hegemonic ideologies and allows texts to be used to challenge dominant cultural norms and values. These theorizations opened up the field of audience studies and, from an emphasis on media texts as ideological apparatuses, Cultural Studies shifted to an emphasis on the active audience. The best-known works in this area are David Morley's *The nationwide audience* (1980), Ien Ang's *Watching Dallas* (1985), and Janice Radway's *Reading the romance* (1987), all of which used ethnographic studies of audiences to examine the relative power of the text versus the reader in cultural struggles over meaning. Polysemy and the extent of the audience's control over ideological meaning is still a topic of considerable debate in the Cultural Studies literature.

The notion of the active audience has been criticized by political economists as well as others who are skeptical about the valorization of audience agency and textual polysemy. During the 1990s, Cultural Studies became the site of intense controversy, as these and other concerns were voiced by a variety of critics in different disciplines and political spheres. Most famously, at a 1993 meeting of the International Communication Association, the political economist Nicholas Garnham excoriated Cultural Studies for its failure to recognize the capital imperatives underlying mass cultural production. A couple of years later, in 1995, the journal *Critical Studies in Mass Communication* published a "Colloquy" including essays by Garnham, Lawrence Grossberg, Graham Murdock, and others interrogating the divide between Cultural Studies and political economy. In the wake of these highly publicized and heated debates, attempts have been made to reconcile these paradigms; current scholarship acknowledges that Cultural Studies must necessarily be multiperspectival and multimethodological in order to adequately analyze the meanings and effects of culture in society. These understandings echo the "circuit model" of Cultural Studies outlined by CCCS director Richard Johnson (1986/87), in which he asserted that the study of culture

necessarily involves the analysis of the conditions of cultural production, the text/content, and audience reception, as well as the complex articulations among these elements.

Cultural Studies goes global

As influential as it was, it is important to note that the CCCS was not the sole site of scholarship in Cultural Studies, though it was the first institution dedicated to this discipline. Elsewhere in Great Britain – at the University of Leicester, the University of Leeds, the University of Glasgow, and London's Open University for example – similar scholarly developments were taking place, and the academic exchanges among scholars at these institutions mobilized the development of the field.

Media studies in the United States were also impacted by the British schools of thought. The social movements of the 1960s and 1970s, including the **civil rights** and black power movements, second-wave feminism, gay liberation, and (perhaps most importantly) anti-Vietnam War protests, gave rise to academic theorizations of **identity**, power, and politics. In 1982, the *Journal of Communication* published its landmark "Ferment in the Field" issue, in which the challenges posed by Cultural Studies to traditional mass communication scholarship were deliberated. US Cultural Studies is broad-ranging in its scope, dealing with a variety of social issues, historical configurations, and cultural artifacts. Certain strains of US Cultural Studies follow the "active audience" tradition of British Cultural Studies in their celebration of the construction of identities via popular culture; other strains are descended from the populist tradition of the Chicago School of sociology and tend to focus on the problems of community and common culture.

Worldwide, Cultural Studies has traced different trajectories in different national, social, and political contexts. Latin

American Cultural Studies is concerned with the roles of the media, the state, and popular culture in society as they pertain to identity formation and to globalization, migration, borderlands, and deterritorialization. Australian Cultural Studies is intensely involved with law and policy. African Cultural Studies focuses on national liberation and the relationship between state and nation, global and local. In India, postcolonialism and subaltern studies are hallmarks of Cultural Studies.

Cultural Studies proliferates internationally; it is a flexible, eclectic, and dynamic discipline with the potential to address virtually any contemporary topic. But its roots in political, economic, and social critique are central to its mission. It is an academic practice that, in Stuart Hall's words, "aims to make a difference in the world." [MGD]

Key readings

Agger, B. (1992). *Cultural studies as cultural theory*. London: Falmer Press.

Bennett, T., Martin, G., Mercer, C. & Woollacott, J. (1981). *Culture, ideology and social process*. London: Batsford Academic and Educational in association with the Open University Press.

Centre for Contemporary Cultural Studies. (1982). *The empire strikes back: Race and racism in 70s Britain*. London: Routledge.

Davies, I. (1995). *Cultural studies and beyond: Fragments of empire*. London: Routledge.

Durham, M. G. & Kellner, D. M. (2006). *Media and cultural studies: KeyWorks*, 2nd ed. Malden, MA: Blackwell

Ferguson, M. & Golding, P. (1997). *Cultural studies in question*. London: Sage.

Gitlin, T. (2003). *The whole world is watching*. Berkeley, CA: University of California Press.

Grossberg, L., Nelson, C., & Treichler, P. (Eds.). (1992). *Cultural studies*. London: Routledge.

Hall, S. (1980). Encoding/decoding. In S. Hall, D. Hobson, A. Lowe, & P. Willis (Eds.). *Culture, media, language: Working papers in cultural studies*. London: Hutchinson/CCCS, pp. 128–138.

——. (1980). The rediscovery of ideology: Return of the repressed in media studies. In Gurevitch, M., Bennett, T., Curran., J. & Woollacott, J. (Eds.), *Culture, society and the media*, pp. 52–86. London: Routledge.

——. (1992). Cultural studies and its theoretical legacies. In L. Grossberg, C. Nelson, & P. Treichler (Eds.), *Cultural studies*. New York: Routledge, pp. 277–294.

Hebdige, D. (1991). *Subculture: The meaning of style*. New York: Routledge

Hoggart, R. (1958). *The uses of literacy*. Harmondsworth, UK: Penguin.

Lewis, J. (2002). *Cultural studies: The basics*. London: Sage.

McRobbie, A. (1991). *Feminism and youth culture: From "Jackie" to "Just Seventeen"*. Boston, MA: Unwin Hyman.

Radway, J. (1991). *Reading the romance: Women, patriarchy, and popular literature*. Chapel Hill, NC: University of North Carolina Press.

Turner, G. (1996). *British cultural studies*, 2nd ed. London: Routledge.

Williams, R. (1976). *Keywords: A vocabulary of culture and society*. New York: Oxford University Press.

——. (1989). *Resources of hope: Culture, democracy, socialism*. Ed. R. Gale. London: Verso.

CULTURE Culture is a society's *crystallized intelligence* – the capacity to use skills, knowledge, and experience for problem solving. A culture's contents consist of a coalescence of shared ideas/practices that human groups construct to coordinate their goal-oriented activities under a set of physical and human-made constraints. Because all individuals of a group have some (albeit imperfect) knowledge of its culture, culture can provide this collection of interconnected individuals with a common frame of reference to make sense of the reality, coordinate their activities in collective living, and adapt to the external environment. According to this definition, a culture can be a national culture (such as Indian culture) or other forms of knowledge traditions (for example, a religion).

Cultural ideas/practices are passed down from one generation to another and are externalized in institutions (e.g. the Church), cultural legends, and myths (e.g. the miracles), scriptures (e.g. the Holy Bible), customs (e.g. Midnight Mass on Christmas Eve), rituals (e.g. baptism), cultural narratives (e.g. acts of the Apostles), the icons of the culture (e.g. the Crucifix), and external memory devices (e.g. pictograms, books, audiotapes, videotapes, CDs, DVDs, or the Internet). In short, three defining features of a culture are: (1) sharedness (but not diffuse sharedness), (2) historicity, and (3) externalization.

Most cultures are complex rather than homogenous. Disparate systems of beliefs and practices are often found in the same culture, with some being more popular than others. For example, a culture can esteem both secular values (the belief in progress, science, and logic) and spirituality.

Finally, cultures are dynamic; they change in response to changes in the physical and human ecology and are a result of innovation and intercultural contacts.

Societal functions of culture
Some ideas/practices wax and wane in human history, while others are transmitted across generations, are externalized in various public media, and become parts of the cultural tradition. The ideas/practices that survive the test of time are usually those that can address the fundamental needs of the society and its people.

Culture plays an important role in social control. People are often motivated by self-interest to exploit the public goods, and excessive exploitation of the public goods could threaten the survival of the group. For example, in Garrett Hardin's influential essay "Tragedy of the Commons," it is in the interest of each herdsman to outsmart his competitors by allowing his herds to consume more grass on the common pasture, in spite of the long-term benefits to the group if all herdsmen cooperate to allow the grass to grow back and avoid accelerated depletion of the common resource.

In part, culture is an evolved mechanism for preventing exploitative selfish behaviors. For example, the culture of honor condones violence against transgressors – defending the properties or the name of one's family is regarded as an honorable act, whereas failure to avenge a transgressor would bring disgrace to the individual. In the culture of face, people are expected to closely monitor their neighbors' and relatives' wrongdoings. Once a wrongdoing is detected, news of it will spread in the community, and the wrongdoer's reputation is ruined. In some variants of face culture, failures to monitor and prevent the wrongdoing of others who are under one's watch are punishable. In the culture of dignity, people are expected to have internalized the value of justice and to experience guilt when they engage in exploitative selfish behaviors.

Societies differ in how much they rely on honor, face, and dignity as social control mechanisms. For example, the culture of honor is a widely used social control mechanism in unstable settlements where law and order are poorly established (e.g. frontier settlements). The culture of face is widely used in stable settlements with established social hierarchy and low residential, job, and relational mobility. Mutual monitoring is practicable in such settlements because people tend to stay in the same community and are tied up in the same relational network throughout most of their lives. In contrast, industrial societies with high residential, job, and relational mobility tend to rely on the culture of dignity as a social control mechanism.

Psychological functions of culture

Ideas/practices that become parts of a culture are usually those that can also address people's basic psychological concerns effectively. For example, ideas/practices that can satisfactorily address the meaning of human existence despite its inevitable finitude (e.g. world religions) have a high chance of becoming a part of the culture. Likewise, ideas/practices that provide firm answers in uncertain situations (e.g. conventional wisdom) are also likely to be transmitted across generations. Patriotic ideas and practices that confer a sense of belongingness, group **identity**, and collective pride (e.g. core national values, patriotic practices, fictions and legends of national heroes) also tend to propagate in culture.

According to this analysis, people would increase their adherence to cultural norms when the quest for existential meanings, the craving for firm answers, and the need for collective pride/identity are evoked in the situation. Likewise, the motivation to follow cultural norms would decrease when these personal concerns are not salient in the situation. From this perspective, people are not passive recipients of cultural influences. Instead, they create and use cultural ideas/practices to address their psychological needs.

Responses to foreign cultures

The above analysis of the functions of culture has important implications for understanding people's reactions to other cultures. Culture is an important intellectual resource; it provides people with time-honored and conventionalized solutions to problems. Not surprisingly, people often use cultural norms as behavioral guides.

However, culture can also create mental sets. People who rely on conventionalized cultural perspectives to define, approach, and solve problems tend not to step back from the problem, question their current assumption, and look at the problems from new perspectives.

The cognitive constraints of culture on problem solving can be readily felt when people are exposed to alternative perspectives in foreign cultures. Extensive experiences with foreign cultures foster critical reflections on the limitations of one's own culture. In addition, such experiences can help to break mental sets, offer alternative perspectives on the problems, increase behavioral flexibility, and promote creativity.

Despite the intellectual benefits of **multiculturalism**, some people, because of their strong psychological attachment to their heritage culture, may refuse to accept or learn from other cultures. To these individuals, their heritage culture confers meanings in life and is the foundation of their self-identity. Thus, they may view infusion of foreign culture as a threat to established meanings and to their identity. When coupled with culturo-centrism (the belief that one's culture is the most important and superior to other cultures), this sentiment may turn into **xenophobia**, or the exaggerated fear that "heretic" foreign cultural ideas/practices may contaminate one's heritage culture and cause erosion of cultural identity. Xenophobia, in turn, can fuel emotional, exclusionary reactions to foreign cultures.

Cultural change

Cultures are constantly evolving despite motivated resistance from some people some of the time. Even in the absence of foreign cultural influence, cultural change may take place as a result of random variation and selective retention. A cultural idea/practice is seldom reproduced faithfully. Instead, random variations and selective retention of the original idea/

practice will emerge in the reproduction. An idea/practice that works well may be replaced by a variant that works slightly better, and the positively selected variant will propagate in culture. In short, selective retention and propagation of the positively selected variants is a process that gives rise to cultural evolution.

Cultural change may also occur when intercultural contacts bring into the society ideas/practices that can more satisfactorily solve society's problems and address people's psychological needs. Intercultural contacts often involve direct interactions with members of other cultures. However, with globalization and rapid development of electronic communication, ideas/practices from one culture can move to another through various media (e.g. Internet, music, advertisements, and products) without direct interactions. For example, some aspects of American culture move to other countries when Hollywood movies are shown there. Intercultural contacts may also take place when individuals move from one culture to another, as in the case of migration. Immigrants from foreign countries are often acculturated into the host country's dominant culture. However, they also carry with them their heritage cultures, and hence are also agents of cultural diffusion.

Cultural change involves modification, abolishment, and reestablishment of a society's formal and informal institutions and life practices. Once a new cultural idea is found to be valuable in coordinating collective life, it will be crystallized and integrated into various institutions and life practices. For example, in the Southern states of America, there is strong support from the legal institutions (e.g. gun control laws, self-defense laws) for the culture of honor and condoned violence.

In summary, culture is the crystallized intelligence of a human group. It consists of knowledge that is selected for reproduction because of its functional values to the society and the individual. At the individual level, navigating cultures involves a dynamic process of negotiating for better psychological benefits through adhering to the heritage culture and learning from other cultures. At the society level, culture is constantly evolving as a result of internal differentiation and cultural diffusion. [CC & ZL]

Key readings

Barth, F. (2002). An anthropology of knowledge. *Current Anthropology*, 43, 1–18.

Braumann, C. (1999). Writing for culture: Why a successful concept should not be discarded. *Current Anthropology*, 40, S1–S27.

Chiu, C-y. and Hong, Y-y. (2006). *The social psychology of culture*. New York: Psychology Press.

Lehman, D., Chiu, C.-Y., & Schaller, M. (2004). Psychology and culture. *Annual Review of Psychology*, 55, 689–714.

Rohner, R. P. (1984). Toward a conception culture for cross-cultural psychology. *Journal of Cross-Cultural Psychology*, 15, 111–138.

Wyer, R. S. Jr, Chiu, C-y., & Hong, Y-y. (2009). *Understanding culture: Theory, research, and application.* New York: Psychology Press.

DIASPORA In its broadest understanding, a diaspora is constituted of any group of individuals, usually defined by common national, ethnic or religious affiliation, who feel some common attachment to or identification with a place beyond the place in which they are living. Diaspora has captured the imagination of researchers in disciplines as varied as economics and literary theory, providing a clear focus for interests in hybrid **identities** and challenging accepted geopolitical understandings of a world neatly divided into mutually exclusive nation-states. As an alternative explanatory framework for a series of interconnected cultural, social, economic and political processes that occur at a global scale but go beyond the state system, it has become tremendously influential. Its popularity has developed in conjunction with broader public awareness of global interconnections at all levels and forms part of the powerful narrative of globalization. Diasporas have also attracted interest from governments, civil society and the private sector. As Khachig Tölölyan wrote in the inaugural editorial of the journal *Diasporas*, diasporas are "the exemplary communities of the transnational moment."

Yet, as the variety of contexts in which it is used and the relatively recent popularity of its modern usage suggest, diaspora is invested with a wide variety of meanings, not all of which are mutually compatible. Substantial disagreement remains, particularly around the potentially essentialist understanding of concepts of **race** or ethnicity inherent in diaspora, the nature of the place to which the group feels common attachment and the extent to which this is compatible with any attachment they may feel to the state in which they are resident and/or hold citizenship. The potential alternative that diaspora offers to the historical dominance of the nation state is undermined by the increasingly widespread use of diaspora to refer simply to individuals from a particular country, temporarily or permanently resident elsewhere (the "Turkish diaspora" as a new label for "Turkish emigrants," for example). The enthusiasm with which some states set about "building" diaspora as a way of boosting inward investment from emigrants is viewed by many as instrumentalizing the success of those who left. Culturally this process is analogous to nation building and may be similarly exclusionary, often portraying ethnically homogenous and frequently masculine versions of the state.

History and development of the diaspora concept

The term "diaspora" has been in existence for more than 2,000 years but its widespread use in social science only dates from the mid-1980s and its broader popularity in public policy and beyond only really since 2000. It is derived from the Greek verb *speiro*, to scatter and *dia* meaning thoroughly and first appears in the Septuagint, the Greek translation of Hebrew scriptures that became the Old Testament, referring to the Babylonian exile of the Jews from Palestine. Diaspora therefore became most strongly associated with the Jews, though it was always used to refer to other groups who were forced to flee an original "homeland" as a result of some major tragedy that became a significant element in their own understanding of who they were, such as African Americans, Armenians or Palestinians.

To an extent, the modern use of diaspora highlights a completely different form of community from this traditional understanding. The notion of diasporas arose in a world in which territorially based states had yet to become the norm; a vastly different political context from the present day. The modern tendency to equate diaspora with emigrant groups from particular nation-states reflects these changes. Yet part of the attraction of the term is historical, referring to a period before the nation-state and acting as a reminder that nation-states are social constructs, a context that is absent from the closely related term of transnational community. In this sense, the idea of diaspora is supportive of relatively recent trends in social theory that question the function of the nation-state and highlight the importance of marginality and hybridity. This leads on to a third explanation for the growth of interest in diaspora – in addition to changing realities and changing awareness of this reality, changing academic fashion inevitably plays a role. As diaspora was elevated to a popular and potentially empty buzzword, appropriate cautionary notes were sounded about the "hype of hybridity," to quote Katherine Mitchell's term.

The relatively restricted association of diaspora with the Jews, and to a limited extent some other groups, began to broaden in the mid-1980s, as diaspora was used more widely in the social sciences. In 1991, William Safran set out six criteria for diaspora that focus on the ongoing relationship between members of the diaspora and places of origin and residence. Safran broadened the understanding of diaspora beyond groups that attribute their initial dispersal to an original tragic event. In an influential study published in 1997 (2nd edition 2008), Robin Cohen set out a typology for this new broader range of diasporic groups, which includes virtually any group of dispersed individuals with a collective consciousness relating to an enduring relationship to their place of "origin." This is a position that now receives very broad acceptance across the social sciences.

The dangers of homogeneity and essentialism

Diaspora is now used extremely widely to refer to dispersed groups, often even in the absence of continued distant engagements, though some argue that an enduring relationship should be a minimal requirement for consideration as a diaspora. These groups may be defined by belonging to a particular nation state, such as the Moroccan, Filipino or Turkish diasporas, either through formal citizenship or as children of citizens who may not have taken up citizenship themselves. Alternatively, diaspora membership may involve sub-state or trans-state ethnic groups, such as the Tamil diaspora or the Berber diaspora or religious communities such as the Sikh diaspora. In these cases, the formal membership of citizenship is absent and the diaspora is a more loosely defined

institution, resembling a social movement. However membership is defined, it is now widely accepted that, within these over-arching characterizations, diasporas are highly heterogeneous collectives with substantial variations in the nature and degree of engagement, most obviously relating to gender but also class, age and sexual orientation. To emphasize this plurality, it is common for the term to be used in the plural to refer to, for example "Italian diasporas."

The centrality of ethnicity or nationality to the meaning of diaspora has raised concerns that there is a degree of essentialism inherent in the concept. The link between particular ethnic groups and certain "homelands" or "origins" to which they feel some attachment enhances these concerns, suggesting a fossilized understanding of identities as bound to particular locations. This is perhaps the most significant challenge to the idea of diaspora. Floya Anthias, for example, argues that diaspora relies on a static conception of **culture** and ethnicity and Dominique Schnapper is critical of the fact that its broad use has provided a more acceptable alternative to terms such as "racial and ethnic minorities." Those authors who counter these charges conceptualize diaspora in a slightly different way. In the influential book *Cartographies of Diaspora*, Avtar Brah argues that diaspora "places discourses of 'home' and 'dispersion' in creative tension, inscribing a homing desire while simultaneously critiquing discourses of fixed origins." **Paul Gilroy's** idea of the "changing same" carries the same idea of a dynamic tradition, justifying and valuing elements of an ethnically defined identity without recognizing it as fixed or immutable.

Government usage and changing meanings
Perhaps the clearest sign of the growing significance of diaspora is the new influence of the concept outside academia. In

August 2000, the Indian government established the High Level Committee on Indian Diaspora, one of the most significant indications of the important shift in the way governments, civil society and private companies relate to migrants and their families. The governments of Armenia, Somalia, Serbia and Georgia, amongst others, all have Ministers of Diaspora, private financial companies offer services to gain access to some of the estimated $350 billion annual global remittance transfer and large development agencies have established strategies to harness some of this potential for development activities. The financial power of diaspora is the chief motivating factor for this interest, but it is leading to new ways of engaging with diaspora groups, an increasing value of their status and, to some extent, an awareness of the difficulties they face, though this typically only applies to groups linked to established nation states.

The initial Greek third century BCE reference to diaspora found its way into the English language Old Testament as "outcast." This reflects the long-standing status of emigrant communities around the world, which have too often been seen as unwanted or surplus to requirement both by the countries from which they migrated and those in which they made new homes. The newly awakened government interest in diaspora groups is, of course, largely motivated by self-interest but it represents an important change in the symbolic value of many diasporas. This applied aspect of the theories of diaspora presents many problems for theoretical understandings, but it is challenging concepts of diasporas in new ways which will ensure the whole issue remains vital and dynamic. [MC]

Key readings

Anthias, F. (1998). Evaluating "diaspora": Beyond ethnicity? *Sociology*, 32, 557–580.

Brah, A. (1996). *Cartographies of diaspora*. London: Routledge

Braziel, J. E. (2008). *Diaspora: An introduction*. Blackwell: Oxford.

Carter, S. (2005). The geopolitics of diaspora. *Area*, 37, 54–63.

Clifford, J. (1994). Diasporas. *Cultural Anthropology*, 9, 302–338.

Cohen, R. (2008). *Global diasporas: An introduction* (2nd ed.). London: Routledge.

Schnapper, D. (1999). From the nation-state to the transnational world: On the meaning and usefulness of diaspora as a concept. *Diaspora*, 8, 225–253.

DISCRIMINATION Discrimination is the unfair treatment of an individual or group on the basis of their essentialist ascriptive factors (e.g. ethno-racial background, gender, age, class at birth). The act of discrimination involves excluding or rejecting an individual, or members of a group, from opportunities which are available to others.

Discrimination on the basis of ascriptive factors is regarded as a source of economic inefficiency, not to mention overtones of social injustice which challenge the normative principles of equality of opportunity. For instance, in a market economy model it is irrational to discriminate against a member of a racial or ethnic **minority** with higher productivity solely on the grounds of ascriptive factors, since this implies a failure to maximize profits.

For this reason, a theory of discrimination was developed arguing that discrimination occurred as a result of an employer's "taste for discrimination." In effect, employers were willing to pay a premium to avoid association with certain groups. Given that such firms will be operating at higher costs than those firms which do not practice discrimination, the discriminatory firm can only continue this practice if the practice is pervasive in the industry or if the firm does not face competition from competitors. Further, the theory suggests that discrimination would be greatest during periods of economic transition, when markets are less developed.

While the "taste for discrimination" theory has achieved prominence, the theory's view that the market is one of impersonal exchange is incomplete, since it underplays the social and psychological elements that are involved. When it comes to the employment of labor, it involves direct personal relations between the employee and employer, as well as among employees, which has the potential to add a discriminatory element. In this regard, to amply examine discrimination there must first be recognition that the concept can manifest itself through statistical and exclusionary dimensions.

The theory of statistical discrimination is an information-based theory which assumes that employers have imperfect information. In practice, statistical discrimination may occur at each stage of the hiring and promotion process, as an employer may fail to fully assess the relevant occupational abilities of a member of a group and make generalized assumptions about the value of their human capital. This can be operationalized in overlapping forms, with one example being the employer, consciously or not, perceiving an employee's ascriptive status as a proxy for lower quality of human capital.

Exclusionary discrimination, on the other hand, can be a more difficult proposition to prove and measure than statistical discrimination, given its predominantly anecdotal nature. Exclusionary discrimination occurs when a member of a group is impeded at a potential or current position due, not to their capacity, but to an external barrier that inhibits their growth. For instance, if an employer raises questions about an individual's racial or ethnic minority background in a fashion that may potentially reduce or eliminate that person's chances of being hired or promoted on the basis of their skills and experiences, this can potentially be a case of exclusionary discrimination. [RH]

Key readings

Allport, G. W. (1954). *The nature of prejudice*. Reading, MA: Addison-Wesley Publishers.

Arrow, K. J. (1998). What has economics to say about racial discrimination? *The Journal of Economic Perspectives*, 12(2), 91–100.

Becker, G. S. (1957). *The economics of discrimination*. Chicago: University of Chicago Press.

Feagin, J. R. (2006). *Systemic racism: A theory of oppression*. New York: Routledge.

Wellman, D. T. (1993). *Portraits of white racism*. New York: Cambridge University Press.

DOUBLE CONSCIOUSNESS Double consciousness refers to an understanding of oneself through the eyes of another, a doubling wherein an individual's sense of self is mediated by how he believes himself to be perceived. Discussed alternately as the gift of second sight and the burden of unreconciled strivings in a double life, double consciousness is inextricably linked with the figure of the **minority** in the majority **culture**. **W. E. B. Du Bois** explores this notion in *The souls of black folk* by both articulating its nature and exemplifying its reach. In addressing his white audience, his "Gentle Reader," Du Bois extends himself, perhaps on behalf of the **race**, to ease his majority audience into an understanding of the minority position. The reader may find his ameliorative language on the subject of American slavery troubling, for example, and worthy of intervention; however, his position simply makes clear what is afforded, and perhaps what is compromised, by this double sight.

This notion of a double life – in Du

Bois's case identifying as both a Negro and an American – and its unreconciled aims are thought to be a precursor to a damaging self-doubt with far-reaching social implications. The student of race and ethnic studies will recall the incisive inward critique, yet another outcome of double consciousness, in the work of figures from Du Bois to contemporary comedian and philanthropist Bill Cosby. In a 2004 address to the NAACP, Cosby made public his dissatisfaction with the state of Black striving. His speech, and the ensuing outcry, were the inspiration for Michael Eric Dyson's *Is Bill Cosby right? Or has the black middle class lost its mind?* Cosby's posture raised as much ire as did the failures he found in a post-*Brown* v. *Board* America, in no small part because his speech was seen by many as a capitulation, an attack without context. Regardless of where the contemporary student sides in the ongoing debate on Black striving, the very nature of the conversation, both public and aware of its audience, speaks to the lasting nature of this double consciousness.

The reader will find the self-questioning that follows this consciousness in many facets of life. In art and literature, the question of derivation and classification were prominent in the 1920s, as George Schuyler and Langston Hughes published pieces debating whether one could speak of Negro art as independent of American art. Richard Wright and Ralph Ellison are also noted for dealing with the unreconciled aims of this double life, as is contemporary novelist Percival Everett, showing the influence of his literary forebears in grappling with this issue. Indeed, stage performance is no different, as figures from Bert Williams to Dave Chappelle have struggled with the gift of second sight.

Ultimately, the quest for reconciliation must address the fundamental question: what does it mean to be an American? What is the place of the minority in the majority culture? The persistence with which "one feels his two-ness" gets right down to the essence of self-realization and, while the resolution may not yet be apparent, the reader can take solace in Du Bois's assurance that an awakening will one day come. The reader may consider just what that would mean for race as a concept, and all that has been made of it. [BM]

Key readings

Du Bois, W. E. B. (1995 [1903]). *The souls of black folk: Essays and sketches*. New York: Signet Classic.

——. (2009 [1924]). *The gift of black folk: The Negroes in the making of America*. Garden City Park, NY: Square One.

Dyson, M. E. (2005). *Is Bill Cosby right? Or has the black middle class lost its mind?* New York: Basic Civitas Books.

Ellison, R. (2002 [1952]). *Invisible man*. New York: Random House.

Everett, P. L. (2001). *Erasure*. Hanover, NH: University Press of New England.

Forbes, C. F. (2004). Dancing with "racial feet": Bert Williams and the performance of blackness. *Theatre Journal*, 56, 603–625.

Hughes, L. (1926, June 23). The negro artist and the racial mountain. *The Nation*, 122, 692–694.

Schuyler, G. S. (1926, June 16). The negro-art hokum. *The Nation*, 122, 662–663.

Wright, R. (1940). *Native son*. New York: Harper & Brothers.

ETHNIC CLEANSING (SEE GENOCIDE/ ETHNIC CLEANSING)

ETHNOCENTRISM Ethnocentrism is a term commonly used to describe a group-held belief that one's group is the center of everything, and that all others should be rated with reference to it. This term has been extended to understand in-group/

out-group violence, intolerance and the presence of **authoritarianism** in certain members of society. In the fields of sociology, urban politics, political behavior, and psychology much research has been conducted to determine the extent of ethnocentric attitudes in society.

Sumner held that groups in society are naturally in conflict and that peace between warring factions could be explained by the demands of war by the in-group on an out-group to maintain peace. This situation of open and constant warfare produces, within the in-group, sentiments of loyalty, superiority, and approval of distinct beliefs coupled with disdain, hatred, and contempt for the out-group. Extending the definition further, Sumner states that for group cohesion to last it must be well-disciplined; therefore discord within the in-group could result in expulsion. Thus, the creation of internal institutions that promote **solidarity** and similar belief structures to hold the group together against outside influences fosters attitudes of ethnocentrism.

By the mid-1900s, ethnocentrism had come to stand for individual's unsophisticated reactions to cultural differences. Research by Allport and the Berkley group confirmed this allegiance to in-group norms. Individuals exhibiting ethnocentric ideology tend to divide humanity into groups, and then determine whether he/she identifies or "counter-identifies" with them. If a group is counter-identified, the individual reacts by rejecting the out-group's legitimacy. Ethnocentric persons will express their disdain by criticizing the out-group in moralistic or pseudo-patriotic terms. They also tend to shift in-group/ out-group distinction depending on the issue being discussed. For example, studies in urban politics have shown that whites' attitudes towards issues related to civil rights have shifted over time from outright **discrimination** to specific grievances with social programs aimed at redressing social inequities. By asking respondents to state the degree to which they feel close to or far from other groups or individuals in society, researchers have been able to reliably identify anti-Semitism, racism and sexism, as well as ethnic discrimination in respondents and the traits connected to the formation of ethnocentric attitudes. These traits include: authoritarianism, egalitarianism, strict adherence to discipline, moral superiority, and intense feelings of group threat. [DCD]

Key readings

Adorno, T. W., Frenkel-Brunswik, E., Levinson, D. J., & Sanford, R. N. (1950). *The authoritarian personality*. New York: Harper.

Allport, G. W. (1954). *The nature of prejudice*. Cambridge, MA: Addison-Wesley.

Campbell D. T. & Levine, R. A. (1972). *Ethnocentrism: Theories of conflict, ethnic attitudes and group behavior*. New York: John Wiley and Sons.

Schuman, H., Steeh, C., Bobo, L., & Krysan, M. (1997). *Racial attitudes in America: Trends and interpretations*. Cambridge, MA: Harvard University Press.

Sumner, W. G. (1906). *Folkways: A study of the sociological importance of usages, manners, customs, mores and morals*. Boston, MA: Ginn.

ETHNOGENESIS Ethnogenesis refers to the creation of a new ethnic **identity**. It was not until the social construction of ethnicity began to replace primordialist or essentialist understandings that ethnogenesis became a topic of research. The primordialist or essentialist view of ethnic identity sees it a something that is just there, rooted in biological facts. In recent decades this approach has been replaced, for the most part, by social constructionist approaches. That is, understanding that what humans define as ethnic identity and/or **race** is socially constructed via historical, political, and cultural changes over time. To some this seems counterintuitive, but some thought reveals that it is not. Consider people who are citizens of the United States, often referred to as "Americans," both as an ethnic group and as a nationality. Before 1776 there were no "Americans," though many people who became "Americans" certainly were alive before 1776. The key point here is that ethnic definitions and boundaries are malleable and change through time. Often such changes are slow, so that ethnic identity "seems" primordial and unchangeable. In recent decades, ethnic identity and **identity politics** in general have become hotly contested issues. These conflicts highlight the mutability of ethnic identity.

If ethnicity is mutable, how do ethnic groups originate? There are many processes that lead to the formation of new ethnic groups and identities. These processes are called ethnogenesis. Briefly, there are several ways in which an ethnic group might originate. Merging or amalgamation of two or more groups into one group is one source. Mixing of various peoples through intermarriage is another source. Relative isolation of a group apart from its origin group can, given sufficient time, generate a new group. If a group takes up a special occupational niche, and again remains in it for sufficient time, it might come to be seen and to see itself as an ethnic group. Finally, a group might change its identity and name if it takes up a new occupation. This list is far from exhaustive, but does reveal many common paths to ethnogenesis.

These processes have occurred throughout history, but have been most common in zones of conquest, especially those that become frontier territories. Also, the timing of a group's acceptance of a new identity often does not coincide with the timing of outsiders' acceptance of the new identity. This can be a source of ethnic

conflict. Conversely, ethnic conflict can be a source of ethnogenesis. A few examples illustrate these processes.

Probably the most widely known instance of merging multiple groups into one is the emergence of the Native American or American Indian peoples as a single group. The merger began when Columbus mislabeled the **indigenous peoples** he first encountered. In the United States, over time, various Indian nations began to cooperate to pursue their rights. This led to the emergence of an "Indian" identity. This instance is especially interesting in that the "Indian" identity has not replaced individual Indian nation identities, but has added an additional layer of identity.

Other examples are groups, known by many names, but most often as "Maroons" composed of escaped African slaves and local indigenous peoples in the Americas. Both groups sought isolation: Africans to escape re-enslavement; Indian groups to avoid conflict and extermination. Over time, extensive interbreeding and intermarriage gave rise to a new group. Interestingly, the term "Maroon" emerged from the Spanish term for the color of iron ore, *cimarón*. The term was used to describe the color of these mixed background people, then came to mean runaway people, and eventually to mean very isolated, "lost" people.

Two other types of mixed background peoples are *Genízaros* and *Métis*. *Genízaros* are doubly interesting in that they formed from peculiar border processes at the northern edges of New Spain, which later became northern Mexico, and then American Southwest. *Genízaros* then later melded into the general population and "disappeared." Spanish settlers on the northern frontier were in the habit of taking indigenous women and children captive and raising them as servants within their communities. Gradually, these people formed their own communities since they were not fully accepted into Spanish society and, because of their long captivity, often could not return to their native or home communities. Some, through extensive military or other service, came to be accepted into Spanish society. After the United States seized northern Mexico in the Mexican–American War (1846–1848) and slavery and taking of captives was banned, no new *Genízaros* were formed, and they gradually blended into the general Hispanic population. The origin of the term *Genízaro* itself remains a matter of some dispute.

The *Métis* formed from the common marriages between European fur traders (typically French) and women in various First Nations. These marriages facilitated trade but also resulted from the usual range of reasons that people marry. At first, their offspring were viewed as "mixed" but eventually developed their own separate identity. This was, in part, because they were able to mix elements from European and Native **cultures** into a distinctively different culture and identity. Late in the twentieth century, the Canadian government recognized *Métis* as a separate **aboriginal** people.

Sometimes ethnicity comes to be associated with occupational specialization. This is a particularly interesting instance since individuals, families, or groups intentionally change identities when they change occupations. Most typically, this occurs along an ecological boundary that shifts, or over which people shift, due to climatic or political pressures. To the extent that such people give up one identity and replace it with another, this process can be seen as a type of ethnogenesis.

Ethnogenesis is often associated with ethnocide and culturicide. Ethnocide is the destruction of an ethnic identity, but not necessarily the culture; culturicide is the destruction of a culture, but not necessarily the ethnic identity. Either can occur with, or more often without, **genocide** – the

actual killing of members of the group. Clearly, ethnogenesis is a complex historical process. It needs to be studied in detail to understand any specific instance. While general description of ethnogenesis is difficult, it is not a rare occurrence. [TDH]

Key readings

Hall, T. D. (2000). Frontiers, ethnogenesis, and world-systems: Rethinking the theories. In T. D. Hall (Ed.), *A world-systems reader: New perspectives on gender, urbanism, cultures, indigenous peoples*, and ecology. Lanham, MD: Rowman & Littlefield, pp. 237–270.

Hill, J. D. (Ed.). (1996). *History, power, and identity: Ethnogenesis in the Americas, 1492–1992*. Iowa City: University of Iowa Press.

Hudson, M. J. (1999). *Ruins of identity: Ethnogenesis in the Japanese Islands.* Honolulu, HI: University of Hawaii Press.

Miller, D. H. (1993). Ethnogenesis and religious revitalization beyond the Roman frontier: The case of Frankish origins. *Journal of World History*, 4, 277–285.

Mulroy, K. (1993). Ethnogenesis and ethnohistory of the Seminole Maroons. *Journal of World History*, 4, 287–305.

EUGENICS In 1883, Francis Galton defined eugenics as "the study of agency under control that seeks to improve or impair the racial qualities of future generations either physically or mentally." Hence, it is possible to improve the quality of the human population by discouraging persons with genetic defects or undesirable traits from reproducing. This is referred to as negative eugenics. Positive eugenics, on the other hand, encourages reproduction by persons presumed to have inheritable desirable traits. Since the main purpose of eugenics was to enhance only the positive traits of the white race, positive eugenics must, therefore, occupy a prominent position. The emphasis of eugenicist discourse of racial preservations made it particularly desirable in the United States. The United States, from the beginning of its formation, promoted the idea of Anglo Saxon whites as superior. Blacks, other nonwhites, and ethnic groups, including Jews and Southern and Eastern Europeans, were viewed as hereditarily inferior.

The purpose of this entry is to examine race, ethnicity, and eugenics in America from the late nineteenth century until the end of the Second World War, when the eugenic movement, for reasons that will not be elaborated here, came to a standstill. In fact, the eugenicist discourse provided a social milieu in which racism, which already existed in the United States, could flourish. Racism cast ethnic groups, blacks and other nonwhites as "unfit" races and promotes unsubstantial notions of **white supremacy** and purity. Hence, in order to maintain the purity of the white race, eugenicists later determined who should and should not reproduce. As if this were not enough, the government implemented laws that restricted marriage between whites and nonwhites. In addition, the government's immigration laws constrained people of nonwhite races and ethnic backgrounds from entering the United States. Intense racism was intimately linked to the eugenicist movement and, as such, blacks, other nonwhites, Jews, and Southern and Eastern Europeans were looked upon as America's undesirables.

The beginning of eugenics in the United States

In 1859, Charles Darwin's *On the origin of species* was published. It drew attention to the inborn differences in the human species and other living forms, which can only be explained by natural selection. Put simply, the idea was that natural selection would end these differences by making it possible

for living forms to survive and reproduce successfully. Even though the survival of the fittest would necessarily entail an inhumane sacrifice of the unfit, it did not deter many scholars from being influenced by Darwinism. Galton for one, in 1869, published *Hereditary genius*, where he argued that great ability is hereditary. Also, in 1871, Darwin published *Descent of man*, in which he maintained that superior selection was important. In addition, it was important "to improve the race of man," Galton convincingly asserted in his essay, "Hereditary improvement." Improving "the race of man" (in this sense, the white race) was an idea that was warmly received in the United States. And, partly as a result, the first major federal immigration law, the Act of 1882, prohibited entry into the United States to any "lunatic, idiot, or any person unable to take care of himself or herself without becoming a public charge." At the end of the nineteenth century, many States followed the lead of Connecticut, which, in 1896, prevented anyone who suffered from certain mental and/or physical defects from marrying. This restriction on legal cohabitation provided fertile soil for the endorsement of eugenics.

In 1910, in Cold Spring Harbor, New York, the Eugenics Record Office opened. Charles B. Davenport, a eugenicist, was the Director. The beginning of the twentieth century marked the spreading of eugenics with the work of Davenport and Harry H. Laughlin, which continued the perpetuation and reinforcement of America's tradition of promoting white supremacy. Leaders such Woodrow Wilson and Theodore Roosevelt were supportive of eugenics. In 1907, Indiana had already adopted mandatory sterilization for certain individuals including the "insane, idiotic, imbecile or epileptic." And, even though this was a crime against humanity, for the purpose of eugenics, soon after, more than 37 States adopted a legislation that promoted mandatory sterilization. In 1927, in Virginia, in *Buck* v. *Bell*, the Supreme Court upheld the mandatory sterilization of Carrie Buck, an apparently "feeble minded" woman who was no longer capable of taking care of herself. Justice Oliver Wendell Holmes, in his ruling, stated that the interest of the state was to promote the purity of the white race in America. The idea was that "feeble minded" parents would, without a doubt, produce "feeble minded" children. *Buck* v. *Bell* declared mandatory sterilization in the United States to be constitutional. Furthermore, it was claimed to be ethical to kill children with severe disabilities as proposed by Foster Kennedy's "The problem of social control of the congenital defects – Education, sterilization, euthanasia," which was published by the *American Journal of Psychiatry* in 1942. Eugenics was to encourage only upper-class white men and women to reproduce in order to maintain a racially pure white race in America. More importantly, it was to promote the notion of Anglo-Saxon whites as inherently superior.

Eugenics and racism in America

Given that eugenics promoted the idea that Anglo Saxon whites were superior to all other races, their supremacy had to be legitimized. Those in **power**, as well as ordinary white Americans, voiced (orally and in writings) their contempt for nonwhites and ethnic groups. More importantly, America had to inoculate itself against racial pollution and promote the means, to use the words of the 1912 editorial title of *The world's works*, "To Improve the Race" – meaning the white race. In fact, there was a decreasing birthrate of the pure white stock. Amongst America's elite, even though white racial purity was already defined in existing State laws, banning interracial marriage (miscegenation laws), there was a public fear that this racially pure white stock would be out-bred by the inferior nonwhite and ethnic groups. As popular fears about the decline of the white stock gathered strength, those in power had to come up with a solution to preserve America's racial purity. Restriction on immigration was among the many solutions. The Immigration Act of 1924 restricted immigration from Southern and Eastern European countries and Asia. Other solutions to promote the purity of the white race included anti-miscegenation laws and mandatory sterilization programs. However, these discriminatory laws and programs did not solve the problem of the demise of the purely white race or, to use Madison Grant's 1916 book title, *The passing of the great race*. Grant's book had inspired the creation of Adolph Hitler's Nazi Germany. On several occasions, Hitler had referred to this book as his "bible."

The demise of the pure white race was labeled as "race suicide" by Roosevelt. In fact, Davenport and his colleagues were burdened by the problem of what to do about "race suicide." In an attempt to deal with "race suicide," the elite worked towards encouraging upper-class white women and men to reproduce. This racially pure America filtered through a huge part of the twentieth-century American culture. And those eugenicists whose preoccupation was centered on race found solace in Gregor Mendel's law on heredity, which he developed in 1865, to put forward the argument that certain traits, such as criminality, pauperism, and intelligence, were passed down from one generation to another.

For these eugenicists, however, it was certain individuals and social groups, including blacks, Asians, **Latinos**, Jews, and Southern and Eastern Europeans who had inherited these undesirable traits. Calvin Coolidge, who was then the President of the United States, put forward the idea that white purity ended when whites mixed with blacks and other nonwhite races. On March 20, 1924, Virginia, for example, implemented the Racial Integrity Act that provided for the illegality of marriage between a white and a nonwhite person. And in situations where an offspring was produced through this union of white and nonwhite, especially blacks, the child was considered to be black, and he/she suffered the oppression that was associated with blackness unless that child passed for white. Nonetheless, the "one-drop" rule legally determined that a person was black. It was not until 1967, in *Loving* v. *Virginia*, that the Supreme Court overturned this Act and declared it unconstitutional. In addition, the Immigration and Restriction Act of 1924, which provided quotas for people entering the United States, was clearly racist in its orientation.

The future of eugenics in America depended on the discriminatory practice of heredity. The eugenics movement flourished until the end of the Second World War, when the practice of eugenics was abandoned. However, the idea of whites as the superior race continues to impact the thinking of American scholars even to this day. As in the 1920s, when the use of test scores was employed by the eugenicists to draw negative conclusions about immigrants, today, test scores are used as a measure to test the intelligence of the assumed inferior groups. Richard J. Herrnstein and Charles Murray, *The bell curve: Intelligence and class structure in American life*, is a case in point. Using statistical evidence (IQ test scores), they attributed certain social ills such as crimes, homelessness, illiteracy, and poverty as direct markers of intelligence. Like the eugenicists of the early twentieth century in America, Herrnstein and Murray see intelligence as genetically based. [SOP]

Key readings

Black, E. (2007). *War against the weak: Eugenics and America's campaign to create a master race*. Morrisville, NC: Dialog Press.

Boas, F. (1916). Eugenics. *The Scientific Monthly*, 3, 471–478.

Currell, S. & Godell, C. (Eds.). (2006). *Popular eugenics: National efficiency and America's mass culture in the 1930s*. Athens, OH: Ohio University Press.

Fields, J. A. (1911). The progress of eugenics. *The Quarterly Journal of Economics*, 26, 1–67.

Grant, M. (1916). *The passing of the great race*. New York: Charles Scribner's Sons.

Hankins, F. M. (1931). Civilization and fertility: Has the reproduction of Western people declined? *Eugenics Review*, 23, 145–150.

Hasian, M. A. (1996). *The rhetoric of eugenics in Anglo-American thought*. Athens, GA: University of Georgia Press.

Herrnstein, R. J. & Murray, C. (1994). *The bell curve: Intelligence and class structure in American life*. New York: Free Press.

Kennedy, F. (1942). The problem of social control of the congenital defects – education, sterilization, euthanasia. *American Journal of Psychiatry*, 99, 13–16.

Kevles, D. J. (1985). *In the name of eugenics: Genetics and the use of human heredity*. New York: Knopf.

Kline, W. (2001). *Building a better race: Gender, sexuality, and eugenics from the turn of the century to the Baby Boom*. Berkeley, CA: University of California Press.

Kühl, S. (1994). *The Nazi connection: Eugenics, American racism, and German socialism*. Oxford: Oxford University Press.

Pernick, M. S. (1996). *The black stork: Eugenics and the death of "defective" babies in American medicine and motion pictures since 1915*. New York: Oxford University Press.

Thompson, W. S. (1924). Eugenics as viewed by a sociologist. *Monthly Review*, 18, 11–25.

Yule, U. G. (1920). *The fall in the birth rate*. Cambridge, MA: Cambridge University Press.

FRANTZ **F**ANON Though his principal occupation was psychiatry, Frantz Fanon was an author and revolutionary best known for his writings about the psychopathology of colonization and issues surrounding decolonized subjects – primarily Africans colonized by the French. Fanon himself was born in one of these colonies (Martinique) and did much of his work in France and other French colonial hubs.

In the summer of 1960, a few months after he was appointed Ambassador to Ghana for the Provisional Algerian Government, Fanon took a trip through Mali on a mission to set up a possible base for a supply line to the Algerian revolution. He wrote that the work he had chosen was "to put Africa in motion, to cooperate in its organization, in its regrouping, behind revolutionary principles." He also warned, at the moment of Africa's decolonization, that the greatest threat to its liberation was not simply external. Six months later, Patrice Lumumba, the first prime minister of newly independent Congo, was murdered. In just a few years Africa's liberation had gone from "no longer being in future heaven" (as he declared in *A dying colonialism* [1959]) to becoming a "misadventure." Yet Fanon's concern with such a development was not new; indeed, this was the focus of his first book, *Black skin white masks* (1952), which engaged major schools of European thought in a quest to disalienate the Black from the internalization of anti-Black racism and inferiority complexes.

Fanon was born on July 20, 1925, in Fort-de-France on the Caribbean island of Martinique. Aimé Césaire was one of his high school teachers. In 1943, he escaped Martinique, joined the free French forces and ended up fighting in North Africa and on the European front, where he was cited for bravery. After working on Césaire's Fort-de-France election, he went to Paris in 1947, leaving shortly thereafter to study medicine in Lyon. He completed his psychiatry studies with François Tosquelles, who was associated with sociotherapy. In Lyon he also attended lectures by Merleau-Ponty and read major works on phenomenology, including those by the young Marx.

Wary of social and economic realities, Fanon attempts in *Black skin* to find a "psychoanalytic interpretation" of the "Black problem." He engages Freud, Jung and Adler and employs Merleau-Ponty and Sartre to speak of the lived experience of the Black under the racial gaze. In a racist society, the Black is not; the Black is a problem, an object walled in by Blackness caricatured, for example, by the constantly smiling African on the box of Banania cereal. In France, Fanon himself became a phobogenic object, a product of the racial gaze looking out from the depths of its **culture** and history. Thus, Fanon's analysis focuses on the doubleness of the Black experience in a racist world, grounded by the "Black myth" where the individual is a **representation** of the naturalized "fact of Blackness." That is, the Antillean is French, but suffers a complete dissociation upon being perceived as Black and thus not wholly French. Confronted with this dilemma, Fanon turned critical of Hegel's dialectic (which, among other qualities presumes dialogue between individuals sharing similar status and acceptance as interlocutor) arguing that when "**race**" is added to the equation there is no reciprocity between master and slave. He also became critical of Sartre's "dismissal" of negritude as a passing stage of the dialectic and moved the focus of his analysis from the individual to the social, and from the abstract universalism of European liberal humanism to the poetics and lived experience of Black consciousness. Fanon employs a dialectic that is more open-ended and less synthetic – an untidy movement through negation. He concludes *Black skin* with a quote from Marx's *Eighteenth Brumaire* and with an imperative to experience the struggle for freedom.

In early 1954, Fanon took up an appointment at Blida-Joinville Hospital in Algiers. By the end of the year, the Algerian revolution had begun. Fanon continued to see patients, while secretly joining the national liberation front (FLN), becoming close to the leaders of the radical wing who formulated the Soummam Platform. As the French employed more torture techniques during the Battle of Algiers, Fanon treated the torturers by day and the tortured at night. This split life became untenable, and he resigned in December 1956, declaring that Algeria had become a nonviable society because it systematically dehumanized Algerians. He moved, by way of France, to Tunis and became an editor for the FLN paper *El Moudjahid*. His writings for the paper are collected in the posthumous *Toward the African Revolution*. During this time he presented papers at two congresses of the Black Writers and Artists.

If *Black skin* is an analysis of the social psychopathology of colonization, *The wretched of the earth* (1961) is a phenomenology of decolonization. They are different books, born from different problems and experiences in different contexts, but the methodology of each is similar. If, in *Black skin*, Fanon's dialectic unfolds from the Manicheanism of racism, in *The wretched* Fanon's dialectic unfolds from the Manicheanism of colonialism. While *The wretched* begins with a discussion of colonialism's violence and the necessary counter-violence of anti-colonialism, Fanon's overall concern is with the direction of the anti-colonial movement. If the anti-colonial movement exhausts itself by taking over positions of **power** vacated by colonialism, national liberation, he feared, would create a vacuum which would ultimately be filled by a re-emergent, colonially crafted ethnic and racial politics. National consciousness is, thus, not the goal of the struggle but the form in which the struggle develops. But such a development comes by humanizing the movement, by shifting the ground of debate away from **nationalist** elites to the wretched of the earth, because only they can concretely understand colonialism's truth.

The nationalist elite threatens national liberation because, at the crucial moment of liberation, they will fail to create anything new; alternatively, educated elites reduce themselves to militant functionaries who silence oppositional voices. Fanon concludes *The wretched* with a plea to foster new beginnings, encouraging their own agency in producing their own liberation.

In late 1960, Fanon was diagnosed with leukemia. Traveling to the Soviet Union for treatment, he returned to Tunis and dictated *The wretched* to his wife, Josie, and delivered a part of it at lectures to officers of the Algerian National Liberation Army. He went for further treatment in the United States but died at Bethesda naval hospital. Since his death, Fanon has become one of the most important anti-colonialist activist-thinkers of the twentieth century. Embraced as a founder of **postcolonial** studies, his work also continues to influence liberation movements in Africa and the Americas. [NCG]

Key readings

Cherki, A. (2008). *Frantz Fanon: A portrait*. Ithaca, NY: Cornell University Press.

Fanon, F. (2008). *Black skin, white masks* [*Peau noire, masques blanc*]. (R. Philcox, Trans.). New York: Grove Press.

——. (1965). *A dying colonialism* [*L'An Cinq de la Révolution Algérienne*]. (H. Chevalier, Trans.). New York: Grove Press.

——. (2005). *The wretched of the earth* [*Les damnés de la terre*]. (R. Philcox, Trans.). New York: Grove Press.

——. (1967). *Toward the African Revolution* [*Pour la Révolution Africaine*]. (H. Chevalier, Trans.). New York: Grove Press.

Gibson, N. C. (Ed.). (1999). *Rethinking Fanon: The continuing dialogue.* Amherst, New York: Humanity Books.

——. (2003). *Fanon: The postcolonial imagination.* Oxford: Polity Press.

Gordon, L. R., Sharpley-Whiting, T. D., & White, R. T. (Eds.). (1996). *Fanon: A critical reader.* Oxford: Blackwell.

Sekyi-Otu, A. (1996). *Fanon's dialectic of experience.* Cambridge, MA: Harvard University Press.

Sharpley-Whiting, T. D. (1998). *Frantz Fanon: Conflicts and feminisms.* Lanham, MD: Rowman & Littlefield Publishers Inc.

GENOCIDE/ETHNIC CLEANSING The most violent and savage offenses a government can perpetuate against its own people are genocide and ethnic cleansing. Genocide is the destruction of a nation or ethnic group. The 1948 Convention on the Prevention and Punishment of Genocide defines the core of genocidal crimes, in Article 2, as killing members of the group, causing serious bodily or mental harm to members of the group, and deliberately inflicting on the group conditions of life calculated to bring about physical destruction in whole or in part. In addition to destruction of a people by mass extermination, as was true for European Jews under the Nazi regime in the Second World War, genocide is also any intentional program that destroys the foundations of life of a people and kills them gradually (for example, food deprivation).

Ethnic cleansing is the use of force or intimidation by a government to expulse members of an ethnic group, **race**, nationality or religion from a territory, usually their homeland. It used to be called "mass deportation." The goal of perpetrators is to render the territory ethnically homogeneous for the majority or the dominant group. Expulsions also occur when rival ethnic groups lay claim to their own state over the same territory. During ethnic cleansing, many criminal offenses are committed, such as massacres, killings, rape, robbery, destruction of cultural property, and other crimes against humanity. These crimes create panic and cause mass flight by the target population. Such crimes also occur during genocides prior to the mass killings themselves.

The perpetrators of genocide and ethnic cleansing are a state or regime; the victims are typically racial, national, ethnic, or religious minorities. Episodes of limited violence against these groups are massacres, pogroms or ethnic riots. Political purges with large loss of life, as in the Chinese Cultural Revolution under Mao and Soviet purges under Stalin, had millions of victims but lacked the genocidal intent to destroy an entire nation or ethnic group.

Genocide and ethnic cleansing in the twentieth century and later are not rare. The most destructive genocides have been the Armenian genocide (0.5 to1.5 million victims), the Nazi genocide against the Jews (the Holocaust, 5.7 million), the Cambodian (1–2 million) and the Rwandan (500–800,000) genocides. Prominent cases of ethnic cleansing in the twentieth century are the mutual expulsions of Greeks and Turks in the early 1920s, the mass deportations of Chechens, Crimean Tatars, and other groups in the Soviet Union under Stalin, the expulsion of 12–15 million German ethnics from Poland, the Baltics, Czechoslovakia and Yugoslavia at the end of the Second World War, expulsion and mass killings of Muslims and Hindus during the partition of India, expulsion of Palestinians and mass flight during the Israeli war of independence, the expulsion of French settlers from Algeria after the war for independence, multiple ethnic cleansings during the Yugoslav wars of the 1990s, and ethnic cleansing in the South Sudan and Darfur by the Sudanese government. Scholars' estimates of victims, based on research, are disputed by adversaries and advocates who inflate or minimize numbers in blame and recrimination accusations.

Genocides and ethnic cleansing are not spontaneous. Perpetrator regimes plan and organize them by mobilizing the full resources of the state. These regimes promote a racist and extreme **nationalist** ideology of ethnic or national domination over alleged inferior and subversive minorities which are blocking the glorious realization of a homogeneous nation state. State propaganda manipulates perceived threats, fears and hostility against **minority** targets, vilifies and dehumanizes the target groups, and justifies removing the legal protections and normal cultural restraints against killing innocent civilians. Extreme measures are chosen by perpetrators after the failure of milder repression to achieve domination. Proximate causes that increase the risk of genocide and ethnic cleansing are the threat of armed invasion in wartime or insurgency by disaffected minorities.

Victims in the target groups include adult males, children, women, old people, religious and medical workers: no one is exempt. Places of religious worship, schools, books, monuments and other cultural artifacts are destroyed for the purpose of erasing the target groups from the collective memory of the perpetrators. The perpetrators are led and organized by regime and state leaders, and assisted by lawyers, bureaucrats, military officers, academics, media professionals and religious leaders. The actual killers and ethnic cleansers are young men and adult males, who are recruited, indoctrinated and organized into armed units by the regime, and possess distinctive names and uniforms, symbols and privileges. They are assisted by the regular army and the police. In some cases, like the Rwanda genocide, neighbors and fellow villagers are organized into extermination bands by the regime. These killers are largely ordinary men, considered normal by their peers and by the psychiatric profession. Their reasons and justifications for violence against innocent civilians range from obedience to authority, conformity to peers, hatred of the targets, ideological fervor to fear and profit. Bystanders are principally classified as three groups: regime supporters who approve of the mass killings and expulsions; opponents who are intimidated and silenced; and confused people who are either apathetic or go along with the authorities. A small number of "good Samaritans" take great personal risks to help victims hide or escape, but their numbers and means are limited and their overall impact slight.

In the aftermath of genocide and ethnic cleansing, the authorities and much of the public in the perpetrator state evade responsibility: they deny that it happened, assert that the number of victims is vastly exaggerated, insist they were victims as well, accuse the victims of starting mass violence, and claim self-defense. Denials are affirmed despite overwhelming evidence from international criminal trials, the exhuming of mass graves and the testimony of survivors. Some killers are glorified as saviors of the nation and treated as heroes. School books and the media ignore these events or falsify the historic record.

Because diplomacy alone seldom deters or stops mass killings, governments (referred to as the "international community") and NGOs have constructed a body of international law for legitimizing humanitarian intervention against states that massively oppress and persecute their own people violently. Such intervention by the UN or by external states is inhibited by the right of states to sovereignty and territorial integrity under Article 2 of the UN Charter. Nevertheless, under Chapter 7, if a conflict presents a "threat to international peace and security," the UN Security Council can decide to intervene, for example by imposing sanctions or sending peacekeeping forces to protect victims. The permanent members of the Security Council can veto UN action and often have partisan interests in ethnic conflicts that override humanitarian intervention. They do not wish to have precedents set that might apply to their own and their allies' ethnic problems. Domestic public opinion reacts negatively to casualties of its nationals for peacekeeping in distant places. Economic sanctions imposed on perpetrators are often evaded. Protection of civilians, aid convoys, safe havens and refugee camps necessitates interposition of peacekeeping forces between attacking armies, paramilitaries, criminal gangs and potential victims and humanitarian aid workers, with risks to the protectors. Endless diplomacy becomes a cover for avoiding effective measures to stop mass violence. The default option of the international community is to concentrate on relief efforts for the victims in refugee camps, provide them with food, medical and other services, and hopefully also protection against aggressors, until some political solution is achieved.

The recent history of humanitarian intervention is disheartening: failure to stop the Rwanda genocide; failure to stop ethnic cleansing in the Yugoslav wars, despite the presence of thousands of UN peacekeepers, a NATO air war and troops in Kosovo; persistent failures in the Congo and in Darfur. The Cambodian genocide was stopped by the Vietnamese army, not the UN. However, some UN interventions in civil wars, as in Namibia and Mozambique, did eventually bring them to an end, thus stopping the killing of civilians and enabling refugees and displaced persons to return home. Plans for a UN-sponsored rapid reaction military force for crisis intervention and deployment when mass violence is imminent have not progressed beyond the talking stage.

Another response to genocide and ethnic cleansing by the international community is to bring the perpetrators to justice in international criminal tribunals (for the former Yugoslavia, for Cambodia and for Rwanda) and in the International Criminal Court. Their function is to administer justice and to establish historical truth of these crimes in the face of denial. Such international trials are expensive, take years, and try mostly top political, military and paramilitary leaders. The vast majority of lower-level perpetrators who killed and cleansed, rather than those who organized and ordered these crimes, have to be tried in state courts, if they are tried at all. Whether these international courts and trials will have a deterrent effect on ethnic cleansing and genocide remains to be seen. As with diplomacy, UN sanctions and peace intervention, the courts' effectiveness depends on cooperation from states that are reluctant to surrender offenders, and sometimes actively help them to evade justice. [AO]

Key readings

Chirot, D. & McCauley, C. (2006). *Why not kill them all? The logic and prevention of mass political murder.* Princeton, NJ: Princeton University Press.

Fein, H. (1979). *Accounting for genocide.* New York: Free Press.

Mann, M. (2005). *The dark side of democracy: Explaining ethnic cleansing.* New York: Cambridge University Press.

Naimark, N. (2001). *Fires of hatred: Ethnic cleansing in the 20th century.* New York: Cambridge University Press.

Valentino, B. (2004). *Final solutions: Mass killings and genocide in the 20th century.* Ithaca, NY: Cornell University Press.

Weiss, T. G. (2007). *Humanitarian intervention.* Cambridge, UK: Polity Press.

HISPANIC (SEE LATINO/HISPANIC)

HUMAN GENOME DIVERSITY PROJECT The Human Genome Diversity Project (HGDP) was created in 1992 as a consortium of mainly molecular biologists, geneticists and biological anthropologists. The project was conceived as a means to study human genetic diversity by collecting DNA samples from approximately 500 different populations. The HGDP's focus on genetic diversity was developed by the project's principal figures – geneticists Luca Cavalli-Sforza, Mary-Claire King, Charles Cantor, Bob Cook-Deegan, the late Allan Wilson and **population geneticist** Kenneth Kidd – who were critical of what they perceived to be the limited scientific parameters of the multi-billion dollar Human Genome Project (HGP) launched in the United States in October 1990.

Sponsored by the National Institute of Health (NIH) and the Department of Energy (DOE), the HGP proposed to chart the roughly 100,000 genes that make up the human genome. The HGDP scientists, however, argued that the HGP was utilizing genetic sampling that was focused on largely white, northern populations, thereby betraying an **ethnocentric** bias by being too narrowly focused on Anglo-European groups. Seeking to correct this, HGDP proponents felt that a broader sampling of ethnic populations would not only better the project's goal to combat common human diseases, but also help anthropologists reconstruct the story of human evolution, as well as patterns of human migration across the globe. In a letter to *Genomics* (1991: vol. 11: 490–491), Cavalli-Sforza and his colleagues proposed that a team of researchers worldwide should be established to collect DNA samples from a wide variety of human populations, and that researchers should extract blood samples from 15–25 individuals in each population to be preserved in permanent cell lines for further research and study.

Subsequent to the *Genomics* letter, the idea of an HGDP attracted the support of the Human Genome Organization (HUGO) and received financial assistance from the US government to fund three planning workshops in 1992 and 1993. The workshops focused on collection methods, sampling from isolated genetic populations that were in danger of "disappearing," and ethical and human rights issues related to conducting the research. In the second workshop, held at Pennsylvania State University in October 1992, HGDP geneticists, anthropologists and linguists identified 722 indigenous populations from around the world that they believed constituted highly desirable candidates for genetic study.

In September 1993, the HGDP held what became its inaugural meeting in Alghero, Sardinia and, in the same year, established an International Executive Committee along with two standing committees (one on ethics and the other on informatics). As the HGDP began to encourage member countries to establish regional committees, groups began to form in North America, South America, Europe, Africa and Oceania. The North American Executive Committee was among the first regional boards to form and its original 13-member directorate consisted of anthropologists, geneticists, a law school professor and a sociologist.

The HGDP surfaced at a time when bio and genetic technologies were becoming highly politicized, especially in terms of intellectual property rights and gene-patenting. As a result, when the HGDP released its list of desirable genetic populations to the public, it generated considerable controversy as well as opposition. One of the most vocal opponents to the HGDP was the Rural Advancement Foundation International (RAFI) – a Canadian-based NGO that had, throughout its 20-year history, forcefully opposed the commercial exploitation of Third World plant and animal resources. RAFI's adverse reaction to the list was immediate and marked. Noting that many of the populations on the HGDP list were peoples who had suffered any one of a number of social ills at the hands of Western colonialism, RAFI accused the HGDP of engaging in "bio-piracy" and denounced scientists who were complicit with commercial efforts to "mine" indigenous communities for raw materials, which now included their DNA. RAFI quickly disseminated the HGDP population list over the Internet to many of the groups specified in the document, calling it a "hit list." As a result, RAFI was quickly supported by several other activist coalitions and widespread opposition to the project (re-labeled by some as "the Vampire Project") ensued.

Many HGDP organizers were initially caught off guard by the negative response of various non-governmental organizations. In 1993, RAFI began to publicize several cases of gene patents filed on the DNA of indigenous persons, including cell-lines derived from a Guaymí woman in Panama and a Hagahai man in Papua New Guinea. Despite protests by members of the North American Regional Committee, the HGDP was linked to these examples of gene-patenting and was widely condemned by civil society organizations. Additionally, an often supercilious and defensive attitude adopted by some the HGDP scientists toward the NGOs fuelled further opposition. In February 1993, partly in response to widespread criticism, the North American Committee held a workshop on social and ethical issues related to the project's goals and came up with a set of guidelines. In 1996, after further discussion, the North American Committee posted a 15,000-word "Model Ethical Protocol" on its website, outlining procedures for collecting DNA samples and introducing the concept of "group consent." Not all the regional HGDP committees adopted the protocol, and critics continue to argue that the HGDP

remained inadequate in a variety of areas, including clarity over the relationship between HGDP research and the commercialization of results. In 1996, a special committee that included three ethicists (George Annas, Eric Juengst and Katherine Mosley) was formed to review the HGDP and evaluate whether or not the project should go forward with government funding. The committee's report, released in 1997, was in many respects highly ambiguous and failed to offer an unequivocal verdict on the project. Partly owing to the controversy it generated, HGDP research stalled during the 1990s and was widely criticized by anthropologists – many of whom connected their critique of the HGDP to broader concerns about the relationship between contemporary forms of racism and geneticized discourses.

Despite the many setbacks that the HGDP has faced and the political controversy that it has generated, its research on human population genetics has continued, albeit in a somewhat low-key fashion. The HGDP continues to be overseen by HUGO and is currently housed at Stanford University's Morrison Institute for Population and Resource Studies. Currently, an unspecified number of laboratories located around the globe contribute cell-lines to a repository known as HGDP-CEPH located in Paris, France, and the Centre d'Etude du Polymorphism Humain maintains the samples. [HC]

Key readings

Cunningham, H. (1998). Colonial encounters in postcolonial contexts: Patenting indigenous DNA and the Human Genome Diversity Project. *Critique of Anthropology*, 18(2), 205–233.

——. (2004). Nations rebound? Crossing borders in a gated globe. *Identities*, 11(3), 329–350.

——. (2009). Of genes and genealogies:

Contesting ancestry and its applications in Iceland. In S. Bamford and J. Leach (Eds.), *Genealogy beyond kinship: Sequence, transmission, and essence in ethnography and social theory.* Oxford: Berghahn.

Scharper, S. B. & Cunningham, H. (2006). The genetic commons: Resisting the neo-liberal enclosure of life. *Social Analysis,* 50(3): 195–202.

IDENTITY Identity has multiple meanings and multiple values. Identity is not only about who we are and how we see ourselves, but also how others see us and how we see others seeing us. Such a position means that, at any given time, we are carrying multiple identities and at each social encounter or action a part of our identity may change, whereas the core may remain the same. For example, a male student at a university, while lecturing other students, is a male lecturer. On finishing his activity his identity shifts back to being a student but his maleness does not necessarily change. Some aspects of identity are visible, such as gender, **race** and biological features, but others may remain hidden, such as sexual orientation. Religious identity may become visible only if certain symbols reflecting a religious proclivity are worn, such as a turban or a cross. Identity, by and large, remains a social construct. Identity is often related to the creation of the **other**: all of us carry an identity in response to the other. For example, male is opposite to the female, older is opposite to the younger, black and white are opposites and often in clinical settings this becomes a major problem in trying to identify an individual. There are cores of identity that are solid and remain the same, such as age and gender, whereas others may shift according to acculturation, etc.

Social psychology of identity: who am I?
Every individual develops a sense of identity that is usually multi-dimensional.

However, there is a hierarchy within this complex sense of individuality and this may differ from how others view the person. A Hispanic female doctor, working in New York, who is a mother of three may be identified by her various roles by others; but, when asked, she might identify herself primarily as a good Catholic. A sense of identity starts to develop from an early age by virtue of one's gender and associated physical and psychological make-up, as well as social and cultural environment. Some features of identity may come naturally or instinctively, while others are attributed and then accepted. These forms may not always fit well together and could bring about internal conflict, especially when they differ from societal expectations. This has a great bearing on individuals' mental health and, if unresolved, may cause a significant amount of continuing personal and social distress. On the other hand, this could also give a person a strong sense of individuality and resolve. Once formed, the main sense of self remains generally intact while other aspects evolve, reflecting changes occurring in one's personal life and aging process.

Religious identity
Religion continues to play a central role in the social, personal and spiritual part of many people's lives. Unlike racial identity, which physically distinguishes people, religious identity is less overt. Religious identity is not biologically determined and so is a social construct. Persons belonging to any given religion may choose to express themselves in a way (for example, dress codes) that distinguishes them from others. Within a religious community this may be a means of conveying a sense of community, cohesion and identity. However, people often attribute possible religious backgrounds by identifying people's physical features or distinctive names. These may be used as a way of discriminating against people, both overtly and covertly,

most significantly within populations with ethnic and religious diversity and conflict.

Cultural identity

Cultural identity is integrated in one's sense of self from one's upbringing, family, peers, education, society, art, literature, folk tales, and so on. This process goes on throughout most of one's lifetime. **Culture** not only influences the cognitive schema, but also moulds the way one thinks of oneself and sees others. It is also important in the way people deal with interpersonal relationships. There is no doubt that culture defines people and distinguishes them from others by their social behavior, religious beliefs, clothes, cuisine, entertainment, arts (high culture), etc. Cultures can also overlap at various levels; for example, students from various ethnic backgrounds attending a certain college may feel that the culture of their college and their identity as a student in that institution are far more relevant. Identity, on the other hand, is another multifaceted aspect of social and personal functioning, which identifies the individual and gives them credibility and some self-esteem. Cultural identity highlights a person's uniqueness and could include gender, ethnicity and occupation. Cultural identity, its preservation and differences, especially in a **multicultural** setting and in a more globalizing world, can potentially bring about conflicts and contribute to mental health problems. It is important for mental and social care professionals to remember this while dealing with those in their care.

Sexual identity

Gender and sexual identities are at the core of one's understanding of oneself. Gender awareness develops relatively early and is both biologically and socially reinforced. Gender identity has an influence on sexual identity, which develops in late childhood and adolescence, when one starts to relate to others in the sexual and emotional context. Sexual orientation is determined by the level of sexual attraction to either or both sexes. Non-concordance of sexuality with the norm can often cause anxiety, especially in cultures with less accepting attitudes towards alternative sexualities. This could lead to changing identities, for example Internet, where other identities can be developed and used, as in Second Life.

Many aspects of one's identity are fluid and influenced by one's interaction with the outside world. In an increasingly globalized world and with the growth of electronic media and information technology (such as the Internet), there is unprecedented interaction between people of various cultures and identities. Though this can bring about better awareness and understanding of other cultures, it might also lead to possible conflict within one's own existing sense of self. This is especially true for those from non-Western cultures, as the globalized culture is primarily Western.

Migration and identity

Migration over the past few centuries has led to the establishment of multicultural societies in various parts of the world. The flow of influence of one culture to another is a two-way process, though it is expected that the flow would be greater from the dominant culture of the host. This confluence can lead to different degrees of acceptance of the dominant culture, resulting in **assimilation**, acculturation or deculturation. Conflict between different cultural values may cause separation or alienation in vulnerable individuals. Hence, the identity of migrants is heavily influenced both by the attitudes of the host culture and by their own. Often there may be pressure to assimilate and this can give rise to internal conflict. The level of assimilation may also differ between generations of migrants. Biculturalism may lead to at least two identities, where the individual may move between the culture they are born in and the culture they are surrounded by.

People have always chosen to develop alternate identities, such as writing under a nom de plume, wearing clothes of a different gender, etc. However, with the advent of the Internet this has changed. In chat rooms and on blogs people create alternative identities that may be very different from their other identities. In these situations people change their age, gender, social status, etc. In some ways this is like a histrionic or multiple identity where, depending upon circumstances, individuals can be whoever they want to be. In collectivist societies, individuals with ego-centric values may find it difficult to assert themselves as such and, consequently, hide those values. The advantages are that they can have an increased cohesion, deal with stress in an anonymous manner and transcend safely into an identity that may overcome or generate **prejudices**. The disadvantages of alternate identities are that there may be inherent dangers that add to stress: "cyberbullying" may occur, or they may lead to addictions. With the use of alternate names and identities, and with individuals having more than one name and identity through their blogs, games or social networking sites, confusion may well be created about who they are and what their role and social contract is.

Conclusions

Identity is both fluid and solid. In response to a number of factors, the individual's identity may change totally through over-compensation or only slightly through adjustments. Often, the identity is created in response to the society and social mores, although some individuals may carry a very rigid perception and demonstration of their identity. In clinical settings the clinician must be sensitive in exploring these in order to ascertain the actual and false identities so that appropriate interventions are set in place. [DBhugra & SG]

Key readings

Appiah, K. A. (2007). *The ethics of identity.* Princeton, NJ: Princeton University Press.

Bhugra, D. (2004). Migration, distress and cultural identity. *British Medical Bulletin*, 69, 129–141.

———, Bhui, K., Mallett, R., Desai, M., Singh, J., & Leff, J. (1999). Cultural identity and its measurement. *International Review of Psychiatry*, 11, 244–249.

———, Leff, J., Mallett, R., Morgan, C., & Zhao, J.-H. (2010). The culture and identity schedule – a measure of cultural affiliation: Acculturation, marginalization and schizophrenia. *International Journal of Social Psychiatry* (in press).

Burke, P. J. & Stets, J. E. (2009). *Identity theory.* New York: Oxford University Press.

Gupta, S. and Bhugra, D. (2009). Cultural identity and its assessment. *Psychiatry*, 8(9), 333–334.

Heidegger, M. (2002). *Identity and difference.* (Trans. J. Stambaugh). Chicago: University of Chicago Press.

Jenkins, R. (2008). *Social identities* (3rd ed.). New York: Routledge.

Tilly, C. (2006). *Identities, boundaries and social ties.* Boulder, CO: Paradigm.

IDENTITY POLITICS Over the past century, the world has witnessed increasing demands for group recognition, respect, equal treatment, opportunity, and rights sought by women, diverse ethnic, racial, religious groups, and, more recently, gays and lesbians. A clear understanding of these social movements requires a thorough consideration of the concept of identity politics.

In the course of such identity-based social movements and the tensions associated with group struggles for political recognition and equality, the world also became the stage for a large number of violent conflicts with **nationalistic**, ethnic, and religious dimensions. Particularly in the post-Cold War era, ethnic conflicts have been among the most serious threats to international security and order. Above all, ethnic conflict has been a primary source for tremendous levels of human suffering; the **genocide** in Rwanda in 1994, the massacre in Srebrenica in 1995, the endless treks of refugees due to the Kosovo War (1998–99), and the ongoing atrocities being committed in Darfur are a few examples of events that shocked the international community.

In light of these developments, identity politics has become the object of a heated debate within academic as well as non-academic circles, and a major subject of scholarly research. Identity politics figure prominently in discussions and investigations regarding a wide array of issues such as social movements, ethnic conflict and conflict resolution, political psychology and behavior, immigration, citizenship, **minority** politics, transnational alliances, democratization, nation building, and globalization.

Defining identity and identity politics
In order to understand identity politics, it is important to first grasp the concept of **identity**. Social identity can simply be associated with membership of a group. Several scholars also link social identity with the value and emotional significance attached to group membership. That said, individuals often possess multiple social identities, which may overlap and intersect, and are almost never exclusive. The layering and ranking of an individual's identities and loyalties is variable, depending largely on context as different issues tap different identities. To illustrate, a person might prioritize the identity of an "African-American" when dealing with issues of racial equality, of a "feminist" when joining a protest against sex **discrimination** in the workplace, of a "Christian" when participating in a public debate over the

issue of prayer in public schools, or of a "lesbian" when writing a petition in support of same sex marriage.

Identity politics is often used interchangeably with minority politics. Accordingly, some scholars define identity politics as the tendency of minority groups to define issues exclusively or primarily in terms of their own group-related social, economic, and political interests, values, and priorities. On a parallel basis, others describe identity politics as an impulse towards forming an organization to imbue denigrated group-identities with more positive meaning or to develop an exclusive group **culture** by drawing strict boundaries around group members based on ascriptive characteristics. Several scholars study the politics of identity under alternative rubrics such as the "new social movements," the "new political culture," the "politics of difference," or the "politics of recognition."

The role of identity in politics
A growing body of research has shown the importance of identity politics for understanding a wide range of political dynamics and outcomes. Specifically, an individual's political identity can have a major impact on political participation, political ideology, and opinion on policy issues. Moreover, an awareness and sensitivity to issues such as human rights, **multiculturalism**, and diversity may be associated with the rise of identity politics and identity-based social movements.

One's identification with a group has cognitive, affective, attitudinal, and behavioral consequences, as well as implications for group formation, cohesion, and political mobilization. Through participation in identity-based social movements, people who are normally discriminated against and/or ignored come to think of themselves as a collectivity with particular needs and goals to be met, thus leading to feelings of empowerment. At its best, identity politics may help individuals to overcome exclusion, silencing, and disparagement, which can result in a replacement of negative **stereotypes** with strong and positive images of the members of such mobilized groups.

Studies on intergroup relations have shown that membership of a group increases in-group favoritism and out-group bias and discrimination. Strong identities have been found to undercut national unity and promote intolerance and intergroup antipathies. In extreme cases of inter-group polarization, one identity can only be constituted or confirmed by repression of another. This constitutes one of the main obstacles to the resolution of identity-based clashes such as the Israeli–Palestinian conflict.

Criticisms of identity politics
Some scholars question the value of identity politics by asserting that organizing politics around historically marginalized group identities can divide a society into rival factions and create an environment of victims and villains. Accordingly, these scholars tend to focus on the dysfunctional, destabilizing, and conflict-generating effects of negative social identity. They also suggest that organizing around separate identities weakens social movements rather than strengthening them. From such a point of view, identity politics often divides social movements, reduces their political effectiveness, and prevents the construction of a common political agenda. Instead, it produces insular, sectarian, and divisive movements, incapable of expanding membership, broadening appeals, or negotiating with prospective allies. As an example, some scholars of identity politics attribute the decline of the radical feminist movement to disputes over sexuality, class, and **race**.

Proponents of identity politics, on the other hand, argue that many organizations are favorably disposed to coalition and cooperation notwithstanding the existence of radically separatist identity groups, and draw attention to the cooperation-inducing potential and transformative power of positive social identity. According to this perspective, national, ethnic, and transnational identity can transform exclusion into inclusion, separation into integration, and conflict into cooperation, if properly channeled and accommodated.

Identity politics in the United States
The United States is a nation of immigrants with multiple ethnic, religious, and cultural groups who mostly view themselves in terms of hyphenated identities such as Mexican-American, Italian-American, Irish-American, etc. Historically, the groups which are not from an Anglo-American ancestry were socially, economically, and politically marginalized. Given such socio-demographic structure, it is not surprising that identity has been a major factor in influencing US politics, particularly since the 1960s. Group identities have had a growing and significant influence on political beliefs, attitudes, and actions, as well as voting behavior. For instance, studies of public opinion generally find that racial identification influences one's policy preferences. To illustrate, African-Americans show greater support for affirmative action policies. More evidence of the importance of identity in politics lies in the media coverage of exit polls that almost invariably report which candidate won the "women's vote" or the "**Latino** vote."

The impact of identity politics in the United States has particularly manifested itself in major social movements that are closely tied to the politics of equality, recognition, **reparation**, and redistribution. The **Civil Rights Movement**, the Black Power Movement, the American Indian Movement, the Japanese American Redress Movement, and protests by Latinos over historical portrayals of the Alamo are all cases where racial/ethnic identity and consciousness instigated political mobilization. However, identity-based social movements in the United States are not limited to just ethnic minorities; two noteworthy examples of non-ethnic minority social movements are the Women's Movement and the American Gay Rights Movement.

Politics of "supranational" identity: The case of the European Union

The European Union is today the deepest form of regional integration that is driven primarily by economic goals. Still, an element of Europeanness is seen as being necessary to validate and legitimate the process of political and economic integration. Accordingly, the creation of a common European identity has critical implications for the survival capacities of the EU. Nevertheless, the EU has had difficulties with its own politics of identity, partly because its attempt to construct a supranational identity that transcends other social identities occurs precisely within the same symbolic terrain as national identities. A unified European identity has been lost over the centuries. Consequently, the definition of who a European is has become the subject of intense political and academic debate.

Transformations in identity politics

Since the rise of the nation-state, national identity had been the primary source of identification for many. However, contemporary trends – particularly globalization – are eroding the state and the state system and instigating significant shifts in identities and loyalties. Major transformations regarding identity politics include, but are not limited to, the de-territorialization of identity, the creation of global **diasporas** by massive international migration, the growth of bi-national communities, some rejuvenation of regional identity-based movements, and, somewhat paradoxically,

a revival of localism. Transnational institutions ranging from formal organizations such as the North Atlantic Treaty Organization (NATO) to less formal international regimes and corporate networks provide functional integration while offering alternatives to ethnic or national communities that seek to secede or win autonomy from existing territorial states.

Several scholars suggest that the increased globalization of the economy, politics, and human affairs has made individuals and groups more insecure and uncertain. Individuals seek reaffirmation of their self-identity by drawing closer to some collective group that may help to reduce such feelings of insecurity and anxiety. Local government, religion, ethnicity, professions, and even urban street gangs offer places of refuge and revitalized identity. Given the complexity and uncertainties tied to these issues, scholarly debate is sure to continue for years to come. [CVS]

Key readings

Balfour, L. (2005). Reparations after identity politics. *Political Theory*, 33(6), 786–811.

DeLeon, R. E., & Naff, K. C. (2004). Identity politics and local political culture: Some comparative results from the social capital benchmark survey. *Urban Affairs Review*, 39(6), 689–719.

Du Plessis, A. (2001). Exploring the concept of identity in world politics. In Report on the Proceedings of a Workshop on *Politics of Identity and Exclusion in Africa: From Violent Confrontation to Peaceful Cooperation* (University of Pretoria, 25–26 July 2001), pp. 13–25. Retrieved from www.kas.de/db_files/dokumente/7_doku ment_dok_pdf_5094_2.pdf#page=12.

Gitlin, T. (1995). *The twilight of common dreams: Why America is wracked by culture wars*. New York: Metropolitan Books.

Kinnvall, C. (2004). Globalization and religious nationalism: Self, identity, and the search for ontological security. *Political Psychology*, 25(5), 741–767.

Preston, M., Cain B., & Bass, S. (Eds.) (1997). *Racial and ethnic politics in California.* Berkeley, CA: University of California Press.

Weldon, S. L. (2006). Women's movements, identity politics, and policy impacts: A study of policies on violence against women in the 50 United States. *Political Research Quarterly*, 59(1), 111–122.

Wong, C. & Cho, G. E. (2005). Two-headed coins or Kandinskys: White racial identification. *Political Psychology*, 26(5), 699–720.

IMPERIALISM Imperialism is a much-contested, complex concept that eludes simple definition and interlocks with other structural developments in world history, such as globalization and capitalism. The ebb and flow of empires goes far back into antiquity but, from the sixteenth century, imperialism was linked exclusively to expansion of European modernity. Unlike Empire, which denotes a geographical space with boundaries, as does the concept of a colony, imperialism is a relationship of **power** that structures **identities** and social relationships in both colonies and imperial centres. The economic, political and cultural aspects of this imperial power dynamic are inseparable and, whilst colonies cannot exist without imperialism, imperialism can, arguably, exist without formal colonization. Imperialism, then, can be defined only loosely as an unequal relationship whereby a more powerful state exerts economic and political influence beyond its boundaries that is backed up by military power. Imperial systems differ between epochs and within empires at any given time, but commonalties also exist. All empires have justified expansion by the need to "civilize the barbarians" through spreading the benefits of a superior **culture/** religion. From the sixteenth century, European justifications of empire became imbued with ideas of racial and cultural superiority, and racism and imperialism became intimately interlinked. In effect, the economic gain of elites in the imperial centre was a prime motive for imperial expansion. Thus, common to imperial systems is land expropriation, exploitation of indigenous labor and taxation. In modern European empires this resulted in the destruction, or undermining, of indigenous cultures and global migrations, forced (as in the transatlantic slave trade) or free, to meet colonial labor needs and secure profits. All empires encountered resistance and maintained their power through military might but also employed more subtle strategies of "divide and rule," cultural imperialism and the co-option of certain sectors of the indigenous population who benefited from such collaboration. Finally, all empires have declined through imperial overstretch and challenges from the dominated peoples.

Modern imperialism is dated from Christopher Columbus's "discovery" of the Americas but this has been criticized as a Eurocentric conception that assumes no important global developments existed before that date, erases the contribution of non-European empires and civilizations to such developments, and emphasizes the rise of unique, and implicitly superior, modern European/Western societies. Before the eighteenth century, many parts of Asia and the Middle East were more advanced than Western Europe, in Africa powerful empires prevented European penetration and, in the Americas, the Spanish conquistadors encountered the Inca and Aztec empires. European imperial expansion was facilitated initially by the European Enlightenment and related technological, maritime, intellectual and political developments but the "great divergence" in the eighteenth century between Europe and the Chinese, Mughal and Ottoman empires was ultimately a consequence of the rise of European capitalism and modernity.

European empires included the seaborne empires of Portugal, Spain, Holland, France and Britain and, later, the Russian and Austro-Hungarian land empires. By 1800, Britain was the leading power but, by 1900, Germany, Italy, Belgium, Japan and the United States competed with the older European empires for territory and influence. European imperialism was transformed into Western imperialism where "West" may be defined as a space of power – geographic, in mapping the wealthy "developed" areas of the world and ideological, in defining the "advanced" West against the less developed "non-West." These networks of imperial power were strengthened by the tighter integration of global markets, more intensive cash-crop and mineral production, and the rise of finance capitalism. This resulted in more intense global economic and cultural dominance, consolidating and expanding processes that mutually shaped the lives of people in the imperial centres and colonized peripheries.

Definitions of imperialism are thus complicated by the interactions between imperial expansion, capitalism and globalization. World systems theorists such as Immanuel Wallenstein prioritize capitalism, rather than imperialism per se, as the dynamic behind global expansion since the sixteenth century. In this context, imperialism is simply a vehicle for the growth of the capitalist world system. As the system expanded, the powerful "core" in the West became wealthier at the expense of the peripheral "non-West," resulting in deepening global inequalities that endure today. Whether we prioritize imperialism or capitalism as the motivating factor, these developments had a massive and irreversible impact and left a legacy of racial inequality, poverty and social injustice that reverberates into the present.

Campaigns to tackle this legacy revived interest in imperial history from the 1970s reflected in the fierce, and often vituperative, arguments between **postcolonial** and orthodox historians. Edward Said's critique of Western constructions of knowledge about the orient and, more widely, colonized subjects, stimulated new academic research into the cultures of imperialism and the intimate link between colonial knowledge and the maintenance of imperial power. Postcolonial studies prioritized the ways in which imperialism mutually shaped the cultures of colony and metropolitan centre and created **race**, class and gender identities that endured after the ending of formal empires. These new perspectives on the imperial past raised the contentious question of whether the long-term impact of Western imperialism was good or bad. Critics claimed that imperialism was exploitative and adversely impacted on indigenous cultures and environments in contrast to the argument that European/Western expansion fostered cultural interchanges and brought development and progress.

To conclude, imperialism was indispensable to the creation of the modern world. Strongly polarized positions exist, however, over the nature of imperialism, its causes and consequences for human societies, questions of periodization, and why empires decline. Additionally, since the 1980s, a number of analysts of contemporary global relations have pointed to the continued relevance of imperialism. Thus, there is an ongoing and contentious debate as to whether imperialism ended with the formal decolonization of the European empires or endured in the global military and economic power of the United States of America, thus perpetuating the dominance of the "West" over the "rest." However, with the rise of China and India as major economic powers, and more intense globalization, the hegemony of the West may now be coming to an end. [BB]

Key readings

Bayly, C. A. (2003). *The birth of the modern world, 1780–1914: Global connections and comparisons.* Oxford: Blackwell.

Bush, B. (2006). *Imperialism and postcolonialism.* London: Pearson Education.

Cain, P. & Harrison, M. (Eds.). (2001). *Imperialism: Critical concepts in historical studies.* London: Routledge, 3 vols.

Cain, P. & Hopkins, A. J. (2001). *British imperialism, 1688–2000.* New York, NY: Longman.

Harvey, D. (2003). *The new imperialism.* Oxford: Oxford University Press.

Osterhammel, J. & Petersson, N. P. (2005). *Globalisation a short history.* Princeton, NJ: Princeton University Press.

Pomeranz, K. (2000). *The great divergence: Europe, China and the making of the modern world economy.* Princeton, NJ: Princeton University Press.

Said, E. (1995). *Orientalism: Western conceptions of the Orient.* London: Penguin.

Sampson, J. (2005). *Race and empire.* Harlow, Middlesex: Pearson Education.

Wallerstein, I. (1996). *Historical capitalism with capitalist civilisation.* London: Verso.

INDIGENOUS PEOPLES We use the term "indigenous peoples" here to refer to those peoples who live, or have lived within the past several centuries, in non-state societies. Examples are the Maori in New Zealand, **Aboriginals** in Australia, Adevasi in India, Saami (formerly known as Lapps in northern Scandinavia), many peoples native to Melanesia and Polynesia, and so on. In North America, we alternate among Native Americans, American Indians, or Indian. Where possible we use the name that the group prefers. We note that official names are political and historical constructions that often are erroneous, and sometimes controversial. There are the historical accidents of naming and spelling, or a name derived from a derogatory term used by others. Recent official name changes are the result of indigenous peoples' efforts to reclaim control of their appellations, such as Diné for Navajo, Ho-Chunk for Winnebago, or Tohono O'odham for Papago. Disputes over names typically result from responses to internal processes or encounters with outsiders. In North America, and many other places around the world, native peoples held a collective sense of **identity**, but did not recognize a single political organization. Resistance to the encroachments of other groups or outsiders often fostered the formation of socio-political structures that constituted groups, and often led to new names and identities.

European invasion and settlement of the Americas had dire consequences for the indigenous populations of both continents. Warfare, enslavement, diseases, and forced displacement from homelands severely reduced native populations. Historical demographers estimated the pre-contact population of North America at several million; by 1900, the US Census reported fewer than 300,000 Native Americans in the lower 48 states. The factors leading to the early decline in the American Indian population characterized colonial–indigenous relations around the world.

The late nineteenth and early twentieth century growth of industrial resource extraction, large-scale agriculture, urbanization, officially sanctioned religious proselytization, and coercive educational programs led many scholars to predict the eventual complete disappearance of indigenous peoples and **cultures** around the world. These predictions were both accurate and inaccurate. In the global system today there is a widespread decline in native languages and traditional cultural practices and increasing numbers of indigenous peoples live outside traditional communities in cities. Despite these changes and the adoption by native peoples of colonizing languages, foods, and cultural practices, there has been not only a survival, but a resurgence of indigenous populations around the world. The United Nations estimates that there are over 350 million indigenous people in the world. This is not only a demographic revival, indigenous groups are organizing, making land claims, petitioning for political rights, and demanding control of resources. Some indigenous communities are having remarkable success given their limited numbers, votes, money, or military capacity. Many indigenous groups are using modern institutions and practices to advance their interests through organizations like the UN and technologies like the Internet.

The creation of new indigenous organizations and identities can be a form of reorganization or resistance resulting from efforts to eliminate particular groups through **genocide**, **assimilation**, or amalgamation with other indigenous groups. The resulting new communities are examples of ethnic reorganization or "**ethnogenesis**," that is, the creation of new ethnic groups. The histories and activities of indigenous peoples offer insights into long-term social change and social evolution. To overlook these many historical and modern groups biases the sample of societies considered by researchers. This is especially important since indigenous peoples are not simply "living fossils" because they have survived centuries, and in parts of Asia millennia, of contact and interaction with many states. Those interactions have reshaped current indigenous social, economic, cultural, and political organization. It is impossible to know the extent and trajectories of these reorganizations since reliance on "first contact" accounts of indigenous peoples can be misleading as early intergroup contacts often lead to rapid and significant change. Thus, while first-hand accounts can be useful, they cannot be presumed to be unbiased snapshots of a pre-contact past. In order to understand the demo-

graphy of indigenous peoples, it is important to recognize the politics of numbers and their uses. There has been a common tendency among historians to underestimate the populations of indigenous peoples prior to contact with states. This serves to minimize the extent of depopulation that resulted from contact. Sometimes this underestimation serves a political end, but often it is unintentional since early observers encountered populations that had already been decimated by diseases and conflicts. Estimates of the indigenous population of the United States and Canada range from 1 million to 30 million. Seven million is a commonly cited figure, based on reconstruction of population densities, early population counts, and the effects of known epidemics. Native populations in the United States reached a nadir of about a quarter of a million around the turn of the twentieth century. Since then, the Native American population has grown to nearly 2.5 million.

Since the Second World War there has been considerable demographic change in the Native American demographic landscape. From 1960 to 2000, the number of Americans who reported their **race** to be "American Indian" in the US Census grew from 523,591 to 2,366,639. This dramatic increase is due to improved enumeration techniques, a small decrease in death rates, and an increased willingness on the part of individuals to identify themselves as Native American. American Indians intermarry with other groups more than any other ethnic group in the United States, and identifying the race of the resulting offspring can greatly complicate official enumerations. There are many controversies about who is and is not "Indian" in tribal governments, among federal officials, and among Indian communities and individuals. Economic issues surrounding gaming, land rights, or natural resources add importance to these debates.

The period since the end of the Second

World War also has been marked by the most political active period in American Indian history. Urbanization, education, and increased participation in the paid labor force contributed to the formation of activist organizations such as the American Indian Movement and Women of All Red Nations, legal defense organizations such as Native American Rights Fund and Native Action, and lobbying groups such as National Congress of American Indians and National Tribal Chairmen's Association. These organizations provided an infrastructure for Indian rights movements that blossomed during the US Civil Rights era during the 1960s and 1970s. These efforts helped to usher in an era of "self-determination" in federal Indian policy.

Self-determination policies have contributed in recent decades to increased economic development on reservations and in American Indian communities from mineral resources, gaming, and tourism. Even with these improvements in native economies, Native Americans remain the poorest ethnic groups in the United States. The growth in economic resources has led to a debate within many Native American nations, and among indigenous peoples globally, about how to participate in economic development without destroying traditional values. Efforts to preserve traditional cultures can be aided or undermined by economic development. Increased wealth can allow indigenous communities to build museums to preserve their heritage, hire linguists to document and provide instruction in native languages, and litigate to protect their rights. Increased participation in modern economic activities, however, also can threaten cultures and communities because of the internal and external consequences of gaming, tensions over the distribution of collective resources, increased tourism, and non-native expropriation and disruption of indigenous spiritual practices. These and other issues associated with development and its consequences are especially acute in the United States. Because of American Indian tribes' special relationship with the US federal government, Indian reservations are able to sponsor gaming, sell gasoline and cigarettes without paying local and state taxes, and sell other typically locally- or state-interdicted or regulated products such as fireworks. The growth of Indian casinos and the desire of non-Indian governments and businesses to compete with Indian enterprises have led to public opinion and social mobilizations that are nominally anti-gaming, but are often thinly-disguised anti-Indian movements. Similar non-Indian opposition has resulted from Native American land claims. Debates about Indian rights can intensify **identity politics** within and among indigenous groups, and between indigenous groups and the general population.

Economic development and land rights are not the only arenas where indigenous rights and community boundaries are debated. Culture is an important domain in historical and contemporary indigenous life around the world. In the United States, the appropriation and frequent misrepresentation of American Indian religious traditions and claims to **authenticity** have generated a backlash by native communities seeking to retain control over their spiritual practices. The market in American Indian art has led to efforts to certify the authenticity of Indian art and the right to be considered an Indian artist. The popularity and lucrative sale of New Age and World music, which use elements (and occasionally performers) from various indigenous populations, has spawned analogous controversies globally. A key point of contention is that it is non-Indian performers and producers who are making large profits from the use of indigenous instruments, themes, music, and performances. A similar, and much more serious, issue involves cultural heritage and intellectual property rights of traditional medicines and plants, as many transnational pharmaceutical corporations attempt to develop and patent the use of plants and chemicals discovered and developed by indigenous peoples or located on indigenous lands. These controversies have led the United Nations to set up guidelines for relations with indigenous peoples and to establish international conventions designed to protect indigenous rights. [TDH & JN]

Key readings

Cornell, S. (1988). *The return of the native: American Indian Political Resurgence*. New York: Oxford University Press.

Hall, T. D. & Fenelon, J. V. (2009). *Indigenous peoples and globalization: Resistance and revitalization*. Boulder, CO: Paradigm Press.

Mann, C. C. (2005). *1491: New revelations of the Americas before Columbus*. New York: Alfred A. Knopf.

Nagel, J. (1996). *American Indian ethnic renewal: Red power and the resurgence of identity and culture*. New York: Oxford University Press.

Snipp, C. M. (1986). Who are American Indians? Some observations about the perils and pitfalls of data for race and ethnicity. *Population Research and Policy Review*, 5, 237–252.

INSTITUTIONAL RACISM Common perceptions of "racism" involve individual-level distaste, resentment or outright hostility toward persons of **races** or ethnicities different from one's own. In reality, though, this describes "**prejudice**" or "bigotry." As a concept, "racism" is rooted in systems, not individuals; it has been described as "prejudice + **power**." Specifically, "institutional racism" refers to the idea that disadvantage has been built into political, social and economic systems in ways that work

separately from the conscious or subconscious prejudice of individuals.

We might consider an analogy: if being "successful" within a given cultural context can be likened to reaching the summit of a mountain, we can imagine a number of people from different races all starting at the base, looking toward the top. In a socially just environment, each climber would have roughly the same chance of making it to the top – the same equipment, food and water, and opportunity for training – with the only differences relating to individual physical ability and mental strength. In such a circumstance, most people would feel fairly comfortable accepting the results of the climb to the top, however it turned out. Because of institutional racism, however, each of the climbers does not start with the same chance. Some of them – climbers who are non-white – have extra weight in their backpacks, while others have more advanced equipment. Whites, for instance, have not historically been denied access to education or job experience that will provide for the "tools" necessary to be successful in life, so their backpacks are more likely to be stocked with important items that will help their climb, while persons of color are burdened by useless weight in the form of prejudice, disproportionately high incarceration rates, disproportionate poverty, etc. While many individual whites also face disadvantage, as a group they have benefitted in various ways from **white supremacy**.

Moreover, the climbers of color were required to help the advantaged climbers to get up the mountain. As the climbers ascended, the whites required the black and **Latino** climbers to take some extra weight, which simultaneously made the climb easier for those who were already advantaged and harder for those who were already disadvantaged. During slavery in America, for example, blacks worked with no pay to help white landowners make profits. Those whites sent their (male) children to school, and the cycle was able to continue. Blacks were prohibited from gaining an education, thus dooming generations to low-wages, dangerous work conditions and poverty, even after slaves were freed.

Emerging conscious norms of equality resulted in the white climbers taking their own backpacks back from the climbers of color (e.g. civil rights legislation), but some would also argue that the advantaged climbers should do more. After all, there is still a long way to the summit and the disadvantaged climbers have been hauling more than their share of the load for a good part of the climb. Others, however, would argue that any effort designed to aid the previously disadvantaged climbers (such as affirmative action policies) would be "reverse **discrimination**" and, therefore, unfair to the advantaged climbers.

Another way to consider how institutional racism works is to analyze the norms upon which dominant institutions were built and are maintained. In 2010, officials in England and Wales were moved to address findings from a series of annual surveys pinpointing some concerns that they thought might be reflective of institutional racism. **Minority** groups were more likely to be involuntarily admitted to hospitals for mental illness, experienced longer stays in hospital, and were reportedly more likely to be coerced into treatment. Additional findings suggested that members of certain minority groups were disproportionately diagnosed with particular mental illnesses and that there were disparities with respect to treatments offered and/ or readily available to members of ethnic minority groups, irrespective of socioeconomic differences. While the answers to the "why" questions – Why are members of racial minority groups treated differently? Why is the diagnosis of particular mental illnesses higher among members of those groups? – are not simple, one must consider the role of institutional racism and the medicalization of cultural difference.

Anecdotal evidence of police misconduct or "profiling" in England, France and other parts of Europe, as well as in the United States, often hinges on discussions of institutional racism that explicitly differentiate the attitudes of individual officers from systemic racism. More generally, members of systemically disadvantaged groups face countless institutional barriers that link together and are related to elements of racism that abound in the creation and maintenance of social structures. This is not to say that many individuals do not or cannot overcome strife or even acute mistreatment, but when systemic stagnation stymies progress in our most fundamental institutions, which continue disproportionately to fail minorities – schools, banks, health care, criminal justice, the workforce – it is essential that we consider the extent to which the goal of meritocracy is compromised. Frequently, systems are "sick," and research has demonstrated that sick systems create illness in the individuals who are oppressed by them, as well as in those who benefit.

In these ways, racism is built into institutions. Students whose parents benefitted from **white privilege** go to better schools than students of color, whose parents (to return to our analogy) were hauling heavier bags. The white students (or their parents, for that matter) did not seek privilege – it was bestowed upon them by a system that worked to their benefit. Their children will experience similar privilege; the children of the burdened climbers will not. The resultant cycle is institutionalized racism, a concept quite distinct from "prejudice." [JC & SMC]

Key readings

Barndt, J. (2007). *Understanding and dismantling racism: The twenty-first century challenge to white America.* Minneapolis, MN: Fortress.

Better, S. (2007). *Institutional racism: A primer on theory and strategies for social change.* New York: Rowman and Littlefield.

Commission for Health Care Audit and Inspection (2008). *Count me in census 2008.* London: Author. Retrieved from www.thecareforum.org/publication_uploads/Marvin%20Rees%20Presentation%20-%20Count%20Me%20In%20Census%202008.pdf

Feagin, J. S. (2006). *Systemic racism: A theory of oppression.* New York: Routledge.

Ridley, C. R. (2005). *Overcoming unintentional racism in counseling and therapy: A practitioner's guide to intentional intervention.* Thousand Oaks, CA: Sage.

Twine, F. W. (1997). *Racism in a racial democracy: The maintenance of white supremacy in Brazil.* New Brunswick, NJ: Rutgers University Press.

ISLAMOPHOBIA Islamophobia is a social anxiety about Islam as a religion and/or Muslims as a group. Although fears may appear specifically connected to particular **races** (e.g. Arab) and/or ethnicities (e.g. Pakistani) associated with the term "Muslim," such concerns tend to stem, ultimately, from the behaviors and predispositions that the core teachings and practices of Islam purportedly promote. These lead to apprehensions regarding such presumptions as the violence of Muslim men, their oppression of women, their intolerance toward all non-Muslims, and their unwillingness to accept anything but an Islamic state and legal system. In turn, these views rely on the erroneous concepts of a singular Muslim community or world and a monolithic, monovocal religion that universally demands such commitments.

Islamophobia tends to be rooted in barely conscious social memories of political, religious, and economic competition that have been reiterated and reinterpreted in contemporary circumstances. For example, while the term "crusade" continues to resonate favorably among Americans and many Christians alike, few recognize the origins of much current Islamophobic imagery (e.g. the scimitar, the fanatical warrior) in Crusader ideology and sentiment. Nevertheless, historical evidence demonstrates the pervasiveness of Islamophobic themes in Europe and European-influenced **cultures**, even if the strength of their expression varies according to fluctuating domestic and international circumstances.

American Islamophobia has existed for centuries (beginning, at the latest, in polemics during the post-Revolution period), while European Islamophobia, from which it derives, has roots more than a millennium old. Their **prejudices** historically have manifested themselves variously, usually correlated with shifts of self-perception within the dominant culture. As an example, Western **representations** of women victimized by supposed Muslim male misogyny often expressed their moral condemnation using prurient, erotic scenes in the nineteenth and early twentieth centuries. However, with the rising consciousness among Westerners about the patriarchal oppression of women in their own societies, subsequent representations on this theme have shifted to an entirely oppressive image. Evidently, the durability of the Islamophobic truism regarding women's subjugation can sublimate and obscure for non-Muslim Westerners the similarities of gender inequality among patriarchal cultures, including their own.

A variety of forms of Islamophobia exist. One manifestation is racial and ethnic. Among many Europeans and North Americans, "Muslim" has been equated with "Arab" (and vice versa). Although only 20 percent of Muslims are Arab and many Arabs profess Christianity, the image of "the Muslim" – whether Saudi, Afghan, or Indonesian – often relies on racial **stereotypes** of Arab (male) physiology (heavy facial hair and large, hawk-like nose), clothing (jalabiya and kaffiyeh), and behavior (irrational anger and unmitigated lustfulness).

A newer expression of Islamophobia – especially common in nations struggling with recent Muslim immigration – manifests itself as a pro-active resistance to alleged Islamic intolerance. For instance, in 2005, the Danish newspaper *Jyllands-Posten* published cartoons of the Prophet Muhammad, which it had commissioned following an editor's concern that some artists were unwilling to transgress Muslim sentiments in their art. The violent response by some Muslims fulfilled Islamophobic expectations (especially as the media preferred to focus on these, instead of the more numerous peaceful protests) and justified a deepening Islamophobia. Although most Muslim outrage stemmed from one particularly insulting caricature of Muhammad, Western news media have continued to trace the response instead to a purportedly universal prohibition against depicting the prophet, hence reasserting an image of Muslims as intolerant of "Western" freedoms, such as that of expression. Simultaneously, the publication's decision a few years earlier not to publish cartoons ridiculing Jesus' resurrection in deference to Christian sentiment shows how Christian normativity often factors into Islamophobia, though with faint visibility. The double standard demonstrates how Islamophobia can generate proof of its own conclusions regarding Islam and Muslims, using one or both as a foil to define and promote certain social norms. [PG & GG]

Key readings

Esposito, J. (Ed.). (forthcoming). *Islamophobia: A challenge to pluralism in the 21st century*. New York: Oxford University Press.

Farouqui, A. (Ed.). (2009). *Muslims and media images: News versus views*. New Delhi: Oxford University Press.

Gottschalk, P. & Greenberg, G. (2008). *Islamophobia: Making Muslims the enemy*. Lanham, MD: Rowman & Littlefield.

Malik, M. (Ed.). (2010). *Anti-Muslim prejudice: Past and present*. New York: Routledge.

Reeves, M. (2000). *Muhammad in Europe: A thousand years of Western myth-making*. New York: New York University Press.

Said, E. (1997). *Covering Islam* (revised edition). New York: Vintage.

Shaheen, J. (2007). *Guilty: Hollywood's verdict on Arabs after 9/11*. Northampton, MA: Olive Branch Press.

LATINOS/**H**ISPANICS Latinos/Hispanics are the largest **minority** group in the United States, and it is projected that by the year 2050 they will constitute one-quarter of the country's population. This demographic explosion has sparked controversies around several topics, including the labels used to refer to them, Latino/Hispanic **identity**, criteria of identification, and challenges they pose to the nation.

"Latinos" vs "Hispanics"
The English term "Hispanics" is a translation of the Spanish *hispanos*, whose origin goes back to the name the Romans gave to the Iberian peninsula, *Hispania*. The Spanish term has a long history in Spain and Latin America, where it has been used most frequently to designate Spaniards and their descendants, or, as an adjective, to refer to anything that has to do with Spanish or Iberian **culture**. Something similar applies to the English term and its derivatives in the United States but, in the mid-1970s, the Census Bureau adopted the term to refer to the minority population, with ties to Latin America in particular.

This decision has been criticized by those who resent the use of a term that goes back to Spain and Iberian culture for a population that suffered under the **imperialism** and colonialism of Iberian powers. Those who oppose the use of the label "Hispanics," often favor "Latinos" as an alternative.

"Latinos" was originally used in Spanish to refer to the inhabitants of ancient Rome and its derivatives were applied to Roman culture and language. In its contemporary use in the United States, however, the term has come to label a population that traces its roots to the territory of the Americas located south of the United States border. The use of the term in its neutral or masculine form, or in its feminine form "Latinas," is favored in particular by those who wish to de-emphasize the connection of Latin America to Europe and to emphasize its colonial and marginal status. Both terms have advantages and disadvantages. "Hispanics" recognizes the cultural ties of Latin American to Iberia, and "Latinos/as" recognizes the unique political, social, and economic situation of Latin America.

General vs specific labels
The controversy concerning the use of these labels extends beyond the question of choice between them. Some argue that the use of all general labels, such as "Latinos" or "Hispanics," is counterproductive because it treats a diverse population as if it were homogenous, by assuming that all members of the group share important ethnic and racial properties. For example, ethnically, they are often thought to share such cultural phenomena as language, food, music, and social customs; and, racially, they are frequently thought to be darker, shorter, and physically different from Europeans. But the facts contradict these assumptions. Latinos/Hispanics differ not only as individuals, but also as groups. Ethnically, some of them speak Spanish or Portuguese, but some do not;

some like hot food, but others dislike it; some enjoy dancing salsa, but others prefer the tango; and the attitudes of Brazilians and Peruvians toward the family differ in significant ways. And when we come to racial markers such as descent or phenotypical features, they also differ: some Latinos/Hispanics are of Irish descent, whereas others are of Mayan or African descent; and some have dark skin, whereas others do not. These differences support the view that it is a mistake to lump all these people together, and that it is much better to separate them in terms of smaller groups, such as nationalities or specific ethne, to which they are closest. It makes more sense to talk about Mexicans, Puerto Ricans, Cubans, or Tarahumara, than about Latinos/Hispanics.

Identity and identification
These concerns have, in turn, sparked a discussion about Latino/Hispanic identity and the effective identification of the members of the group. The issues involved may be formulated in the following questions: Is there a Latino/Hispanic identity? If there is, is it a matter of fact or a matter of opinion? And, whether one or the other, how is it to be conceived? Among the positions taken on these issues, three are most common. *Essentialism* holds that there is a Latino/Hispanic identity, that it is a matter of fact, and that it consists of a set of properties shared by the members of the group. *Eliminativism* maintains that there is no such identity, except in people's minds, and that it is best to do away with the use of the notion of identity in referring to Latinos/Hispanics; the term "identity" should be reserved for individuals. And *relationalism* claims that there is a Latino/Hispanic identity, but that it is a mater of both fact and opinion and, ultimately, depends on context.

Each of these positions offers a different view of membership identification. For essentialism, Latinos/Hispanics are effectively identified in terms of the properties that characterize the members of the group – such as, for example, a language or a certain physical appearance. For eliminativism, any attempt at effective identification is bound to fail, insofar as there are no objective grounds on which to base membership in an overall Latino/Hispanic group. And relationalism holds that identification is contextual and can take place effectively only under certain conditions, insofar as there is no essence that characterizes the group, but context can be sufficient for identification.

Challenges

The demographic growth of Latinos/ Hispanics has sparked charges that they pose certain serious challenges to the nation. One of these is that their values and culture pose a threat to the values and culture that are fundamental to America. Indeed, some argue that the fabric of American society, based on the Protestant work ethic and democratic ideals, is being undermined by Latino/Hispanic culture. This is exacerbated by the fact that, unlike previous waves of immigrants to the United States, Latinos/Hispanics do not integrate into the mainstream culture of the country, but continue to practice their culture, speak their own language, and put pressure on American society to recognize their differences. Nowhere is this controversy more acute than in reference to linguistic rights. These have become a battleground between those who argue, for example, in favor of recognizing that Spanish-speaking children should be allowed to maintain their language and to be educated in it, and those who claim that such recognition would ultimately split the nation in two. [JJEG]

Key readings

Alcoff, L. M. (2006). *Visible identities: Race, gender, and the self.* New York: Oxford University Press.

Gracia, J. J. E. (2000). *Hispanic/Latino identity: A philosophical perspective.* Malden and Oxford: Blackwell Publishers Ltd.

——. (2008). *Latinos in America: Philosophy and social identity.* Oxford: Blackwell Publishing.

——. (Ed.). (2010). *Forging people: Race, ethnicity, and nationality in Hispanic American and Latino/a Thought.* Notre Dame, IN: Notre Dame University Press.

Gracia, J. J. E. & De Greiff, P. (Eds.). (2000). *Hispanics/Latinos in the United States: Ethnicity, race, and rights.* New York: Routledge.

Huntington, S. P. (2004). The Hispanic challenge. *Foreign Affairs* (March–April).

Idler, J. E. (2007). *Officially Hispanic: Classification policy and identity.* Lanham, MD: Rowman & Littlefield.

MANIFEST DESTINY The term "Manifest Destiny" first appeared in print in 1839. It was invoked in 1845 to call for the annexation of Texas, and later used to explain that the United States' westward expansion from the Atlantic seaboard to the Pacific Ocean was destined, or divinely ordained. It was revived in the 1890s, as a theoretical justification for US expansion outside of North America, including the eventual absorption of Canada, Mexico, Cuba, and Central America.

Speaking globally, Manifest Destiny is closely associated with the concept of American exceptionalism, which is the belief that America is distinctive in its founding principles, the supremacy of its political institutions and moral character. Both concepts incorporate a belief in the natural superiority of white Americans. Historian William E. Weeks noted three key themes which advocates of Manifest Destiny advance:

1 the virtue of the American people and their institutions;

2 the mission to spread these institutions, thereby redeeming and remaking the world in the image of the United States; and

3 the destiny under God to accomplish this work.

Territorial expansion of the United States from 1812 to 1860 is often associated with Manifest Destiny. Key events that represented the national commitment to notions of Manifest Destiny were the Aroostock War of 1839, the dispute with Great Britain about the Oregon boundary in 1846, the fight for Texan independence from Mexico and subsequent annexation (1836–1845), and the Mexican War (1846–1848). Westward expansion was encouraged by the Homestead Acts of 1841 and 1862, and supported by various efforts to blaze trails to the Pacific Coast, most notably the Oregon and Santa Fe Trails. Between 1849 and 1860, more than 250,000 people made the trek westward.

Territorial annexation and acquisition impacted nonwhite groups and individuals because racial rhetoric increased during the era of Manifest Destiny. The Wilmont Proviso of 1846, the Missouri Compromise (1820–1854), the Nebraska–Kansas Act of 1854, and the Supreme Court decision in Dred Scott v. Sandford (1857) specifically grappled with slavery and the territorial balance of free and slave states. In 1830, President Andrew Jackson signed the Indian Removal Act of 1830, leading to forced relocation of Native Americans from their homelands to Indian Territory in the west on what was is known as the Trail of Tears (1831–1837). Many Mexicans and Mexican Americans lost claim to their lands during the Mexican–American War and the Texas Revolution.

After 1848, disagreements over the expansion of slavery made further territorial annexation too divisive to be official government policy. Without official government support, the most radical advocates of Manifest Destiny increasingly turned to unauthorized military expeditions and encouraged unrest or revolution. While there had been some expeditions into Canada in the late 1830s, the primary target was Latin America, particularly Mexico and Cuba. [TF]

Key readings

Burns, E. M. (1957). *The American idea of mission: Concepts of national purpose and destiny*. New Brunswick, NJ: Rutgers University Press.

Haynes, S. W. & Morris, C. (Eds.). (1997). *Manifest Destiny and empire: American antebellum expansionism*. College Station, Texas: Texas A&M University Press.

Morrison, M. A. (1997). *Slavery and the American West: The eclipse of Manifest Destiny and the coming of the Civil War*. Chapel Hill, NC: University of North Carolina Press.

Schuck, P. H. & Wilson, J. Q. (Eds.). (2008). *Understanding America: The anatomy of an exceptional nation*. New York: Public Affairs.

Weeks, W. E. (1996). *Building the continental empire: American expansion from the revolution to the Civil War*. Chicago: Ivan R. Dee.

MARTIN LUTHER KING, JR Martin Luther King, Jr, was a Baptist minister and president of the Southern Christian Leadership Conference (SCLC). He emerged as one of the most prominent African American leaders in the **Civil Rights Movement** of the 1950s and 1960s.

King was born in Atlanta, Georgia, on January 15, 1929, to Alberta Williams and Martin Luther King, Sr. King grew up in the family home, just a block from his father's Ebenezer Baptist Church. After graduating from Booker T. Washington High School in 1944, King enrolled at Morehouse College. In February 1948,

King Sr ordained his son as a Baptist minister. After graduating from Morehouse in June 1948, King studied for a divinity degree at Crozer Theological Seminary in Upland, Pennsylvania. King graduated from Crozer in May 1951 and the following September he enrolled at Boston University in the PhD program in systematic theology. There he met his future wife, Coretta Scott, who was from rural Perry County, Alabama. King and Coretta were married by King Sr on June 18, 1953. King accepted a position at Dexter Avenue Baptist Church in Montgomery, Alabama in April 1954. In June 1955, King received his PhD. The Kings' first child, Yolanda Denise, was born November 17, 1955.

On December 1, 1955, Rosa Parks, a respected member of Montgomery's African American community, refused to surrender her seat on a city bus to a white passenger when she was asked to do so. She was arrested for breaking laws that required **segregation** on buses. Community activists proposed a bus boycott in protest. King was asked to head the Montgomery Improvement Association (MIA), a new organization formed to run the bus boycott. The boycott ran for 381 days. After the U.S. Supreme Court ruled segregation on Montgomery buses unconstitutional, they were desegregated on December 21, 1956.

The bus boycott made King a national symbol of African American protest. In August 1957, the SCLC was launched with King as president. The SCLC, headquartered in Atlanta, initially focused on supporting bus boycotts and voter registration drives. These campaigns made little impression. At the end of 1959, King resigned from his position at Dexter and, in early 1960, moved back to Atlanta, sharing the pastorate at Ebenezer with his father.

Developments elsewhere drove the newly-emerging Civil Rights Movement forward. In February 1960, four black students staged a sit-in at a segregated lunch counter in Greensboro, North Carolina. The sit-in movement rapidly expanded to other cities, where it met with some success in persuading local communities to desegregate facilities. In April 1960, the Student Nonviolent Coordinating Committee (SNCC), based in Atlanta, was formed to support student protest. In 1961, the Chicago-based Congress of Racial Equality (CORE) held interracial freedom rides to test the court-ordered desegregation of bus terminals. The freedom rides ultimately led to federal action to uphold the court order.

The success of the sit-ins and the freedom rides demonstrated the relevance of nonviolent direct action to the Civil Rights Movement and helped to develop King's rudimentary understanding of the technique. King and the SCLC embarked upon their first nonviolent direct-action campaign in 1961 in Albany, Georgia, with little immediate success. Learning lessons from the Albany campaign, in 1963 King and the SCLC targeted Birmingham, Alabama, for a civil rights campaign. A dramatic conflict with Birmingham's Public Safety Director Theophilus Eugene "Bull" Connor, who deployed police dogs and water from high-power fire hoses to break up demonstrations, brought national news headlines and federal intervention and pulled local white businessmen to the negotiating table.

The years between 1963 and 1965 represented the high-point of King's leadership. In August 1963, the Civil Rights Movement staged its largest gathering ever, with as many as 250,000 participants at the March on Washington for Jobs and Freedom. King's "I have a dream" speech was the most enduring emblem of the day and confirmed him as the movement's most prominent spokesperson.

In July 1964, U.S. Congress passed the 1964 Civil Rights Act, outlawing segregation in public facilities. In December 1964,

King was awarded the Nobel Peace Prize in Oslo, Norway. In February and March 1965, King and the SCLC campaigned in Selma, Alabama, for African American voting rights. The campaign led to the passage of the 1965 Voting Rights Act in August, which abolished legal impediments to voting rights for African Americans and initiated greater federal protection at the polls.

In the last few years of King's life, he and the Civil Rights Movement began to take different trajectories. Between 1965 and 1967, **race** riots erupted in a number of US cities. In 1966, some young activists began to embrace the militant "Black Power" slogan. The escalation of the Vietnam War shifted public debate, material resources, and political will away from the Civil Rights Movement. Conservative politicians, playing to a white backlash against African American gains, were increasingly successful in advocating a tougher law-and-order stance to subdue protest.

King responded to these developments in a variety of ways. In 1966, he took the SCLC into the northern ghettos of Chicago in an unsuccessful attempt to alleviate the conditions that caused the urban riots. He opposed much of the angry rhetoric of Black Power and continued to stress the importance of nonviolence. He spoke out ever more stridently in opposition to American involvement in the Vietnam War. He opposed conservative politicians who sought to exploit white racial fears. He also gained new insight about black problems in the United States as the movement shifted from tackling segregation to confronting the larger problem of racial **discrimination**.

King increasingly came to believe that many of the problems faced by African Americans were due to fundamental economic inequalities in American society. Consequently, he called for a redistribution of wealth and resources, advocating a move away from the harsher aspects of capitalism toward a society modeled on some form of democratic socialism. The last campaign King planned with the SCLC was a Poor People's March to Washington DC to dramatize the problem of poverty in the United States. But, on April 4, 1968, before the march took place, King was assassinated in Memphis, Tennessee, where he was supporting striking sanitation workers. King was survived by his wife, Coretta, and four children, Yolanda Denise, Martin Luther III, Dexter Scott, and Bernice Albertine. [JAK]

Key readings

Branch, T. (1988). *Parting the waters: Martin Luther King and the Civil Rights Movement, 1954–63*. New York: Simon and Schuster.
——. (1998). *Pillar of fire: America in the King years, 1963–65*. New York: Simon and Schuster.
——. (2006). *At Canaan's edge: America in the King years, 1965–1968*. New York: Simon and Schuster.
Fairclough, A. (1987). *To redeem the soul of America: The Southern Christian Leadership Conference and Martin Luther King, Jr*. Athens: University of Georgia Press.
Garrow, D. (1986). *Bearing the cross: Martin Luther King, Jr. and the Southern Christian Leadership Conference*. New York: William Morrow, 1986.
Kirk, J. (2005). *Martin Luther King, Jr*. New York: Pearson Longman.
——. (Ed.). (2007). *Martin Luther King, Jr. and the Civil Rights Movement: Controversies and debates*. London: Palgrave Macmillan.

MESTIZOS/MESTIZAS Derived from the Latin *mixtus*, Spanish *mesto*, the Spanish *mestizo* (masculine), *mestiza* (feminine), plural *mestizos/mestizas*, originally referred to hybrid plants and animals. It was only after the establishment of the Spanish viceroyalties in the Americas in the six-teenth century that the term was applied to the mixed **race** populations that originated during colonization. Despite progressively becoming the majority in much of the American possessions, *mestizos/mestizas* were outside official classifications of Indian and White. Furthermore, the forced arrival of Africans also contributed to the development of this mixed race popula-tion, not only in the Caribbean or in Portuguese Brazil, but also in the viceroy-alties of New Spain, Peru, and Argentina.

The stigma associated with *mestizaje* (miscegenation) became stronger during the nineteenth century due to "scientific" belief in the degenerative consequences of racial mixing. However, the celebration of the *mestizo/mestiza*, not only as the charac-teristic inhabitant of Latin American soci-eties, but as the basis for future regional and even world progress, was first pro-posed in 1870 Eugenio María de Hostos (1839–1903), a major nineteenth century Puerto Rican and Caribbean intellectual. In 1870, he published an article signifi-cantly titled "El cholo" – a term sometimes used derogatorily for Andean Amerindians and *mestizos/mestizas.*

However, it was only in the early twen-tieth century that the celebration of the *mestizo/mestiza* became central to ideas of nationhood throughout much of Latin America. By then, Latin American intellec-tuals – such as José Martí – and European and (North) American scholars – such as Franz Boas – had begun a consistent cri-tique of scientific racism. Another factor undermining racialism was the impact of the Mexican Revolution (1910–20), seen by many as a process of political and cul-tural regeneration led by the *mestizo/mes-tiza* and indigenous majority.

The Mexican philosopher José Vasconcelos (1882–1959) reformulated Hostos's ideas, giving them his own vision-ary and near-mystical spin in his work *The Cosmic Race* (1925). For Vasconcelos, the *mestizo/mestiza* constituted the forerunner of what he called the "cosmic race," which, through miscegenation, would not only aggregate what he believed were specific racial virtues, but also usher in a new age of peace and collaboration among racially mixed individuals. But, despite his rejec-tion of racialism, Vasconcelos's writings exhibit a patriarchal and anti-indigenous view of Latin American history. It is the Spanish conquistadors who, out of "an abundance of love," began the process of *mestizaje* that would ultimately lead to the cosmic race. Indigenous populations, on the other hand, are bizarrely described as degraded descendants of the "red race" of Atlantis.

There has frequently been a conservative aspect to discourses of *mestizaje*, in that they justify nations in which non-white majorities are subordinated to Westernized elites and frequently slight the contri-butions of black populations to national **identity**. *Indigenismo*, the political and lit-erary defense of indigenous **cultures**, has frequently been seen as a radical alterna-tive to discourses of *mestizaje*. However, *indigenismo*, like the celebration of the *mestizo/mestiza*, has implicitly proposed **assimilation** into national versions of Hispanic culture and, therefore, can be seen as ultimately justifying the disappear-ance of the Amerindian cultures it claims to defend. A perhaps different kind of *indi-genismo* and *mestizaje* was proposed by the Peruvian novelist José María Arguedas who, in *The Fox from Up Above and the Fox from Down Below* (1970), celebrated Spanish/Quechua biculturalism. However, since the 1980s, invigorated indigenous movements – in particular in Guatemala, Ecuador, and Bolivia and, since the rise of the *Zapatista* rebellion, Mexico – have rejected the homogenizing ideologies of *indigenismo* and *mestizaje*.

Given US racial hierarchies, the celebra-tion of the *mestizo/mestiza* has been seen by many **Latinos**/Latinas as empowering.

A popular self-designation among descendants of Mexicans was *la Raza* (the Race), which, in addition to echoing the "cosmic race," may also have had as one of its origins Vasconcelos's motto for the Mexican University system: "Through my race the spirit will speak." Vasconcelos was a major influence on the writings of the Chicano (the name taken by politically-active descendants of Mexicans) civil-rights movement in the late 1960s. In fact, *El plan de Santa Bárbara* (1969), one of the documents that first proposed Chicano studies as a distinct academic field, has as an epigraph Vasconcelos's phrase. "I Am Joaquín" (1967), an influential agit prop poem by Rodolfo Corky González, traces the history of Mexican and Chicano *mestizaje* from the encounter of the Aztecs and Spaniards to the Chicano movement. While the poem stresses the historical and psychological ambiguity of the *mestizo* – the poetic persona claims alternatively to have been Aztec and Spaniard, exploited and exploiter – there is the clear implication that this "confusion," a word repeated throughout the poem, will be overcome through participation in the Chicano struggle. The Young Lords, the radical US-based Puerto Rican civil-rights group of the 1960s, also adopted *la Raza* as a communal nominator, for instance in their "13-Point Program and Platform."

By the 1980s, there was a reaction against the **nationalist** and patriarchal ideas frequently present in Latino versions of the discourse of *mestizaje*. The key figure here is the Chicana poet and scholar **Gloria Anzaldúa**. In her *Borderlands/La Frontera: The New Mestiza* (1987), Anzaldúa undermines Chicano nationalism by redefining Aztlán, the mythical geographic origin of the Aztecs frequently identified with the US Southwest, as the borderlands, that is as the location of cultural, racial, and gender hybridization. Moreover, Chicano patriarchy is contested by proposing the new *mestiza*, not the implicitly male *mestizo*, as the active conduit for cultural change. Vasconcelos is explicitly referred to as an **anti-racist** thinker, though his famous motto is rewritten as: "Through the woman of my race the spirit will speak." In fact, *Borderlands* reinterprets Vasconcelos's utopianism and mythic writing style from a radical queer feminist perspective, in which cultural, racial, and gender in-betweenness are seen as undermining binary thinking and as making a more just society possible. Instead of the celebration of the *mestizo*, as incarnating nationalist values, the (new) *mestiza* is seen as both the product of a history of struggle and as going beyond the dualities that underlie the dyad exploitation/resistance.

A conservative critic of *Chicanismo*, Richard Rodriguez, also exhibits the direct influence of Vasconcelos. His first book, *Hunger of memory: The education of Richard Rodriguez* (1982) is a call for the complete acculturation of ethnic subjects. However, in his subsequent writings, in particular *Days of obligation: A conversation with my Mexican father* (1992) and *Brown: The last discovery of America* (2002), he makes use of Vasconcelos's ideas to celebrate "browning," that is processes of incorporation, including *mestizaje*, that change individuals in both the source and target cultures.

Despite their ideological differences, Anzaldúa and Rodriguez respond to the social changes of the past 20 years: immigration from Latin America, Africa, and Asia into Europe and North America, economic globalization, the rise of a world mass culture industry, the instantaneity of communication, etc. These have undermined notions of racial and cultural purity throughout the world. The processes set in motion by the first colonial globalization of the sixteenth century have become radicalized both in intensity and extensity, as no area of the world is isolated. Cultural and actual *mestizos/mestizas* are rapidly becoming the majority, not only in Latin

America but throughout the world. [JEDC]

Key readings

Arrizón, A. (2006). *Queering Mestizaje: Transculturation and performance.* Ann Arbor: University of Michigan Press.

De Castro, J. E. (2002). *Mestizo nations: Culture, race and conformity in Latin American literature.* Tucson, AZ: University of Arizona.

Miller, M. G. (2004). *Rise and fall of the cosmic race: The cult of Mestizaje in Latin America.* Austin, TX: University of Texas.

Pérez Torres, R. (2006). *Mestizaje: Critical uses of race in Chicano culture.* Minneapolis, MN: University of Minnesota Press.

Sanjinés, J. (2004). *Mestizaje upside-down: Aesthetics policies in modern Bolivia.* Pittsburgh, PA: University of Pittsburgh.

MINORITY A minority group is one that is socially, politically, and economically subordinated by the dominant (majority) group in a given society, due to the stigma that the majority attaches to their perceived physical or cultural characteristics. Minority groups frequently suffer **discrimination**, racialization, and marginalization at the hands of majority group individuals and majority-controlled social institutions. These unequal **power** relations lead to disparities between members of minority groups and the majority group in key indicators of life chances, such as levels of educational and occupational attainment. Minority group status is both subjective and objective. Minorities are identified as different by the majority; and they also often see themselves as a group sharing a common burden. However, just as **"race"** is recognized as a social construct, many scholars have likewise deconstructed the assumptions involved in the various conceptualizations of the term "minority."

Indeed, the terms "majority" and "minority" can be malleable and dynamic. Their conceptualization varies across time and space.

Generally, minority groups are determined on the basis of perceived ethno-racial differences. They are then placed by the majority at or near the bottom of an ethno-racial hierarchy. Will Kymlicka makes a useful distinction between voluntary immigrant minorities, and involuntary, territorially concentrated, and often conquered national minorities, such as the indigenous groups of the Americas. In addition, distinct and isolated religious groups such as the Amish, or, ethnic groups whose ethnic **identity** cannot be separated from a religion – such as Irish Catholics or Jewish people – may be called *ethno-religious* minority groups. In Western Europe, *religious* boundaries trump other markers of minority status, since Muslim minorities there are stigmatized on that basis. Gay people and disabled Americans are other examples of non-ethnic minorities: they may be of any race, but are still disadvantaged by the majority.

A minority group in the sociological sense need not even be a numerical minority in a given locale. Thus, given the criterion of subjugation by a dominant group, women and black South Africans also fall under the rubric of minority groups. Women often suffer from pay and employment discrimination. South African blacks were disenfranchised under **apartheid** and they remain severely socio-economically disadvantaged today.

In the United States, a major change has occurred in the post-war era in the legal treatment of minorities. In 1954, the Supreme Court's *Brown* v. *Board of Education* decision prohibited the *de jure* **segregation** of schools; and the Civil Rights Act of 1964 (along with other subsequent acts of Congress) extended voting rights for minority groups and prohibited segregation and discrimination on the basis of race, color, religion, sex, or national origin. These were followed by more race-conscious policies, such as affirmative action, school busing, bilingual education, and race-based electoral redistricting, resulting in a government-sanctioned classification of Americans into what Hollinger calls the "ethnoracial pentagon." Four official minority groups were identified (alongside non-Hispanic whites): African-Americans, Hispanics, Native Americans, and Asian-Americans, who were all regarded as being in need of affirmative state action to remedy the effects of ethno-racial subordination. Thus, while original efforts were arguably targeted primarily at African-Americans, civil rights policies have gradually come to expand to other groups designated as disadvantaged ethno-racial minorities that were deemed analogous to African-Americans. Globally, countries like Canada, Australia, the United Kingdom, and the Netherlands have also implemented similar group-conscious civil rights policies in recent decades, while France has been ideologically averse to designating official minority groups, due to its universalist republican model of citizenship.

A number of complications arise in the conceptualization of American minority groups. For instance, first, official groups constructed by policymakers may be too broad to have conceptual utility: a poor immigrant from rural Laos may belong to the same "racial" group as, say, a mixed-race, US-born Japanese-American professional. However, these constructed categories may nonetheless still foster a group identity among the classified. Second, the term "minority" implies a "white" majority, which is itself not an organic, cohesive group that is uniformly privileged. Scholars have also shown that Southern and Eastern European immigrants, who were non-Protestant and were once perceived as "racially" different, have now gradually **assimilated** into the white majority, thus changing the definition of the majority. Third, an apparently distinct minority racial or ethno-religious background need not equal socio-economic subordination: even though Asian-Americans and Jewish-Americans are racial or religious minorities, their average incomes surpass those of most other groups.

Finally, groups and the social boundaries between them can be fluid and malleable. Immigration from Africa and the Caribbean may complicate the heretofore cohesive African-American group identity built on a shared experience of oppression and resistance. Furthermore, the fact that half of all **Latinos** identify themselves as "white," as well as the rapidly increasing rates of socio-economic assimilation and intermarriage with non-Hispanic whites among US-born Latinos and Asians, may also complicate received concepts and perhaps necessitate a redefinition of the terms "majority" and "minority" in the United States in the near future. On the other hand, the continuing structural disadvantages suffered by many African-Americans and Latinos, and their continuing racialization and stigmatization, are proof that ethno-racial stratification is alive and well in American society. [US]

Key readings

Alba, R. (2009). *Blurring the color line*. Cambridge, MA: Harvard University Press.

Bleich, E. (2003). *Race politics in Britain and France: Ideas and policymaking since the 1960s*. New York: Cambridge University Press.

Gleason, P. (1991). Minorities (almost) all: The minority concept in American social thought. *American Quarterly*, 43(3), 392–424.

Hollinger, D. (1995). *Postethnic America: Beyond multiculturalism*. New York: Basic Books.

Kasinitz, P., Mollenkopf, J., Waters, M.C., & Holdaway, J. (2008). *Inheriting the city: The children of immigrants come of age.* Cambridge, MA: Harvard University Press.

Kymlicka, W. (1995). *Multicultural citizenship: A liberal theory of minority rights.* Oxford: Oxford University Press.

Omi, M. & Winant, H. (1989). *Racial formation in the United States: From the 1960s to the 1980s.* New York: Routledge & Kegan Paul Inc.

Skrentny, J. (2002). *Minority rights revolution.* Cambridge, MA: Harvard University Press.

MODEL MINORITY The term "model minority" refers to **minority** groups that have ostensibly achieved a high level of success in contemporary US society. The term has been used most often to describe Asian Americans, a group seen as having attained educational and financial success relative to other immigrant groups. The "model minority" label on its surface seems to be an accolade because it appears to praise Asian Americans for their achievements. However, a critical analysis of the way the term is used and the consequences of its use suggest that there are pernicious effects of classifying Asian Americans, or any racial group, as a model minority.

History of the term
The term "model minority" was coined in 1966 by sociologist William Petersen in an article he wrote for *The New York Times Magazine* entitled "Success story: Japanese American style." Petersen emphasized that family structure and a cultural emphasis on hard work allowed Japanese Americans to overcome the **discrimination** against their group and achieve a measure of success in the United States. Numerous popular press articles subsequently appeared describing the "successes" of various Asian American groups. Explanations for the

seeming success of Asian Americans focused variously on Confucian values, work ethic, centrality of family, and genetic superiority. One factor that was often overlooked in these accounts was US immigration law. The 1965 Immigration Act reversed years of restrictive immigration policies that virtually banned all immigration from Asia, allowing for a greater number of immigrants to enter the United States from non-Western countries, including countries in Asia and Latin America. Although this act lifted previous geographic restrictions, it allowed only those with certain backgrounds to enter the United States. After immediate family members of those already in the United States, the second priority was recruiting professionals and scientists. As a result, a large influx of highly-educated professionals (such as doctors and engineers) and scientists from Asia left their home countries after 1965 and immigrated to the Unites States. It is this group of Asian Americans, and their children, that make up a significant portion of the Asian American community today. A radical change in US immigration policy can thus explain some of the individual success stories profiled in popular press articles describing Asian American success.

Model minority myth?
Although there are national statistics that suggest that Asian Americans have achieved some measure of success in US society, disaggregating the statistics reveals a different story. According to the 2006 Census data, when combined into one group, Asian Americans earn a greater household income than Whites ($66,060 vs $53,910), Blacks ($32,876), and **Latinos** ($38,853). Educational attainment from the 2000 Census shows a similar pattern: a greater percentage of Asian Americans attend college than Whites (65 percent vs 54 percent). On the face of it, the Asian American community may appear to be

doing quite well. However, the term "model minority" is often accompanied by the word "myth" because many scholars have argued that the assumptions that Asian Americans are doing well is overgeneralized and inaccurate. First, the use of household income statistics obscures the fact that many Asian American families have larger households with more adults who are employed than White families. Second, although some Asian American ethnic groups may be doing relatively well, there are many Asian American ethnic groups that not doing well compared to the rest of the US population. For instance, according to the 2000 Census, Cambodians have a per-capita income of $10,215, and over 90 percent of their population does not have a bachelor's degree, significantly lower than the comparable statistics for the US overall ($21,587 per capita income and 76 percent without a bachelor's degree). Third, Asian Americans make up a disproportionately high percentage of those living in poverty; the 2005 Census data reveals that 11 percent of Asian Americans live below the poverty line, compared to 8 percent of Whites. Asian Americans are also uninsured at a higher rate than Whites (18 percent vs 11 percent). Focusing on the Asian Americans who have "made it" renders invisible those in the community who continue to struggle.

Relying on aggregate household income and education statistics also obscures the fact that White Americans still hold a disproportionate number of the top positions in US society. Even today, there is only one Asian American governor and two Asian American senators (both from Hawaii). Similarly, the top-level positions in business are still overwhelmingly filled by Whites. Asian Americans have also encountered a glass ceiling, making up less than 1.5 percent of the top executives in Fortune 1000 firms. Perhaps most telling, Asian Americans realize lower returns on their education than Whites, meaning that Asian Americans require more years of education to achieve the same level of income as Whites. Asian Americans, like other minority groups, have not yet achieved a level of success that is commensurate to the success of Whites, even when education differences are controlled for across the two groups. Moreover, this is true even of Asian Americans born in the United States, suggesting that a lack of facility with English does not fully explain the greater achievement of Whites. Taken together, these observations reveal that the model minority **stereotype** is problematic because it masks many of the struggles faced by Asian Americans.

Consequences for Asian Americans

While some Asian Americans embrace the seemingly positive characterization of their group, others resist it because of the negative consequences it has for the Asian American community. On the one hand, social psychological experiments have shown that being stereotyped as smart may benefit Asian Americans in test-taking situations because positive stereotypes about one's group can boost performance. On the other hand, the model minority myth can be harmful to Asian Americans who may feel pressure to live up to unrealistic expectations. In addition, believing that Asian Americans are a model minority diverts attention away from any discrimination they may have faced and continue to face. Asian Americans who mention discrimination may seem to be complaining about something that does not exist or is not serious. However, discrimination against Asian Americans is real. Asian Americans are often mistaken for foreign citizens, are believed to be more loyal to Asia than to the United States, and have little political support among other Americans. Moreover, although being stereotyped as smart may seem like a good thing, seeming too competent garners feelings of envy and competition, especially in situations where resources may be scarce (such as during bad economic times). Envied groups are also often viewed as cold and unsociable, reflecting a tradeoff between competence and likability in perceptions of social groups. Thus, although the model minority's high competence may be (begrudgingly) admired, it can at the same time undermine liking for the group and lead to **prejudice**. Whites have initiated hate crimes against Asian Americans because of a belief that Asian Americans were achieving too much and taking resources, such as jobs, away from Whites. The model minority myth can also obscure socioeconomic diversity within the Asian American community and prevent Asian Americans who need assistance from getting it. More research is necessary to identify the situations in which the model minority label benefits as opposed to harms Asian Americans.

Consequences for relationships between minority groups

Scholars argue that the model minority label serves to undermine positive relationships between ethnic groups. The model minority myth reinforces the American dream by promoting the image that hard work pays off. This rhetoric can be divisive, because it can be used as a tool to reinforce the subordinate position of other minority groups ("they made it, why can't you?") and prevent cooperation between Asian Americans and other minorities. In addition, the characterization of Asian Americans as a model minority can be used to undermine support for programs that help other minority groups to achieve success, such as affirmative action, by suggesting that affirmative action beneficiaries should be able to work hard and achieve success without any assistance.

Consequences for majority groups

Asian Americans' status as the model minority also has negative effects on Whites. Referring to Asian Americans as a model minority not only compares them to other minorities, but it has also been used to suggest that Asian Americans are, in the words of a *Newsweek* article "outwhiting the Whites." Reminding White men about the stereotype of Asian superiority in math results in White underperformance because they are fearful of confirming the stereotype that their racial group has inferior abilities in math. In some parts of the country, this fear is manifested in White parents pulling their children out of schools with high Asian American populations so that their children do not have to compete with Asian American students.

Summary

The model minority label characterizes Asian Americans as a hard working and docile racial group that has achieved financial and educational success in the United States. On the face of it, this label may seem to be an accolade, but a closer examination of the assumptions and the consequences that accompany such a label reveal the problematic nature of this construct. The model minority label renders invisible Asian Americans who are not successful, creates resentment by other groups, and pits racial groups against one another. Taken together, the evidence suggests that the use of the term "model minority" to describe any racial group is problematic. [SC & GB]

Key readings

Aronson, J., Lustina, M. J., Good, C., Keough, K., Steele, C. M., & Brown, J. (1999). When White men can't do math: Necessary and sufficient factors in stereotype threat. *Journal of Experimental Social Psychology*, 35(1), 29–46.

DeNavas-Walt, C., Proctor, B. D., & Lee, C. H. (2006). *U.S. Census Bureau: Current population reports, P60-231: Income, poverty, and health insurance coverage in the United States, 2005*. Washington, DC: U.S. Government Printing Office.

Lin, M. H., Kwan, V. S. Y., Cheung, A., & Fiske, S. T. (2005). Stereotype content model explains prejudice for an envied outgroup: Scale of anti-Asian American stereotypes. *Personality and Social Psychology Bulletin*, 31(1), 34.

Maddux, W. W., Galinsky, A. D., Cuddy, A. J. C., & Polifroni, M. (2008). When being a model minority is good … and bad: Realistic threat explains negativity toward Asian Americans. *Personality and Social Psychology Bulletin*, 34(1), 74.

Mervis, J. (2005). US workforce: A glass ceiling for Asian Scientists? *Science*, 310(5748), 606–607.

Shih, M., Ambady, N., Richeson, J. A., Fujita, K., & Gray, H. M. (2002). Stereotype performance boosts: The impact of self-relevance and the manner of stereotype activation. *Journal of Personality and Social Psychology*, 83(3), 638–647.

Wu, F. (2002). *Yellow: Race in America beyond Black and White*. New York: Basic Books.

MULTICULTURALISM The first decade of the twenty-first century in the West has been marked by a profound re-evaluation of multiculturalism as a prescription for living together in complex, **postcolonial**, multiethnic societies. Paradoxically, globalization – the spread of the neoliberal economic doctrine around the world – while certainly resulting in increased cultural diversity, has often been met with a retreat into a narrow, ethnoracial **nationalism** that eschews the inevitability of hybridization. In Europe, since 2004 in particular, states such as the United Kingdom, the Netherlands, and Denmark, once advocates of multicultural policy, have declared multiculturalism to be "in crisis." They now espouse the integration of "national values" to replace what is seen to be the permissiveness of multiculturalism past which, according to Trevor Phillips, resulted in societies "sleepwalking into **segregation**."

However, the multiculturalism which today is deemed to be beset by crisis relates not so much to the policies put in place by various governments in recognition of cultural, ethnic and religious pluralism in their societies, but to the fact of diversity itself. As David Goodhart wrote in his controversial 2004 article, "too much diversity" discourages social **solidarity** in a welfare state: the more different someone is from oneself, the less likely an individual is to want to share resources with her. The notion that Western societies risk disintegration from an excess of diversity reveals the problematic definition of multiculturalism itself, which this article addresses.

David Goldberg (2004) distinguishes between descriptive and normative multiculturalism. The former describes the ethnic, cultural, religious and national plurality of Western, postcolonial, urban spaces resulting from increased global migration since the end of the Second World War. The second is a prescriptive outlook which actively celebrates the proliferation of diversity, even insisting on the relative value of different **cultures** to each other, thus resisting the hegemony of national(ist) culture. As Goldberg notes, "'The multicultural' has been caught in an oscillation between these two understandings: description and prescription." In reality, the often begrudging recognition of the former resulted in a variety of policy arrangements that sought to appease "minority communities" in the interests of maintaining social harmony in the face of "racial" unrest and without revoking a commitment to a narrative of the homogeneous nation.

Anthias and Yuval-Davis, in their 1992 work *Racialized Boundaries*, portray multicultural policy as a response to the realization that the "melting pot does not melt." US-American strategies of **assimilation** assumed that the linguistic, cultural and ethnic differences of immigrants from across the globe would fade once incorporated into the great American "melting pot." Effectively, this meant less desirable racialized minorities denying their heritage and assimilating the values of white America. The multicultural response of the 1960s conceded the impossibility of complete assimilation. Hence, the melting pot metaphor is replaced with that of a "salad bowl" of distinct cultural groups, each finding their place within the "mosaic" of society.

The move from assimilation to multiculturalism, however, is not due to a straightforward recognition of the failure of the melting pot to bring about an end to the supremacist status of white Europeans and the ongoing **discrimination** against blacks and other racialized minorities. Calls from civil rights and **anti-racist** activists, in the United States and the United Kingdom most notably, did not focus on cultural recognition but on equality of rights and, more radically, an end to racist oppression. To understand why multiculturalism is posited as a solution to racial discord, for example following the 1958 anti-black Notting Hill "**race** riots" in London, attention should be paid to the roots of culturalization.

The origins of contemporary multiculturalist policies can be found in the post-1945 anti-racism of international institutions, specifically in the emphasis placed by organizations such as UNESCO on the principle of cultural relativism as a means of combating racism.

This stance formed the background for the elite response to racism among many Western governments, and played an important role in elevating the discourse of culture to its current status. The group of anthropologists and anti-racist scientists who drafted the UNESCO "Statement on the nature of race differences" (1951) set out both to disprove race as a scientific theory and to propose an alternative concept for understanding human difference. This alternative concept was culture. In accepting that race as a categorization of humanity was scientifically false, the UNESCO scientists nevertheless understood that human diversity – especially in an era of immigration – needed explaining.

Culture was seen as a means of capturing the differences between human groups. No superiority or inferiority was inferred; rather, the uneven spread of "progress" created a coexistence of equal-but-different groups, each bringing to the world its own competencies. UNESCO promoted the idea of intercultural knowledge as a means of combining cross-cultural understanding and cultural diversity with the slogan: "reconciling fidelity to oneself with openness to others."

For the UNESCO approach, the continuing realities of racism were attributed to individual **prejudice**; the historic role of the European nation-state in utilizing the category of race in its political projects was ignored. Thus, by replacing race with culture, the UNESCO project failed to engage with the realities of **imperialism**, slavery, class inequalities or tight migration controls. In this, UNESCO permitted European states to deny the centrality of the idea of race to their formation – an evasion that persists, in the post-racial vision popularized today.

Multicultural policies were set in motion by governments eager to by-pass the conflictual terrain of racial injustice. These policies, rather than diversity itself, have indeed sown the seeds of segregation by relying on a reified view of "ethnic minority communities" that refuses to see the extent of their internal diversity. Policies drawn up in collusion between governments and, often traditional and patriarchal, community leaders encouraged a unilinear view of minority culture as distinctly unmodern. The current focus on the incompatibility of Muslims with Western "culture" exemplifies the lack of attention paid within a mainstream multiculturalist vision to identity formation within all groups in "super-diverse" societies. Insistence on integration into national values reveals less of a return to universalism, but the favoring of a distinctly national particularism over the recognition of the extent to which migration and globalization lead to an "expansion of identity" in us all. [AL]

Key readings

Anthias, F. & Yuval-Davis, N. (1992). *Racialized boundaries: Race, nation, gender, colour and class and the anti-racist struggle.* London: Routledge.

Badiou, A. (2008). The communist hypothesis. *New Left Review*, 49 (January–February), 29–42.

Goldberg, D. (2002). *The racial state.* Oxford: Blackwell.

——. (2004). The space of multiculturalism. *OpenDemocracy*, 16 (September), www.opendemocracy.net/arts-multiculturalism/article_2097.jsp

Goodhart, D. (2004). Too diverse? *Prospect*, 95 (February).

Kundnani, A. (2007). *The end of tolerance: Racism in twenty-first century Britain.* London: Pluto Press.

Vertovec, S. (2007). Super-diversity and its implications. *Ethnic and Racial Studies*, 30(6).

NATIONALISM Nationalism is a term with complex and variant meanings. However, it can be usefully defined as an ideology or movement that cultivates and affirms a profound commitment to a people or country, and places primary importance on the protection and promotion of its interests. The central focus and motive force of nationalism is the nation, which can be a people, called an ethno-nation or cultural nation, or the country, which is called a nation-state. A key principle of nationalism in its various forms is the basic assumption that a distinct people has the right and responsibility of self-determination. This principle of self-determination in its fullest form requires state sovereignty. But other forms of nationalism might seek community control, political and/or cultural autonomy or a protected status within a sovereign state.

Given the negative history of pernicious, even pathological, forms of nation-state nationalism, such as jingoism, chauvinism, Nazism and fascism, there has been an effort to distinguish nationalism from patriotism. Patriotism is seen as a "civic commitment" to constitution and country, and nationalism is posed as an ethnic commitment to a people. But patriotism and nationalism often overlap, are used interchangeably and can both be excessive in ideology and practice. Also, it is difficult to separate loyalty to the country from loyalty to the people, if one is patriotic.

Nationalism has been a powerful force in human history that, arguably, can be traced from the evolution of the nation-state in ancient Egypt and its ethical ideal and concept of mission. However, most of the literature focuses on emergence of nationalism and nation-states in Europe and the French and American Revolutions in the late eighteenth century and into the nineteenth century. But the Haitian Revolution (1791–1803), in spite of its uniqueness, was based on similar ideas of freedom, equality, justice and **solidarity** of persons and peoples and prefigured the revolutionary and liberation struggles against colonialism in Latin America in the nineteenth and twentieth centuries and in Asia and Africa in the twentieth century. Also, in the United States in the 1960s, emancipatory or liberational nationalism was the central ideology of the Black Power phase (1965–75) of the Black Freedom Movement, which succeeded the

Civil Rights phase (1955–65). It also played a major role in the subsequent Native American, Chicano and Asian American Movements.

From its inception, nationalism fought an internal tension between inclusive and exclusive approaches to nation-building; liberation and oppression; universalism and isolationism; peaceful co-existence and war for expansion, domination and resource seizure, involving occupation, **ethnic cleansing**, **genocide** and holocausts. It is these horrific and destructive excesses that tend to make many scholars view nationalism as problematic and pernicious and reduce it to its most pathological forms, denying its positive and emancipatory role in history.

In its complexity, nationalism can be understood and studied in various ways. In terms of varieties of nationalism determined by its social emphasis in defining, directing and shaping the nation, it can assume religious, political, cultural or economic forms for both states and ethnic groups. Likewise, in evaluative terms that suggest the quality or character of its social thought and practice, it can be considered revolutionary, liberational, liberal or reactionary.

In its most positive form, nationalism upholds the nation – cultural and/or political – as the central context for **identity**, **culture** and the unfolding narrative of a people. The nation is also posed as the indispensable communal context for achieving and sustaining basic goods of self-determination, justice, equality and human flourishing for its members. Indeed, nation, defined as a people, becomes a morally compelling context for expressing a people's right to exist, to pursue its interests, preserve its culture, defend itself, live in a state of solidarity with its members, as well as with others, and work in cooperative projects of common good with its members and with others in society and the world. This form of nationalism opens itself up to the dynamics and demands of both a **multicultural** society and world, offering a critical alternative to nationalism's most pernicious forms, and pointing toward self-affirmation without denying the equal dignity and rights of others. [MK]

Key readings

Chavez, E. (2002). *"Mi raza primero!" (My people first!): Nationalism, identity, and insurgency in the Chicano movement in Los Angeles, 1966–1978*. Berkeley, CA: University of California Press.

Couture, J., Nielsen, K., & Seymour, M. (Eds.). (1998). *Rethinking nationalism: Canadian Journal of Philosophy*. Supplement Volume 22.

Karenga, M. (2008). *Kawaida and questions of life and struggle*. Los Angeles, CA: University of Sankore Press.

Liu, M. (2008). *The snake dance of Asian American activism: Community, vision, and power*. Lanham, MD: Lexington Books.

McKim, R. & McMahan, J. (Eds.). (1997). *The morality of nationalism*. Oxford: Oxford University Press.

Moore, M. (2001). Normative justifications for liberal nationalism: Justice, democracy and national identity. *Nations and Nationalism*, 7(1), 1–20.

Pinkney, A. (1976). *Red, black and green: Black nationalism in the United States*. New York: Cambridge University Press.

Smith, P. C. & Warrior, R. A. 1997, *Like a hurricane: The Indian Movement from Alcatraz to Wounded Knee*, New Press, New York.

NAWAL EL SAADAWI Nawal El Saadawi was born in 1931, in the small rural village of Kafr Tahla, to a prominent local family. She proved to be an excellent student and was able to enter Cairo University's medical school, from which she graduated in 1955. While practicing medicine in Kafr

Tahla, and later Cairo, she began writing short stories and personal accounts, including *Memoirs of a woman doctor*. In Cairo, she was appointed Director of Public Health within the Ministry of Public Health. Her experiences with counseling patients on medical and sexual issues led to her seminal text, *al-Mar'a wa al-Jins* (*Women and sex*). She could not publish it in Egypt, due to that country's limited press freedom, but was able to publish it in Lebanon, in 1972. The book created a sensation because its language and content were far more graphic than was customary and the issues nearly unrecognized in public life. After her book appeared, she was summarily dismissed from the Ministry of Health. She then joined the Faculty of Medicine of Ain Shams University where, from 1973–76, she specialized in women's psychiatry. She later became editor of a health journal and the Assistant General Secretary of the Medical Association in Egypt.

El Saadawi first came to the attention of Western readers in the context of the international women's movement, which was expanding rapidly in the early 1980s. Her account of her early childhood experiences growing up in rural Egypt, *Al Wajh al-ari lil-Mar'a al-Arabiya*, was translated by her husband, Sherif Hetata (who is also a prominent physician, writer, and public intellectual). *The hidden face of Eve: Women of the Arab world*, became an instant bestseller and was widely assigned in the burgeoning women's studies classes of that era. Her account of being "circumcised" or subjected to female genital mutilation (FGM) brought the practice to the attention of Western readers. Many have argued that the practice of FGM then became a lightning rod for those anxious about Muslim societies in general and a means of masking wider geopolitical challenges impacting Muslim women and men in Africa and the Middle East. On the other hand, the success of her writings led

to the writing, publication, and translation of other books by Arab and Muslim women, and readers now have available a far more nuanced and varied selection than when she began writing.

El-Saadawi was among the prominent intellectuals and Islamists arrested in 1981 for their opposition to the regime. She was released shortly after Sadat's assassination by Islamist militants and wrote an account of her prison experiences *Memoirs from the women's prison*. She was an outspoken opponent of Egypt's participation in the US-led Gulf War of 1991. Under threat from Islamists and the Egyptian government, she accepted teaching positions at Duke University and Washington State University. During this period, she spoke widely to university audiences and appeared at numerous conferences. In 1996, she returned to Egypt where she continued her political activity. Islamists charged her with apostasy, but she was able to defeat them in court. In recent years, she has continued her writing, political activism, and championing of women's rights in Egypt and abroad. She is a pioneer of the women's rights movement in Egypt, a prominent writer, and a longtime defender of international human rights. [NG]

Key readings

Amireh, A. (2000). Framing Nawal El Saadawi: Arab feminism in a transnational world. *Signs*, 26(1), 215–249.

El Saadawi, N. (1982 [1979]). *Woman at point zero*. (S. Hetata, Trans.) London: Zed Books Ltd.

——. (1985 [1974]). *The death of the only man in the world* (S. Hetata, Trans.). London: Zed Books.

——. (1985 [1983]). *Two women in one*. (O. Nusairi and J. Gough, Trans.) London: Al Saqui.

——. (1987 [1980]). *Death of an ex-minister*. (S. Eber, Trans.). London: Methuen.

——. (1987 [1979]). *She has no place in paradise.* (S. Eber, Trans.). London: Methuen.

——. (1988 [1987]). *The fall of the imam.* (S. Hetat, Trans.). London: Methuen.

——. (1989 [1978]). *The circling song.* (M. Booth, Trans.). London: Zed Books.

——. (1991 [1968]). *Searching.* (S. Eber, Trans.). London: Zed Books.

——. (1994). *The innocence of the devil.* (S. Hetata, Trans.). Berkeley, CA: University of California Press.

——. (1994 [1984]). *Memoirs from the women's prison.* (M. Booth, Trans.). London: Methuen.

——. (1997). *The Nawal El Saadawi reader.* London: Zed Books.

——. (1999). *A daughter of Isis: An autobiography of Nawal El Saadawi.* London: Zed Books.

——. (2001 [1960]). *Memoirs of a woman doctor.* (C. Cobham, Trans.). San Francisco, CA: City Lights Books.

Tarabishi, G. (2001). *Woman against her sex.* London: Saqi Books.

NIGGER "Nigger" is a complex term that has been the focus of much interest and debate over the years. However, there is little consensus about either the origins, meaning or multiple meanings of this word. Most involved in the debate, however, agree that "nigger" stands alone when it comes to the ability of an ethnic epithet to hurt those at which it is hurled. Harvard Law School professor and author Randall Kennedy stated "it is arguably the most consequential social insult in American history." The word is so offensive and derogatory to some that it is sometimes referred to as the "N-word" in speech or "n*gger" in written communications because individuals do not want to either say or write the word.

Origins – epistemology
"Nigger" appears to have derived from words that meant "black" in various European languages, for example, from the Latin term "niger," the French term "nègre" and the Spanish word "negro." Some contend that the term was in early use to refer to individuals from Africa, India, Australia and Polynesia, and was merely descriptive of skin color void of negative connotation. Others suggest that the description was not a reference to skin color, but rather an indication of the physical location from whence some of the enslaved dark skinned people came – areas along the Niger River in East Africa. During the early 1800s, authors of slave narratives referred to themselves, their family members and other slaves and former slaves as *niggers*. In these narratives (some written by slave owners) there appeared to be no intention to insult or denigrate, as illustrated by the title of what is believed to be the first book written by a black-American female, *Our Nig or Sketches from a life of a free Black* (published in 1859).

It is not clear when "nigger" came to be used and understood as pejorative or derogative to blacks. In 1884 Mark Twain published *The adventures of Huckleberry Finn*. The book was a satire of an earlier era and spoke of white-on-black racism. The *adventures of Huckleberry Finn* was banned from libraries when Twain was alive, and criticized then and later for his frequent use of the word "nigger" when he referred to "Huck" Finn's companion as the "runaway nigger named Jim," and to other black characters in the novel. At some point prior to the publication of Twain's book, "nigger" seemed to have crossed the line from descriptive of either skin color or geographic region of origin to an insult that was a code word that suggested and communicated beliefs of black inferiority held by the white majority. This sensitivity to the use of "nigger" in Mark Twain's novels suggests that Twain's contemporaries understood the code embedded in "nigger," and this code was intended to convey a less-than-positive image of the former enslaved individuals from African descent. It is important to note that, rather than dismiss it, authors such as Langston Hughes and Richard Hughes use *Finn* to capture and convey the hatred and contempt Southern whites had for blacks.

Current use and meaning

"Nigger" is but one of many ethnic epithets used to refer to members of numerical **minority** groups in the United States and beyond. Examples of other derogatory terms for numerical minority groups include "spic," "chink," "wetback" and "wop," to name a few. An Internet search using the search engine Google.com revealed almost five million references to "nigger." Other searches resulted in almost two million references to "spic," more than one million mentions of "chink" and more than three hundred thousand references to "wetback." While spic and chink results were not solely in reference to derogatory terms for members of ethnic groups, all results for "nigger" and "wetback" alluded to terms for African-Americans and Mexicans, respectively. The universal understanding that "nigger" refers to black people is quite interesting; however, it should be noted that not all the references to "nigger" could be characterized as negative. Just as there appear to be multiple potential origins and meanings of the term "nigger" from the distant past, we may be no closer to understanding what "nigger" means today.

Consistent with this previous lack of precision, dictionaries include multiple definitions of "nigger." These include: a black person (usually offensive), a member of any dark-skinned ethnic group (also usually offensive), and/or a member of a socially disadvantaged group. Interestingly, the last example is not designated as offensive. Regardless of these multiple definitions, the Merriam-Webster Online Dictionary indicates that "nigger" "now ranks as perhaps the most offensive and inflammatory racial slur in English."

An interesting aspect of ethnic slurs and racial epithets is that their meanings can be vague, fluid and based on the manner in which these terms are used. For example, when "nigger" is used by a non-black to address a black individual, the black individual might interpret the term "nigger" as threatening, debasing and/or insulting. However, when an African-American uses "nigger" in conversation with another African-American, the word may be viewed as a term of endearment or, in some cases, an expression of respect as suggested by Kennedy and others. This latter usage is understood by some as an attempt by African-Americans to rob the term of its ability to hurt them by changing the meaning of the word. Our understanding of "nigger" is further complicated because some contend the meaning of the term varies with the spelling. That is, some people suggest that "nigger" or "nigra" are insulting terms used primarily by whites and that "nigga" can be a friendly term used by blacks to refer to each other.

Additionally, the meaning or degree of offensiveness of "nigger" seems to vary according to the **culture** of the individuals participating in the communication, even when all are black individuals of African descent. For example, African-Americans might consistently perceive "nigger" spoken by a non-black to be denigrating. However, Afro-Caribbeans might not consider hearing "nigger" from the same non-black as insulting because of differences in historical experiences of racism among African-Americans and Afro-Caribbeans. In addition, the emotional reactions of African-Americans to the term "nigger" differ from those of other people from the African **diaspora**. When the context suggests that "nigger" is meant as an insult, many African-Americans might be more likely to respond with physical violence than others. [CMM]

Key readings

Asim, J. (2007). *The n word: Who can say it, who shouldn't and why.* Boston, MA: Houghton Mifflin Company.

Kennedy, R. (2002). *Nigger: The strange career of a troublesome word.* New York: Pantheon.

Motley, C. M. & Craig-Henderson, K. M. (2007). Epithet or endearment? Examining reactions among those of the African Diaspora to an ethnic epithet. *Journal of Black Studies, 37,* 944–963.

NUREMBERG LAWS Almost immediately after their seizure of power in January 1933, Nazi officials began placing restrictions on Jewish life in Germany. The Nazis persecuted Jews through violence and terror on one hand, and through legislation that stripped them of their rights on the other. On April 1, 1933, the government instituted a nationwide boycott of Jewish businesses. On May 10, Goebbels staged a public burning of books by democratic, socialist, and Jewish authors in Berlin. Thousands of intellectuals, including the luminaries of Weimar **culture** and science, left Germany. But, both the boycott and the book burnings were not widely popular; not necessarily because of sympathy for the victims, but because of the inconvenience and chaos on the street; after all, the Nazis had gained their popularity on their promise that they would restore law and order to a decadent, violent interwar Germany.

Learning from public reaction, the Nazis decided to embark on an official policy of legislating Jews out of their jobs, marriages, and citizenship. In the spring of 1933, laws banning Jews from public office and forbidding them to practice as lawyers and physicians (except for other Jews) took effect. Then, in September 1935, the Nazis unveiled a much more wide-reaching anti-Jewish policy at their annual party rally in Nuremberg. The "Nuremberg Laws" defined and identified Jews in order to exclude them from public life. Included among them was the "Law for the Protection of German Blood and German Honor," which prohibited marriages and affairs between Jews and Germans. Jews were classified by a series of convoluted pseudo-scientific rather than religious definitions, in which anyone with three or four Jewish grandparents was considered a Jew. Once Jews were defined, then the Germans began to publicly identify them so that everyone would know who was an Aryan and who was not. Those who were then defined as Jews were subject to the second pernicious law, the "Reich Citizenship Law," which stripped Jews of their citizenship in Germany and made them stateless "nationals." In addition to these two laws, Jews were removed from many parts of German life such as the military, graduate school, and some civil service positions.

The Nuremberg Laws ushered in a new era of official, state-legislated persecution, and opened the door to many other persecutory measures that the Nazis would enforce. The regime carefully documented public reaction to its policies through reports conducted by the security services and regional and district reports; this intelligence shows that the public reaction to these laws was indifferent if not positive, and that people were generally pleased with the reestablishment of law and order and the stabilizing of the regime through official means. The Nuremberg Laws, together with the German reaction to them, signaled to the members of the Jewish community of Germany that they were completely alone, unprotected, and vulnerable; they signaled to the outside world that Jews were in terrible danger in Germany but, sadly, the warning was not heeded. [RW]

Key readings

Allen, W. S. (1984). *The Nazi seizure of power: The experience of a single German* town, 1922–1945. New York: Franklin Watts.

Burleigh, M. & Wippermann, W. (1993). *The racial state: Germany 1933–1945.* New York: Cambridge.

Friedlander, S. (1997). *Nazi Germany and the Jews: The years of persecution, 1933–1939 (vol. 1).* New York: HarperCollins.

Hilberg, R. (1985). *The destruction of the European Jews.* New York: Holmes & Meier.

Kershaw, I. (1993). *The Nazi dictatorship: Problems and perspectives of interpretation* (2nd ed.). London: E. Arnold.

Marrus, M. R. (1987). *The Holocaust in history.* Lebanon, NH: University Press of New England.

Peukert, D. J. K. (1987). *Inside Nazi Germany: Conformity, opposition and racism in everyday life.* New Haven, CT: Yale University Press.

ORIENTALISM The term "orientalism" generally refers to prejudicial, even demeaning, self-reflective Western interpretations of Eastern cultural practices. Edward Said, in his ground-breaking *Orientalism* (1978), systematically studies Western scholarship on and **representation** of the Near East or the Arab world. Focusing on British, French, and American thinkers and artists since the nineteenth century, Said argues that, rather than pure, objective, and disinterested scholarship and cultural practices, Orientalism aims to discursively subjugate the East. It belongs to the **imperial** drive to, paraphrasing Socrates, "know thy colony" and control it. Said incisively diagnoses Orientalist representations as projecting Western desires onto the Orient, rendering the **Other** as shadow of the Self. The Orient is thus turned into **stereotypes** of extremities, or the Western Self's aspirations for beauty and love (such as the Islamic harem or Madame Butterfly), and abject fears (such as barbarism and opium). As a result, the Orientalist formula dictates that the Orient is polarized, emptied of psychological depth and subjectivity. The extremes of Samuel Taylor Coleridge's "A sunny pleasure-dome with caves of ice!" in "Kubla Khan" is split between the demonic and the domestic, with the exotic unfolding in the most predictable manner. The West projects its own neuroses onto the opposing constructs of, among others, "Khans" and "Shangri-las," of the Mongolian horde and Tibetan religiosity. Inherent in both ends of Orientalist stereotypes are transgressions and taboos that the West must shun. At a time when science and reason are secularizing the West, the need for myth and what lies beyond reason is displaced onto the Orient. Orientalism, hence, allows the West to articulate its own repressions in the name of representing the East.

The theoretical framework of *Orientalism* derives primarily from Michel Foucault's discourse theory and Antonio Gramsci's concept of hegemony. Foucault inspires Said to cross the distinction between non-political and political knowledge, in that Western Orientalists are vested in the maintenance of **power** over their subject-matter of the East. Accordingly, no such thing as "true," apolitical knowledge exists. Gramsci, on the other hand, demonstrates that consensus or hegemony can be forged in a civil society without resorting to coercion or violence. Foucauldian discursive power is woven into Gramscian hegemony to buttress Saidian Orientalism.

Iconoclastic and controversial, Said's *Orientalism* has been credited by some as having single-handedly inaugurated **postcolonialism**. Said provides a counter-hegemonic theoretical basis for Western liberals and non-Western academics in search of an alternative to canonical criticism. Many postcolonial scholars build on Said's foundational work: Gayatri Chakravorty Spivak links Said with Derridean deconstruction and the subaltern group, arguing for the need for strategic essentializing; Homi Bhabha yokes **Fanonian** psychoanalysis with Saidian colonial stereotypes, interrogating the ambivalence of nation and narration. Other scholars have taken Said to task for creating yet another totalizing, master narrative. Instead of Orientalism, critics accuse Said of Occidentalizing, to the extent of employing anti-Western rhetoric from a Western-trained elite of Palestinian descent. Critics cite as an example Said's fervent devotion to the Palestinian cause in *The question of Palestine* (1979), which Said supporters see as engaged scholarship.

Politics aside, Said does ignore counter-hegemonic voices within the colonies as well as within the Western discourse itself. Said's monolithic *Orientalism* fails to account for, in particular, inner tensions within artistic expressions. A host of scholars have challenged Said from various angles: Aijaz Ahmad from the local conditions in India and from the global theory of Marxism; Lisa Lowe from ethnic studies marked by hybridity and hetereogeneity; Dennis Porter from the ambivalent genre of travel writings; John M. MacKenzie from historicism, among others. The fact that one must contend with *Orientalism* in order to stake out a territory attests to the centrality of Said's book, its flaws notwithstanding. Any rehearsal of Said's flaws without acknowledging his potential suggests a conservative, reactionary position, one that is in denial of the fundamental power dynamics of knowledge production. After all, Said himself hints at some blind spots within his work. With the caveat that Europe sets itself off "against the Orient as a sort of surrogate and even underground self" (1978: 3), Said points away from an antithetical and mutually exclusive relationship between the West and the Orient to a symbiosis, with a sense of self-reflexivity shot through the manifest and

hegemonic as well as the subterranean and repressed half. Said elaborates in *Culture and imperialism* (1993: 51):

> As we look at the cultural archive, we begin to reread it not univocally but *contrapuntally*, with a simultaneous awareness both of the metropolitan history that is narrated and of those other histories against which (and together with which) the dominating discourse acts.

As if minor, the parenthesis, nonetheless, suggests a possible symbiotic relationship between the metropolitan and the subaltern, since "We are, so to speak, *of* the connections, not outside or beyond them." Just as the imperialist instinct propels the West to study and hence gain control of the Orient, the contrapuntal instinct leads the West to absorb, to identify with, and to *be* the Orient. Scholarship in the new millennium ought to expand Said's work to tease out the cultural complexity Said has intimated. [SM]

Key readings

Ma, S.-M. (2000). *The deathly embrace: Orientalism and Asian American identity.* Minneapolis, MN: University of Minnesota Press.

Said, E. (1978). *Orientalism.* New York: Pantheon.

OTHER "Other" is a term sometimes used by members of the dominant group to refer to members of the non-dominant or marginalized groups. Typically, group relationships in society have always been an issue of supremacy, specifically the belief that the dominant group is superior to groups or civilizations that are labeled, implicitly or explicitly, as "other." Early **assimilation** theorists and scholars specializing in world civilizations were quick to point out how clashes between **cultures** usually began with **ethnocentric** judgments of one group against another group. According to leading **race** scholars, such as Eduardo Bonilla-Silva, Joe R. Feagin, and Abby Ferber, the issue in the United States has mostly been one of **white supremacy**. Moreover, the notion of viewing outsiders as "others" has historically been used to justify the mistreatment and oppression of one group of people by another. For instance, the notion of **Manifest Destiny** in the middle 1800s was dependent on the view that the United States, as the more "civilized" nation, had a right to expand westward and assimilate or eliminate other "less civilized" or racially inferior groups in the process. Similarly, chattel slavery and the systematic theft of resources and oppressive treatment of indigenous populations under colonialism were deemed to be justifiable, based on the idea that the oppressed group represented a "less civilized" or subhuman group of people.

Orientalism and assimilation

One way to view the term "other" is through Edward Said's concept of **orientalism**. According to Said, orientalism refers to the image of the "Orient" or Eastern-based cultures as a completely different, and often inferior, system as compared to that of Western thought or ideals. Made famous in his 1978 book, *Orientalism*, Edward Said was critical of Western philosophy and **prejudice** against Eastern cultures. Said's central argument was that all discourses and philosophical stances are ideological in nature. As such, any discourse by Westerners creates a biased divide between the West and the East. Thus, Westerners typically hold the opinion that Eastern cultures and societies are untrustworthy, irrational, dangerous, and have anti-Western mentalities; specifically, they are an inferior group compared to their Western counterparts. Although orientalism is often used as a term to refer to

mostly European **imperialistic** attitudes and prejudice towards Eastern cultures and people in the eighteenth and nineteenth centuries, it has recently been used to describe the mostly negative views of Westerners towards Arabs and other Middle-Easterners. In general, orientalism refers to the "otherization" of Eastern cultures by the Western world.

Assimilation refers to the process by which people or groups voluntarily adopt or are forced to adopt the language and cultural norms and values of another group. In almost all cases, the **minority** group is expected to conform to normative practices and ideals associated with the majority group. Those who refuse to assimilate into the larger culture are typically viewed as anti-American or somehow different from or "other" than "typical" Americans. However, like most matters of group relationships in the United States, the issue of assimilation is often an issue of white supremacy. That is, who is allowed to assimilate into the dominant culture largely depends on whether that group will fit into the political, social, and economic desires of the dominant group, a group that has historically been (and continues to be) comprised of European white ethnic groups. In the United States, for example, Native Americans, African Americans, and Mexican Americans have lived there much longer than most European American groups. Unfortunately, instead of being viewed as the normative culture (or part of the normative culture), these groups continue to be viewed as "others" who have cultures that differ from the "American" or "white" culture.

Citizenship

Another way to examine how groups become or remain "otherized" is to look at the issue of citizenship. For instance, United States citizenship was once legally denied to Chinese immigrants, as well Chinese born in America. Although the law has changed so that Chinese Americans today are legal citizens, they continue to be viewed as outsiders and foreigners because of their race. One recent study exposed how Asian Americans continue to be "otherized," even those who have lived in the United States for several generations. The study illustrated that, when Asian Americans were asked where they were from, the answer that was most unsatisfactory to whites was "America." Unsatisfied that Asians can be "Americans," many whites will continue the conversation by asking, "No, where are you *really* from?" As Frank Wu has pointed out, Asian Americans are often seen as "perpetual foreigners" in the United States. For example, during the 1998 Winter Olympics ice skating competition, Michelle Kwan, a United States Olympic ice skater lost to Tara Lipinski, a white American. Following that event, MSNBC published a headline that read "American Beats out Kwan," suggesting that Kwan was not as "American" as Lapinski. Four years later, in the *Seattle Times*, a similar headline appeared again when Kwan lost to another white American, Sarah Hughes in the 2002 Winter Olympics, "Hughes Good As Gold: American Outshines Kwan, Slutskaya in Skating Surprise." Both of the above are examples of how minority groups, especially Asian Americans, continue to be relegated to "other" status by the dominant group in society.

Group threat and the future of race relations
There have been numerous studies on the relationship between minority group size and racial prejudice and discrimination. As some scholars, such as Herbert Blumer, Mark Fossett, and Lincoln Quillian have suggested, the perceived "racialized" threat of the dominant group toward a minority group, even if the threat is unfounded, leads to increased prejudice against the minority group. Other researchers, such as

Gary Becker, have argued that there is an increase in the dominant group's prejudice against minority and immigrant groups during economic downturns. Hence, during economic difficulties, there is a tendency for the majority group to blame "others" for their perceived loss of jobs, economic insecurities, and threat of job competition.

Recent debates indicate that there is no clear consensus on the future of race relations in the United States. For some scholars, such as George Yancey, future race relations in the United States will largely remain a black/white issue. Thus, future race relations will continue to be largely centered on black versus non-black issues. Other scholars, however, argue that we are moving towards a multi-racial society similar to that in many South American countries. These researchers conclude that the United States will be further racially stratified, with white groups at the top, groups such as those who identify themselves as multi-racial serving as a buffer group in the middle, and darker-skinned groups at the bottom of the racial hierarchy. Depending on which of these sides is correct, we may be witnessing a largely collective black population that represents the "other" in United States society, or a more complex tiered system with various levels of "others" who differ from one another in terms of their access to economic, political, and social resources in society. [DGE]

Key readings

Becker, G. S. (1971). *The economics of discrimination.* Chicago: University of Chicago Press.

Blumer, H. (1958). Race prejudice as a sense of group position. *Pacific Sociological Review*, 1, 3–7.

Bonilla-Silva, E. (1997). Rethinking racism: Toward a structural interpretation. *American Sociological Review*, 62(3), 465–480.

——. (2001). *White supremacy & racism in the post-Civil Rights era*. Boulder, CO: Lynne Rienner Publishers.

——. (2006). *Racism without racists: Color-blind racism and the persistence of racial inequality in the USA*. Boulder, CO: Rowman and Littlefield Publishers.

Bonilla-Silva, E., & Embrick, D. G. (2006). Black, honorary white, white: The future of race in the United States? In D. L. Brunsma (Ed.) *Mixed messages: Multiracial identities in the color-blind era*. Boulder, CO: Lynne Rienner Publishers, pp. 33–48.

Feagin, J. R. (2006). *Systemic racism: A theory of oppression*. New York, NY: Routledge.

Ferber, A. (1998). *White man falling: Race, gender, and white supremacy*. New York, NY: Roman & Littlefield.

Fossett, M. A. & Kiecolt, K. J. (1989). The relative size of minority populations and white racial attitudes. *Social Science Quarterly*, 70, 820–835.

Quillian, L. (1996). Group threat and regional change in attitudes toward African-Americans. *American Journal of Sociology*, 102(3), 816–860.

——. (1995). Prejudice as a response to perceived group threat: Population composition and anti-immigrant and racial prejudice in Europe. *American Sociological Review*, 60, 586–611.

Said, E. (1978). *Orientalism*. New York: Random House.

Wu, F. H. (2002) *Yellow: Race in America beyond black and white*. New York: Basic Books.

Yancey, G. (2003). *Who is white? Latinos, Asians, and the new black/nonblack divide*. Boulder, CO: Lynne Rienner Publishers.

PAUL GILROY Although initially affiliated with British **Cultural Studies** – as a member of the group of critics associated with the influential British-Jamaican thinker **Stuart Hall** at the Centre for Contemporary Cultural Studies at Birmingham University – Paul Gilroy has become arguably its foremost product, if not its most influential apostate. As perhaps its most well-known practitioner, his work has gone far beyond its limits, primarily in refusing the national boundaries that Cultural Studies in its initial formulations acknowledged as porous but not central to a neo-Marxist intellectual and political project.

Gilroy's work has become apostatical, then, in identifying national, cultural and *racial* boundaries as in fact constituting the primary problems of materialist analysis and of classic Cultural Studies itself. These are problems in which **race**, racism and attendant notions of **identity** and ethnicity are themselves symptomatic; and so his apostasy goes to the heart of not just the **ethnocentrism** of British Cultural Studies, but of long-standing Marxist tensions between race and class that can be traced back to the British New Left. Rather than accept that class is the primary unit and value in this tradition, Gilroy and others asserted race as one of the ways that class and nation are fundamentally produced. This was particularly the case in an England that, from the late 1950s, began to be increasingly remade, not only by Caribbean and other non-white immigrants, but also by complex white responses to that immigrant presence, particularly among the working-class.

The first significant expression of these ideas is his co-authored *The Empire strikes back: Race and racism in 1970s Britain* (1982), which emerged under the auspices of the Birmingham center. His *"There ain't no black in the Union Jack": The cultural politics of race and nation* (1987) then provides an analysis and history of how race functioned in the 1960s and 1970s in both political discourse and popular **culture**. These were decades in which Great Britain found itself wracked with the anxieties of both post-**imperial** and post-industrial decline. In Gilroy's analysis this was also a period when class opposition was absorbed or superseded by an increasingly racialized and multi-ethnic youth culture that used the "profane" spaces of the popular as an "alternate public sphere."

This period was also one where competitive constructions of race, nation and sexuality were central to both semiotic play and "subaltern" attempts at transforming capitalist commodification into meaningful modes of lived resistance, as much through pleasure as through classic modes of refusal. Due to Antonio Gramsci's influence on the Birmingham center – particularly his flexible conception of hegemony – race for Gilroy is a productive and malleable construction. As such, it is easily absolutized by all sides of political and cultural argument, representing more than the threat of difference or national decline that characterized much British post-war cultural conversation. Indeed, race is too complex even to be claimed by the various black **nationalisms** that have long crisscrossed the Atlantic with England as a central node in **anti-racist** and anti-colonial agitation.

Gilroy's work identified a distinctly Black British inflection of Cultural Studies that emerged in the 1980s alongside popular movements and cultural tendencies that were loosely termed "UK Black" or the "Black British Renaissance." This agglomeration of styles, events, texts and sounds featured a distinct formulation of Black British cultural identity in which the cross-cultural impact of West Indian and African American literary and popular culture came to bear on a generational self-naming. Amidst a harsh conservative retrenchment, symbolized most conspicuously by Prime Minister Margaret Thatcher and the rise of the racist National Front, the work of Gilroy and others served as a commentary on Black British culture in the 1980s and early 1990s.

Central to the political valence of his work was the impact of race and immigration on sacrosanct notions of "British-ness." And central to this increasingly threatened sense of white national identity was the epochal shift from biological racism to plural forms of cultural racisms that attempted to contain an already transformed England. Though rooted in Black Britain, it is in this work that his commitment to the *diasporic* begins to cohere into a model of analysis. This model would be clearly articulated in his most notable work, *The Black Atlantic: Modernity and double consciousness* (1993). Informed by art history, anthropology and rooted in the work of African-American thought, this model is racial but not bound by the sacred structures of nation and class. *The Black Atlantic* also critiqued those identitarian political and cultural tendencies that increasingly narrowed black New World thinking, particularly in an often-recalcitrant African-America.

The now ubiquitous "black Atlantic" framework took movement as its fetish, the Atlantic Ocean as its heuristic unit and was produced and reproduced by transnational exchanges between and amongst black communities in the New World. It is too often forgotten that this model was hardly new, being essentially rooted in a pan-Africanism that had become increasingly marginalized by academicians in Europe and America due to its commitment to bio-cultural notions of race and nation. But, once articulated in the anti-nationalist language of contemporary critical and cultural studies, this framework would prove to be as intellectually threatening to racism as to the black nationalisms formulated to combat it.

Gilroy would then specify a challenge to race itself as a category of analysis, a mode of thinking and unit of political or cultural or organization in 2000's *Against race: Imagining political culture beyond the color line* (published in the UK as *Between two camps*). Proving to be his most controversial work, it sharply critiques the black political and cultural traditions that were central to the "black Atlantic" paradigm, but which were and are too intimate with uniquely twentieth-century forms of tyranny and violence through the ossifying language of racial nationalism. His most recent book *Post-colonial melancholia* (2006) explores the fate of multi-culturalism in the wake of a "war on terror" that would exploit the 9/11 attacks to obfuscate the legacies of colonialism that were arguably at the source of those very attacks. [LCS]

Key readings

Carby, H. V. (1999). *Cultures in Babylon: Black Britain and African America.* London: Verso.

Fryer, P. (1984). *Staying power: The history of black people in Britain.* London: Pluto Press.

Gilroy, P. (1993). *Small acts: Thoughts on the politics of black cultures.* London: Serpent's Tail.

Mercer, K. (1994). *Welcome to the jungle: New positions in black cultural studies.* New York: Routledge.

Morley, D. & Chen, K.-H. (Eds.). (1996). *Stuart Hall: Critical dialogues in cultural studies.* London: Routledge.

Owusu, K. (Ed.). (1999). *Black British culture and society: A text reader.* London: Routledge.

POLITICAL CORRECTNESS Early in the twentieth century, the term political correctness (PC) was used mostly on the Left. Those who adhered closely to the official position of the Communist Party were often chided by less orthodox persons as politically correct. But, in the 1990s, this phrase was adopted by the Right to criticize those who were advancing a post-structural, postmodern, or **multicultural** agenda. The basic idea is that these theories are pursuing a line of thought that jeopardizes traditional

values and undermines society. PC should thus be rejected.

In this cultural battle, conservatives championed the cause of truth, objectivity, and disinterested research, while PCers, they claimed, were relativists and trying to recreate society. Conservatives were neutral and non-ideological; PCers were clandestine and proposing unsavory, left-wing political interventions.

Critique of modernity

At the core of modern PC is an epistemology that is antagonistic to modernism. Often the work of Thomas Kuhn is mentioned by PCers to suggest that all knowledge is mediated by theory. The dualism that supports the objectivity coveted by modernists is thus undermined. As a result, the realism – represented by a reality *sui generis* – that is invoked by modernists to establish a reliable base of knowledge and order is not viable. Modernists claim that the result of this theoretical démarche is radical relativism which culminates in chaos. Supporters of PC, nonetheless, contend that such a foundation is not needed to establish order; order can be based, instead, on inter-subjective negotiation.

Contrary to the claims made by conservatives, PCers are not trying to destroy society. Their point is that order does not have to be monolithic to survive. A new vision is possible that does not require the submission of persons to a single, universal, and glorified cultural framework.

Anti-essentialism

With respect to **identity**, the rejection of dualism undercuts essentialism, or the belief that specific persons or groups have primordial traits that separate them categorically from others. Essentialism, for example, has been used to justify the differential treatment of women and minorities, including their marginalization. Minorities, stated simply, have been identified as lacking intelligence, reason, and moral character. Consequently, they do not deserve to be treated like Europeans, even in a democracy.

But now that all knowledge is shaped by the human presence – for example, through theory, language, or praxis – so-called essential traits cannot be protected from contingency and interpretation. Therefore, the seigniorial position claimed by supremacists does not have the stature necessary to dominate other viewpoints. There is no inherent hierarchy of persons; all persons are "**other**" and deserve recognition and respect. Simply stated, no traits are inherently faulty and therefore subject to being repressed.

Decline of social realism

In the absence of dualism, social ontological realism cannot survive. In line with modernism, such realism is predicated on a-historical or neutral norms that unite society. But, without the implied absolute norms, order cannot be enforced in the usual manner. Traditionally, the belief is that order cannot be established unless everyone **assimilates** to a particular normative ideal. Hence, order does not thrive in the presence of diversity. For this reason, all immigrants must abandon their ethnic heritage, so that a more perfect order can be created. Any challenge to this assimilation, furthermore, is a direct threat to society.

In the PC lexicon, essentialism and social ontological realism are representative of foundationalism. Foundationalists believe that truth, identity, and social **solidarity** can only be predicated on objective standards, disconnected from personal or collective experience. The aim is to create an all-encompassing, or totalistic, normative referent that does not favor any constituency. According to PCers, however, this foundation has no justification beyond the respective claims made by particular persons or groups. Contrary to the claims of conservatives, institutional order is neither autonomous nor neutral.

PC and race relations

The guiding principle of American **race** relations has been assimilation. This idea sustains the three primary models of racial or ethnic integration: Anglo-conformity, melting pot, and pluralism. In each case, all persons must internalize particular norms, so that society has a uniform foundation. The general result of this strategy is the homogenization of society. Additionally, certain racial or ethnic characteristics are accepted as universal and imposed on everyone, regardless of their relevance.

To avoid the resulting supremacy, PCers promote multiculturalism. Metaphors such as the quilt, rhizome, and salad bar are used to describe the resulting order. The point is that without a reality *sui generis*, different racial or ethnic traits must be juxtaposed. The resulting order does not extend from an eternal core, but instead reflects various, complementary perspectives. The message conveyed by this new social imagery is that social integration does not require the sacrifice of diversity.

Conclusion

Nathan Glazer declared that now we are all multiculturalists. PCers argue that this insight is liberating and consistent with democracy. What PCers are saying is that democracy involves more than voting, and that the cultural conditions must be established to foster this wider, and more profound, participation.

Democracy is extolled to represent government by the people. But how can a wide variety of voices be heard, ask PCers, if good ideas are presumed to originate only from certain segments of society? If select persons or groups are inferiorized through assimilation, how can democracy be said to exist? Because multiculturalism does not rely on assimilation, and maintains that order exists at the nexus of diversity, this new model of race and ethnic relations is consistent with the aims of democracy.

That is, a radically plural society might finally be proposed and realized.

PCers do not see themselves as a threat to **culture** or social order, but believe they are making a philosophical maneuver that is necessary to create a more inclusive society. In the absence of essentialism and social ontological realism, persons can create their own identities, along with institutions that do not encourage supremacy. In this way, PCers aim to generate a more open, less hierarchical society. [JWM & JMC]

Key readings

Berman, P. (Ed.). (1993). *Debating PC.* New York: Dell.

Choi, J. M. & Murphy, J. W. (1992). *The politics and philosophy of political correctness.* Westport, CT: Praeger.

Feldstein, R. (1997). *Political correctness: A response from the cultural left.* Minneapolis, MN: University of Minnesota Press.

Fish, S. (1989). *Doing what comes naturally.* Durham, NC: Duke University Press.

——. (1995). *Professional correctness.* New York: Clarenden Press.

Gitlin, T. (1995). *The twilight of common dreams.* New York: Metropolitan Books.

Glazer, N. (1997). *We are all multiculturalists now.* Cambridge, MA: Harvard University Press.

Huntington, S. (2004). *Who are we?* New York: Simon and Schuster.

Kuhn, T. (1996). *The structure of scientific revolutions.* Chicago: University of Chicago Press.

POPULATION GENETICS Population geneticists focus on the genetic basis of evolutionary change within species: they describe existing genetic variation within and between populations and explain these patterns by appealing to various evolutionary forces (mutation, selection, migration, drift).

The origins of population genetics lie in the early twentieth-century controversy between Mendelians and biometricians. Mendelians rejected Darwin's theory of evolution by natural selection, holding that evolution occurs in saltations (jumps) due to discontinuous mutations. Biometricians rejected Mendel's theory of heredity, holding that evolution occurs gradually due to natural selection acting on continuous variation.

Mendelism and Darwinism ultimately proved to be compatible. In 1908, Hardy and Weinberg demonstrated that genetic variability in Mendelian populations remains constant across generations (assuming infinite size, random mating, and absence of mutation, selection, and migration), thus providing raw material for selection (which Darwin's blending theory of heredity failed to do). In 1918, Fisher demonstrated that the continuous variation favored by biometricians could arise from many Mendelian factors of small effect. Fisher's 1930 *The genetical theory of natural selection,* Wright's 1931 "Evolution in Mendelian populations," and Haldane's 1932 *The causes of evolution* mark the founding of theoretical population genetics as a synthesis of Mendelism, Darwinism, and biometry. Fisher, Wright, and Haldane incorporated the biometricians' quantitative approach to the study of evolution, using changes in gene frequencies in populations to demonstrate how evolution by natural selection could occur.

Many biologists remained skeptical. Paleontologists supported saltationism (evolution proceeds in jumps) and orthogenesis (evolution is inherently progressive) because they believed these approaches better explained patterns in the fossil record. Naturalists discounted the importance of Mendelian factors in evolution, favoring the Lamarckian inheritance of acquired characteristics. Only with the modern evolutionary synthesis of the

1930s and 1940s was biology's acceptance of Mendelism and Darwinism consolidated. Population genetics played a central role in this second, more empirically based synthesis. This was largely due to the influence of Dobzhansky's 1937 *Genetics and the origin of species* and its redefinition of evolution as a genetic process.

Early empirical studies in population genetics during the 1930s–40s were shaped by disagreement among the founding theoreticians about the relative importance of selection (changes resulting from organisms' differing abilities to survive and reproduce) and drift (changes occurring by chance in finite populations). Fisher and Haldane held that evolution proceeds deterministically with selection operating on single genes in large populations. In Britain, Ford collaborated with Fisher to provide evidence for the importance of selection in butterflies and moths (the order Lepidoptera). Wright held that natural selection acts on favorable gene combinations that happen to arise in subdivided populations due to drift. In the United States, Dobzhansky launched his Genetics of Natural Populations studies in collaboration with Wright, initially finding evidence of drift in populations of the fruit fly *Drosophila pseudoobscura*. In France, Lamotte found support for Wright's shifting balance theory in populations of the land snail *Cepaea nemoralis*.

Selectionism predominated during the 1950s and 1960s: the selection–drift debate was replaced by the classical–balance debate, over whether natural selection operates to eliminate or preserve genetic variation in populations – Muller's and Dobzhansky's respective positions. The matter looked to be decided in favor of Dobzhansky when significant levels of protein polymorphism were detected in humans and *Drosophila* using electrophoresis in 1966. However, in 1968, Kimura proposed his neutral theory of molecular evolution, which held that most amino acid substitutions in the evolution of species involve the fixation of neutral, or nearly neutral, mutations due to drift; consequently, protein polymorphisms observed within species are likely to be neutral variants on a random path to eventual fixation or loss, not of adaptive significance.

Over the past few decades, coalescent theory has transformed population genetics. In finite populations, some lineages for a given segment of DNA become extinct in each successive generation because their bearers have no offspring; when a present-day population is sampled for that segment, lineages coalesce in increasingly fewer ancestors going back in time, until the most recent common ancestor (MRCA) is reached. The occurrence of mutations along these lineages helps to recover this history. Studies using mitochondrial DNA and Y-chromosomal DNA have established MRCAs for everyone alive today: an African woman who lived 120,000–200,000 years ago and an African man who lived 35,000–89,000 years ago. These efforts lend support to the "Out of Africa 2" theory of human origins: that *H. sapiens* evolved in Africa about 200,000 years ago, leaving Africa to populate the globe about 50,000 years ago, replacing the *H. erectus* groups they encountered. The Genographic Project seeks to reconstruct this migration history, as did the failed **Human Genome Diversity Project**.

Around 1950, population genetics brought physical anthropology into the evolutionary synthesis, a development considered by historians to mark the retreat of scientific racism associated with nineteenth-century anthropology, early twentieth-century **eugenics**, and Nazi "**race** hygiene." Arguably, biological race was not eliminated at this time but redefined as a populational rather than typological concept.

Population geneticists like Dobzhansky, Lewontin, Feldman, and Cavalli-Sforza have taken **anti-racist** public stances. They have criticized misuse of the concept of heritability in claims that IQ differences among racial groups are genetic. Such claims receive widespread media attention and are used to justify persisting socioeconomic inequalities (e.g. Jensen's 1969 article in *Harvard Educational Review* and Herrnstein and Murray's 1994 *The bell curve*). Heritability is a local measure of the proportion of variation in a quantitative trait (such as height, weight or IQ) that is due to genetic variation for a specific population. Even if two populations exhibit high heritability for a trait, average differences between them can be entirely due to environmental factors.

Population geneticists also emphasize that genetic diversity within groups is far greater than between groups and, consequently, an individual's ethnicity or race is not a reliable predictor of genetic makeup. Recent studies estimate that 85–95 percent of genetic diversity lies within national or ethnic groups, 2–6 percent lies between national or ethnic groups within the same racial group, and 3–10 percent lies between racial groups.

Nevertheless, between-group differences are of great interest to researchers, who work in increasingly commercialized settings. In medical genetics, isolated, founder, consanguineous, and "admixed" groups facilitate the mapping of disease genes; in pharmacogenomics, racial and ethnic group differences furnish a shortcut to "personalized medicine"; in forensics, racial and ethnic databases are used to establish DNA match probabilities and make predictions about an unknown perpetrator's race or ethnicity from DNA left at the crime scene; in genetic genealogy, African Americans submit DNA swabs hoping to trace their African ethnic roots and DNA tests are marketed to Native Americans as proof of tribal **identity**.

The use of racial and ethnic categories in genetic research suggests the unraveling of any previously existing academic consensus about the social construction of race and ethnicity. But this does not mean that race and ethnicity have been validated as biological categories. Geneticists use group categories to capture the ways in which human genome diversity is distributed across space and time. Social scientists and humanists are tasked with examining the ways in which these categories are embedded in cultural and historical ways of knowing. [LG]

Key readings

Allen, G. E. (1978). *Life science in the twentieth century*. New York: Cambridge University Press.

Gayon, J. (1998). *Darwinism's struggle for survival: Heredity and the hypothesis of natural selection*. New York: Cambridge University Press.

Hartl, D. L. & Clark, A. G. (2007). *Principles of population genetics* (4th ed.). Sunderland, MA: Sinauer.

Koenig, B. A., Lee, S. S.-J., & Richardson, S. S. (2008). *Revisiting race in a genomic age*. New Brunswick, NJ: Rutgers University Press.

Mayr, E. & Provine, W. B. (Eds.). (1980). *The evolutionary synthesis: Perspectives on the unification of biology*. Cambridge, MA: Harvard University Press.

Provine, W. B. (1971). *The origins of theoretical population genetics*. Chicago: University of Chicago Press.

Reardon, J. (2005). *Race to the finish: Identity and governance in an age of genomics*. Princeton, NJ: Princeton University Press.

POSTCOLONIALISM As the word implies, postcolonialism is the study of the cultural effects of colonization evidenced after independence. More specifically, in academic circles the term has generally come to designate the study of countries once referred to as the Third World (and, thus, always defined in relationship with the

"First" World that sets the terms) after the European powers have technically relinquished control. Neocolonialism, as a corollary, calls the concept into question by recognizing the ongoing **power** the colonizer maintains in relations with the former colony through financial, linguistic, educational, and various other social ties. In this latter school of thought, the only "post" in the term is the temporal rather than consequential demarcation of a legal cutting of legislative subservience to the former master – thus it is a distinction without significant difference.

Edward Said, Gayatri Spivak, and Homi Bhabha are considered lynchpins in postcolonial theory, building on the work of **Frantz Fanon**, Edouard Glissant, Aime Cesaire, Antonio Gramsci, and a good many others who protested colonial domination. Drawing variously on Marxism and poststructualism, central to postcolonialism is an analysis of the embattled ability of individuals to represent themselves (even *to* themselves) as having **identities** independent of that assigned them by the colonizer. This question has informed the work of the Subaltern Studies Group in India and others who seek to write a history "from below," in which the voiceless of societies are written back into national histories.

Postcolonialism therefore asks questions that foreground issues of **power** and significance, and even of timing: how is it, for example, that an island like Britain came to dominate the world? In postcolonialism, this plays itself out in an examination of technologies of production and social control, of centers and margins: of metropolitan hubs like London and Paris, and peripheries and margins – like the colonies. This physical expression of significance replicates the symbolic gradation of meaning, as expressed in global domination in the here and now, and in the extension of that declared meaning through the writing of Eurocentric histories.

Discourse itself, then, becomes an object of study for postcolonial writers – ranging from the choice of language in which one will write (English? Kikuyu?), to the demands of the "master narrative" that one must echo or against which one must struggle. An analogous struggle is that for **authenticity**, whereby an individual is designated as the spokesperson for a larger community: who makes this decision, and how? What are the various discourse communities in which one operates, and which are the "imagined" communities wherein one defines one's "nation"?

Among the insidious effects of colonialism have been the imposition of a comprador class, the intellectual elite and bourgeois merchants who have vested interests in the maintenance of colonial structures of power. Thus, even after technical independence, the cultural residue from Great Britain, France, and lesser colonizing powers is enshrined by their stepchildren in the new nations. A similar dynamic prompts a mimicking of metropolitan standards of civilization among those who have spent some time in universities like Oxford and the Sorbonne and then returned home to assume positions of power in government, in business, and in academe: an apparent conversion of local citizens into **stereotypically** British and *très* French compatriots. But mimicry is a two-sided sword: mockery is its underside, and can offer the subaltern an avenue to critique the master with less fear of chastisement. Appropriation of the colonizer's tools can appear to be a caving in, an **assimilation**, but in fact can also be a mastery of the tools that can then be turned against the master.

On the other hand, the romantic notion of a precolonial pristine **culture**, unified and egalitarian, is criticized in later postcolonial theory as nativism; an essentialist bias that has been frequently mobilized in defense of a militant **nationalism** that necessarily excludes difference among citizenry. Countering this approach is the concept of hybridity, which celebrates the mixing of cultures and **races** and points to the multiple identities of each person in an age of expanding globalization. But the valorization of hybridity itself comes under attack from those who see it as elitist, an outcome of greater mobility and wealth than is common in postcolonial countries except among the comprador class – who lack "authenticity."

Travel, in its several forms, comes under intense examination in postcolonialism. There is the travel of the explorer, who records "first contact" with the "native" and, in that recording, objectifies and establishes the terms by which future generations of westerners imagine the object of that study. This process has been called **orientalism**, the setting in stone of the alterity (**otherness**) of the colonized individual – who, in the process, is rarely actually seen as an individual, but rather as an example of a type. Aware of being observed, the native develops a **double consciousness**: a prior self-understanding, and a secondary recognition of the script that others, more powerful than he or she, prepare and present for enactment on a daily basis.

There is also the travel of the migrant, and this is of various sorts depending upon motivation and circumstances. At one end of the scale is the global citizen with access to wealth and leisure, education, political sway. At the other end of the scale is the migrant worker, with great need for employment and little sense of belonging. In this group there are gradations of security, with some possessing green cards or their equivalent, with others serving as modern indentured servants, and with still others flying under a host nation's surveillance. Postcolonial theorists are intrigued by these many individuals living outside their native lands, and they designate them members of a **diaspora**: a people flung far from home, having to accommodate themselves to often unwelcoming communities,

seldom settling in to a new culture in any secure way, often yearning for return to a remembered time and place of fuller meaning and greater sense of self. This sense of displacement often dominates their creative work.

Women play a special role in postcolonialism, since they often find themselves doubly colonized: subservient as members of a large brutalized community, and more pointedly colonized by the males of their own societies. Understandably, in their novels and poetry such women have less romanticized depictions of a return to carefree precolonial states than do some of their male compatriots.

Outside the United States, there has been some resistance to applying postcolonial theory to the various populations that make up its national identity, though the case for doing so has been most easily made with regard to native Americans – who, everyone would agree, were colonized by invading armies. In their case, though, the counterargument is that there is absolutely no "post" involved in the equation. As with the other ethnic American literatures, the crucial factor is the resistance to assimilation and homogenization that is, or is not, apparent in the fiction and poetry produced. This provides plenty of leeway for the sorts of hybrid self-definition that are evident in the postcolonial literatures of Africa, South Asia, the Caribbean, etc.

The feature common to postcolonialism and United States ethnic studies is the historic and ongoing privileging of **whiteness** and the collapsing of difference: discussing "Arab Americans," for example, as if all subsets were roughly identical, or "Asian Americans" as if Chinese Americans and Indian Americans had a great deal in common – and a great deal that sets them apart from "Americans." As with other versions of postcolonialism, US ethnic studies seek to avoid a false universalism by extending to all minorities characteristics which are, rightly or wrongly, attributed to the majority population. Most scholars who work in both fields point to US borders studies as the most fruitful point of exchange between postcolonialism and ethnic studies. The borders in question are literal, and symbolic, representing the stratification in US society that is not only class-based but also dependent upon ethnicity.

Proponents of globalization seem to suggest that the time of nations has passed, and **identity politics** are no longer relevant. In such a world, postcolonialism may seem less relevant. There is a similar "post-ethnic" school of thought that obscures the concerns of the borders school with claims that individuals can, and should, constantly reinvent themselves. But, like globalists, such thinkers open themselves to the charge of elitism, apparently ascribing far greater agency to individuals than that delineated in postcolonialism or US ethnic studies. The globalized utopian (or dystopian) view of our world would seem to falter when confronted with the daily ongoing social struggles in the countries of the former European colonies – including the United States. [JCH]

Key readings

Desai, G. & Nair, S. (Eds). (2005). *Postcolonialisms: An anthology of cultural theory and criticism*. New Brunswick, NJ: Rutgers University Press.

Morley, D. (Ed.). (1996). *Stuart Hall: Critical dialogues in cultural studies*. New York: Routledge.

Omi, M. & Winant, H. (1986). *Racial formation in the United States: From the 1960s to the 1990s* (2nd ed.). New York: Routledge.

Schueller, M. J. (2009). *Locating race: Global sites of post-colonial citizenship*. Albany, NY: State University of New York Press.

Singh, A. & Schmidt, P. (2000). *Postcolonial theory and the United States: Race,* *ethnicity, and literature.* Jackson, MS: University Press of Mississippi.

POWER In the social sciences, a power relation involves a set of actions that structure the field of the actions of another. I will return to this deceptively simple definition below. By way of introduction, consider that power is both fundamentally relational and is saturated throughout the social. Power is, therefore, immanent to material practices, social relations, discourses, knowledges, institutions and ideologies. It is little surprise then that for many scholars, posing the question of power necessarily invites the questions of subjects, societies and states.

One of the earliest and most influential conceptions of power in the modern period appeared in Thomas Hobbes's *Leviathan*. For Hobbes, the power of an individual rests in his or her means to obtain some future "good." However, the warlike and selfish nature of human beings (not to mention their possessive individualism) necessitates that the collection of individuals sacrifice power to a commonwealth via numerous acts of covenant. Thus it is that power becomes centralized in the sovereign. In his *Second treatise of government*, John Locke does away with the absolute power of Hobbes's sovereign, returning to the consent to power by rational individuals. While the consent of individuals continues to give the sovereign the right to govern, and while the obligations of individuals following from this consent give the sovereign the capacity to act, in Locke, individuals retain the right to liberty (to remove the sovereign). The sovereign cannot be both judge and participant in the disputes between what Locke saw as essentially peaceful individuals. Although an important study by Hindess (1996) convincingly demonstrates that, in both Locke and Hobbes, there are alternative views of power that go beyond a simple view of capacity, power relations for these writers nonetheless remain external to the formation of individual subjectivity – a key issue to which I return below.

Many scholars, wrestling with the nature of political power, have built upon this early modern "power as capacity" approach. Consider the work of C. Wright Mills, Robert Dahl and Anthony Giddens, to name but a few. Max Weber is an important example in this context due to his enormous influence. Although seeing the concept as "sociologically amorphous," Weber went on to define power as the pushing forward of one's will in a relationship despite resistance. With the state at the helm of all legitimate use of force and with bureaucrats (often seated beyond the state) increasingly ushering in a "polar night of icy darkness," Weber's "people of vocation" were quickly being replaced by a conformist citizenry.

Useful in coming to terms with these many approaches to power is Steven Lukes' well-rehearsed multi-dimensional view of power. The first dimension of power, or the "liberal" view, reduces power to the active political arena where conflicts are overt and the decisions of power brokers are in evidence. Well-known writers in this dimension are Robert Dahl and Nelson Polsby. The second dimension, which was worked out by "reformists" such as C. Wright Mills, along with Peter Bachrach and Morton Baratz, widens power beyond the actual halls of decision making to the countless struggles through which interests either do or do not enter the arena. Finally, Lukes delineates a third, "radical" dimension where the analysis of power moves to subjugation and where certain actors are seemingly unaware of their "real" interests. This facet of power can be seen in Karl Marx's notion of false consciousness and in Antonio Gramsci's concept of hegemony. Even with Lukes' "radical" conception, however, the human subject remains formed prior to his or her involvement in relations of power.

Throughout much of the modern period, then, power has largely been approached as a thing to be possessed or quantified, a simple ability and a zero-sum game. Further, power was thought to be negative in its effects, fundamentally disabling and opposed to freedom (Ricken 2006). Michel Foucault termed this constellation of attributes the "juridical-discursive" model of power and, due to his critical clarification of its unity along with his own evolving contributions to a novel approach, Foucault has emerged as the most important theorist of power to date.

In his early work, Foucault stepped back from the political theory questions of who is or is not in possession of power and how this possession supports various sovereign/citizenry contracts, social hierarchies and laws governing property and deeds. These were the solidified outcomes of what he saw to be mobile, constantly shifting force relations that are immanent to specific spheres of the social and which assure continuous struggle. Focusing on these terminal points of force tends to lead investigation away from the more revealing mechanisms of power. Acknowledging the importance of Carl von Clausewitz's early embedding of warfare in modern power strategies, Foucault reasoned that force relations gain orientation and consistency from strategic forms while marshalling concreteness from tactical maneuvers. Strategies, for their part, are mostly captured by discernible rationalities and even larger apparatuses of power, such as state practices, laws and hegemonies (indeed, entire social orders). However, such strategies are irreducible to the larger rationalities and technologies. Of particular interest here is the argument that resistance is not external to power. Rather, for the early Foucault, the exertion of one force is in some *direct* relation to the work of another. From within this "strategic conception of power," Foucault argued that critique should best concern itself with the "rule of the double conditioning" of tactics and strategy. Resistance at just the right tactical moment has the potential to render questionable the organization of the power ensemble as a totality. Foucault termed this the tactical reversal of power relations. In reaction, many scholars – most notably feminists, concerned with alternative formations of gendered **identities** – were critical of the ubiquity and saturation of Foucault's conception of modern power and feared the proverbial iron cage.

In the mid-1970s, Foucault began to rethink his ideas on power and critique, being especially concerned that the strategic model did not allow him to properly understand struggles against subjugation. Foucault revisited his idea that forces are always in direct relations. In his strategic model of power, resistance was forever reactive and answered only to the movement of rising forces. He therefore shifted his terms from force to conduct and from the strategic to the governmental model of power. In the neologism "governmentality" (a term used decades earlier by Roland Barthes), Foucault combines "*gouverner*" (governing) and "*mentalité*" (modes of thought). Governing, in this sense, involves structuring the field of knowledge and power so that power itself is seen to be rational. Foucault argues that governing people involves a "versatile equilibrium" between coercive techniques and self-modification processes. One now acts upon another through his or her free conduct, shaping the realm of possibilities whereby others conduct themselves. Importantly, the other is always assumed to retain the capacity to act; thus, freedom and power constitute one another. For Foucault, power has always sought to form individual actions via specific social norms. With the governmental approach to power (and with the subject free to relate to herself), subjectivity is no longer the product of

power *tout court*, but a provisional result of subjectivization techniques. Resistance to such governmental power now entails refusing the results of the normalizing forces that move between the poles of individualization (disciplinary strategies that focus on the training and surveillance of the individual body) and totalization (biopolitical techniques that work through the population and biosociological processes to massify and secure). Just as important, resistance requires the second step of cultivating and employing novel, alternative forms of subjectivity. The resulting formations of self, of course, are never fully autonomous as they are both the product and critique of existent discourses. Taken as a whole, such practices of resistance are what Foucault called the "aesthetics of existence." Readers might be reminded here that Foucault's aesthetics owe a debt to Weber's insistence that the "man of vocation" has resources to offer in the ongoing struggle against rationalization.

Foucault died before reaching the age of 60 in 1984. His work on power, however, continues to generate important new conceptions. One example is the debates between Giorgio Agamben and Michael Hardt/Antonio Negri over Foucault's concept of biopower (and biopolitics) – that is, modern society's capturing of our species' being as an object for political strategy. Agamben's *thanatopolitics* (politics as death) and Hardt and Negri's *biopotenza* (biopolitical production), although very different, represent exciting new explorations of power mechanisms outside the terms set by sovereignty. [PH]

Key readings

Agamben, G. (2005). *The State of exception*. Chicago: University of Chicago Press.
Foucault, M. (1982). The subject and power. In H. L. Dreyfus & P. Rabinow (Eds.), *Michel Foucault: Beyond structuralism and hermeneutics*. Chicago: University of Chicago Press, pp. 208–228.

Foucault, M. (1991). On governmentality. In C. Gordon, G. Burchell, & P. Miller (Eds.), *The Foucault effect: Studies in governmentality*. Chicago: University of Chicago Press, pp. 87–104.

Hindess, B. (1996). *Discourses of power: From Hobbes to Foucault*. Cambridge, MA: Blackwell.

Lukes, S. (1974). *Power: A radical view*. Houndmills: Macmillan.

Ricken, N. (2006). The power of power – questions to Michel Foucault. *Educational Philosophy and Theory*, 38(4), 541–560.

Thompson, K. (2003). Forms of resistance: Foucault on tactical reversal and self-formation. *Continental Philosophy Review*, 36, 113–138.

PREJUDICE "Prejudice" has traditionally been defined as an attitude reflecting antipathy, or ill-feelings toward a group and its members, based on over-generalizations about the characteristics of the group. More recent definitions have emphasized the dynamic and situational nature of prejudice, noting that these negative feelings are primarily aroused when members of a group violate **stereotypic** expectations or roles.

Bases of prejudice

The foundation of prejudice is established by the act of merely categorizing people into groups: the ingroup (which contains the self) and outgroups. Work using the *minimal group paradigm*, in which groups are formed on an arbitrary basis (for example, whether people overestimate or underestimate dots on a drawing) and have no direct functional relationship with each other, reveals that people spontaneously evaluate ingroup members more favorably than outgroup members. In addition, people think in deeper and more complex ways about ingroup members and excuse negative behaviors more for ingroup than for outgroup members.

The nature and degree of prejudice that people experience, however, are further determined by: (a) the characteristics of the other group being perceived; (b) the personality and ideology of the perceiver; and (c) the context. In terms of the qualities of the target group, the feelings elicited toward a group and its members are determined by where the group is perceived to fall on two dimensions: warmth and competence. Groups perceived to be high in warmth and high in competence (e.g. one's own group, close allies) elicit pride and admiration; groups perceived to be high in warmth but low in competence (e.g. housewives, the elderly) produce pity and sympathy; those perceived to be low in warmth but high in competence (e.g. Asians, Jews) evoke envy and jealousy; and groups perceived to be low on both warmth and competence (e.g. welfare recipients and poor people) are associated with feelings of disgust, anger, and resentment. Thus, prejudice can involve a range of different emotional reactions that vary as a function of the group's perceived qualities.

Because prejudice is an attitude held by individuals, considerable research has focused on personality differences related to prejudice. The classic work on the **authoritarian** personality represents one of the most influential lines of research on this topic. Extensive research published by Theodor Adorno and his colleagues in the early 1950s on authoritarianism identified a number of distinctive qualities of people who were prejudiced. High authoritarians, who are prejudiced against a range of other groups, tend to be intolerant of ambiguity, are rigid and concrete in their thinking, and typically over-generalize in their characterization of other groups. High authoritarianism develops from people's experiences in childhood with parents who are hierarchical and punitive in their orientations.

An alternative approach to individual

differences in prejudice focuses on people's worldviews about how groups relate to each other. Research on social dominance theory has revealed that people who believe that it is appropriate for some groups to dominate other groups and who see the world as "zero-sum" (in which gains for one group mean losses for another) tend to be highly prejudiced. Whereas a recent measure of authoritarianism, right-wing authoritarianism, is a particularly good predictor of prejudice toward individuals perceived to violate the traditional standards of one's group (e.g. homosexuals), social dominance orientation is the primary predictor of *inter*group prejudices (e.g. prejudice toward immigrants).

Other theories have emphasized the relationship between groups in a given context as a determinant of prejudice. Social **identity** theory proposes that, because people derive their personal esteem through their group membership and collective identity, they are motivated to perceive the "positive distinctiveness" of their group relative to others. Prejudice helps to satisfy this need psychologically, and to the extent that it leads to **discrimination** in action, it can also produce tangible advantages for one's own group. From a social identity perspective (consider also self-categorization theory), the context determines prejudice: the circumstances under which social comparisons between one's own group and other groups occur determine how individuals establish positive distinctiveness, thereby shaping the nature of the prejudice.

Beyond meeting psychological needs, realistic group conflict theory views prejudice as the consequence of actual competition between groups for material resources. In the classic Robbers Cave research by Muzafer Sherif and colleagues in the early 1950s, prejudice quickly developed when two different groups of boys at a summer camp engaged in competitive activities.

Further, consistent with the proposition that functional relationships between groups shape intergroup attitudes, an intervention that required both groups to cooperate to achieve desired goals (i.e. "superordinate goals") significantly reduced prejudice. However, competition with members of other groups to generate biases does not have to be demonstrated in practice. People typically presume that members of other groups are competitive and greedy. In addition, when members of other groups deviate from their stereotypically prescribed roles, they arouse feelings of threat anxiety, which generate greater prejudice.

Manifestations of prejudice

Traditionally, prejudice has been measured using standardized scales that assess people's beliefs about attributes of a group, feelings about the group, and orientations toward policies that affect the group. Feeling thermometers, in which people rate their degree of warmth for a group, are also used to compare the degree of prejudice across groups. Scales that measure **minority** group members' bias toward the majority group reveal some differences between the prejudices. Prejudice of minority group members toward the majority group is characterized by a strong reactive component, related to the anticipation of being stigmatized by majority group members, and involves an explicit emphasis on the distinctive ways that the minority group is better than the majority group.

However, people's actual level of prejudice may not be fully captured by these self-report scales because they may not be fully aware of their prejudices. Socialization processes and media exposure that repeatedly associate negative qualities with certain groups create overlearned or "habitual" negative responses – implicit prejudice – which are activated automatically, without intention or awareness. In contrast to the conscious, explicit prejudice, which can be measured with self-report, assessments of implicit prejudice utilize a variety of techniques, including psychophysiological measures, brain activity as indicated by functional magnetic resonance imaging (fMRI), and response latency measures of association (e.g. the Implicit Association Test).

Moreover, one basic thesis of contemporary theories of prejudice, such as aversive racism, is that increasingly egalitarian norms have facilitated the development of conscious, nonprejudiced self-images among many people who appear nonbiased on explicit measures but who still harbor unconscious negative feelings toward and beliefs about other groups. Consistent with this proposition, implicit measures show generally higher levels of prejudice than do explicit measures, and implicit and explicit measures are only modestly correlated with each other.

Whereas explicit prejudice predicts direct and blatant forms of discrimination (e.g. exclusionary acts), implicit prejudice predicts more spontaneous or subtle manifestations that are difficult for a person to monitor or control (e.g. negative nonverbal behavior). Considerable research on aversive racism reveals that contemporary prejudice, which is more unconscious than intentional, predicts systematic discrimination in situations in which right or wrong is not clearly defined or in which people can justify a negative response on the basis of some factor other than the person's group membership (e.g. **race**).

Combating prejudice

Because prejudice involves emotional reactions and implicit beliefs and evaluations, one of the most effective ways of reducing prejudice is experientially. In particular, intergroup contact theory specifies ways to structure interactions between members of different groups to ameliorate prejudice. The most important features are: (a) equal status within the contact situation; (b) intergroup cooperation; (c) common goals; (d) support of authorities, law, or custom; (e) opportunities for personal acquaintance between the members; and (f) formation of intergroup friendships. Intergroup contact under these conditions can lead people to change the way they categorize the groups, either by encouraging them to view the groups within a common ingroup identity or by making group boundaries secondary to positive personalized relationships. It also reduces negative emotional reactions, such as anxiety and feelings of threat, previously elicited by the other group, while increasing empathy for members of the other group. In addition, sustained positive intergroup contact can reduce implicit prejudice by producing greater distinctions in how members of another group are viewed (i.e. subtypes) and by creating new favorable, counter-stereotypic associations with the other group.

Conclusion

Prejudice is an over-generalized negative attitude toward another group and its members. It involves what people feel about others as well as what people believe about them. The level of prejudice experienced toward another group varies as a function of the characteristics of the target group, the personality and worldview of the perceiver, and the psychological and material relationships between one's own group and other groups. Moreover, people may not be fully conscious of their biases: prejudice is implicit as well as explicit. As a consequence, prejudice often produces subtle discrimination, which often occurs unintentionally, as well as open and blatant discrimination. Because prejudice is such a multifaceted phenomenon, it is combated most effectively by interventions that involve direct intergroup interaction in ways that can change emotional reactions and alter the way people think about the group and its members in personally relevant ways. [JFD]

Key readings

Cuddy, A. J. C., Fiske, S. T., & Glick, P. (2008). Warmth and competence as universal dimensions of social perception: The Stereotype Content Model and the BIAS map. In M. P. Zanna (Ed.), *Advances in experimental social psychology* (vol. 40). New York: Academic Press, pp. 61–149.

Dovidio, J. F. & Gaertner, S. L. (2004). Aversive racism. In M. P. Zanna (Ed.), *Advances in experimental social psychology* (vol. 36). San Diego, CA: Academic Press, pp. 1–51.

Nosek, B. A., Banaji, M. R., & Greenwald, A. G. (2002). Harvesting implicit group attitudes and beliefs from a demonstration web site. *Group dynamics: Theory, research, and practice*, 6, 101–115.

Pettigrew, T. F. & Tropp, L. (2006). A meta-analytic test of intergroup contact theory. *Journal of Personality and Social Psychology*, 90, 751–783.

Sherif, M., Harvey, O. J., White, B. J., Hood, W. R., & Sherif, C. W. (1961). *Intergroup conflict and cooperation: The Robbers Cave experiment*. Norman, OK: University of Oklahoma Book Exchange.

Sidanius, J. & Pratto, F. (1999). *Social dominance: An intergroup theory of social hierarchy and oppression*. New York: Cambridge University Press.

Tajfel, H. & Turner, J. C. (1979). An integrative theory of intergroup conflict. In W. G. Austin and S. Worchel (Eds.), *The social psychology of intergroup relations*. Monterey, CA: Brooks/Cole, pp. 33–48.

RACE

Practically every academic discipline has something to say about "race." Some focus on its origins, some on permutations over time and **cultures**, others on its relationship to other phenomena, whether diseases,

academic achievement, marriage patterns, or inequality.

Yet the term "race" is illusive, confusing, and inconsistently used across disciplines. It has referred to everything from one's nationality, religion, ancestry, or class status to biological sub-categories. The American Anthropological Association's exhaustive 2005 review of academic sources could not identify a coherent, unified definition, even within anthropology.

The scientific community has long struggled with multiple meanings of "race." The "scientific" concept of "race" emerged in eighteenth-century Europe, coinciding with the growth of colonialism and the trans-Atlantic slave trade. Naturalists, such as Johann Blumenbach, classified humans into five geographically distinct "races," hierarchically ordered by their resemblance to God's original forms, supposedly to be found in the Caucasus Mountains. Europeans belonged to this highest "race": the "Caucasians."

By the nineteenth century, scientists incorporated the "race" concept into reconstructions of human cultural evolution. Physical and cultural evolution purportedly moved in tandem: biological "advances" in human mental capacity were responsible for cultural "advances," such as new technology and social institutions. According to this logic, more "advanced" cultures were biologically and intellectually more evolved. Skull size was used to rank human groups from more "primitive" to more "advanced."

Christian theologians believed in a single source for human origins [Adam and Eve] but argued that non-"Caucasian" races subsequently "degenerated." Some evolutionary scientists, however, proposed multiple human origins, with distinct races evolving at different places and times. By the beginning of the twentieth century, what is now called "racial science" – the belief in natural, long-standing divisions of the human species, evolving at different rates biologically and, hence, culturally and intellectually – had taken hold in North America. This "cultural logic," conveniently, naturalized and legitimized racial inequality.

Yet, there have always been challenges to the biological concept of race. The rise of genetics and modern evolutionary theory in the 1930s and the post-Nazi era repugnance for racism accelerated this critique of racial science. An alternative definition emerged of race as a human invention, a "social construction," a set of social practices, institutions, **identities**, and beliefs; a way of classifying and ranking human groups; and, for many, an ideology and system of social inequality based on ancestry. This is the prevailing scientific view of race today. Indeed, organizations, such as the American Sociological Association and the American Anthropological Association, have official statements that reject race as a biological concept in favor of race as a cultural and social invention, created in specific cultural, historical, and political contexts.

However, despite consensus that "race" is a human invention, confusion persists among the public, and even the scientific community. Race is deeply embedded in the US society and psyche. But we are also dealing with comprehensive, multi-layered, complex concepts. Unraveling the myth of race as biology requires knowledge of human biological variation and genetics. The idea of race as a "social" or "cultural" "construction" rests on understanding how profoundly historical, social, and cultural processes impact lived reality.

Most academic disciplines treat only one side of the "race as biology or culture-social construct" question. Within the last decade, however, anthropology has developed an integrated "biocultural" approach, which incorporates perspectives from its major subfields – biological and cultural anthropology. The American Anthropological Association's traveling

museum exhibit, *RACE: Are we so different?* weaves together historical, biological and social scientific evidence to make three major points: (1) race is a recent human invention; (2) race is about culture, not biology; and (3) race and racism are deeply embedded in institutions and everyday life. A complementary book, *How real is race? A Sourcebook on race, culture, and biology*, offers more detailed evidence that race is about culture not biology, including a systematic exploration of the fallacy of race as biology and how culture has "created" race.

The fallacy of race as biology

The idea that race is not "biologically real" seems contrary to many people's experience. If race is biological fiction, why are we so often able to classify people racially? Doesn't President Barack Obama look racially different than George Bush?

Scientists are not arguing that there is no biological component to what we call "race. Human biological variation exists and a combination of geography, history, and social restrictions on mating have produced some superficial visible markers of common ancestry. But scientists reject the concept of race as a scientifically valid description of human biological variation.

Scientists now know that modern humans originated in Africa, as one species, and remained a single species, despite migrations to different parts of the world. All contemporary human populations are subsets of this single African lineage. Local populations, through natural selection as well as random genetic mutation, acquired some distinct genetic traits, such as shovel-shaped incisor teeth, hairy ears, or paler skin. At the same time, continuous migration and inter-mating between local populations prevented us from branching into distinct subspecies or species and, instead, produced a richer, more variable gene pool.

In short, the idea of between three and

six "original" or "natural" human sub-divisions, "archaic" races, "mixing" in recent centuries is fiction not fact. There have been thousands and thousands of populations throughout human history, fusing, disappearing, re-emerging in new configurations of human variability. All contemporary human populations are historically specific mixtures of the human gene pool.

For biological races to be scientifically "real" they must be based on objective, consistent, reliable, and meaningful biological criteria. The race concept historically envisioned clear-cut, discrete, homogeneous, and easily identifiable human subgroups into which people could easily be categorized; but this is not the case.

There are no biological traits that will consistently and reliably divide the human species into the same set of racial groupings. There are thousands of potential "racial" traits. Some are visible, such as skin, eye and hair color, height, and body shape. Others are not: saliva components, enzymes for milk tolerance, substances in blood. There are at least ten human blood systems that show significant genetic variations among humans (e.g. ABO blood system). These can have significant medical consequences, as anyone seeking a blood transfusion knows.

North American racial categories historically utilized a few visible traits – skin color and other genetic-based features of physical appearance. These constitute only a small fraction of human genetic variation. A system of "race" based on these traits (and not others) is totally arbitrary, biologically speaking. In addition, most "racialized" traits, like skin color, are not discrete categories but are continuous; that is, there are infinite degrees of lightness–darkness. The dividing line between categories and the number of racial categories is, again, purely arbitrary.

Most important, so-called "racial" traits do not co-vary. In order to create biologically distinct groups, each racial trait must have approximately the same distribution. Thus, populations with particular forms of one trait, such as darker skin, should also have straighter hair or noses, or share the same blood types. Yet the distribution of traits across populations in different geographic regions of the world ("clines") shows that no two traits have the same distribution. Using different traits produces a different "racial" classification or division of the human species. A population's "race" shifts depending on the trait used.

Neither do "race" traits co-vary with other, more biologically significant forms of genetic variation, such as blood type. Yet, if we wanted to classify people by genetic traits, it would make more medical sense to form races based on ABO blood type or lactose intolerance than on skin color or eye shape.

There is far more genetic variability within so-called "races" than between races. Scientist Richard Lewontin showed that nearly 94 percent of all human genetic diversity occurs within the populations we call races. Indeed, more genetic variability occurs within communities, and even within families, than between races. Most variability in DNA is at the individual level and is "unexpressed." That is, it is part of an individual's total genetic makeup ("genotype") and is transmitted to offspring but it has no biological impact on the organism.

Current US racial categories are arbitrary, unstable and, arguably, biologically meaningless. Individuals cannot reliably be "raced," because the criteria are so subjective and unscientific. And the meanings of "race" have changed over time. The 1900 US Census included "mulatto, quadroon, or octoroon" along with "Black" and "White" races. Asian Indians were initially categorized as "White" until the *Thind* Supreme Court case designated them "Caucasian" but not "White." Shifts in the number and definitions of "race" occur regularly, as in the latest US Census. And US racial classifications do not work in other countries, such as in Brazil or South Asia. "Race" is not a universal concept.

Biological definitions of race are not useful in understanding other phenomena. There is no convincing evidence that "racial" characteristics are causally linked to behavior, capacities, individual and group accomplishments, cultural institutions, or activity preferences. On the contrary, focusing on racial explanations can mask other environmental causal factors.

Race as culturally and socially real

Race may be a biological fiction but that does not mean that race does not exist. The concept of race is a cultural invention, a culturally and historically specific way of thinking about, categorizing, and treating human beings. Race, and what Smedley calls the North American "racial world view," developed to legitimize and maintain social inequality between groups with different ancestries, national origins and histories.

But cultural inventions are "real," experientially. Indeed, the human world is largely a cultural and social invention – but one that is obviously quite real. Race in the United States has profoundly shaped social life and social institutions, **power** relationships, mating, dating and reproduction, our social identities, our experiences, and our perceptions.

Like other cultural inventions, "race," once learned, feels "natural," like a seven-day "week," a 60 "minute" hour, or a "lunch" of turkey, not rat. Without thinking, we perceive people through a "racial" lens. We unconsciously "notice" racially marked features, like skin color or eye shape, while ignoring other visible traits. We "race" strangers and feel uneasy if our racial categories do not "fit." It is the deep cultural and social reality of race in the United States that makes it difficult for some people to accept that races are not biologically "real." But scientists are not saying that race is not "real." Race is both a biological fiction and a social-cultural reality.

Race in the US context can trick us into thinking that there are biological races. Geographically localized populations, as a result of adaptation, migration, and chance, may develop characteristic physical traits. Some, (such as skin color) reflect climatic conditions; others reflect random, historical processes and migration patterns. The United States was peopled by populations from geographically separated regions of the world – immigrants, African slaves, and indigenous American groups. Dominant European ethnic groups drew upon visible differences, especially skin color, as racial status "markers" in a race-based social hierarchy.

Preserving racial "markers" required control of mating and reproduction, so European American elites created elaborate social and physical barriers to racial interaction. Anti-miscegenation laws outlawed interracial sex and marriage until declared unconstitutional in 1967. Children of interracial (often forced) matings acquired the racial status of their racially lower-status parent, usually the mother – the "one-drop" rule ("hypodescent").

In contrast, there were relatively few barriers among Americans of European ancestry – English, Germans, Swedes, etc. With intermarriage, previous intra-European genetic and cultural differences disappeared into the macro-racial category "White" or, more accurately, European American.

There is, then, a biological component in US racial groups. But it is the result of recent socio-cultural processes – namely, formal and informal barriers to mating and marriage. Current "racial" markers, like skin color, reflect the triumph of culture over "nature," reflect biology shaped by culture and society. But then "race" has always been about manipulating biology for social, political, and economic ends. [CCM]

Key readings

American Anthropological Association, 2007. *RACE: Are we so different*. See website: www.understandingrace.org; see especially Resources/Bibliography, www. understandingrace.org/resources/pdf/ annotated_bibliography.pdf and Teachers Guides.

Marks, J. (2008) Race: Past, present and future. In B. Koenig, S. Lee, & S. Richardson (Eds.), *Revisiting race in a genomic age*. New Brunswick, NJ: Rutgers University Press, pp. 21–38.

Mukhopadhyay, C. C., Henze, R., & Moses, Y. T. (2007). *How real is race? A sourcebook on race, culture and biology*. Lanham, MD: Rowman and Littlefield Education.

Omi, M. A. & Winant, H. (1994). *Racial formation in the United States* (2nd ed.). New York: Routledge.

Smedley, A. (2005). *Race in North America: Origin and evolution of a worldview*. Boulder: Westview Press.

RACE CARD Like the concept of race, the notion of the "race card" is contested. The [im]possibilities and discomfort of speaking about **race** have often displaced the intellectual necessity to theorize "race card" as a concept embedded in **power** and domination. Are all human social relations a form of race relations? I would say "yes," to the extent that race has become a key principle of social organization, **representation** and identity formation in today's society. Race is often the silent elephant in the room that no one wants to speak about. A history of discomfort around, and, particularly, the silence of the dominant's complicities in race/racism have

often led to accusations of "playing the card" whenever race is injected into discussions that call into question a racist moment and/or encounter. To most people (especially the dominant) that incident has no bearing on race relations. Thus, "playing the race card" has come to embody a particular hegemonic discourse deployed from the dominant body/geography/space that counters, as an absolute, talk about racism as experienced by the racialized and minoritized body. As a strategic discursive tool, playing the race card has come to be vibrant in the present neo-liberal democratic epoch, where globalization is prominent, and where the de-legalization of racial **segregation** (in particular in 1994 in South Africa), has contributed to the increasing difficulty of talking about race and racism. Instead, there is much talk of a post-South Africa, post **apartheid**, post-racial era. The election of Barak Obama as President of the United States, the first person of color to hold that office, has further contributed to this difficulty. In the public sphere of the West, talk of affirmative action has come to be diffused/diluted and even silenced through particular discursives (for example civil rights/equal opportunity for all, the discourse of meritocracy, the discourse of class and overcoming) by certain racialized peoples. Importantly, we need to think of these discourses as different cards from the same deck. We need to ask: what are the consequences and implications, when such discursive practices are taken up by the racialized body? That is, what are the implications when racialized bodies come to be unintentionally complicit in taking up these cards as their own (for example, when racialized bodies claim the discourse of overcoming race)? We need to think about the ways in which the "race card" presents itself in everyday moments, through the dominant as well as through the racialized body. Consequently, in this entry I begin with the premise that the race card is invoked, and proceed to question the location of the speaker/subject evoking the race card? And, which body has the authority to claim race-card politics?

The race card offers a particular moment that accords a certain body the opportunity to take up an ahistorical politic, that is allowing one to speak, in an uncompromising manner, of a moment, to speak of an experience as devoid of material, historical colonial relations. We need to discus this "race card" as a problematic discursive technology that works to diffuse the saliency of race within the governing neoliberal public sphere. In our contemporary pluralist epoch, the deployed "race card" negates the everyday historic colonial communicative exchanges as experienced by the racialized body. We need to understand the "race card" in, and of itself, as constitutive of epistemic violence against the different geo-racialized bodies. I am asking us to consider the manner in which the "race card" disseminates a particular humanism in which the said body experiences myriad exigencies of alienation. What are the ways in which the deployed "race card" speaks to the historic-socio-cultural material conditions of the dominant group? How does the "race card" come to de-race the dominant subject and simultaneously appear neutral, innocent, benevolent/humanitarian? How does the "race card," as embodied, appear as not being complicit, privileged, or responsible for the existing racial division? Equally important is the question of the tacit de-politicization of racial oppression. Ultimately, the "race card" resides in questions of race and power and the immanent asymmetrical relations of power. In discussing the "race card" we need to locate the body, the speaker, the context of the relationship and the myriad loci of talking about the lived experience of race. What then is the relationship concerning **identity** formation, the politics of representation and race? What are the points of divergence and convergence when the "race card" is discussed from the dominant and from bodies of the oppressed? How do bodies of difference come to work with and against the discursive temporality of the "race card?" Take as an example the situation when the "black" body is admitted to competitive programs within elite schooling. From the well-to-do med schools, to the much talked about law schools, the acceptance becomes easily dismissed as acts of charity by the dominant group. But this sentiment is also shared by some racialized bodies who have bought into the campaign the purposefully constructed notion that "'black' folks don't know what they are doing nor where they are going." On the contrary, recently a case was sent to the Supreme Court in which white firefighters cried alleged "reverse **discrimination**" when they were not promoted to the next rank. The race card was an integrative factor in the white firefighters' victorious outcome. Needless to say, the black firefighters appealed. The point here being that, in discussing the "race card," we must dialogue about the material historic conditions of our existence; we cannot continue to simply accept the governing contemporary moment as existing within some historical vacuum. We cannot continue to proceed with historical amnesia regarding socio-historic development. We must consider a dialectical historical materialism to engage the here, the now and the before, if we choose to collectively pursue emancipatory pedagogies and social justice for all.

While there may be some justification for the accusation when race is invoked to win sympathy in an otherwise non-racist context, for the most part race has been invoked to gesture to particular racialized and racist experiences. By far, the majority of the allegations of "playing the race card" are misplaced when the sub-text is that calling on race involves inserting emotions into an otherwise rational/credible discussion. The play on race is also intended to win sympathy and avoid a critical interrogation of the issues on the table. Hence, calling on the race card is a form of silencing. It is also important to note, however, that it is not always the minoritized who has been accused by the dominant of playing the race card. The majority can play the race card in ways that maintain their privilege and power. Conversely, the whole idea of dismissing claims of the racially minoritized as merely playing the race card can be a way for the dominant to avoid discussions of their complicities and privileges which have helped to sustain a racist moment, encounter, or practice. So we can have dominant groups playing the race card when they intend to maintain their privileges regarding the distributions of social goods and services (e.g. employment and schooling opportunities).

In effect, "playing the race card" can be viewed as a set of contested and conjectural knowledges that can only be understood in a dialogical encounter between the dominant and the oppressed. The understanding of the phrase cannot be located in a fixed/static metaphoric space, one that is removed from practice, performance, power and process. It is important for us to understand how power relations are articulated in society in ways that construct and validate certain experiences while denying and invalidating others. There are some "power-saturated aspects of race" that allow the dominant to name certain experiences as race/racial experiences but not others. The notion of the "race card" is articulated in a place and within a particular politics. Therefore, our understanding must deal with the situated political and social practices through which names and meanings are contested, produced and reworked in particular historical moments. The power to define a particular experience and social practice is an essential part of the larger social framework of understanding race and racism in society.

Resistance to racism and racist codes is more than a social and spatial encounter. These are important historical moments as well. Throughout human history, the sites and spaces of resistance are constructed by, and for individuals, groups and collectivities by the dominant. The intellectual agency of the minoritized to resist such dominance is often negated or down played with powerful and seductive discourses. Playing the race card is one of such discourses. It is about definitions of what constitutes a racist moment, racist name-calling and a racist/racial encounter. The phrase is about producing and [in]validating knowledge, ideas, images and imagining social relations and encounters as either racist/racial incidents or encounters. Through counter discourses, the racially minoritized search and produce other discursive resources and practices that speak to the ideological context in which their experiences and social readings are either framed or framing their "new" world.

In effect, challenging the naming of the race card cannot simply be understood as a discursive practice. It is about the political and linguistic struggles of the racially minoritized to ensure that their experiences and understandings are not understood exclusively as questions about identity. There are significant economic, political, symbolic and spiritual considerations that need to be taken into account in order to move beyond Eurocentric and dominant interpretations of the race card. By simultaneously emphasizing the issues of **culture**, identity, history and politics, we can begin to understand why and how racially minoritized bodies continue to resist and become subjects and actors of social change. [GJSD]

Key readings

Dei, G. J. S., Karumanchery, L., & Karumanchery-Luik, N. (2004). *Playing the race card: Exposing white power and privilege.* New York: Peter Lang.

Dei, G. J. S. (2008). *Crash* and the relevance of an anti-racism analytical lens. In G. J. S. Dei & S. S. Howard (Eds.), *Crash politics and antiracism: Interrogations of liberal race discourse.* New York: Peter Lang, pp. 13–23.

Cheng, A. A. (1997). The melancholy of race. *The Kenyon Review*, 19(1), 49–61.

Hurwitz, J. & Peffley, M. (2005). Playing the race card in the post-Willie Horton era: The impact of racialized code words on support for punitive crime policy. *Public Opinion Quarterly*, 69 (Spring), 99–112.

Nelson, T., Sanbonmatsu, K., & McClerking, H. K. (2007). Playing a different race card: Examining the limits of elite influence on perceptions of racism. *Journal of Politics*, 69, 416–429.

Williams, L. (2001). *Playing the race card: Melodramas of black and white from Uncle Tom to O.J.* Princeton, NJ: Princeton University Press.

RACIAL PROFILING Racial disparities in the American criminal justice system have been of interest for researchers, legislators, and society due to the documented disproportionate numbers of racial and ethnic minorities at every stage of the criminal justice process. For instance, police departments have been sharply criticized for their response and service to the **minority** community since the post-**Civil Rights** era and, recently, researchers documented a similar issue in the consumer industry.

The documentation of issues involving law enforcement and in the consumer industry has led to a substantial amount of energy being focused on the intersection between **race** and the use of profiles. For instance, citizens, police administrators, policy makers, and legislators of all levels of government have been particularly interested in this issue. The issue of profiling has been problematic because there has been some indication that race has been the sole reason for the profile. Thus, since the late 1990s, law enforcement racial profiling has been an area of significant interest.

Definitions of racial profiling
Racial profiling is not easily defined and is generally controversial. In fact, racial profiling generally has been defined based on context. The number of definitions may be best understood as emanating either from law enforcement or the consumer industry. Racial profiling in law enforcement has several different definitions that are based on individual perception, which muddle the understanding of the issue. For instance, profiling is the use of a combination of physical, behavioral or psychological factors that, after being subjected to careful analysis, improve the probability of identifying and apprehending a suspect. While this is a general definition it has a positive tone. Others are not so positive in tone when defining racial profiling. For example, profiling refers to the tendency of police officers to stop and cite a disproportionate number of minorities. Some scholars define racial profiling as including specific targeting of minorities for unwarranted stops or any police-initiated action that relies on race, ethnicity, or national origin rather than a behavior. While these definitions are more negative in tone, they do not provide a substantial degree of clarity about racial profiling because they do not make it clear if the officers' behavior is mandated by the police department or is a reflection of their own bias. For the present study, while not clarifying the role of the police department or the officer, racial profiling is the practice of making law enforcement decisions based on race or ethnicity. Yet others define profiling as having two parts, hard profiling (race is used as the only factor in a police officer's decision-making) and soft profiling (when race is only one factor used in a police officer's decision-making).

In the consumer industry, racial profiling

does take place and scholars are beginning to research this issue. The genesis of consumer racial profiling (CRP) is defining the event. Unlike defining racial profiling in law enforcement, the definition of CRP has not been debated. The general definition of CRP is the discriminatory treatment of racial and ethnic minorities in retail establishments. While this definition may be vague, CRP is evident in two ways. First, poor treatment is a consistent practice for those that are victims of CRP. Second, those that are victims of CRP usually receive unwanted and unnecessary discriminatory attention in retail settings.

Overall, the definition of racial profiling seems to be most controversial in the context of law enforcement, but the definition of CRP may become more controversial as a greater number of scholars begin to research this issue. When researching racial profiling, regardless of the context, several issues need to be understood and, if possible, addressed to explain racial profiling.

Issues in explaining racial profiling

Regardless of the context in which racial profiling takes place, a number of issues need to be understood or addressed. The issues that will be discussed here are the implications of the lack of theory and methodological issues when studying racial profiling.

Unfortunately, little research into racial profiling has directly applied theory to allow for an understanding. To be clear, researchers of racial profiling have consistently used a number of variables (i.e. operationalized concepts) to attempt to understand racial profiling. Methodologically, researchers have several issues to overcome to provide an understanding of racial profiling. First, law enforcement researchers, have to determine what part of an encounter are they will use to understand racial profiling. For instance, law enforcement researchers need to determine

if they will be studying the traffic stop itself or some other portion of the traffic stop (i.e. search or arrest). While seemingly minor, this determination has implications for how the data are collected. For example, the researcher will need to have data that are theoretically derived before a traffic stop occurs to accurately capture intentions to perform or use racial profiling. This would mean that researchers would not be able to rely on agency-collected data. The same may be said for researchers that are studying CRP.

Second, the racial profiling literature contains a debate on the use of "benchmarks." Benchmarks pose a substantial challenge because researchers have been occupied with the attempt to develop a fraction in understanding their data. The fraction would place the recorded traffic stops in the numerator and a baseline or benchmark as the denominator. Thus, three potential outcomes are possible. First, if the racial composition in the numerator is the same as the denominator, then no racial profiling has taken place. Second, if the racial composition in the numerator is smaller than the denominator, then no racial profiling has taken place. Third, if the racial composition of the numerator is greater than the denominator, then racial profiling has taken place. While this seems simple, to date, there has not been any consensus on the proper baseline or benchmark among practitioners or academics. Therefore, the fraction approach is limited due to the lack of benchmarks or baselines.

Overall, consumers and researchers of racial profiling need to consider a few issues when reviewing or studying this behavior. First, the researchers need to know if it is theoretically driven. Second, researchers need to know what methodologies have been used in collecting and analyzing the data. Understanding these issues will allow for better research and understanding of racial profiling.

Literature on racial profiling

The literature on racial profiling has been developing for nearly a decade – especially from the law enforcement side, but has also been growing from the consumer side. From this literature, some discernable themes have arisen. First, the lack of theory and methodological issues discussed before has been confirmed and is glaringly obvious in both types of literature. Second, the law enforcement racial profiling literature has seen a shift away from the use of benchmarks. Importantly, the literature shows that the focus of racial profiling has moved away from the traffic stop alone. Early racial profiling researchers would attempt to understand why the traffic stop took place. This has been a rather fruitless effort, given that the officer makes the decision, and few have shown good results that speak to this issue.

While this is still an important area, many researchers have now shifted their focus to examine other outcomes of the traffic stop. For instance, a growing body of research is focused on the racial implications of the decision to search an individual. Others are now focusing on the decision to arrest an individual. Unfortunately, these efforts are methodologically driven and not theoretically driven. Thus, the results of these efforts are still devoid of solid understandings of racial profiling.

In the consumer portion of racial profiling (CRP), researchers are just beginning to show some research interest in this topic. Researchers of this genre usually examine the behavior using literature reviews of the legal cases which show that CRP does take place, while a small body of research empirically shows that African-American individuals are much more likely to be victims of CRP. Different from the research on law enforcement racial profiling, the CRP empirical literature appears to focus more on the comments and responses of the actual victims, rather than relying on official reports from agencies, as is typical in law enforcement racial profiling studies.

Research directions

Few will argue that racial profiling is a controversial issue. Defining racial profiling is not only difficult, but it is complicated by being context-specific. The empirical literature has shed some light on this behavior, but it has been lax in establishing theoretical understandings that have hampered empirical efforts. Unfortunately, methodologies that researchers have employed to understand racial profiling have also been underdeveloped. While these are issues, the controversy that surrounds the issue demands that additional research be conducted to reduce instances, or perceptions of instances, of this behavior.

The racial profiling phenomenon is important because it is ripe for additional research. Researchers of racial profiling should consider the theoretical issues in making sense out of their racial profiling data. Further, researchers should consider the implications (i.e. strengths and weaknesses) of their research methodologies. That is, researchers need to be creative in employing theories that push the boundaries of understanding and use methodologies based on the theories that may provide solid evidence that is supportive or contradictory in order to maximize the ability to reduce racial profiling. [GEH]

Key readings

Engel, R. S. (2008). A critique of the outcome test in racial profiling research. *Justice Quarterly*, 25, 1–36.

Engel, R. & Calnon, J. (2004). Examining the influence of drivers' characteristics during traffic stops with police: Results from a national survey. *Justice Quarterly*, 21(1), 49–90.

Gabbidon, S. L. & Higgins, G. E. (2007).

Consumer racial profiling and perceived victimization: A phone survey of Philadelphia Area residents. *American Journal of Criminal Justice,* 32, 1–11.

Withrow, B. L. (2006). *Racial profiling: From rhetoric to reason.* Prentice Hall: Upper Saddle River, NJ.

RAP MUSIC Rap music is a central feature of hip hop **culture**, comprising just one of hip hop's four basic elements: graffiti, break dancing, DJing and rapping (or MCing). First appearing in New York City's Bronx neighborhoods in the late 1970s, hip hop began as a youth-oriented, working-class and largely Black American urban cultural movement. Since its inception, rap music has served as hip hop's most culturally recognized and commercially successfully component.

While rap's artistic lineage can be traced back to rhythmic sounds and speech of African and Caribbean musical traditions, rap music is popularly understood as a unique African American art form, resulting from the distinctly Black American social and cultural context in which it was born. Politically defined as post-**civil rights** and culturally understood as post-soul, rap music's originators were a generation of predominantly Black and **Latino** youth who came of age in an era where, while civil rights had been formally granted, new and more subtle – though no less devastating – racial barriers had been erected. Cloaked in a language of **color blindness**, new social and economic policies created an environment where poor and working-class Black and Latino urban youth faced high levels of unemployment, incarceration, police brutality, **racial profiling**, unaffordable and segregated urban housing, and a racially discriminatory War on Drugs policy. Both an incorporation of and reaction against 1970s disco music, rap's post-soul aesthetic reflected the changing values within Black culture in the late 1970s, moving away from a 1960s optimism concerning the achievement of racial equality through collective political action and moral persuasion, to a more cynical and self-involved ethos. In this social and cultural context, marginalized African American, Caribbean American and Latin American adolescents voiced frustrations and aspirations through the newly emerging hip hop aesthetic.

Musically, rap's rhythms are a product of two technological influences: the introduction of the "mixer," which allowed disco DJs to seamlessly flow recorded music from one song to another; and early hip hop artists' incorporation of Jamaican sound mixing – a style called "dub" – which isolated and then emphasized the strong, pulsating drum and bass lines running through reggae music. Over these beats, MCs provided spoken words, reciting rhymes often pertaining to a MC's musical, sexual, and/or intellectual prowess; this spoken-word quality of rap music has roots in various American – and specifically African American – oral narrative traditions, most evident in the African American tradition of "toasting."

The early years

While artists were already experimenting with precursors of hip hop music throughout the 1970s, it was the commercial popularity of the Sugarhill Gang's 1979 song "Rapper's Delight" that introduced rap's unique sound to a world beyond New York's inner city neighborhoods. The early 1980s ushered in an era of rap music characterized by the mixing and sampling of previous musical traditions, and lyrics served as soundtracks for party-like atmospheres, as well as more serious testimonials of the harsh social conditions of America's urban poor. It was also during this time that rap music began to garner attention from major record labels (beginning with rapper Kurtis Blow's contract with Mercury Records in late 1979), and experience crossover success in pop music. By the beginning of the mid-1980s, rap music had began to make a definitive move outside the boroughs of New York, and Los Angeles rappers emerged with their own distinct hip hop sound, dance, and style.

As the 1980s came to a close and the Reagan Administration's trickle-down economic policies took a toll on America's inner cities, particularly affecting Black and Hispanic youth, rap music's lyrics became more socially critical and increasingly hardcore. Rap groups, such as Public Enemy, emerged with lyrical messages informed by a Black **Nationalist** perspective, and Los Angeles rappers such as Ice-T and N.W.A. highlighted the perils of the American ghetto and the corruption of society, particularly targeting law enforcement and elected officials. By the end of the decade, the unique characteristics associated with New York and California rap music had laid the groundwork for what would later become important regional differences. Today, general regional flavors are evident in hip hop music of the Northeast, the West Coast, the Midwest, and the so-called "Dirty South."

By the turn of the decade, rap music had unequivocally become associated with big business and the commercial success of rap music was drawing considerable attention, not only from devoted fans, but also from cultural, social and political critics, both within and outside the hip hop community. More and more rappers were becoming critical of the corporate music industry's influence on the direction of the music and on rap artists' increasing acquiescence; this critique within hip hop laid the groundwork for the sub-genres of alternative, socially conscious and underground hip hop music. During this time, the contradictions and confrontations that had always been a part of rap music began to emerge as controversial sites of debate outside the hip hop community as well.

Debates and controversies

The 1990s witnessed several high-profile cases in which rap disputes around censorship, partisan politics and family values took center stage. These include: the 1990 obscenity charges against rap group 2 Live Crew, who were eventually acquitted; the 1992 political attack on Ice-T's band Body Count's "Cop Killer;" and Bill Clinton's 1991 denouncement of Sister Souljah's critique of Black-on-Black crime, in which she satirically suggests that Black people take a break from killing each other and have a week where they kill White people instead. These culturally visible moments in the early 1990s underscore the rising political and cultural stakes becoming associated with hip hop music.

Gang wars and the politicized rap of the 1980s translated into financial fortunes for 1990s rappers and music executives, who capitalized on the media's seductive depiction of Los Angeles gangster culture, breathing life into the musical genre of gangsta rap. Rap music of this persuasion laid claims to street credibility and gangsta **authenticity**, and the genre quickly received criticism not only for its portrayal (and glorification) of violence and drug culture, but also for its reinforcement of **stereotypes** pertaining to the dangerous nature of poor Black and Latino youth. Yet, by mid-decade, gangsta rap was charged with being co-opted by not-so-real gangstas trying to find success in the changing music scene. This infiltration of allegedly wannabe or artificially-cultivated gangstas challenged the integrity of a genre that relied heavily on notions of authenticity and lived gangsta experience.

The commercial and musical success of Los Angeles gangsta rap, most notably ushered in by Dr Dre's *The Chronic* (1992) followed by Snoop Doggy Dogg's *Doggystyle* (1993), served to legitimate, for the first time, West Coast rappers' claims to lyrical and musical authority, which fueled an East Coast–West Coast rap rivalry that had been smoldering for years, fanned further by the media's sensationalized coverage and industry executives' encouragement. The untimely murders of superstar rappers Tupac Shakur in 1996 and the Notorious B.I.G. in 1997 served as wake-up calls for the antagonistic coastal rap rivalry, in which the world lost two of hip hop's greatest, most talented rappers.

Today, in addition to its explicit lyrical – and real-life – portrayals of violence and drug culture, rap music stands at the center of other serious social and cultural debates, including concerns over the music's misogyny and heterosexism; detachment from political roots; accommodation to industry pressures and a majority-White consumer base; the hyper-materialism of its "bling-bling" ethos; and portrayals of hyper, exploitative sexuality, or "hip hop pornography." But rap music has never suffered from a lack of fans willing to defend various aspects of the music's most controversial features and hip hop music, either in spite of or perhaps because of its contentious characteristics, remains a central force in the lives of its devotees.

Future directions

Rap music's success in the decades since its inception in the late 1970s is a strong indication of its sustaining presence and unforgettable mark on the world of music. Artists from around the globe are creating new and distinct styles of rap, infusing it with other cultural and national music traditions. These rap-inspired offshoots integrate hip hop sensibilities with local musical aesthetics, producing such creations as reggaeton music, influenced by Puerto Rican and Panamanian traditions, Japan's nip-hop and South Africa's kwaito. Strong hip hop music communities thrive in Cuba, Ghana, France, Germany, Kenya, Brazil, New Zealand, Poland, Uganda, Turkey, Italy, Spain and many other locations across the world.

Since the debut of "Rapper's Delight" in 1979, rap music has gone through many changes, innovations and, some might argue, regressions. Nonetheless, rap music continues to serve as a source of social critique and artistic expression. Rap music also continues to function as a powerful component of hip hop culture, and the incredible mobilizing potential of hip hop is increasingly tapped as an organizing force for various political, activist, civic engagement and youth education projects. Hip hop fans, frustrated by negative portrayals of women in the music, as well as by rap's often monolithic and homophobic **representations** of sexuality, are talking back under the banner of hip hop feminism. Hip hop and hip hop music have spawned in more directions than ever imagined back in the Bronx in the late 1970s when the borough's youth made music – and history – with just "two turntables and a microphone." [VC]

Key readings

Basu, D. & Lemelle, S. (Eds.). (2006). *The vinyl ain't final: Hip hop and the globalization of black popular culture*. London: Pluto.

Chang, J. (2005). *Can't stop, won't stop: A history of the hip-hop generation*. New York: St. Martin's Press.

George, N. (1998). *Hip hop America*. New York: Viking.

Kitwana, B. (2002). *The hip hop generation: Young blacks and the crisis in African-American culture*. New York: BasicCivitas.

Ogbar, J. O. G. (2007). *Hip hop revolution: The culture and politics of rap*. Lawrence, KS: University Press of Kansas.

Pough, G. D. (2004). *Check it while I wreck it: Black womanhood, hip hop culture, and the public sphere*. Boston: Northeastern University Press.

Rose, T. (1994). *Black noise: Rap music and black culture in contemporary America*. Hanover, NH: University Press of New England.

REPARATIONS Reparations is a concept historically connected with dues owed by one state to another in recompense for damages in the aftermath of war. The concept has broadened more recently to become a centerpiece of claims by certain ethno-racial groups for compensation for historical wrongs committed against them. Such claims are most typically brought against states, but sometimes against corporate and religious entities as well. Efforts directed toward exacting reparations have proliferated since the 1990s. Such proliferation is owed, in large measure, to the growing influence of the international human rights paradigm and the rise of **identity politics**. Claimants, in turn, have been buoyed by a host of successful Second World War-related reparations cases involving, for example, Holocaust victims (**genocide**), Korean comfort women (sexual exploitation), and Japanese-Americans and Japanese-Canadians (internment). Alongside these developments has grown a burgeoning academic literature on reparations politics, transitional justice, and public apologies. The literature highlights the fact that reparations can be of many types, and is useful in drawing distinctions based on, for example, time (whether or not the victims/perpetrators are still living), scope (whether or not the crimes violated the rights of individuals or groups), and type of repair (symbolic, financial, or rehabilitative).

Reparations for slavery in the United States
Demands for reparations in the United States have been brought forward predominantly by African Americans who have sought remedy against the legacy of slavery and, to a lesser extent, that of Jim Crow. There exist many historical precedents for reparations politics in the United States. In 1866, Thaddeus Stevens proposed the famous "forty acres and a mule" for every freedman. In 1915, Cornelius J. Jones filed an unsuccessful lawsuit against

the U.S. Department of the Treasury to recover $68 million for former slaves in what became known as the Cotton Tax Case. In 1969, **Civil Rights** activist James Foreman read out "The Black Manifesto" before an audience at the Riverside Church, which demanded $500 million from the country's churches and synagogues for African Americans as recompense for centuries of racism. Since 1988, congressman John Conyers (D-Michigan), along with the National Coalition of Blacks for Reparations, has lobbied for reparations for slavery and **segregation**. Although reparations have not been paid to date, the U.S. House of Representatives did offer a public apology in 2008 for slavery and **discrimination** during the era of segregation.

Present-day demands for reparations on the part of African Americans build on precedents set by other groups. Many of these are borrowed from the international arena surveyed below, but domestic examples register too, such as the US Government's apology in 1988 to Japanese-Americans for internment during the Second World War and the payment of $20,000 to each survivor as compensation for the wartime loss of property and liberty. The moral case revolves around the claim that the nation's wealth owes a historic debt to the labor provided by enslaved blacks, and that modern-day differentials in socio-economic and cultural status between racial groups are owing to this inadequately redressed historical legacy.

Yet, in the post-Civil Rights era United States, the politics of reparations remains mired in controversy. Proposals for direct payments to the descendants of slaves by the US Government become stymied by the question of how to properly identify descendants, especially given that the US Census does not track such descent but relies on racial self-identification. An added problem is how to calculate what is owed and by whom. Here, the passage of time fuels the criticism that reparations are being asked to be paid by those who are not themselves the perpetrators and to individuals who are not themselves the direct victims. When the focus of reparations politics shifts from individual payments to more systemic programs aimed at community rehabilitation, white discourses of victim-blaming and racial innocence abound. Even proposals for a public apology for slavery and/or segregation, with no link to monetary payouts, evoke white anger. Conservative critics such as David Horowitz argue that reparations politics serve only to fuel racial resentment and an overall deterioration in **race** relations.

The emergent field of "White Studies" helps to contextualize such negative responses. Surveys of white racial attitudes reveal that the majority of white people today feel that slavery – and, by extension, racism – occurred so very long ago that it has nothing to do with them. A common theme is the denial of historic responsibility or even acknowledgement of the accumulative benefits of **whiteness**. Tales of the hardships faced by white ethnic ancestors further attempt to cement white innocence in the face of demands for reparations. The fetish for innocence is revealed in repeated assertions that Africans also participated in and profited from the slave trade and, more controversially, that African Americans are better off in the United States today than if they had been left in Africa. Some combatants in white backlash **culture** opine that white people are, in fact, the new victims of the present-day racial spoils system.

For now, reparation politics enters the mainstream of American political discourse and policymaking mainly in the form of debates over affirmative action. The policy does represent one form of systemic reparations for the history of institutionalized racism against black Americans.

Even as the basis for affirmative action has tapered and shifted from redress to diversity, some argue that, since blacks were historically disadvantaged by government policy, the best way forward is to embrace affirmative action as the vehicle for appropriate and just compensation.

International perspectives

Outside the West, reparations politics has sat at the heart of debates concerning transitional justice in the aftermath of democratization. Transitional justice became a somewhat peripheral focus for political scientists in the 1980s in the aftermath of a series of democratic transitions in Latin America, and then, in the 1990s and beyond, increased in profile with an expanded geographic reach across Africa, Asia, and Central/Eastern Europe. Reparations in this context refer to wrongs committed during the colonial era or in the context of **authoritarian** regimes, past and present. Here, the debate revolves less around themes of racial guilt and innocence, as above, but rather on the tradeoffs between securing justice for victims and perpetrators alike, on the one hand, and negotiating a smooth transition to a new socio-political order on the other. Closely associated is the question of how best to consolidate democratic reforms and invest in national healing – via exorcising the ghosts of the past or adopting a forward-looking universalistic platform.

South Africa's Truth and Reconciliation Commission (SA-TRC) stands as a model, even though it was not the first such established truth commission. The TRC was established as part of the negotiated transition to democracy in 1994, a moment when the world stood in awe at the so-called miracle of racial reconciliation and magnanimity of spirit on the part of then President Nelson Mandela after nearly three decades as **apartheid's** most infamous political prisoner. The formation of the new unity Government was vexed from the start by the question of what to do about the crimes of the apartheid past. Real concern existed that, if aggressive prosecutions were to be pursued, the fragile unity would give way to the prospect of renewed political strife and even Civil War. While the TRC did not avoid criminal prosecutions altogether, the master narrative was one of trading confession for amnesty. The tropes of confession, absolution and forgiveness were further underscored by the chosen Commission Head – Archbishop Desmond Tutu. For several years following the transition to democratic rule, the TRC presided over highly public and emotionally charged sessions that sought to air the dirty laundry of the past so that the post-apartheid future could be free of such weighty historical baggage. In the end, many more victims gave testimonials than perpetrators, pitifully few of whom came forward in the process. The TRC ultimately secured from the government $74 million for 19,000 victims in financial reparations.

Academics and practitioners alike continue to explore and weigh the balancing of truth and justice. New comparative work on truth commissions and public apologies is helping to add empirical leanings to what can otherwise become a quite philosophical discussion. Also pertinent is an evolving set of international norms on reparations for victims of gross human rights violations, the most recent of which is commonly referred to as the "Bassiouni Principles," established and disseminated under the auspices of the United Nations (2005). Another trend is the hope proffered by a new generation of class action suits claiming reparations against corporations, such as the apartheid-era lawsuits brought by a group of black South African apartheid victims against multinationals that did business with the apartheid regime. Psycho-social research is just beginning the task of determining whether or not the aspirations of reparations politics are in

fact met, measured in terms of goals such as healing and forgiveness on the individual level, and reconciliation in the social arena. There is still much work to be done, in scholarship and practical policymaking, to protect groups of persons historically overlooked, such as the women who are victimized during armed conflicts. [AEA]

Key readings

Brophy, A. (2008). *Reparations: Pro and con.* New York: Oxford University Press.

Horowitz, D. (2002). *Uncivil wars: The controversy over reparations for slavery.* New York: Encounter Books.

Martin, M. & Yaquinto, M. (Eds.). (2007). *Redress for historical injustices in the United States: On reparations for slavery, Jim Crow, and their legacies.* Durham, NC: Duke University Press.

Minow, M. (1999). *Between vengeance and forgiveness: Facing history after genocide and mass violence.* Boston, MA: Beacon Press.

Thompson, J. (2003). *Taking responsibility for the past: Reparation and historical injustice.* Cambridge, MA: Polity Press.

Torpey, J. (2004). *Making whole what has been smashed: On reparations politics.* Cambridge, MA: Harvard University Press.

Wilson, R. A. (2001). *The politics of truth and reconciliation in South Africa: Legitimizing the post-apartheid state.* New York: Cambridge University Press.

REPRESENTATION Representation is the social process of making sense of the many signifying systems within a **culture**. It refers both to the active process and to the products of the process of representing. This process of interpreting signs is central to how we see other people and ourselves. The relationship between representation and the "real" is complex. What is representation? The word has several meanings:

to depict, to present, to offer a portrayal of...but at the same time it means to "re-present," to show again something that is already there, and to stand in for some-thing, or somebody, in the way a lawyer might represent the interests of her client, or a politician act on behalf of a country. While culture organizes and regulates the meanings we make, no two people will interpret the meaning of a representation in exactly the same way. The "real" mean-ing of something depends on what people make of it. Arguably, then, no "real" meaning can be attributed to something until it has been represented; so, in a sense, the thing that is being represented is consti-tuted by the representation.

Two complex, interrelated systems are central to the process of interpreting cultural meanings. First, a system of correspondences, a conceptual map that we have internalized, this provides a guide to the distinctive features of those things or people we perceive. For example, our inter-nalized map of what constitutes "a dog" and differentiates it from other categories of animals and animal behaviors, or within the category "furniture," the differentiation between the concept "table" from a writing desk, bench or sideboard. Second, the con-cepts need to be rendered into a shared lan-guage so that they can be recorded, expressed, shared and perhaps negotiated and modified. It is these arbitrary, conven-tional signs through which elements in our conceptual map are represented.

All available signifying systems produce representations of phenomena: spoken, written, electronic media, film, literature, news media and so on. For example, if rep-resentations of "**race**" were being investi-gated, many examples could be uncovered across a range of different media – for instance, the representation of characters in soap operas, of people in advertising, in news stories, an overheard joke in a bar or a university lecture. An analysis of these varied representations, and their different

forms of authority, further reveals that they are organized within different dis-courses. These representations may be articulated through apparently authorita-tive discourses such as scientific research, government policy and legislation or educational practices, or they may be the less formal, popular meanings of enter-tainment and celebrity culture. Paradoxically, in addition to the specific form of the media and message, the *absence* of portrayals can equally be a powerful representation. Just as the scar-city of African-Caribbean academics is a representation of inequality in the UK, the absence of African actors in sitcoms, com-edies or dramas (other than in exotic or aggressive criminal roles) may demon-strate dominant **stereotypes**.

It soon becomes apparent that terms like "race" and "ethnicity" (or, equally, "mas-culinity" and "sexuality") do not describe some static or "natural" social reality; rather, their meanings are constantly changing, reflecting the political and social contexts of the place and time. In current sociological discourse in the UK, "race" often appears in "scare quotes" because, as a representation of a social reality, its validity is heavily contested, and its very use might appear to lend credence to cate-gories that have been largely dismissed as illusory. Yet, to pretend that "race" is an illusory social construct and pursue a **color-blind** approach is equally problem-atic, as racism is an everyday reality for many. In many ways this is a clear demon-stration of how conventional, cultural signs that represent something become part of the **identity** they are representing.

Take the example shown here from a CRE (Commission for Racial Equality) poster campaign. A number of conven-tional codes are combined in an attempt to problematize and expose mainstream per-ceptions of "race." Yet the effectiveness of the campaign is questionable because the meaning of this poster is unclear. Certainly the result was a confronting image, but how does the viewer interpret the image of this eerily lit Black face? How should the text elements be linked with this image? First, we might consider the internalized map we have of, for example, Black culture, African or African Caribbean males; this particular image is understood intertextually from our existing lexicon/experience of similar faces, people, and our own subject location and background.

Source: reproduced with express permission from the Equality and Human Rights Commission, formerly the Commission for Racial Equality.

Second, this rather abstract visual image is also associated with language, generating connotations that locate the image culturally, historically and politically. All of this produces a complex interpretation of the meanings in a shared language that we can communicate to others. At the level of shared language, how do the text elements affect the perception of this image? Do these words anchor, modify, shape, affirm or contradict the more immediate sense impressions of the image? What is the role of the color, size, font choice, etc.? Here is a "representation gap," as perhaps the image and text are too ambiguous to form a coherent message. The rhetoric of the large word (in red) "SCARED?" is pivotal and suggests perhaps a collective fear of blackness as part of the cultural baggage of the reader. The use of a much smaller script size for the message (in white) "YOU SHOULD BE. HE'S A DENTIST." is intended to hold up our stereotypical

assumptions to scorn. Perhaps these were admirable aims but the sign vehicle for this exposé of stereotypical views was open to other interpretations: is this a revelation of small mindedness (which could seem insulting to many of us) or is it even serving to affirm racist beliefs? The CRE did not receive the many outraged complaints they had hoped for, apart from a few from dentists!

Several prominent scholars have commented on the relentlessly distorted representation in the West of Black and **minority** ethnic "**others**." **Postcolonial** writers, such as **Fanon** (1974), recognized that the colonialist language is permeated by White ideological meaning, which automatically positions the "Others" as marginal and inferior, and that this system of representations is internalized, leading to a divided psyche – "black skins/ white masks." Edward Said demonstrates the manner in which European and American media, including Hollywood films, cartoons and news reports, portray the Arab world as barbarous, primitive, mystical and exotic. There is nothing innocent in these systems and their consequences for foreign policy are arguably disastrous.

In a wider sense, some scholars may argue that the system of representation in the West is one that renders the experiences of Black history and culture invisible or inferior (see Asante's concept of "Eurocentricity"). The importance of understanding the dimension of representation is that it allows a critical appraisal of the hegemonic process by which divisive ideas may begin to be perceived as "natural." [SS]

Key readings

Asante, M. K. (1987). *The Afrocentric idea.* Philadelphia, PA: Temple University Press.

Fanon, F. (1974). *Black skin, white masks.* Boulder, CO: Paladin.

Fiske, J. (1989). *Understanding popular culture*. London: Unwin Hyman.

Hall, S. (Ed.). (1997). The work of representation. In S. Hall (Ed.), *Representation: Cultural representations and signifying practices*. Thousand Oaks, CA: Sage, pp. 13–74.

hooks, b. (1992). *Black looks: Race and representation*. New York: South End Press.

O'Sullivan, T., Hartley, J., Saunders, D., Montgomery, M., & Fiske, J. (Eds.). (1994). *Key concepts in communication and cultural studies*. London: Routledge.

Said, E. (1978). *Orientalism*. New York: Vintage Books.

——. (1981). *Covering Islam: How the media and the experts determine how we see the rest of the world*. London: Routledge & Kegan Paul.

Spencer, S. (2006). *Race & ethnicity: Culture, identity and representation*. London: Routledge.

Webb, J. (2009). *Representation*. Thousand Oaks, CA: Sage.

Woodward, K. (1997). *Identity & difference*. Thousand Oaks, CA: Sage.

SEGREGATION Segregation, or, the strategic isolation of individuals as a result of such characteristics as **race**, religion, social class, or sexual orientation, represents the aim of this concept. In the United States, for example, racial segregation has been the most pervasive form of human dissociation, dating back centuries. Whether prohibiting interracial relationships or upholding the "separate but equal" doctrine, segregation has been at the forefront of American socio-political development, especially pertaining to African Americans. Examples of segregation can best be illustrated through its longstanding legal history. By examining the Supreme Court cases of *Plessy* v. *Ferguson*, and *Brown* v. *Topeka Board of Education*, segregation can better be explained.

In the 1896 case of *Plessey* v. *Ferguson*, John Ferguson, who was one-eighth African American, was forcibly removed and jailed for trying to occupy the White section of a Louisiana railway train, defying the pro-segregationist doctrine of "separate but equal." In court, Ferguson argued that "separate but equal" violates the equal protection clause of the fourteenth amendment along with the rights essential to his freedom as guaranteed under the thirteenth amendment. Given the dominant nature of segregation in nineteenth-century America, the majority opinion, written by Justice Brown, upheld the "separate but equal" doctrine. Of particular interest to segregation, Justice Brown famously noted that "separate but equal" does not violate the fourteenth amendment on the grounds that the fourteenth amendment was not intended to "abolish distinctions based upon color or a comingling of the two races." In Justice Brown's eyes, not only was segregation legally permissible, but he affirmed the popular social doctrine that upheld a racial hierarchy in America that places African Americans at the bottom. In turn, *Plessey* v. *Ferguson* provided the foundation for the continuation of legal segregation until the 1954 ruling of *Brown* v. *Topeka Board of Education*.

The 1954 Supreme Court case of *Brown* v. *Topeka Board of Education* represents a class action on behalf of several African American students who were denied admission to their respective community public schools on the basis of race, requiring them to attend segregated schools according to their race. Until this court case, segregation had been legally upheld on the grounds of "separate but equal." To this extent, the common argument stated that, although African Americans and Whites were segregated, both races enjoyed equal access to facilities and other societal amenities. However, in a rare moment of unanimity, the Supreme Court overturned the longstanding doctrine of legal segregation. Writing on behalf of the court's unanimous decision was Justice Thurgood Marshall. In the court's majority opinion, Justice Marshall argued not only that "separate but equal" violates the fourteenth amendment, the same reasoning previously argued by John Plessey in his 1896 case, but Justice Marshall also contended that to segregate children of similar age and qualifications solely on the basis of their race generates a feeling of inferiority that may affect their hearts and minds.

If nothing else, an examination of these landmark Supreme Court cases illustrates how the "separate but equal" doctrine shaped segregation in America. [DBrown]

Key readings

Jackson, J. (2005). *Science for segregation: The case against Brown v. Board of Education.* New York: New York University Press.

Litwack, L. (2009). *How free is free? The long death of Jim Crow.* Cambridge: Harvard University Press.

Medley, K. (2003). *We as freemen: Plessey v. Ferguson.* Gretna, LA: Pelican Publishing Company.

Ritterhouse, J. (2006). *Growing up Jim Crow: How black and white Southern children learned race.* Chapel Hill, NC: University of North Carolina Press.

Tischauser, L. (2002). *The changing nature of racial and ethnic conflict in United States history.* Lanham, MD: University Press of America.

SOCIAL DARWINISM Social Darwnism is the application of Charles Darwin's theory of evolution by natural selection to human history, behavior and psychology. Social Darwinists argue that, like all organisms, humans are engaged in a struggle for existence generated by the pressure of population on resources, hence psychological and behavioral traits that enhanced adaptation and reproductive success (e.g. aggression and incest prohibition) would spread through the population. This perspective has been used to support different ideological positions, such as patriarchy and feminism, militarism and pacifism, totalitarianism and anarchism. One of the most notorious examples is the application of Social Darwinism to racial theories.

During the last four decades of the nineteenth and well into the twentieth centuries, Social Darwinism was mobilized to support two distinct but related racial doctrines. The first of these was the idea of **race** war. Its proponents argued that races were analogous to species and were engaged in an unending struggle to acquire the necessities of life – territory, raw materials and food. This produced conflict in the form of economic competition for markets and resources, and outright warfare. In this struggle, the strongest races would prevail and the weaker ones would either be colonized or exterminated. This argument received wide support in the Western world, where it was seen not only as a "scientific" rationale for **imperialism**, but also for an aggressive foreign policy with respect to other Western powers who were regarded as powerful competitors in the struggle for survival.

The second association between Social Darwinism and race was in the area of 'racial hygiene or **"eugenics**." During the latter half of the nineteenth century, many nations were preoccupied with "racial degeneration," a decline in vigor and creativity allegedly caused by industrial and urban civilization and/or procreation with "inferior" races. Some Social Darwinists augmented these fears by arguing that natural selection, which ensured the survival of the fittest, was being replaced by "social selection" (e.g. advances in medicine), which enabled the "unfit" to survive and procreate. This necessitated measures to encourage breeding by the "best" and to prevent the proliferation of those deemed unfit (a heterogeneous category which included the mentally and physically handicapped, criminals, alcoholics, the unemployed, and "less evolved" ethnic groups). By the early twentieth century, eugenics societies had sprung up in many countries and eugenics policies involving involuntary sterilization were enacted in the USA. Racial hygiene reached its zenith in Nazi Germany (1933–45) where Social Darwinism was used both to legitimate race war (especially on the Eastern Front), and to justify the extermination of "unfit" ethnic groups (the Jews and Roma) and even Germans who threatened the purity and vitality of the race (e.g. homosexuals, communists and the congenitally physically and mentally handicapped).

Since the Second World War, Social Darwinist theories of race have declined dramatically in popularity, although they are still evoked by racist and **white-supremacist** groups. The modern disciplines of socio-biology and evolutionary psychology insist that human nature has evolved through natural selection, but invariably refuse to give credence to the idea of race. [MH]

Key readings

Barkan, E. (1992). *The retreat of scientific racism: Changing concepts of race in Britain and the United States between the World Wars*. New York: Cambridge University Press.

Crook, P. (2002). American eugenics and the Nazis: Recent historiography. *The European Legacy*, 7, 361–381.

Hawkins, M. (2006). Social Darwinism and race. In S. Berger (Ed.), *A companion to nineteenth century Europe 1789–1914*. Oxford: Blackwell.

Richards, R. (1987). *Darwin and the emergence of evolutionary theories of mind and behavior*. Chicago: Chicago University Press.

Weikart, R. (2004). *From Darwin to Hitler: Evolutionary ethics, eugenics, and racism in Germany*. New York: Palgrave Macmillan.

SOLIDARITY The *Oxford English Dictionary* defines "solidarity" as the fact or quality, on the part of communities, etc., of being perfectly united or at one in some respect, especially in interests, sympathies, or aspirations; specifically with reference to the aspirations or actions of trade-union members or nation-states involved in international and regional organizations revolving around specific interests. Starting in the 1950s, leaders in developing countries began to construct divergent modes of Third World solidarity to challenge global inequality that characterized the world system. While our contemporary globalized system of geopolitics have given way to more expansive, intersectional grounds for solidarity, early expressions of the term and its practice were linked specifically to matters of racial and ethnic solidarity. Such calls for solidarity were germane to many of the early rights movements in the United States, Europe, Africa and other parts of the world where racial and ethnic minorities lacked basic legal protections based primarily on their racial and/or ethnic status.

When we apply the concept of solidarity to the Third World states, however, we encounter four generations of developing solidarity among these actors. First, *Afro-Asianism* emerged in the 1950s as a Third World response to the racial hierarchy in the world system. Second, *nonalignment* evolved as a reaction by Third World leaders to the Cold War conflict and the bipolar **power** structure in the world system. Third, the East–West conflict was replaced by the *North–South* conflict as the most salient issue confronting the collectivity of states known as the Third World during the 1970s. The quest for a *new international economic order* (NIEO) became the raison d'être for Third World solidarity from the 1970s to the 1980s. Fourth, the *South-to-South dialogue* – that is economic coopera-tion among developing countries – developed in the 1980s as an important catalyst for community building in the South during the epoch of global restruc-turing. Nevertheless, collective self-reli-ance in the South carried the possibility of transforming into sub-**imperialism** within the Third World as the newly industrializ-ing or advanced developing countries sought to carve out their own niches in a changing international division of labor. Starting in the 1990s, the global turn toward neo-liberalism also had a devastat-ing impact on Third World solidarity.

Third World solidarity evolved first and foremost as an issue of **race**, and then pro-gressed to shared determination to avoid Cold War alliances, and during the latter part of the twentieth century it was predi-cated on a mutual interest in terminating poverty and inequality. Third World unity had matured from pan-pigmentationalism (solidarity based on race and geography) to pan-proletarianism (solidarity based on economic disadvantages). Third World solidarity collapsed as the world system made the decisive turn toward neo-liberal-ism in the 1980s and the 1990s.

In order to understand solidarity and the divergent forms it may take, it is impor-tant to examine the milieu and setting in which it operates. Third World solidarity functions within a broader context of global restructuring within the world sys-tem. Periodically, the world system under-goes rhythmic cycles of restructuring, transitioning from one hegemonic order to another, creating new international regimes, and new models of capital accu-mulation for regulating the interstate sys-tem and the world economy. At these junctures, the value systems and ideologi-cal underpinnings that support world structures, such as liberalism under Pax Britannica or neo-liberalism under Pax Americana, undergo change. These cycles of change have influenced the content and direction of Third World solidarity.

In the current wave of globalization that is postindustrial, post-Cold War, transitional, informational, and high-technology-driven, global capitalism has the capacity to produce and distribute any commodity on a global scale. The new capacity of global capital has transformed the existing fragile bargaining power between the North and the South. The new phase of capitalism undermines the ability of Third World states, both individually and collectively, to negotiate in their own interests: that is, better prices for their products, improved working conditions for their workers, environmentally sustain-able industrial policies, and increased employment opportunities for their citizens.

In the age of globalization, the neo-liberal state is hostile to all forms of what we might call social solidarity, for instance trade unions or other forms of social move-ments created by states. The neo-liberal state seeks the reduction of barriers to the movement of capital across borders and the opening of markets to the global forces of capital accumulation along more mono-polistic lines. International institutions, such as the World Bank, the International Monetary Fund (IMF), and the World Trade Organization (WTO) reinforce and facilitate the power of global capital and dictate the terms of order on the South, reducing the capacity for any form of soli-darity. [DCT]

Key readings

Durkheim, E. (1933). *The division of labor in society*. Trans. George Sampson. New York: The Free Press.

Gidden, A. (1972). *Emile Durkheim: Selected writings*. London: Cambridge University Press.

Harvey, D. (2006). *Spaces of global capital-*

ism: Toward a theory of geographical development. London: Verso Press.

Hoogvelt, A. (Ed.). (2001). *Globalization and the postcolonial world: The new political economy of development*. Baltimore, MD: The Johns Hopkins University Press.

Thomas, D. C. (2001). *The theory and practice of Third World solidarity*. Westport, CT: Praeger.

STEREOTYPING Most people think they know what stereotypes are, but relying on definitions from mainstream dictionaries can lead to improper assumptions (i.e. stereotypes) about the precise meaning. But that might not be a bad thing. Webster's defines stereotyping as "a standardized mental picture that is held in common by members of a group and that represents an oversimplified opinion, **prejudiced** attitude, or uncritical judgment." This definition clearly reflects the popular perception of stereotypes as inaccurate and negative overgeneralizations. However, this popular perception is mostly wrong. A better, non-judgmental definition would be that stereotypes are specific traits attributed to people based on group membership.

Research studies conducted by cognitive and social psychologists reveal that stereotypes are often contextually based, meaning that we have different stereotypes for different social contexts. In addition, psychologists generally agree that stereotypes:

- may be accurate or false
- may describe positive or negative characteristics
- may be intentional or automatic
- may be consciously endorsed or rejected (i.e. may or may not result in prejudice)
- may or may not have an impact on behavior (e.g. **discrimination**)
- have both positive and negative functions
- may have either positive or negative outcomes.

Sometimes stereotypes are accurate reflections of reality. For example, men are stereotyped as being violent (relative to women), and data consistently show that a disproportionate number of men commit violent crimes. Sometimes stereotypes are inaccurate. For example, African American men are often stereotyped as "drug users," but data (from community studies that protect the **identity** of respondents) show that a higher percentage of White men report illegal drug use than Black men. Often, we do not know whether the stereotypes are accurate. Existence of a stereotype not only fails to tell us anything useful about a given individual, it does not even tell us anything useful about group differences. All stereotypes tell us is that there is a common shared perception about a group difference.

Stereotypes can describe both positive and negative characteristics, which is something that all groups have attributed to them to one degree or another. For example, in the United States, the White racial majority group is stereotyped as both smart (positive characteristic) and unathletic (negative characteristic). Stereotypes of Asians as "hard working" and African Americans as "athletic" are also considered to be positive stereotypes, but these and other "positive" stereotypes can still be damaging to the members of the target group.

Sometimes stereotypes are held in our conscious minds, especially if we endorse a particular stereotype, but, as research with the Implicit Associations Test (IAT) demonstrates, stereotypes are often unintentional, effortless, and automatic, which is to say that they are not under our conscious control. However, this should not be taken to imply that racial, ethnic, or other social stereotypes are unavoidable. Although people seem to have an innate need to place people (and objects) into categories, the categories themselves are not an essential part of the natural world. They are social creations that are a function of the cultural and political zeitgeist. As the zeitgeist changes, so do the categories.

The connection between stereotypes and prejudice is probably not as strong as most people think. While it is true that stereotypes often pop into our minds automatically, as long as we have some awareness of the stereotypical thought, we can choose to either endorse it or reject it. We might reject stereotypes for all sorts of reasons, including having information that the stereotype is false or understanding that the reason it is true is because of social conditions (e.g. access to resources) rather than group membership. Whatever the reason, when we reject a stereotype, we also make a deliberate choice not to hold a prejudicial attitude. The problem is that we do not necessarily have a conscious awareness of all the stereotypical thoughts that occur to us. It is this lack of awareness that can lead to unintended prejudice.

Stereotypes do not always have behavior implications. Even when we consciously endorse stereotypes, our behavior may be inhibited by a variety of social factors, especially now that explicit racism is no longer publicly tolerated in most **cultures**. And, as explained above, we can choose to reject stereotypical thoughts. However, we are more likely to act on our stereotypes when such action is consistent with social norms or when the situation is sufficiently ambiguous that it is not clear what the socially appropriate action is.

Stereotypes are associated with a variety of different negative outcomes, but they also serve some useful functions. Primary among these is that they serve as heuristics (intellectual shortcuts) in various decision-making contexts and, in so doing, free up our thinking for other things. Such heuristics can get us into trouble but, to the extent that our understanding of group differences is accurate and we realize that group differences cannot be generalized to individual members, stereotypes can help us navigate our social environment.

As noted above, positive stereotypes do not necessarily have positive outcomes. For example, the commonly-endorsed stereotype that Asian Americans have disproportionate aptitude in mathematics can have two negative outcomes. First, it can be damaging to the self esteem of those Asian Americans who struggle with math because of the high (and unreasonable) expectations. Second, it devalues the achievements of Asian Americans who do excel in math because their achievements are attributed to their racial status rather than their hard work. That said, stereotypes can, in fact, work in some people's favor, especially for members of the dominant group. For example, a Harvard graduate probably benefits from some of the stereotypes associated with Harvard, even if he or she is not aware of benefiting in this way. In this way, stereotypes can be a double-edged sword: they can produce prejudice against one group and prejudice in favor of another. The reality is that both contexts are problematic, as the practice of stereotyping undermines individuals' humanity by unfairly creating a set of assumptions based on previous experiences and cultural socialization. [ML]

Key readings

Brown, R. (2000). Social identity theory: Past achievements, current problems and future challenges. *European Journal of Social Psychology*, 30, 745–778

Stangor, C. & Schaller, M. (1996/2000). Stereotypes as individual and collective representations. In C. Stangor (Ed.), *Stereotypes and prejudice: Essential readings*. Philadelphia: Taylor and Francis Group, pp. 64–82.

Tajfel, H. (1982). Social psychology of intergroup relations. *Annual Review of Psychology*, 33, 1–39.

Stuart Hall Stuart Hall (1932–) was born in Jamaica and immigrated to Great Britain in 1951, as a part of the significant post-war migration from the West Indies to Great Britain. A prominent scholar of **cultural studies**, media and communications and sociology, Hall began his formative years as a Rhodes Scholar at Oxford University in the 1950s. Early in his career, Hall was engaged with an emergent group of scholars and public intellectuals on the left. The British New Left emerged in the late 1950s through a commingling of two distinct traditions, one being an active student movement and another rooted in the Communist and Popular Front politics of Britain. This group founded the journal *New Left Review*, and Hall acted as editor between 1960 and 1962. Hall joined the Centre for Contemporary Cultural Studies (CCCS) at the University of Birmingham in 1964 under Richard Hoggart and became director in 1968. Hall remained at the University of Birmingham until 1979 and then left to join the sociology department of the Open University, retiring as Professor Emeritus in 1997. Some of Stuart Hall's intellectual interlocutors include E. P. Thompson, Raymond Williams, Antonio Gramsci, Sigmund Freud, Louis Althusser and Michel Foucault. Hall's most significant influence is surely noted in the area of cultural studies, neo-Marxist critique and studies of hegemony. Foremost, he is a scholar who has contributed to defining **critical race** studies, examining questions of **identity** and difference, **multiculturalism**, **post-colonialism** and **diaspora** studies.

Stuart Hall's work contributes to the development of a post-structuralist reading of **culture**. Hall persuasively argues that popular culture must be seen as constitutive of society, and not something separable. He insisted that, for this reason, popular culture requires a rigorous deconstruction, one based on a system of decoding and encoding forms of popular culture.

The method of encoding/decoding is articulated by Hall in an essay titled "Encoding and decoding in the television discourse" (1973); later an abridged version appeared in *Culture, media, language* (1980) as "Encoding/Decoding." Through this methodological approach, Hall placed an emphasis on the reception of media, how the viewer or audience is also, in a sense, an active subject which, through consuming, reading or receiving media, contributes to or produces meaning.

During his time at CCCS, Hall worked collaboratively with colleagues to develop forms of social analysis strongly informed by a Marxist reading of the social, political and economic context of contemporary cultural formations. The projects undertaken at the CCCS strove to highlight the transformations of post-war British society, examining the social, cultural shifts that gave way under the pressure to a demographically altered society due to large-scale migration and also a shift within the working class culture represented by the proliferation of youth subcultures. Two significant projects produced by the CCCS in the 1970s included *Resistance through rituals: Youth subcultures in post-war Britain* (1976), and *Policing the crisis: Mugging, the state and law and order* (1978). In particular, the work that took place through the *Policing* project proved relevant for examining the emerging crisis of **race** politics in Britain. By investigating the production, circulation and reception of the falsely represented legal categorization of "mugging," Hall and his collaborators revealed the tensions developing due to the resettlement and immigration of large-scale postcolonial Black populations throughout the 1960s and 1970s. This increasing immigration had a strong pro-**nationalist** and racist backlash in Britain. To this end, Hall and others were engaged in analyzing the often hidden and ideological dimensions of both British **culture** and the ensuing forms of racisms encountered in this backlash. For Hall, the understanding of racism is always in the plural, highly contingent on the specificities of historical and social formation, and requires the rigorous reading and interpretation of modes of its production and consumption. For instance, Hall and his collaborators famously investigated the relationship of mugging as both a consequence of the declining economic position of Black communities in Britain and, potentially, as a reaction and form of resistance to the experience of systemic forms of racism.

Hall's continued investigation of the political culture of race and racisms in Britain led to a challenge in many circles regarding forms of essential identities. Through his critique of essentialism, Hall argues for a concept of differences that challenges us to view a mutually exclusive understanding of us/them dichotomies. Instead, he views the necessity to understand the cultural as responsive to dialogic strategies and hybrid forms that are necessary to read the diasporic aesthetic. For Hall, a rigorous reading of Black culture in Britain would not permit a homogenizing **representation** of one singular or unified identity. Rather, through his methodological practices of decoding forms and modes of signification, Hall examines the prescriptive nature and question of race. In a highly acclaimed video production titled *Race, the floating signifier*, Hall speaks to the complicated relationship between the signification of race, challenging biological descriptors and investigating this concept as an inherently discursive construction.

Stuart Hall's contribution to the field of cultural studies, postcolonial critique, and critical race studies holds a particular historical specificity of its own, engaged in the material politics and the culture of everyday life. This does not detract from, but rather bolsters, its significance to contemporary studies of race, ethnicity and culture. [DB]

Key readings

Jhally, S. (Producer; Director). (1997). *Stuart Hall – Race, the floating signifier*. United States: Media Education Foundation.

Hall, S. (1988). *The hard road to renewal: Thatcherism and the crisis of the left*. London: Verso.

Hall, S. & Jefferson, T. (1976). *Resistance through rituals: Youth subcultures in post-war Britain*. London: Hutchinson.

Hall, S., Critcher, C., Jefferson, T., Clarke, J., & Robert, B. *et al.* (1978). *Policing the crisis: Mugging, the state, and law and order*. London: Macmillan.

W. E. B. DU BOIS William Edward Burghardt Du Bois (1868–1963), was a black American sociologist, historian, and one of the leaders of the **civil rights** and human rights movement from the late nineteenth century to the mid-twentieth century. Though he was born in Great Barrington, Massachusetts and wished to attend Harvard, he was unable to do so, but he received a Harvard scholarship, which enabled him to attend Fisk University (1885–88) in Nashville, Tennessee, from which he received his BA. The Fisk experience – from his BA thesis on the German Empire's first chancellor, Bismarck, to the opportunity the college provided for him to immerse himself in the life, **culture** and politics of black Southerners – was the foundation for many of Du Bois's ideas, programs and activities on matters of **race**, ethnicity, and class throughout his life.

Du Bois entered Harvard as a junior in 1888 and graduated with a BA with high honors in 1890, writing a thesis on Jefferson Davis, the president of the Confederate States. At Harvard he studied psychology and philosophy with William James, philosophy with Josiah Royce and George Santayana, and history with Albert Bushnell Hart. It is from a viewpoint inspired by James and literary works of the nineteenth century that Du Bois proffers his views on consciousness, the self, and double consciousness. Ideas and concepts related to the nature of consciousness and the leadership necessary in assisting an impoverished people towards their freedom and a collective sense of themselves as a people emerged in Du Bois's mental landscape as a meeting of theory and history, obtained from Harvard, met and co-joined the politics, culture, economics, and religion of blacks in the South.

Though his Southern experience was a revolutionary force in shaping Du Bois's view of himself and his people, his European experience, both as a student at the University of Berlin and as a traveler throughout Europe, added yet another layer to his attempts to create a role for himself and how the extension of his "self creation," begun at Fisk and Harvard, would have great sociological significance as he sought to place himself and his people in time and history.

At the University of Berlin, Du Bois's views on **nationalism**, Pan-Germanic movements, and the history and economics of a people were developed. The ideas and ideals of the German people and the German state for a place in the sun struck a resounding chord with the young Du Bois. It is with both ideas in mind that we best understand Du Bois's long involvements in Pan-African movements, beginning at the end of the nineteenth century until his death in 1963. And, ironically, we can best understand a part of Du Bois's anticapitalist stance, not so much as an indication of his revolutionary politics, but rather as reflected in both Germany and the South, as a largely agrarian opposition to the economic and cultural destruction and displacement wrought by capitalism. While in Germany, Du Bois also attended lectures by Max Weber, a leading sociologist and scholar with whom he would form a warm personal and academic friendship.

Returning from Europe in 1894, Du Bois was hired as a professor of Greek and Latin at Wilberforce University in Ohio, one of the oldest, predominately black universities in the country, where he remained until 1896, the year he received his PhD degree from Harvard, writing the dissertation, *The suppression of the African slave trade to the United States of America, 1638–1870*. He was then hired as an assistant professor of sociology at the University of Pennsylvania. Working at both schools prompted Du Bois to ponder which path he would travel in selecting his life work, and how the use and role of science could be applied to an assessment of the personal and institutional development of black life. That he desired to do so merely highlighted a prevailing disposition of that time that science would buttress and support the search for truth as it assessed what Du Bois called "the Negro problem." Like many others, Du Bois assumed that science would operate and prove effective in the social world, just as it had in the natural and physical world. And a corollary to this view was the idea that science, and the use of scientific methods, would, of necessity, help to negate human subjectivity and usher in an era of rationality, reason, and objectivity. For Du Bois, this assessment would be pivotal to the solution of the "Negro problem," but it would also be crucial to the social, moral, economic, and political reconstruction of the American nation. It was for these reasons that he agreed to participate in two geographically diverse studies using a variety of social scientific methodologies – census data, life histories, participant observation, questionnaires, and local records – and sought to present a holistic, institutional, individualistically-oriented view of the history and sociology of a people. And, though Du Bois prided himself on the uses of scientific sociology as opposed to "armchair sociology," he himself came to both studies armed with a theory of race which he forthrightly enunciated in an Occasional Paper presented to the American Negro Academy in 1897: "The conservation of races."

His studies and observations gave him acute insights into the mind and manners of the American nation from which he would theorize about a **"double consciousness"** and the search for a "true" consciousness among blacks in *The souls of black folk* (1903). It is also in this book that Du Bois hints at the emergence of, and importance of, the talented tenth and its natural and necessary leadership role. Du Bois juxtaposed this leadership model to the one exemplified by his nemesis, Booker T. Washington, but the contrast is basically unrealistic since Du Bois's model was clearly one most effectively used in the free North, whereas Washington lived in an unfree, repressive, and terrorized South. Nevertheless, Du Bois's leadership model remains a valid strategy for oppressed groups despite the fact that Du Bois discarded the concept in the late 1950s.

Du Bois displayed great prescience and much prophetic and sociological insight when he noted that the **"color line"** would characterize the twentieth century. Because he believed the color line could be altered by scientific data illustrating how **minority** lives are shaped and altered by dominant, majority values and behavior, and because he believed black values, norms, and ideals had an organic genesis in the foundation of black family, institutional, and community life, Du Bois sought to document key features of black life via social scientific research methods.

However, the scientific study of black life was only one phase of Du Bois's concentrated attack on the color line and social injustice, at home and abroad. Another entailed the creation and utilization of organizations and periodicals as ideological weapons in the struggle. From his participation in the American Negro Academy, as a founder and general

secretary of the Niagara Movement, and as one of the original founders of the National Association for the Advancement of Colored People (NAACP), Du Bois saw these groups as frontline battle organizations geared for resisting prejudice and **discrimination**. Likewise, he created journals and reviews for the same purpose: *The Moon Illustrated Weekly*, *The Horizon*, *The Crisis*, *The Brownies' Book*, and *Phylon*. Politically, by the first decade of the twentieth century, Du Bois declared himself a socialist and joined the Socialist Party, but resigned in 1913.

Throughout the 1920s and 1930s, Du Bois was a virtual "protean" man moving back and forth on dialectical shifts while advancing integration, Pan-Africanism (not the Garveyite Back-to-African plan), and in the Depression, proposing a form of collective black separatist economics, the Black Economic Commonwealth. It was also in the late 1940s that Du Bois began to participate in various national and international peace groups and movements that were generally communist-front organizations; he also ran for senator of New York on the Progressive Party ticket, and lost. When Du Bois writes his second autobiographical sketch, *Dusk of dawn*, the tone and tenor of his political views appear to have been solidified, for it is in this book that Du Bois spelled out his virtual acceptance of communism and his reasons for doing so. This acceptance and his involvement in various peace movements caused him to be indicted as an unregistered foreign agent for the Soviet Union in 1950–51. He was acquitted, but he joined the Communist Party in 1961, traveled to Ghana at the invitation of Nkrumah, became a citizen of Ghana in 1963, and died August 27, 1963 on the eve of the massive March on Washington in which Dr **Martin Luther King, Jr** gave his memorable "I have a dream" speech.

At the end of the nineteenth century and for five decades into the twentieth century he painted a portrait of the black and African self, and also the selves of other victims of colonialism as bodies and minds of both defiance and hope. In the end, Du Bois believed that Western civilization had not lived up to its promise to reshape and make the world better. In his sociological works Du Bois dug deeply into the epicenter of black life and, indirectly, the black psyche, opening the doors to its pain as well as its joys and, above all, he provided blacks with voices to express their varied American experiences and to demonstrate that blacks would continue to struggle until they, too, could have their place in the American racial and ethnic mosaic. His scholarly works, journals, reviews, and other periodicals, plus the various Pan-African movements and meetings, and the Niagara Movement and the NAACP all acted in tandem and were orchestrated by Du Bois as a unitary force to fight against injustice. [RD]

Key readings

Alridge, D. P. (2008). *The educational thought of W. E. B. Du Bois: An intellectual history.* New York: Teachers College Press.

Aptheker, H. (1973) *Annotated bibliography of the published writings of W. E. B. Du Bois.* Millwood, NY: Kraus-Thomson.

Dennis, R. M. (Ed.). (1996). *W. E. B. Du Bois: The scholar as activist.* Greenwich, CT: JAI Press.

Du Bois, W. E. B. (1899). *The Philadelphia Negro: A social study.* Boston: Ginn.

——. (1939). *Black folk then and now: An essay in the history and sociology of the Negro race.* New York: Holt.

——. (1968). *The autobiography of W. E. B. Du Bois: A soliloquy on viewing my life from the last decade of its first century.* New York: International Publishers.

——. (1995 [1903]). *The souls of black folk: Essays and sketches.* New York: Signet Classic.

Lewis, D. L. (2009). *W. E. B. Du Bois: A biography.* New York: Henry Holt and Co.

Marable, M. (1986). *W. E. B. Du Bois: Black radical democrat.* Boston, MA: Twayne.

Zuckerman, P. (Ed.). (2004). *The social theory of W. E. B. Du Bois.* Thousand Oaks, CA: Pine Forge Press.

WHITE PRIVILEGE Racial inequality has generally been viewed through the lens of what it means to be in the **minority**, to be non-white. The disadvantages of being non-white, the cultural distinctiveness of non-white groups, and the characteristics of those who are not white have long been the focus of attention. The status of **whiteness** has rarely been scrutinized. What it means to be white in the United States, and particularly the benefits or privileges of whiteness, have either been accepted as given or simply not recognized. But that has begun to change in recent years. The reality of white privilege is emerging as a subject of much **race** relations research, if not a topic of policy debate or public discussion.

Being white in America brings a number of advantages, generally unearned, even in the absence of any prejudicial attitudes or discriminatory behavior. That is, whiteness involves structural realities that translate into virtually automatic benefits for members of the white race. These are privileges that whites enjoy simply because of their status as whites, regardless of any attitudinal or behavioral characteristics on their part. For example, whites can offer to purchase a home, apply for a job, or visit most restaurants, department stores and other commercial establishments, confident that their race will constitute no barrier to their participation in those markets. Not only can they participate but they generally obtain benefits and privileges of those milieu on more favorable terms than is the case for non-whites.

White privilege is particularly striking in the housing market where it leads to many benefits both directly and indirectly related to housing. Without ever expressing a racially biased thought or engaging in any discriminatory actions, whites can purchase or rent almost any housing that they can afford. African Americans and Hispanics encounter some form of unlawful **discrimination** in approximately one out of every five initial meetings with rental or real estate agents. The **segregation** that follows means that whites are significantly more able to translate their housing choices into better schools for their children, safer streets for their families and greater appreciation in the value of their homes, all of which leads to substantial wealth disparities and the transmission of wealth – along with the associated benefits – across generations. Again, these are benefits that whites enjoy even in the absence of any intentional prejudice or discrimination.

Today, the typical white family holds approximately ten times the wealth of typical black and Hispanic families. These disparities reflect a wide range of public policies and private practices over generations. Starting with slavery and the Jim Crow years, then continuing through New Deal policies that favored whites (social security and unemployment compensation initially did not cover agricultural and personal service workers, occupations in which blacks were heavily concentrated) and urban renewal programs that opened up the nation's suburbs primarily for whites while concentrating blacks in central cities, public policy has reinforced private practices, including overt and subtle forms of discrimination. If the far lower level of white demand for homes in non-white and integrated neighborhoods reflects racially and ethnically biased attitudes and practices of a relatively small number of whites, all whites can (and most do) benefit from the greater financial appreciation of homes in white areas and the wealth that brings.

White privilege is a structural reality of life in the United States today. Certainly this reality has been built on a history of bigotry. And while prejudice and discrimination have hardly disappeared from the nation today, such attitudes and practices constitute only part of the scaffolding on which the edifice of white privilege has been constructed. [GDS]

Key readings

Bonilla-Silva, E. (2003). *Racism without racists: Color-blind racism and the persistence of racial inequality in the United States.* Lanham, MD: Rowman and Littlefield.
Brown, M. K., Carnoy, M., Currie, E., Duster, T., Oppenheimer, D., & Shultz, M. M. (2003). *Whitewashing race: The myth of a color-blind society.* Berkeley, CA: University of California Press.
Katznelson, I. (2005). When affirmative action was white: An untold history of racial inequality in twentieth-century America. New York: W.W. Norton.
McIntosh, P. (1992). White privilege. *Creation Spirituality* (January/February), 33–35, 53.
Oliver. M. & Shapiro, T. (2006). *Black wealth, white wealth: A new perspective on racial inequality.* New York: Routledge.

WHITE SUPREMACY White supremacy is the belief that members of the Caucasian **race** are superior in all ways to other ethnic groups or races in the world. The term is usually used to describe a political ideology that advocates white social and political dominance. In the United States, white supremacy was the official law of the land until the Civil War ended in 1865. Until that time, the Constitution denied all rights to black slaves brought to the United States from Africa as they were deemed to be property, not worthy of the same treatment afforded white Americans. From 1948 to 1994, **apartheid**-era South Africa, which was characterized by a system of legal racial **segregation** and **discrimination** against nonwhites, also functioned as a white supremacist system.

After 1865, white supremacy continued de facto in the Deep South of the United States as Reconstruction eventually gave way to a reassertion of white **power** through Jim Crow laws that kept schools segregated and made voting by blacks nearly impossible. It was not just the South that favored whites over **minorities**. Other parts of the country had laws on the books discriminating against blacks and other minorities in such areas as housing, schooling and public accommodation. Racist views about nonwhites were expressed in legislation, particularly as it related to immigration. An example of this was the Immigration Act of 1924, which banned Asians from the United States and instituted a national origin quota system favoring Europeans. It was not until the 1950s and 1960s, as pressure mounted from the **Civil Rights Movement**, that legal provisions allowing for white domination were finally found to be unconstitutional.

The most important white supremacist group in American history is the Ku Klux Klan. Founded immediately after the Civil War and first led nationally by former Confederate General Nathan Bedford Forrest, the group's aim was to re-impose the racial *status quo ante* of the Old South by instilling fear in the black population. The Klan's robes originally served the purpose of making members appear more ominous, particularly when harassing blacks at night from horseback. After virtually disappearing after the imposition of Jim Crow laws, the "second era" Klan was inaugurated in 1915 and reached a membership of nearly four million by the mid-1920s. During that time, the Klan saw itself as a defender of white Protestant Christianity and its concerns had as much

or more to do with anger over a major influx of Irish and Italian Catholic immigrants as they did with blacks.

The 1920s saw other expressions of white supremacy. In the early 1900s, there was a widespread movement in the United States advocating **eugenics**, meaning the "science" of breeding a better human race. Several states, pushed by eugenicists espousing racist views, advocated against nonwhite immigration and discriminated against the mentally ill through forced sterilizations. Eugenicists favored immigration restriction, segregation and, in some cases, even entertained the idea of extermination of nonwhites. These ideas were so respected by Adolf Hitler that he awarded prizes to prominent American eugenicists. Hitler's white supremacist and genocidal National Socialist regime, with its extermination policies for Jews, non-"Aryans," and those with disabilities, represented the most frightening example of where eugenicist thinking could lead.

As the Jim Crow regime came tumbling down in the years after the Second World War with U.S. Supreme Court rulings against segregation and the passage of civil rights laws, organized white supremacists reacted violently. The Klan resurged, engaging in a violent political campaign against civil rights activists, including several murders. A revitalized Klan was joined in its white supremacy by new groups that arose to fight desegregation, most notably the White Citizens' Councils, which earned the moniker, "uptown Klan." White Citizens' Council chapters formed across the South, signing up prominent members of Southern society. In the end, the egalitarian ideas of the Civil Rights Movement, not those of the Klan, prevailed.

White supremacist ideology in the twenty-first century is significantly different than at the time of the Civil Rights Movement, when the explicit goal of white supremacists was to maintain – or reestablish – the dominance of whites in America. As segregation was dismantled and the US population became more amenable to desegregation and extending civil rights protections to minorities, white supremacists had to accommodate their movement to the fact that their views were those of a shrinking minority, and that, increasingly, government, law enforcement, and the communities in which they lived opposed their goals.

From the 1970s forward, white supremacist ideology changed to reflect these conditions. The concept of "white separatism" arose, whereby many white supremacists conceded that whites could no longer dominate all of America and instead focused on various plans to create all-white "homelands." This was a much more defensive and somewhat paranoid ideology, whose main focus was on saving the white race from a supposed "extinction." White supremacists have come to believe that the future of the white race itself is in doubt, about to fall prey to a "rising tide of color" brought on by immigration and other malignant forces. This viewpoint was best captured by the popular white supremacist slogan, "The 14 Words," coined by deceased white supremacist terrorist David Lane. Based on a section of Hitler's *Mein Kampf*, the slogan reads, "We must secure the existence of our people and a future for White children."

Reaction by white supremacists to demographic and other societal changes has ranged from peaceful protest to extreme violence. Groups that label themselves "white **nationalists**," a subset of the white supremacist scene that arose over the last few decades, mostly engage in publishing racist political tracts or holding meetings that, at times, have received support from politicians on the far right (usually Deep South politicians). Other white nationalist outfits put out pseudo-academic "studies" asserting the inferiority of minorities. For those most steeped in neo-Nazi ideology,

demographic and other changes seen as detrimental to white power are viewed as controlled and manipulated by Jews. There have been several instances of violence where neo-Nazi beliefs have enabled domestic terrorists to rationalize taking violent or extreme actions, including mass murder, in the hope of "saving" the white race.

Today, white supremacist groups are found in several countries across Europe and in South Africa, New Zealand, Australia and Canada. They tend to be small organizations with few members that operate far outside the mainstream. However, some of their ideas, particularly their dislike of nonwhite immigrants, have found their way into the ideology of extreme-right parties, including the British National Party and the French National Front. [HB & MP]

Key readings

Black, E. (2003). *War against the weak: Eugenics and America's campaign to create a master race*. New York: Four Walls Eight Windows.

Chalmers, D. (1987). *Hooded Americanism: The history of the Ku Klux Klan* (3rd ed.). Durham, NC: Duke University Press.

Lee, M. A. (1997). *The beast reawakens*. New York: Little Brown & Co.

McMillen, N. R. (1994). *The citizens' council: Organized resistance to the second Reconstruction, 1954–64*. Champaign, IL: University of Illinois Press.

Ridgeway, J. (1990). *Blood in the face: The Ku Klux Klan, Aryan nations, Nazi skinheads and the rise of new white culture*. New York: Thunder Mouth's Press.

Simonelli, F. J. (1999). *American Fuehrer: George Lincoln Rockwell and the American Nazi Party*. Champaign, IL: University of Illinois Press.

WHITENESS It is customary to begin an entry like this with a definition, but who gets to define whiteness? In contemporary progressive circles, it is generally assumed that a group should be able to define itself, but whiteness has historically been defined by non-whites. For example, James Weldon Johnson, an African American poet and anthologist, observed in 1912 that "The colored people of this country know and understand the white people better than the white people will ever know and understand themselves." In the past 20 years, many white writers and scholars have embraced the study of whiteness, but people of color, particularly Black writers and academics, continue to make significant (at times, even primary) contributions to this area of scholarship.

There are several different components of whiteness. These include: (1) racial **identity**; (2) racial bias; and (3) racial privilege.

The "whiteness as group identity" model conceptualizes whiteness as one of many different racial identities, the strength of which is determined by four factors: group size, group **power**, group **discrimination**, and group appearance. According to this model, those who are part of a group that is the numerical **minority**, have less power relative to other groups, experience more discrimination, and less phenotypically resemble the majority group, should have a greater sense of racial identity, while those who are part of the racial majority (with all its privileges) should put very little emphasis on their racial identity. Indeed, though self-identified **white supremacists** and **anti-racism** activists are notable exceptions, many white Americans much more strongly prefer to identify themselves as "American" or as a humanist rather than as "white."

In contrast to the neutrality of the group identity model, a number of writers and activists have equated whiteness with a racist ideology. They argue that US society is characterized by a socially created racial hierarchy that values whiteness above all and that, because whites are socialized (via

family, peers, media) into this society, they cannot help but internalize some of the messages about white superiority, even if they consciously reject racist beliefs. Though controversial (especially in conservative circles), a number of cleverly designed empirical studies, most notably those using the Implicit Association Test (IAT), have supported the notion that most white people show unconscious (and therefore unintentional) bias in favor of those who are white, a bias that is either not evident or significantly smaller, in non-white groups.

Because of the racial socialization described above, the "whiteness as privilege" model posits that whiteness is characterized, not so much by racial bias (i.e. racism), but by racial privilege. In her now classic "Invisible knapsack" paper, Peggy McIntosh identified several dozen specific privileges associated with whiteness, including, for example, the privilege of learning about the important contributions of one's people in schools, but probably the two primary privileges are (1) the privilege to assume that whiteness is the norm against which everyone else should be compared and (2) the privilege to live one's life without ever needing to be aware of one's whiteness and how it might be impacting their life.

In order to describe the various world views associated with whiteness and the developmental process though which these world views sometimes change, a number of white racial identity models have been developed, most notably by Janet Helms who argued that white individuals generally start with a racist identity and must first move away from such an identity before they can develop a non-racist identity. Helms described six different statuses – Contact, Disintegration, Reintegration, Pseudo-Independent, Immersion–Emersion, and Autonomy – and posited that each status is associated with a different way of processing racial data. While research support for this particular model has been mixed, developmental models of white identity continue to be a very active area of research and discussion among psychologists. [ML]

Key readings

Brown, R. (2000). Social identity theory: past achievements, current problems and future challenges. *European Journal of Social Psychology*, 30(6), 745–778.

Gaertner, S. L. & Dovidio, J. F (1986). The aversive form of racism. In J. F. Dovidio and S. L. Gaertner (Eds.), *Prejudice, discrimination, and racism*. Orlando, FL: Academic Press, pp. 61–89.

Helms, J. E. (2005). An update of Helm's White and people of color racial identity models. In J. G. Ponterotto, J. M. Casas, L. A. Suzuki, & C. M. Alexander (Eds.), *Handbook of multicultural counseling*. Thousand Oaks, CA: Sage Publications, pp. 181–198.

McIntosh, P. (1988). White privilege and male privilege: A personal account of coming to see correspondences through work in Women's Studies. Paper#189, retrieved from http://web.clas.ufl.edu/users/leslieh/syg2000/whiteprivilege.html

McIntyre, A. (1997). *Making meaning of whiteness: Exploring racial identity with white teachers*. Albany, NY: State University of New York Press.

Omi, M. & Winant, H. (1989). *Racial formation in the United States: From the 1960s to the 1980s*. New York: Routledge.

Thandeka. (1999). *Learning to be white*. New York: Continuum Publishing.

XENOPHOBIA The etymological meaning of xenophobia comes from the Greek words "xeno" that means stranger and "phobia" that means fear. Thus, xenophobia literally means "fear of strangers." The lexical definition of xenophobia has developed in scientific literature in two ways. First, the stranger has come to be equated with foreigners or immigrants and, second, xenophobia has come to always include a derogatory understanding of immigrants.

Thus, a contemporary understanding of xenophobia is to view it as antipathy toward immigrants or foreigners, based upon fear. Xenophobia is partly an attitude, but it also includes an affective part, fear, that is intrinsic to xenophobia. The fear results from a situation where individuals perceive that their individual, or their group's, position is being threatened. The threat does not have to be based on real circumstances, but is almost always perceived by the xenophobic person as being a real existing threat. For example, many xenophobic people fear that immigrants will put severe strains on the economy; a fear which there is little empirical evidence to support. The threat against the group's position is of greatest importance as xenophobia is closely related to nationality and **identity**, where people may perceive foreigners or immigrants as a threat to the national **solidarity**. The close relation between xenophobia and nation make it very easy to politicize, which can be exemplified by the effective rhetoric of the radical right which accuses immigrants of increasing crime rates and causing unrest.

The demarcation between xenophobia and **prejudice** is sometimes blurred. The difference is the fear component and the close relationship with a nationally based in-group. Prejudice is often understood as being an antipathy based upon faulty generalizations of the group, i.e. prejudice does not include an affective component, nor is it related to the nation. In practice, xenophobia and prejudice are closely related and the theoretical and empirical explanations of prejudice are, in most cases, also applicable to xenophobia. The latter includes individual explanations of xenophobia (e.g. low levels of education, social dominance orientation) as well as institutional contexts (e.g. political articulation, economic circumstances) that counteract or promote xenophobia.

Three things differentiate xenophobia from racism. First, xenophobia does not have to be ideological. Racism is commonly understood as an ideology that claims a racially or culturally based hierarchical order. Xenophobia is related to, though not equated with, the understanding of superiority, but more national superiority than racial superiority. Second, there is no action component in xenophobia even though xenophobia increases the probability of action. That is, xenophobic people do not automatically discriminate against other people, but the risk of them doing so cannot be neglected. Racism is not, by definition, related to action but has an action component built in to the very fabric of the concept. Third, xenophobia is not biological, as negative attitudes can stem from a variety of perceived differences like religion, **culture** and nationality. [MHjerm]

Key readings

Allport, G. (1979 [1954]). *The nature of prejudice.* Cambridge, MA: Perseus Books.

Boehnke, K., Hagan, J., & Hefler, G. (1998). On the development of xenophobia in Germany: The adolescent years. *Journal of Social Issues*, 54(3), 585–602.

Hagendorn, L. & Sniderman, P. (2001). Experimenting with a national sample: A Dutch survey on prejudice. *Patterns of Prejudice*, 35, 19–31.

Hjerm, M. (1998). National identities, national pride and xenophobia: A comparison of four Western countries. *Acta Sociologica*, 41(24), 335–347.

——. (2007). Are we the people? National sentiments in a changing political landscape. In S. Svallfors (Ed.), *The political sociology of the welfare state: Institutions, cleavages, orientations.* Palo Alto, CA: Stanford University Press, pp. 223–257.

Rowthorn, R. (2008). The fiscal impact of immigration on the advanced economies. *Oxford Review of Economic Policy*, 24(3), 561–581.

Rydgren, J. (2008). Immigration sceptics, xenophobes or racists? Radical right-wing voting in six West European countries. *European Journal of Political Research*, 47, 737–765.

Thranhardt, D. (1995). The political uses of xenophobia in England, France and Germany. *Party Politics*, 1(3), 323–345.

Yakushko, O. (2009). Xenophobia: Understanding the roots and consequences of negative attitudes toward immigrants. *The Counseling Psychologist*, 37(1), 36–66.

INDEX

9/11 100, 190

Aberle, David 49
Aboriginal Protection Board, Australia 95
Aboriginals 41, 95–7, 157
acculturation 56–8; strategies for 58–9
Act for the Preservation and Enhancement of
    Multiculturalism in Canada (1985) 16–17
adaptation 56–8
adjustment 56–8
adoption 56–8
Adorno, Theodor 109, 124, 200
Adventures of Huckleberry Finn (Twain)
    181–2
advertising 77–8
affirmative action policies 38–9, 44–5, 115,
    116–17, 161, 172, 207, 217
Africa: colonial style and ethnic conflict
    31–2; cultural studies 127; creating
    ethnicity and ethnic conflict 30–1;
    de-colonized subjects 142–4
African Americans 69–70; identity 120–1;
    reactions to use of term "nigger" 182;
    reparations 216–17; stereotyping 225;
    systematic disadvantage of 7–10
African diaspora 50
African National Congress (ANC) 50, 105
Africanity 97
Afrocentricity 97–8
Against race (Gilroy) 189–90
agenda setting 39, 74–6
Ain't I a woman (hooks) 111
Algerian migrants 16
Algerian revolution 142, 143
Ali, Ayaan Hirsi 18
Altemeyer, B. 110
alternative identities 151
America, slavery and race-making 32–4
American Anthropological Association 204
American culture: demonization of 18;
    export of 130
American evasion of philosophy (West) 120
American exceptionalism 165
American Indians: authenticity 108; current
    population 158; decline of 157;
    discovering race in 35–6; economic

development 159; emergence of identity
    137; and postcolonialism 196
American Revolution 112–13
ancestral classifications 7, 13
Anderson, Benedict 15
Anglo conformity 106, 191
Anglo-Saxon globalism/market racism 86–7
Anthias, Floya 132, 176–7
Anti-Apartheid Movement 47, 50–1, 52–3,
    104–5
anti-colonial movement 143, 189
anti-racism movement 100–2
Anti-Slavery Society 113
Anzaldúa, Gloria Evangelina 99–100, 170
apartheid 7, 44–5, 48–9, 171; ideology of 103;
    legacy of 105; policy program 103–4;
    protest, reform and dismantling of 104–5;
    reparations for 217–18
Arabs 14, 162–3; and orientalism 184–5, 186
Arguedos, José Maria 169
Aristotle 38, 60
Aryans 6–7, 183, 233
Asante, Molefi Kete 97
Asia, assimilation 107
Asian Americans 69–70, 173–4, 187;
    consequences of model minority 174–5,
    226
assimilation 31, 35, 55, 56–9, 106–7, 150,
    158, 169, 172, 177, 185, 191, 195; and
    orientalism 186
attributed identity 56, 149, 225, 226
attribution theory 61
audience studies 125–6
Audre Lord Project 70
Australia: census policy 42; cultural studies
    127; indigenous people 95–7
authenticity 10, 22, 80, 108–9, 120–1, 159,
    195
Authoritarian personality (Adorno *et al.*) 109
authoritarianism 7, 109–10, 136, 200, 201,
    217

"Balkanization," fears of 17–18
Bandura, Albert 61
Barth, Fredrik 15
"Bassiouni Principles" 218

Behrman, J.N. 83
Belgian colonies 31–2
Bell curve (Hernstein/Murray) 4, 141
Bell, Derrick 122
Bend it like Beckham (film) 70
Benford, Robert 48
Berlin Conference (1884–85) 30–1
Berman, Bruce 29
Bernier, François 3
Berry, John 57–8, 59
Bhabba, Homi 14, 185
"bi-racial" 10, 22–3, 34–5
biculturalism 150–1, 169
Big Brother (TV program) 79
biological difference 3–5, 25, 33–4, 203–4;
     fallacy of 204–6
Black Consciousness Movement 50, 52–3
black inferiority, establishment of 5–6
Black looks (hooks) 112
"Black myth" 142
Black power (Carmichael/Hamilton) 6
Black Power movement 71, 168
black pride 27
Black skin, white masks (Fanon) 67–8, 142–3
Black Student Association 120
Blackmun, Harry 116–17
Blanton, Robert 32
blood quantum 108–9
Blumenbach, Johann Friedrich 3, 40
Blumer, Herbert 49, 51
border territories 137–8
Borderlands/la frontera (Anzaldúa) 99, 170
Bosnian War (1992–95) 18
Brah, Avtar 132
Brazil: census policy 43; racial democracy
     34–5; slavery 32–3
Breaking bread (hooks/West) 111–12
British colonies 31–2
British New Left 227
Brown v. *Topeka Board of Education* 114,
     116, 171, 221
Brown, Catherine 114
Buck v. *Bell* 140
bus boycotts 167

"California Civil Rights Initiative" 117
Canada: anti-racism movements 100;
     indigenous people 95–7; multiculturalism
     16–17, 100
Carmichael, Stokely 6
Cartographies of diaspora (Brah) 132
Cavalli-Sforza, Luca 147
census policy and race consciousness 41–3
Centre for Contemporary Cultural Studies
     (CCCS) 124, 125, 126, 188, 227
Chicago School 126
Chicano 170
China, equal opportunities 44

Chinese Exclusionary Act (1882), US 58
Christianity 5, 14, 36, 120, 163, 233
citizenship 8, 87, 103–4, 107, 113, 131–2,
     186–7
civic nationalism 15–16
civic panic 101
Civil Rights Acts, US 52, 113, 114, 115, 167
Civil Rights Movement, US 9, 21, 24, 47,
     51–3, 65, 100, 112–15, 126, 153, 233;
     compromise of 1877 113; and Martin
     Luther King, Jr 166–8
Civil War, US 8–9, 119
"class line" 84
Cliteur, Paul 17
"closeting" 71
coalescent theory 193
cognitive processing 74
Cohen, Robin 132
Coleridge, Samuel Taylor 184
collective action frames 48–9
colonial style and ethnic conflict 31–2
colonialism 29–36; Africa 31–2; Australia
     and Canada 95–7; Fanon on 142–3; and
     migration 16, 101; and race-based
     segregation 5–6; remnants of 40
color blindness 10, 26, 122, 213, 219–20;
     criticisms of discourse 117–18; historical
     origins 115–17; recent debates 117
color line 41, 84, 118–19, 230
"comfort zone" motivation to move away
     from 61–2
conformity 56–8
Congress of Racial Equality (CORE) 50, 167
Connerly, Ward 117
conscious motivation 60
conscious-level thinking 74, 77–8, 79, 229
conservatism 59, 75, 102, 109–10, 115, 122,
     168, 169, 185, 189, 190–1
consumer racial profiling (CRP) 211–12
Convention on the Prevention and
     Punishment of Genocide (1948) 144
Cook, James 95
Coombe, Rosemary 87–8
Cosby, Bill 135
Cosmic race (Vasconcelos) 169
counterstorytelling 123
craniometry 33–4
Crenshaw, Kimberlé 122
critical legal studies (CLS) 122
critical race theory (CRT) 110–12, 121–3, 227
Crusader ideology 162
cultural change 129–30, 137, 170
cultural heritage 159–60
cultural norms 106, 125–6, 129, 186
cultural pluralism 68–9, 106–7, 191
cultural relativism 68–9, 177, 190
Cultural studies and its theoretical legacies
     (Hall) 125

cultural studies: British roots of 124–5; controversies and challenges 125–6; globalization of 126–7; and Paul Gilroy 188–90; and Stuart Hall 227–8
culturally real, race as 206–7
culture 127–30; American Indians 36, 159; borderlands of 99; cognitive constraints of 129; creation of new 106, 107; crises in 97; indigenous peoples 96; and migration 55–62; and orientalism 184–5, 186; preservation of 17; psychological functions of 129; societal functions of 128–9; *see also* rap music
Culture and imperialism (Said) 185
culturicide 138
culturo-centrism 129

Dahl, Robert 106
Dalits 89–90
Darwin, Charles 4, 139
Darwinism 192, 222–3
Davenport, Charles B. 139, 140
De Hostos, Eugenio Maria 169
de-colonized subjects 142–4
Degler, Carl 34–5
democracy 33–4, 121, 191–2
derogatory terms 182
Descent of man (Darwin) 139
descriptive multiculturalism 176
Dewing, M. 16
diacritics 13
diaspora 19, 50, 59, 97, 154, 196; dangers of homogeneity and essentialism 132; government usage and changing meanings 132–3; history and development of concept 131–2
dignity culture 128
disabled people 139, 140
discourse theory 184
discrimination 65, 87–9, 133–4, 171, 173, 177, 201; approaches to 84–6
"divide and conquer" strategies 23–4, 105
"divide and rule" strategies 32, 155
domination 87–9
double consciousness 55, 134–5, 196, 229, 230
drive theory 61
"driving while black/brown" 26
Du Bois, W.E.B. 28, 41, 50, 55, 62, 118, 120, 123, 134, 228–31
dualism 190, 191
Dusk of dawn (Du Bois) 230
Dutch Reformed Church 103
Dyson, Michael Eric 135

Eastern cultures 184–5, 186
Eck, Diana 107
economic disparity 89–90, 231–2

economic equality, Brazil 35–6
economic globalization 82–91
economic status, US immigrants 173–6
editorial media content 78
educated immigrants 173–5
education 111, 112, 114, 120, 123
education policy 39, 44, 116, 117, 221
egalitarian approaches to discrimination 85
Egypt, women in 179–80
El Saadawi, Nawal 179–81
eliminativism 164–5
emancipatory nationalism 178–9
emotional movement 59–60
Empire strikes back (Hall) 125, 188
employment discrimination 133–4
entertainment 78–9
equal opportunity policies 38–9, 43–5
essentialism 64, 66, 131, 132, 136, 164; and anti-essentialism 190–1
ethnic cleansing 18, 87, 144–6, 179; *see also* genocide
ethnic conflict 151–2; Africa 30–1; and colonial style 31–2; and ethnogenesis 137
ethnicity: in Africa 30–1; beyond 18–19; and diaspora 132; and globalization 82–91; and nation state/multiculturalism 15–17; origins of 12–13; policies centring on 43–5; social construction of 13, 29–30, 33–4, 36; theories of 14–15
ethno-religious minority groups 171
ethno-symbolist approach 15
ethnocentrism 18, 110, 135–6, 186, 188
ethnocide 138
ethnogenesis 136–8, 158
eugenics 62, 138–41, 193, 222–3, 233; beginning of 139–40; and racism 140–1
Eurocentrism 67, 68, 97, 147, 155
Europe: anti-racism movements 100–1; assimilation 107; identity politics 154; multiculturalism 17–18, 176; nationalism and nation states 178
European Empires 155–6
European Network Against Racism 102
exclusion 58, 87–9, 134
expectations, violation of 62
explicit discussion of race 76–8
explicit prejudice 202
extrinsic motivation 60–1, 62

face culture 128–9
false equivalency problem 27
Fanon, Franz 41, 50, 55, 62, 67–8, 101, 142–4, 185, 195, 220
female genital mutilation (FGM) 180
feminism 68, 71; bell hooks on 111–12; and racism 101
Fields, Barbara Jeanne 29
financial globalization 86–7

Finland, equal opportunities 44
"First Nations" 70, 96–7, 138
Fiske, John 125
foreign cultures, responses to 129–30
Fortuyn, Pim 17–18
Foucault, Michel 184, 198–9
Fox from up above and the fox from down below (Arguedas) 169
framing 48–9, 74–6, 83–6
France: anti-racism movements 101; multiculturalism 16
Frankfurt School 122, 124
Freire, Paulo 67, 68, 112
French colonies 31–2
French Revolution 16
Freyre, Gilberto 34, 35

Galton, Francis 138, 139
Garnham, Nicholas 126
Garveyism 50
Gay Pride movement 71
Geertz, Clifford 14, 30, 48
Gellner, Ernest 18–19
gender: accomplishments and ongoing struggles 68–9; common issues across 65–6; conceptualising in academic discourses 67–8; and discrimination 17; and identity 150, 199; interstices and hybridities 70–1; politics of 125; relations across communities 69–70; and social change 71
General Allotment Act (1887), US 108–9
genetic diversity 194, 204–6
genetic research 25, 101, 147–9, 193
genetically based intelligence 4, 141
Genizaros 137–8
genocide 7, 18, 31, 73, 80, 138, 144–6, 152, 158, 179
German colonies 31–2
Gilroy, Paul 125, 132, 188–90
globalization: Anglo-Saxon globalism and market racism 86–7; domination, exclusion and discrimination 87–9; economic disparity and denial of opportunities 89–90; framing the issue 83–6; and gender/sexuality 66; and identity politics 154; and imperialism 156; loss of sovereignty 90; and Third World solidarity 224
Goldberg David 176
Goldman, Lucien 124
González, Rodolfo Corky 170
Goodhart, David 176
Gordon, Milton 57, 106
Gotanda, Neil 122
Gramsci, Antonio 184, 189, 198
Grant, Madison 140
Greider, William 88

group conflict theory 201
group identity 129, 153, 182, 202; whiteness as 235
group threat 136, 187, 236
Gudykunst, William 58

Haiti, earthquake in 78
Haitian Revolution (1791–1803) 178
Hall, Stuart 67, 125, 127, 188, 227–8
Hamilton, Charles 6
Hardin, Garret 128
Harlan, John 116
Harris, Cheryl 122
hate crimes 175
hate speech 122
Hatzfeld, Jean 80
Hayes, Rutherford B. 8–9
health issues 4–5, 75–6, 87
hegemony 111, 124, 156, 176, 184, 189, 198, 227
Heider, Fritz 61
Helms, Janet 235
Hereditary genius (Galton) 139
heredity 140, 192–4
Hernstein, Richard 4, 141
Herzberg, Frederick 62
heuristics 226
Hidden face of Eve (El Saadawi) 180
Higginbotham, A. Leon 5–6, 10
hip hop 213–15
Hispanics *see* Latinos/Hispanics
historical construction of difference 13
Hitler, Adolf 6–7, 140, 233, 234
HIV/AIDS 75–6, 87
Hobbes, Thomas 197–8
Hoggart, Richard 124, 125
Holocaust 80, 144
home, meaning of 59
"homeland" system, South Africa 104
homogeneity 131, 132
homophobia 17, 120
honor culture 128, 130
hooks, bell 67, 68, 110–12
Horkheimer, Max 124
"host" culture 55, 56–9, 150
Human Genome Diversity Project (HGDP) 25, 101, 147–9, 193
Human Genome Organization (HUGO) 147, 148
humanitarian interventions 145–6
Hunger for money (Rodriguez) 170
Huntington, Samuel 107
Hurricane Katrina 78
Hutu 31, 79–80
hybridity 16, 70–1, 120, 130–1, 132, 168–71, 196

identity 149–51; crises in 97; creation of new

136–8; defining 51, 53–4; and migration 150–1; role in politics 152–3; social psychology of 149; as socially constructed 13, 29–30, 33–4, 36, 136–7, 149, 150
identity politics 53, 96, 109, 137, 197, 216; American Indians 159; criticisms of 153; EU 154; identifying 152; role of identity 152–3; transformations in 154; US 153–4
Ignatieff, Noel 23
Imagined communities (Anderson) 15
immigrants 55–6; acculturation strategies 58–9; assimilation of 58, 106–7; experiences of 56–8; motivation of 59–62; and multiculturalism 15–19; professionals as 173, 174; as travellers 196
Immigration Act (1965), US 173
Immigration and Restriction Act (1924), US 140, 141
immigration, restrictions on 139, 140
imperialism 101, 111, 112, 121, 155–8, 164, 177, 184, 186, 222
Implicit Association Test (IAT) 235
implicit discussion of race 76–8
implicit prejudice 202
in-groups/out-groups 135–6, 153
indentured servants 33
India, multiculturalism 16
indigenismo 169
indigenous peoples 157–60; Australia and Canada 95–7; colonization of 41; demography of 158; elimination of 24; loss of sovereignty 102; territorial distribution of 29; theft of lands 118; *see also* Aboriginals
institutional diversity 30
institutionalized racism 44, 160–2, 217
Instrumentalists 14
intangible motivators 62
integration 56–9
intellectual property rights 160
intercultural contacts 130, 158
intergroup contact theory 202
intermarriage 96, 104, 137, 138, 172, 183; *see also* miscegenation
international criminal tribunals 146
International Monetary Fund (IMF) 86
intrinsic motivation 60–1
Inuit 9
IQ tests 4, 141, 194
Isaacs, Harold 13, 16
Islam 14, 18–19, 120
Islamophobia 162–3
Israel, equal opportunities 44

Jefferson, Thomas 112
Jewish diaspora 131, 132
Jews 7, 23, 144, 183, 233
Jim Crow laws 9, 48, 113–14, 119, 233

Kagame, Paul 7
Karenga, Maulana 97
Kasinitz, P. 107
Kennedy, John F. 116
Keto, C. Tsehloane 97
Kim, Young Yun 58
Kindleberger, Charles 83
King, Dr Martin Luther 9, 51–2, 112, 115, 166–8
Kinzer, Stephen 31
Kornhauser, William 51
Ku Klux Klan 5, 233
Kymlicka, Will 171

land rights, American Indians 159
language of race 95–6
Lasswell, Harold 39
Latin American Cultural Studies 127
Latinos/Hispanics 22, 42, 64, 69, 74, 106, 140, 153, 160, 169, 172; challenges 165; general versus specific labels 164; identity and identification 164–5; vs Hispanics 163–4
law enforcement, racial profiling 210–12
legal strategy, civil rights 122
Leman, M. 16
lesbian, gay, bisexual and transgender (LGBT) 64, 65–6, 67–72
Leviathan (Hobbes) 197
liberalism 18, 109–10, 224
"linguistic terrorism" 99
location theory 98
Locke, John 197–8
Lorde, Audre 67, 70
Loving v. *Virginia* (1967) 141
Lukes, Steven 198

Maalouf, Amin 14
McDaniels, Hattie 114
McIntosh, Peggy 235
McRobbie, Angela 125
Maddison, Angus 82–3
Making face, making soul/haciendo caras (Anzaldúa) 99
Making of the English working class (Thompson) 124
Mandela, Nelson 52, 105, 217
Manifest Destiny 165–6, 186
marginalization 58–9, 68, 88, 98
market racism 86–7
"Maroons" 137
Marshall, Thurgood 222
Marxism 124–5, 188, 195, 198, 227
mass communication model 125, 126
Mazama, Ama 97
Mbeki, Thabo 75–6
media messages: content of 78–9, 112; effects of 73–8; Rwanda 79–80

"melting pot" assimilation model 106, 107, 176–7, 191
Melvern, Linda 79–80
Mendelberg, Tali 77
Mendelism 140, 192–3
meritocracy 10, 26, 161, 207
mestizaje see miscegenation
mestizos/mestizas 99, 168–71
Métis 96, 137–8
Mies, Maria 88
migration: and colonialism 16, 101; and identity 150–1; motive for 61–2; *see also* immigrants
Milgram, Stanley 80
Minh-ha, Trinh 67, 78
minorities 171–4; bias toward majority group 201; conformity of 186; discrimination against 133–4; and double consciousness 134–5; and genocide 145; policies for 116
minority politics 152
minority rule 44, 48–9, 51, 53
miscegenation 34–5, 70, 104, 158, 169, 170; laws of 139, 140, 141
Mississippi burning (film) 24
mixed-race 22–3, 35, 95, 96, 137–8, 168–71
model minority 69; consequences for Asian Americans 174–5; consequences for majority groups 175; consequences for relationships between minority groups 175; history of term 173; myth of 173–4
modernity, critique of 190
Mohanty, Chandra 67
monocultural societies 17
Montgomery Improvement Association (MIA) 167
moralist approaches to discrimination 84–5
Morton, Samuel 33–4
"motive," etymology of 59–60
motivation: conscious versus unconscious 60; intrinsic versus extrinsic 60–1; to emigrate 61–2
multiculturalism 15–17, 106–7, 152, 176–8, 179, 190, 191; and authenticity 108; Canada 100; critical approaches to 68–9; failure of 17–18; and identity 150; intellectual benefits of 129
multiculturist approaches to discrimination 85
multiple identities 99, 149, 151
Murray, Charles 4, 141
Muslim Americans 100
Muslims 17–18, 162–3, 171, 178; *see also* Islam

nation state: and ethnicity 15–17; as social construct 131
National Aboriginal Day, Canada 96

National Association for the Advancement of Colored People (NAACP) 71, 114, 230
national identity 17–18, 101, 154, 169, 189
National Organization for Women 71
nationalism 13, 176, 178–9, 195–6, 214; African peoples 98; Afrikaners 103; as reaction to 9/11 100; homogenizing tendencies of 18–19
nationalist elites 143
nationalist ideology 145
nationalist movements 50
nationalistic conflicts 151–2
natural selection 139, 192–3
Nazism 6–7, 140, 144, 183, 223, 233
neo-liberalism 207, 224
Netherlands, multiculturalism 17–18
new international economic order (NIEO) 83, 223–4
New Social Movement (NSM) theory 53
news media content 78
Niagara Movement 230
Nigger: current use and meaning 182; epistemology 181–2
non-discrimination policies 43–5
normative multiculturalism 176
North America, white supremacy 23–4
North–South conflict 223
Norway, equal opportunities 44
Nuremberg Laws 183–4

Obama, Barack 9–10, 75, 76, 115, 207
On the origin of species (Darwin) 139
opportunities, denial of 89–90
oppressor/colonializer 67–8, 69
orientalism 184–5, 196; and assimilation 186
Orientalism (Said) 67, 184–5, 186
orthogenesis 192
"other" 3, 12, 65, 76, 149, 191; and citizenship 186–7; group threat and future of race relations 187; orientalism and assimilation 186
"otherness" 55, 75, 96
Ottoman Empire 15
"Out of Africa 2" theory 193

Pan-Africanism 189, 230, 231
Parents Involved in Community Schools v. *Seattle School District No. 1* 117
Park, Robert 56–7, 58, 106
Parks, Rosa 9, 112, 167
Passing of the great race (Madison) 140
patriotism 178
Petersen, William 173
physical attributes 22–3, 25
Plessey v. *Ferguson* 114, 116, 221, 222
policing practices 102
policymaking process 39–40
political activity, American Indians 159

political correctness (PC) 17; anti-essentialism 190–1; critique of modernity 10; decline of social realism 191; and race relations 191
political economy 126
politicization of identities 31
politics 38–45; role of identity 152–3; of race 227–8; of "supranational" identity 154
polyethnic states 16
polysemic texts 125
population genetics 4, 147, 148, 192–4
Portes, A. 106
Portuguese colonies 31–2, 34–5
positive discrimination 38–9
Post-colonial melancholia (Gilroy) 190
post-industrial decline, UK 188–9
"post-racial" era, US 9–10
postcolonial states 30, 176, 188–9; ethnic and racial identity in 32; racial democracy in 34–5
postcolonial studies 67–8, 125, 143, 156, 184–5, 194–7
postmodernism 120
Powell, Adam Clayton 114
power 197–200; and apartheid 104; bipolar structure of 223; class-based analyses of 122; diasporas 133; and domination 110; dynamics of 12; and identity 155; imbalances 101; maintenance of 184, 195; and racial stratification 40–1; unjust distribution of 25
power relations: racial framing of 48; status quo of 49; unequal 171
pragmatism 120
Pratto, F. 110
prejudice 10, 44, 62, 74, 110, 151, 160, 162, 175, 177, 186; bases of 200–1; combating 202; manifestations of 201–2; and stereotyping 225–6; and xenophobia 236–7
priming 74–6
primordialism 14, 30, 136–7
privilege, systems of 26–7
psychometric scale (F scale) 109–10
public policy 38–45, 172; and color blindness 115–18
public services, segregation of 104, 114, 167
purges 144

"queer" 64, 70–1
quotas 41, 44, 233

race biology 101
race card 207–10
race consciousness and census policy 41–3
race hygiene *see* eugenics
race making, America 32–4
"race matters" 5–6

Race matters (West) 120–1
race relations: future of 187; and political correctness 191
race riots 168, 177
race: accomplishments and ongoing struggles 68–9; as analytical tool 122–3; biological justification and implications 3–5, 203–6; common issues across 65–6; conceptualising in academic discourses 67–8; as culturally and socially real 206–7; discovering in American Indians 35–6; explicit and implicit discussion of 76–8; framing in social movements 48–51; and globalization 82–91; interstices and hybridities 70–1; language of 95–6; and media messages 73–81; origins of concept 3–11; paradoxical nature of 101; policies centring on 43–5; relations across communities 69–70; representations of 219; and social change 71; social construction of 13, 29–30, 33–4, 36, 204
race-based social movements 47–54
racial categorization 33, 41–3, 205–6
racial classification 3–6; power of 10
racial declines 51–3
racial democracy, Brazil 34–5
racial differences, UNESCO statement on 177
racial diversity 41
racial failures 51–3
Racial Integrity Act (1924), Virginia 141
racial "markers" 206–7
racial non-recognition *see* color blindness
racial organization in social movements 49–51
"Racial Privacy Initiative" 117
racial profiling: definitions of 210–11; issues in explaining 211; literature on 212; research directions 212
racial stratification and power 40–1
racial successes 51–3
racial traits 205
racialization process 6, 101–2
Racialized boundaries (Anthias/Yuval-Davis) 176–7
racism 6–7; as analytical tool 122–3; and anti-racist movement 100–2; definition of 122; and eugenics 140–1; individualization of 10–11; Rwanda media 79–80; and xenophobia 237
radical democracy 121
Radical Lesbians movement 71
Radio-Télévision Libres des Mille Colines (RTLMC) 79–80
Randolph, Edmond 113
rap music 79, 121; debates and controversies 214–15; early years 213–14
Raza, la (the Race) 170

re-centering/re-positioning 98
"reality" television 79
Reconstruction era, US 8–9, 113
Regents of the University of California v.
    Bakke 116
relationalism 164–5
religion: and apartheid 103; *see also*
    Christianity; Islamophobia
religious dress 101, 149
religious identity 18, 149–50
remittances 133
reparations 153; international perspectives
    217–18; for slavery 216–17
representation 8, 66, 112, 118, 122, 142, 162,
    184, 218–21, 228
"reverse discrimination/racism" 26, 161,
    208
Rhode, Deborah 40
Ricken, N. 198
Right Wing Authoritarianism (RWA) scale
    110
Rodriguez, Richard 170
Roediger, David 24
Roman Empire 13
Rondinelli, D.A. 83
Roosevelt, Theodore 24
Rorty, Richard 120
Rural Advancement Foundation
    International (RAFI) 147–8
Russia, ethnic diversity 41
Rwanda: ancestral classifications 7;
    colonization of 31; genocide 7, 18, 73,
    144–6, 152; radio racism 79–80

Sachs, Jeffrey 86
Safran, William 132
Sagasti, Francisco 82
Said, Edward 12, 59, 67, 156, 184–5, 186, 220
schemata 74, 75–6, 77
Schnapper, Dominique 132
scientific racism 34, 169, 193
Scott, Dred 113
"Scramble for Africa" 30–1
Second treatise of government (Locke) 197
segregation 5–6, 7, 9, 48–9, 70, 113–14, 167,
    171–2, 176, 221–2; *see also* apartheid
self-identification 15, 216, 229
Sen, Amartya 91
"separate but equal" doctrine 113–14, 116,
    119, 222
"separate development" policy 103
settler nationalism 102
sexual discrimination 65, 68, 152, 162,
    179–80, 196
sexual identity 150
sexuality: accomplishments and ongoing
    struggles 68–9; common issues across
    65–6; conceptualising in academic

discourses 67–8; interstices and hybridities
    70–1; relations across communities 69–70;
    and social change 71
Shea, Dan 79
Shills, Edward 14
Shiva, Vandana 88
sickle cell anemia 4–5
Sidanius, J. 110
slavery: abolition of 24; abolitionist
    movements 100; philosophical
    justification 6; racial justification 34;
    reparations for 216–17; US 4, 7–8,
    112–13
slaves, separation from white workers 23
Smith, Anthony D. 15
Snow, David 48
social change 69, 71, 158, 170–1
Social Darwinism 222–3
Social Dominance Orientation (SDO) 110
social identity theory 201
social movements 47–54; framing race in
    48–9; racial organization in 49–51; *see
    also* identity politics
social realism, decline of 191
socially constructed identities 13, 29–30,
    33–4, 36, 136–7, 149, 150, 204
socially real, race as 206–7
societal functions of culture 128–9
socio-economic subordination 25, 172
solidarity 23–4, 25, 136, 176, 191, 223–5
souls of black folk , The (Du Bois) 28, 134,
    230
South Africa Truth and Reconciliation
    Committee (SA-TRC) 217–18
South Africa: Anti-Apartheid Movement 47,
    52–3; apartheid 7, 44–5, 48–9, 103–5;
    Black Consciousness Movement 50, 52–3;
    census policy 43; economic inequality 105;
    equal opportunities 44–5
South Korea, assimilation 107
South-to-South dialogue 224
Southern Christian leadership Conference
    (SCLC) 166, 167, 168
sovereignty: lack of regard for 102; loss of 90
statistical discrimination theory 134
stereotypes 27, 36, 66, 73, 74, 77–8, 79, 88,
    113, 153, 163, 174–5, 184, 195, 200, 219,
    220, 225–6
sterilization 139, 140
structural racism 102, 115, 123
Student Nonviolent Coordinating
    Committee (SNCC) 50, 167
subconscious processing 74, 77, 79, 80
suffrage 65, 113
Sumner, W.G. 136
"supranational identity," politics of 154
systematic disadvantage: African Americans
    7–10; and equal opportunity policies 43–5

Taibi, Anthony 85
Talking back (hooks) 111
Tamil Tigers 19
Tannenbaum, Frank 34, 35
"taste for discrimination" 133–4
Taylor, Charles 108
Teaching community (hooks) 112
Teaching to transgress (hooks) 112
technology 82, 87, 88
territorial expansion, US 165–6
There ain't no black in the Union Jack
   (Gilroy) 188
Third World solidarity 223–4
This bridge called my back (Anzaldúa) 99
Thompson, E.P. 124
Three-Fifths compromise 8
Tilden, Samuel 8
Torres Strait Islanders 96
Transactionalists 14–15
tribal membership 108–9
truth commissions 217–18
Tutsi 7, 31, 79–80
Twain, Mark 181–2
"two-spirit" people 70–1

UK: census policy 43; cultural studies 124–5;
   institutional racism 161; race politics
   227–8; racial diversity 41; re-making of
   188–90
unconscious motivation 60
United Nations 105, 145–6, 158, 160;
   Commission on Human Rights 85;
   UNESCO Statement on nature of race
   differences 177
Universal Negro Improvement Association
   50
Urban League 50
US: anti-racism movements 100; assimilation
   106–7; black consciousness 50; census
   policy 42; citizenship 186–7; color line
   118–19; Constitution 8, 113, 114, 116;
   cultural studies 126; Emancipation
   Proclamation 8; ethnic studies 196–7;
   eugenics 139–41; identity politics 153–4;
   institutionalised racism 44; model
   minority 173–6; multiculturalism 18;
   "post-racial" era 9–10; presidential
   elections 75, 76; racial classification 5–6,
   205–6; racial segregation 48–9; reactions
   to "white privilege" 26–7; reconstruction
   8–9, 119; reparations 216–17; slavery and
   race making 32–4; slavery in New
   Republic 7–8; systematic disadvantage of

African Americans 7–10; territorial
   expansion 165–6; treatment of minorities
   171; white privilege 231–2; white
   supremacy 24–6, 232–4
Uses of literacy (Hoggart) 124

Vasconcelos, José 169, 170
Vietnam War 168
Voting Rights Act (1965), US 115, 168

"wage of whiteness" 23–4
Wallenstein, Immanuel 156
Weaver, Jace 108–9
Weber, Max 13, 14, 198, 199, 229
Weeks, William E. 165–6
West, Cornel 5, 111, 119–21
White Anglo-Saxon Protestant (WASP)
   culture 107
White Citizens' Councils 233
white privilege 9, 22, 161, 231–2, 235; white
   reactions to 26–7
white purity 138–41
white superiority, establishment of 5–6
white supremacist groups 5, 223
white supremacy 21–2, 111, 122, 160, 186,
   232–4; collective resistance to 27;
   emergence of 23–6; and eugenics 138–41;
   maintenance of 41; as root of race
   problems 28
"white trash" 25
whiteness 21–2, 122, 196, 234–6; as de facto
   state of being 101–2; definition of 22–3;
   origins of idea of 23–4; reference points
   of 6; tenacity of idea of 24–6
"whiteness as group identity" model 235
Williams, Raymond 124
Wilson, Pete 117
Wolfe, Thomas 59
Women and Sex (El Saadawi) 180
women: and postcolonialism 196; in Muslim
   societies 162, 179–80
women's movements 65
women's studies 68
World Trade Organization (WHO) 83, 85, 90
worldviews 201
Woubi Chéri (documentary) 71
Wretched of the earth (Fanon) 143

xenophobia 129, 236–7

Yuval-Davis, N. 176–7

Zhou, M. 106